Basel III tiers:

* Capital Standards

* Official Supervision

* Market Discipline

Rethinking Bank Regulation

Banking systems are important not only for countries' finances but also to help spur economic growth. This volume presents and discusses a new database on bank regulation in more than 150 countries. It offers the first comprehensive cross-country assessment of the impact of bank regulation on the operation of banks and assesses the validity of the Basel Committee's influential approach to bank regulation. A key finding is that societies that emphasize market-based monitoring of banks enjoy superior outcomes along a range of criteria. Viewing the reform of bank regulation and supervision as a narrow technical issue is risky because the impact of bank regulation reflects host countries' complex economic and political institutions. The data also indicate that restrictions on the entry of new banks, government ownership of banks, and restrictions on bank activities adversely affect banking system performance.

James R. Barth is the Lowder Eminent Scholar in Finance at Auburn University and a Senior Finance Fellow at the Milken Institute. He also has been Professor of Economics at George Washington University, Associate Director of the economics program at the National Science Foundation, and Shaw Foundation Professor of Banking and Finance at Nanyang Technological University. Professor Barth was an appointee of Presidents Ronald Reagan and George H. W. Bush as Chief Economist of the Office of Thrift Supervision and previously as Chief Economist of the Federal Home Loan Bank Board. His research focuses on financial institutions and capital markets, both domestic and global, with special emphasis on regulatory issues.

Gerard Caprio, Jr., is Professor of Economics at Williams College and, until January 2006, the Director for Policy in the Financial Sector Vice Presidency of the World Bank. He previously served as Manager, Financial Sector Research, in the Bank's Development Research Group and was the senior Bank spokesperson on financial sector issues. Before joining the Bank in 1988, Professor Caprio was Vice President and Head of Global Economics at JP Morgan, previously serving as an economist at the Federal Reserve Board and the IMF and also teaching at George Washington University. His current research explores the links between financial sector regulation and supervision and the performance of financial institutions, as well as financial crises.

Ross Levine is the Harrison S. Kravis University Professor and Professor of Economics at Brown University. He is also a Research Associate at the National Bureau of Economic Research and the Dupee Faculty Fellow at the Watson Institute of International Affairs. After receiving his Ph.D. in economics and working at the Board of Governors of the Federal Reserve System, Professor Levine moved to the World Bank. There he participated in and managed a number of research and operational programs. In 1997 Professor Levine joined the University of Virginia, before moving to the finance department of the Carlson School of Management at the University of Minnesota in 1999. His work focuses on the links between financial sector policies, the operation of financial systems, and economic growth.

Rethinking Bank Regulation

Till Angels Govern

JAMES R. BARTH
Auburn University and Milken Institute

GERARD CAPRIO, JR.
Williams College

ROSS LEVINE
Brown University

CAMBRIDGE
UNIVERSITY PRESS

CAMBRIDGE UNIVERSITY PRESS
Cambridge, New York, Melbourne, Madrid, Cape Town, Singapore, São Paulo

Cambridge University Press
32 Avenue of the Americas, New York, NY 10013-2473, USA

www.cambridge.org
Information on this title: www.cambridge.org/9780521855761

First published 2006
Reprinted 2006 (twice)

Printed in the United States of America

A catalog record for this publication is available from the British Library.

Library of Congress Cataloging in Publication Data
Barth, James R.
Rethinking bank regulation : till angels govern / James R. Barth, Gerard
Caprio, Jr., Ross Levine.
p. cm.
Includes bibliographical references.
ISBN-13: 978-0-521-85576-1 (hardcover)
ISBN-10: 0-521-85576-4 (hardcover)
1. Banking Law. 2. Banks and banking – State supervision. 3. Banks and
banking – Government policy. I. Caprio, Gerard, Jr. II. Levine, Ross. III. Title.
K1066.B37 2006
346′.082 – dc22   2005028138

ISBN-13 978-0-521-85576-1 hardback
ISBN-10 0-521-85576-4 hardback

For Mary, Jeanne, and Maruja

Contents

Figures, Tables, and Appendices

FIGURES

TABLES

APPENDICES

Preface

Although our names appear on the book cover, the contents benefited enormously from insightful conversations with many colleagues, the detailed comments of those who suffered through early versions of the manuscript, seminar and conference participants literally all over the world, and the extraordinary help of many research assistants. At various stages of putting together the database and checking the results, we received excellent assistance from Xin Chen, Dan Goldblum, Andy Kim, and Iffath Sharif; Polly Means assisted with Figure 1.1 and the cover with her usual skill. Daniele Evans kept Jerry organized while he was working on the book and defended him from some bureaucratic demands with great skill, and she and Elena Mehkova helped on parts of the manuscript. We are especially grateful to Cindy Lee and Triphon Phumiwasana for their tireless efforts in assisting us with the database during the past few years. We also benefited from extensive comments from a number of scholars working in this or related areas, and we owe a debt to Thorsten Beck, John Boyd, Charles Calomiris, Maria Carkovic, Stijn Claessens, Asli Demirgüç-Kunt, Bill Easterly, Morris Goldstein, Charles Goodhart, Stephen Haber, Jim Hanson, Patrick Honohan, Ed Kane, George Kaufman, Luc Laeven, Juan Marchetti, Rick Mishkin, Dan Nolle, Larry Promisel, Raghu Rajan, Joao Santos, Augusto de la Torre, Andrei Shleifer, and Greg Udell for comments both general and specific. The authors would like to thank participants at seminars and conferences at the Bank of England, Bank for International Settlements, Brown University, Claremont Graduate University, Columbia University, Dartmouth College, European Central Bank, Federal Reserve Bank of New York, Harvard University, International Monetary Fund, London

Business School, London School of Economics, National Bureau of Economic Research, New York University, Stanford University, Ohio State University, Oxford College, Stockholm School of Economics, University of Minnesota, Tsinghua University, Washington University in St. Louis, the Wharton School, Williams College, and the World Bank, where we presented various elements of the research incorporated in this book.

Ross Levine worked on this book while he was at the Carlson School of Management, University of Minnesota, and he would like to thank all of his colleagues there, who heard more about bank regulation and supervision over lunch and coffee than they might have liked. Jerry Caprio, who worked on this book while at the World Bank, likewise extends thanks to his colleagues there for similar endurance, and he would especially like to thank Cesare Calari, the Vice President and Head of the Financial Sector Network, for his feedback, support, and encouragement. Jim Barth was at the Lowder School of Business, Auburn University, and the Milken Institute while he worked on this book, and he is grateful for the support and encouragement he received from his colleagues at both institutions, especially Glenn Yago. The findings do not necessarily represent the opinions of The World Bank, its management, the Executive Directors, or the countries they represent.

Rethinking Bank Regulation

ONE

Introduction

But what is government itself, but the greatest of all reflections on human
nature. If men were angels, no government would be necessary. If angels
were to govern men, neither external nor internal controls would be necessary. In framing a government which is to be administered by men over
men, the great difficulty lies in this: you must first enable the government
to control the governed; and in the next place oblige it to control itself.

James Madison, *Federalist Papers*, Number 51

1.A. MOTIVATION

When budding entrepreneurs in Brazil, Egypt, Zambia, or Indonesia are
turned down for loans or do not even bother to apply because banks
instead funnel credit to the rich or politically powerful, this stymies
innovation and thwarts economic growth. When households in Georgia,
Nigeria, Russia, or Venezuela avoid placing their savings in financial institutions and instead buy foreign currency, physical commodities, or durable
goods, this reflects queasiness about domestic banks and advertises the
lack of efficient mechanisms for getting savings to productive firms.
When bank managers in too many countries simply take deposits with
one hand and pass them along to friends and related businesses with
the other hand, this discourages business initiative and prevents the
poor and unconnected with good ideas from realizing their dreams and
improving their economic condition. When bad policies ignite or exacerbate banking crises in Argentina, Indonesia, or Mexico, this yields
widespread bankruptcies, rising unemployment, and even soaring street
violence. Thus, our main motivation for studying bank regulation and

1

supervision is that banks matter for human welfare; therefore, we seek
to identify which approach to regulation and supervision best enhances
bank performance.

Formal econometric studies confirm that banks exert a first-order
impact on economic development.[1] When banks direct the flow of capital toward those enterprises with the highest expected social returns
and monitor firms carefully after providing funds, this encourages
entrepreneurship and economic growth. New research further suggests
that banks influence income distribution and poverty. Although sound
banks alleviate poverty primarily by accelerating overall growth and
therefore by "raising all ships," well-functioning banks also exert a disproportionately positive impact on the poor.[2] Countries with better banks
experience faster reductions in poverty as capital flows to those with the
best projects, not simply to those with the most wealth and power. The
reverse is also true. Poorly functioning banks that simply funnel credit to
connected parties and elites slow growth and exert a disproportionately
negative influence on the poor and small businesses by depriving them
of the capital they need to succeed. Unfortunately, billions of people live
in countries with poorly functioning banks. Thus, banking policies matter
because banks influence the ability of people, rich and poor, to improve
their living standards.

Banks also matter when they fail. In Japan, the banking crisis in the
1990s was estimated to cost over 20 percent of GDP (Caprio, Klingebiel, Laeven, and Noguera, 2003). The fiscal costs of banking crises in
developing countries alone exceeded $1 trillion in the 1980s and 1990s. In
present value terms, this is about equal to all foreign assistance transfers
to developing countries over the period 1950–2001 (World Bank, 2001,
and authors' calculations)! The banking crises in Argentina and Chile in
the early 1980s, and Indonesia in the 1990s, were of epic proportions with
estimated costs surpassing 40 percent of a year's Gross Domestic Product
(Caprio and Klingebiel, 1997; Caprio et al., 2003). Banking crises can
completely disrupt economies, and the human costs can be very real, as,
for example, when health and education programs are dramatically cut
to fund a government bailout of the failed banks.

Besides studying bank regulation and supervision to identify policies
that promote economic growth, reduce poverty, and minimize destructive

---

[1] See Levine (1997, 2005) and sources cited therein.
[2] See Beck, Demirgüç-Kunt, and Levine (2004b); and Beck, Demirgüç-Kunt, Laeven, and
Levine (2004); and Honohan (2004).

financial crises, our research is also motivated by the influential "best practice" recommendations advocated by the Basel Committee on Bank Supervision. Virtually all countries adopted the 1988 Basel Capital Accord, which provided guidelines for assuring that banks have sufficient capital. In 2004, the Basel Committee released a new, much more expansive set of recommendations – Basel II. The first and main pillar develops far more intricate procedures than the 1988 Accord for computing minimum capital requirements. The second pillar recommends regulations that empower official supervisory agencies to scrutinize and discipline banks. The third, and least developed, pillar focuses on regulations that require accurate information disclosure and facilitate market oversight and discipline of banks.[3] Although not finalized, within three months of its official announcement, more than one hundred countries already signaled their intention to adopt the Basel II guidelines. Thus, part of our motivation for writing this book is to provide guidance to authorities as they consider whether and how to adopt Basel II or more generally how to reshape their regulatory frameworks.

1.B. OBJECTIVES AND CONTRIBUTIONS

In this book, we:

- Assemble a new, detailed database on bank regulation and supervision in over 150 countries.
- Conduct the first, comprehensive, cross-country assessment of the impact of bank regulatory and supervisory practices on bank development, efficiency, stability, and the degree of corruption in bank lending, including an examination of the three pillars of Basel II: capital regulations, official supervision, and market discipline.
- Provide an empirical evaluation of the historic debate about the proper role of government in the economy by using the laboratory of bank regulation and supervision around the world.
- Analyze why countries make different regulatory and supervisory choices.

The absence of data on bank regulation and supervision around the world has made it impossible to assess empirically which policies boost bank development and efficiency, and which ones reduce the susceptibility

---

[3] Powell (2004) describes the detailed features of Basel II. The underdevelopment of the third pillar was a theme of the 2003 Chicago Fed conference on Market Discipline (Borio, Hunter, Kaufman, and Tsatsaronis, 2004).

of economies to systemic banking crises and limit corruption in finance. Data limitations have impeded cross-country examinations of: (i) why countries choose different banking policies, (ii) whether policies adopted in countries with particular legal and political institutions will work in countries with very different systems, and (iii) which broad approaches to the role of government in society work best in fostering efficient functioning banks. There has been an enormous gap between empirical evidence on the efficacy of different banking policies and the enunciation of best practice recommendations by international experts.

Our main contribution is to assemble a new database on bank regulation and supervision around the world, so that researchers and policy makers can for the first time compare what countries actually do and assess which policies work best to improve human welfare. We use the phrase "bank regulation and supervision" to encompass a wide range of policies and enforcement procedures that apply specifically to the banking sector. Regulation typically refers to the rules that govern the behavior of banks, whereas supervision is the oversight that takes place to ensure that banks comply with those rules.[4] To collect information on both bank regulations and supervisory practices, we conducted two surveys (in 1998/1999 and in 2002/2003). Chapter 3 discusses these data and we provide the data on the CD that accompanies this book.

In addition to constructing a database, we also examine which banking sector policies and strategies enhance bank development and efficiency, and which policies lower banking system fragility and the degree of corruption in lending. Because banks affect economic prosperity, our goal is to provide empirical evidence on which regulatory and supervisory practices improve the functioning of banks. We examine regulatory impediments to the entry of new domestic and foreign banks, restrictions on bank activities, the generosity of the deposit insurance regime, the power of the official supervisory agency to close banks, change managers, stop dividends and other payments, the degree to which regulations force the disclosure of accurate comparable information, the extent of government ownership of banks, rules regarding prompt corrective action and loan classification, and many other policies. We use broad cross-country comparisons, bank-level data, and firm-level data to assess

---

[4] In many cases, we will simply use the term regulation as a generic description of banking sector policies and compliance mechanisms. In some cases, however, we will use regulation and supervision less generically, such as when we discuss particular regulations (e.g., the activities in which banks are permitted to engage) or particular aspects of supervision (e.g., taking corrective actions).

the impact of these different banking sector policies on the operation of the banking system. Throughout, we test whether banking policies operate differently in countries with distinct political and institutional settings.

In assessing which policies work best, we devote special attention to Basel II's three pillars. Basel II was developed primarily by bank supervisors from the world's richest countries, but the recommendations are having worldwide repercussions. Although there is an appealing logic to following the advice of rich-country supervisors, there are two equally compelling concerns. First, there is no evidence that any single set of best practices is appropriate for promoting well-functioning banks in every country. Specifically, practices that appear to succeed in the United States, Europe, or Japan may not succeed in countries with different institutional or political settings.[5] Thus, "one size may not fit" for all countries. Second, the Basel II approach to regulation stresses direct official supervision, which may not work as well as an approach that emphasizes market discipline. In fact, there is a risk that policies developed by official supervisors will unduly emphasize and empower official supervision. Too much trust may be accorded government officials and too little attention devoted to the potential abuse of this trust or to inefficiencies introduced by excessive reliance on supervision. Although it is possible to imagine institutional environments in which abuses are limited (e.g., in which both the judiciary and the media are both independent and honest), the opposite environment may be more common in practice, as posited in Chapter 2 and sources cited therein. Thus, recommendations rooted only in supervisory wisdom may push countries in the wrong direction, as argued for example by the Shadow Financial Regulatory Committee (1999) and Shin et al. (2001). This book contributes to filling the gap between the Basel recommendations and the response of a number of experts in the academic community by providing cross-country empirical evidence.

Although the rationale for the first two objectives – assembling the database and examining which regulations and supervisory practices work best – are clear, many may wonder why this book grants such prominence

---

[5] The point that policy recommendations can vary with the institutional environment was shown for deposit insurance by Demirgüç-Kunt and Kane (2002), and also the World Bank (2001). The point is that if the rule of law, bank regulation and supervision, or the information environment is sufficiently weak, deposit insurance, which reduces market discipline, could so weaken monitoring of banks that it would make the banking system more vulnerable to crises. Where institutions are stronger, and both official supervision and market monitoring better developed, any weakening of market discipline may be less significant.

Institutional Environment
Democratic, Political Structure/System

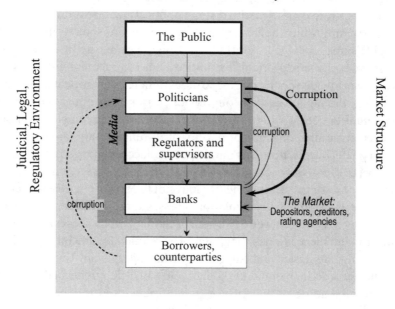

Technology, Information
Infrastructure

Figure 1.1. Framework for Bank Regulation.

to the last two objectives – assessing the proper role of government in society and investigating the determinants of banking policies. Many may consider bank regulation a technical specialty, akin to the mechanics of clearing and settling equity transactions. From this technical perspective, bank regulation and supervision involve defining and measuring capital, determining the number of days a loan needs to be in arrears before classifying it as nonperforming, and similar issues. From that perspective, this book should focus only on assessing which regulations work best. This technical view would not place much weight on viewing bank supervision and regulation within a broader political economy context that stresses how political philosophies and institutions shape both policy choices and the impact of those decisions. Although we began our investigation with this technical perspective, the data quickly induced us to rethink our approach to bank regulation.

Figure 1.1 illustrates a broader framework in which to view bank regulation and supervision that involves a sequence of agency problems surrounded by the entire apparatus of political, legal, cultural, and technological forces influencing the operation of banks.[6] At each level in this figure, there is a principal-agent problem. For example, in the lending relationship, the bank is the principal, the borrower is the agent, and the bank's problem is how to induce the borrower to behave in a responsible way and service the debt. Information asymmetries – the borrower having better information about issues such as their own busines activities, behaviors, and effort than the bank – make this problem difficult, and lead to a variety of loan characteristics, such as the demand for collateral and short maturities. Similar agency problems continue at the next level as bank regulators and supervisors with imperfect information about banks seek to design rules and enforcement procedures that induce banks to behave in desirable ways. At this same level, traditional corporate governance problems plague the oversight of banks: informational asymmetries make it difficult for the market – depositors, equity holders, other creditors, and rating agencies – to monitor and control bank managers. The series of agency problems continues at the next level, where "politicians," including officials from all branches of government, seek to influence bank regulators. Just as regulators face agency problems in controlling banks, politicians face similar problems in controlling the regulators. Regulators have much more information about bank activities, regulatory policies, and enforcement procedures than politicians, which may make it difficult for politicians sitting in national capitals to control regulators throughout the country.

At the highest level of the sequence of complex agency problems lies the most difficult problem: How does the public induce politicians to act in the best interests of society? As explained in Chapter 2, sometimes politicians are motivated to behave with society's best interests in mind (the "public interest" view) and at other times, politicians promote their own private well-being to the detriment of society (the "private interest" view). The ability of the public to monitor and control politicians has key implications for the selection and operation of bank regulations and supervisory practices, and hence for bank performance and economic prosperity.

Beyond this series of agency problems (the straight lines with vertical arrows pointing down), the framework for bank regulation and

---

[6] This is a modified version of the figure in Berger and Udell (2002). Note that among other changes, we have consolidated bank owners, managers and loan officers into one category, "banks," in order to address the issues under consideration. Those interested in more on the principal-agent problems within banks should see their informative discussion.

supervision is further complicated by possible corruption as powerful individuals try to influence the flow of society's savings (the upward-pointing arrows). Bankers may try to influence regulators and supervisors with offers of jobs or other emoluments. Perhaps more commonly, banks may try to buy influence with politicians who in turn can affect the actions of regulators and supervisors. Wallis (2004) refers to this channel as venal corruption, illustrated by the upward-curved arrows in Figure 1.1 from banks to politicians and to regulators and supervisors. Perhaps more insidious is what he describes as systematic corruption, which is when politicians try to use their influence to maintain or augment their political position, such as by leaning on or conspiring with bankers to extend credit only to those supporting the ruling party, restricting entry to those who will play by these rules and so on, as captured in the curved line pointing from politicians to banks. Furthermore, borrowers may seek to influence politicians – lobbying for regulatory/supervisory policies that will favor their own interests. Although many lines may complicate Figure 1.1, the crucial point is that we cannot usefully examine banking policies without considering the private interests of those setting and implementing policies in each country.

In Figure 1.1, we frame the sequence of principal-agent relationships and political connections within an even broader institutional setting. Banks are inextricable parts of a nation's social fabric. For example, the presence and quality of checks and balances in government influence the degree to which politicians behave in a public or private interest manner. The power and independence of the judiciary as well as legal statutes shape the level of corruption, the extent to which rules and regulations are actually followed, and the ability of private market participants to exert corporate control over banks. An independent and active media can play a key role in monitoring corruption and investigating each of the relationships in the sequence of agency problems depicted in Figure 1.1. Furthermore, the level of information technology affects the flow of information about banks, which can influence both official and private oversight of banks. This framework suggests that an array of factors influences the effect of banking policies on social welfare.

Thus, we reject the narrow, technical approach and instead adopt a broader, more complex approach to banking policies for a very simple reason. People have a powerful interest in the supervision and regulation of banks, as these policies influence who gets to use society's savings and who does not, who gets to start a business and who will not fulfill his/her dreams, who can expand and who is thwarted by a lack of capital, who remains economically and politically powerful and who will never realistically experience entrepreneurial and political success. Thus, powerful people will try to influence politicians, supervisors, and regulators in ways that promote their selfish interests. Their ability to manipulate the rules of the banking game depends, importantly, on each nation's political, legal, and cultural institutions. This view suggests that to have banks that promote social welfare, a country needs political and other institutions that "oblige" its officials to develop policies that maximize social welfare, not the private welfare of officials or bankers.

The quotation at the beginning of this chapter from James Madison's contribution to the *Federalist Papers* is consistent with this broad and necessarily complex view of bank regulation. Madison clearly recognizes a role for government, "If men were angels, no government would be necessary." Madison was equally clear in recognizing that government would not necessarily strive to maximize social welfare, "If angels were to govern men, neither external nor internal controls would be necessary." Thus, although recognizing the necessity of government, Madison stressed that to maximize social welfare, political systems must unequivocally reject the presumption that governments naturally maximize public welfare and instead must adopt mechanisms that induce governments to promote the public interest and limit government officials from abusing their power to maximize their private interests: "In framing a government which is to be administered by men over men, the great difficulty lies in this: you must first enable the government to control the governed; and in the next place oblige it to control itself."

Madison's view has direct implications for bank supervisory and regulatory strategies. Popular approaches to bank supervision assume either that bank supervisors and politicians naturally behave like angels or that sufficient institutional mechanisms exist to ensure such behavior. Strengthening official supervision may not have desirable outcomes, however, when politicians and bankers – with or without the cooperation of supervisors – conspire to promote the interests of narrow elites. Strengthening official oversight of banks may only work when political institutions minimize political and regulatory capture, thwart officials from using their public power for private gain, and oblige supervisors to act in the best interests of society. It is an empirical question, therefore, whether countries have sufficiently well-functioning political institutions so that strengthening direct official supervision of banks fosters aggregate growth, stability, and efficient resource allocation, or whether strengthening official oversight advances the interests of the privileged.

The likely connections between political institutions and the origins and implications of banking policies, in conjunction with the view that politicians may attempt to maximize private gain, compel a rethinking of bank supervision and regulation. We use case-studies and our cross-country data to examine the linkages between political institutions and bank supervisory and regulatory choices. In essence, we use the laboratory of bank supervision and regulation to assess different views of the role of government. We do not believe it is possible to understand the basis and hence the implications of banking policies without a comprehensive understanding of the political institutions driving policy choices. Furthermore, we do not believe it is possible to make policy recommendations without a sound understanding of the country's political institutions. For example, during President Suharto's regime in Indonesia, a few families controlled the economy and the government. The media did not enjoy independence, and any formal checks and balances in government simply did not function. In this environment, although formal attempts to increase the independence of supervision could have been made to look great on paper, those with Suharto connections had overwhelming influence and would have circumvented any formal reforms that satisfied international standards. Empowering official supervision would have had at best a nugatory effect, and may have given the elites even greater control over resource allocation.

From this perspective, it is misguided and potentially counterproductive to develop a unified checklist of best practice recommendations with the belief that closer adherence to the checklist will produce better functioning banks. We have more modest ambitions. Rather than construct a checklist of best practices, our goals are to better understand the forces influencing bank regulatory and supervisory choices, identify which broad approaches to bank regulation tend to produce better functioning banking systems, and provide a useful database for comparing and assessing bank regulation and supervision.

1.C. KEY FINDINGS: A BRIEF SYNOPSIS

As emphasized, the key contribution of this book is to assemble, present, and summarize new data on bank supervision and regulation across more than 150 countries. In collecting and summarizing these data, we observe enormous cross-country diversity in bank supervisory and regulatory practices, which advertises the importance of exploiting this information to better understand banking policies. For example, minimum required capital ratios around the world vary from 4 percent to 20 percent. Actual capital ratios vary from almost zero to almost 80 percent (no country stated that the net worth in their banks was negative). About 50 percent of all countries offer explicit deposit insurance, a more than threefold increase in the last twenty years. Government ownership of banks varies from zero to 98 percent of total banking system assets. And, foreign bank presence varies from 0 to 100 percent of a country's banking sector. Although the database also reveals regional coordination and harmonization of bank regulations, Chapter 3 documents the continuing international diversity of banking sector policies.

In terms of what works best, our analyses raise a cautionary flag regarding the foundations of current international best practice recommendations. In particular, our results question the efficacy of Basel II's first two pillars on capital regulations and official supervision. We use an amalgam of cross-country studies, bank-level investigations, and firm-level examinations to assess the connections between banking system performance and banking policies. Chapter 4 presents and discusses the results on many individual regulations; here we focus on "big picture" findings.

Before summarizing those results, we note three caveats. First, neither we nor anyone else has data on how well supervision works on the ground. As Chapter 3 makes clear, most of our supervisory variables relate to statutory powers.[7] Although we collect information on how often these powers have been used in the past five years, we cannot know how often they should have been used. This shortcoming may reduce confidence in our econometric work, and if the primary result of this book is "merely" to encourage greater effort to measure supervisory effectiveness, we will be pleased. Second, we only have data for 1998/1999 and 2002/early 2003.

---

[7] Some information on supervisory effectiveness or enforcement may be available from the regulatory authorities, but is usually treated as confidential, has not been publicly examined or tested, and its ability to describe supervisory efficacy is therefore unclear. Interestingly, Barth and Brumbaugh (1996) prepared testimony for hearings before a committee of the U.S. House of Representatives. Their testimony concerned the condition and regulation of Madison Guaranty S&L, which became the focus of intense scrutiny after allegations were made that Madison received lax state regulatory treatment when President Clinton was governor of Arkansas, and that funds from Madison were inappropriately diverted to support the Clinton's political interests and what has become known as their Whitewater real estate investment. They state that "to our knowledge this is the only instance where a review of the examination reports and supervisory correspondence ... has been made public." They add that "as the Madison case makes clear, the examination reports and supervisory correspondence can reveal a considerable amount of valuable information" and ask "unless regulatory agencies disclose the necessary information, how can they ever be held accountable to the public?"

This not only prevents us from studying how regulation evolves over time, but it also advertises potential problems of reverse causation – perhaps, for example, countries that saw financial crises looming ahead tightened supervision, and we then find a link between stronger supervision and crises not because greater supervisory powers cause crises but, rather, the reverse. In light of these shortcomings, we employ instrumental variables, use different bank-level and firm-level data, and test whether we obtain consistent results using various databases and statistical methods. Nevertheless, as new data become available, future research will need to revisit our analyses and employ more powerful methods to control for potential endogeneity. Finally, our data come from survey responses by government officials, not a third-party assessment. As explained in Chapter 3, we have attempted to minimize coding errors by regularly communicating with the national authorities to clarify our questions, confirming each country's responses with national officials, posting our data on the Web, responding to queries, and providing the data to Bank-Fund teams assessing national financial systems. Rarely did we hear of an inaccuracy in the database, and where one occurred, we corrected it.

Across the different statistical approaches, we find that empowering direct official supervision of banks and strengthening capital standards do not boost bank development, improve bank efficiency, reduce corruption in lending, or lower banking system fragility. Indeed, the evidence suggests that fortifying official supervisory oversight and disciplinary powers actually impedes the efficient operation of banks, increases corruption in lending, and therefore hurts the effectiveness of capital allocation without any corresponding improvement in bank stability.

In contrast to these findings on capital regulations and direct supervisory oversight of banks, bank supervisory and regulatory policies that facilitate private sector monitoring of banks improve bank operations, which endorses Basel II's third pillar on market discipline. One mechanism for fostering private monitoring of banks is by requiring the disclosure of reliable, comprehensive, and timely information. Countries that enact and implement these pro-private monitoring regulations enjoy more efficient banks and suffer from less corruption in lending. Furthermore, laws that strengthen the rights of private investors enhance the corporate governance of banks. In contrast, policies (e.g., deposit insurance) that weaken market monitoring of banks tend to have adverse ramifications on the banking system. These results advertise the importance of using bank supervision and regulation to promote market discipline of banks.

Viewed through the lens of the debate on the proper role of government in the economy, the results (1) expose weaknesses with assuming that politicians and bank supervisors act in a public interest manner and (2) highlight the risks of relying on the strong, helping hand of government to oversee banks directly and produce socially efficient financial intermediation. A public interest view of bank supervision and regulation holds that governments will use regulations and supervisory agencies to boost banking performance. In contrast, do not our analyses support this prediction. The results do not suggest that regulatory restrictions on bank activities, regulatory impediments to the entry of new domestic or foreign banks, greater state ownership of banks, or expansion of a wide array of supervisory powers to discipline banks are associated with improved bank development, efficiency, stability, or integrity of lending relationships. Also, although a stated objective of government sponsored deposit insurance is to stabilize banking systems, we find the opposite: the generosity of the deposit insurance regime is associated with greater banking system fragility, not enhanced stability. Overall, the results in this book cast doubt on the view that granting greater power to official supervisory and regulatory agencies to monitor and discipline banks directly will lead to improvements in banking performance and social welfare.

Rather, the results (1) advertise the benefits of a private interest view of government that reflects concerns about political and regulatory capture and (2) endorse a more limited role for the government that focuses on information disclosure and strengthening private market discipline of banks. Consistent with the private interest view, interventionist supervisory and regulatory policies, such as fortifying official supervisory oversight powers, restricting bank activities, limiting the entry of new banks, and expanding government ownership of banks, tend to reduce bank development, make banks more inefficient, and increase corruption in lending. There are some cases in which the negative impact of official supervisory power vanishes when countries have extremely open, competitive, democratic political institutions. Again, this advertises Madison's insight that sufficient checks and balances on the ability of government officials to exploit their positions of power for private gains are crucial for compelling government to maximize social welfare. Because few countries have highly developed democratic institutions, however, the overriding message is that simply strengthening direct official oversight of banks may very well make things worse, not better, in the vast majority of countries. Importing a checklist of regulatory and supervisory practices from the most developed countries may have undesirable repercussions for the vast majority of the world's people.

This does not mean that there is no role for government. The analyses do not support a laissez-faire conclusion. Rather, the results indicate that governments that implement and enforce policies that hold bank directors responsible for the provision of reliable and timely information tend to produce better-functioning banks. Governments that create legal systems that effectively empower private equity and debt holders tend to boost the governance and hence performance of banks. Thus, there is an important role for the government in creating an environment conducive to effective market monitoring of banks, and in using supervision to assist in verifying the information that is disclosed.

We recognize, however, that many countries do not have the legal and political institutions necessary to support effective market monitoring of banks. Consequently, many readers may conclude that a practical approach involves empowering official supervisors until countries develop the institutional foundations for market monitoring. The cross-country results thus far, however, do not support this conclusion. The results instead indicate that regulatory restrictions on bank activities, impediments to the entry of new banks, government ownership of banks, and reliance on powerful official supervisors to oversee banks have adverse effects on the operation of banks. Moreover, it is exactly in countries with weak political and legal institutions that empowering official supervisors is likely to be most detrimental. In weak institutional environments with few checks and balances on the grabbing hand of government, increasing the powers of government supervisors may exert a particularly pernicious impact on corruption in lending and political cronyism. Thus, the evidence pushes inexorably toward the conclusion that the most successful role for government supervisors is to support the market rather than to supplant it in overseeing banks – at least, as James Madison might have added, until angels govern.

We also acknowledge that these findings confront strong prejudices that are manifest in the common jargon of banking sector policy experts. Official reports of international institutions, central banks, and supervisory agencies typically use the phrase "strengthen official supervision and regulation" as synonymous with policies that improve the functioning of banks. Our results suggest that we need to rethink and make more precise the phrase "strengthen official supervision and regulation." This phrase seems to imply increasing the power of the official supervisory agency to oversee, regulate, and discipline banks. These powers, however, are not associated with better banking. To foster better-developed, more efficient banks that effectively mobilize and allocate society's saving, our results suggest that improving banking policies involves considerably more than empowering official supervisors: it involves reforming political, legal, and regulatory systems in ways that require the disclosure of reliable, comparable information on banks and provide private investors with the incentives and tools to exert effective corporate governance over banks.

In terms of the determinants of bank supervisory and regulatory policies, our analyses indicate that political institutions exert a powerful influence over policy choices. Countries with more open, competitive, democratic political systems that effectively constrain executive power tend to rely more on private monitoring of banks, impose fewer regulatory restrictions on banks, erect less imposing barriers to the entry of new domestic and foreign banks, and give less of a role to government-owned banks. The data are consistent with the view that countries with more closed, autocratic regimes: (1) do not strive to promote the dissemination of transparent information, (2) use government-owned banks to funnel credit toward the interests of the politically powerful, (3) limit competition in banking to protect incumbent banks, and (4) create regulatory restrictions so that bankers need to lobby politicians for special exceptions.

The data suggest that countries are not necessarily choosing policies to maximize social welfare. To the extent that open political systems reflect the interests of broader society and act to check government power, bank supervision and regulation tends to promote market discipline of banks, foster competition in banking, and refrain from excessive government intervention in and ownership of the banking industry. To the extent that political systems reflect the interests of smaller elites, there is a much greater tendency for governments to spurn transparency and competition and use the grabbing hand of government to support narrow interests. Thus, our results (1) suggest that political institutions help explain national choices regarding supervisory and regulatory policies and (2) these choices have huge implications for the operation of banks and the prosperity of countries.

The finding that political economy forces determine banking policies implies that improving bank supervision and regulation in many countries will entail much more than identifying those supervisory and regulatory policies that enhance bank operations and social welfare. If governments choose banking policies to maximize social welfare, then deviations of actual policies from optimal policies reflect limited information or mistakes about what works best. From this perspective, credible information on which policy reforms will boost bank development, efficiency, and stability will induce countries to adopt better policies with positive repercussions on social welfare. This book's analyses, however, suggest that many countries' political systems produce policies that maximize the welfare of the politically powerful, not social welfare more broadly. If policy makers are not maximizing social welfare, telling them which policies maximize social welfare may not have much of an impact. Thus, improving bank supervision and regulation is inextricably linked with the reform of deeply rooted institutions. Accordingly, we do not offer our own checklist of best practice recommendations. We simply observe that political, legal, and regulatory systems that foster private monitoring of banks tend to produce more socially desirable results than systems focused on empowering official oversight.

1.D. GUIDE TO THE BOOK

The remainder of the book is organized as follows. Chapter 2 reviews the conceptual reasons for why countries regulate banks, discusses how this thinking has evolved over time, and explains the history of the Basel Committee's approach to making best practice recommendations. Furthermore, Chapter 2 describes how broad social attitudes toward the role of government in society may shape bank supervisory and regulatory practices. Chapter 3 then describes regulation and supervision around the world, drawing on our database. We document vast cross-country differences in regulatory and supervisory policies. Chapter 4 turns to the evaluation of what works best in bank regulation and supervision from a variety of perspectives. We examine the impact of bank supervision and regulation on the development of the banking system, the fragility of the sector, the efficiency of banks, and the degree of corruption in lending. In Chapter 5, we turn to factors underlying bank supervisory and regulatory choices. Do countries choose policies to maximize social welfare? Do policy decisions represent historical accidents – or the advice of international experts? Or, do international differences in political systems explain observed cross-country differences in bank supervision and regulation? Many might presume that politics matter for bank regulation, although the advice of outsiders frequently ignores such factors and proceeds as though any given reform will have the same impact regardless of the institutional setting. Finally, Chapter 6 summarizes our key results and draws policy conclusions. We relate our findings to Basel II,

WTO agreements on financial services, and the drive to harmonize bank regulation across different groups of countries.

This book does not have to be read from beginning to end. Many with a background in banking and regulation might prefer to skip to Chapters 4, 5, and 6 to read the findings on: (1) which policies boost banking system performance and which ones do not, (2) why countries choose different bank regulations and supervisory practices, and (3) the policy lessons. Others may use this book primarily as a reference guide to the data, in which case Chapter 3, the extensive appendices and the CD are required reading. Still others without much training in the economics of banking will find Chapter 2 a useful introduction to the data, analyses, and interpretation of the results. We also hope that even those steeped in the subject might gain from our treatment of bank regulation in Chapter 2 because it further explains the need to rethink bank regulation. Although the chapters fit together, we believe they stand sufficiently alone so that readers with different backgrounds and interests can use the book to achieve different goals.

TWO

Contrasting Approaches to Bank Regulation

People say that Russia should become like Sweden. Or like China. Or like America. But the problem is that we don't have enough Swedes. We don't have enough Chinese. We don't have enough Americans.

Arkady Volsky, former Soviet official
International Herald Tribune
February 17, 2004, p. 1

Over the course of time and across countries, approaches to bank regulation have varied from extremely light to all encompassing, from highly interventionist regulations and even outright government ownership to episodes of "free" banking. In most countries, the level of regulatory intervention in banking has increased dramatically relative to that in other sectors since the Great Depression (Calomiris, 2003). Before looking in detail in Chapter 3 at current regulatory arrangements around the world, this chapter discusses the ways in which societies approach financial sector regulation, the primary features of regulation and supervision, and how external forces are shaping the regulatory choices that countries make.

The first part of this chapter begins with the broad conceptual foundations for bank regulation. As with government interventions in other sectors, those in banking can be examined from the standpoint of the broader debate on the role of government in an economy. Two mostly opposing camps set the boundaries for this debate.

The *public interest view* holds that governments regulate banks to facilitate the efficient functioning of banks by ameliorating market failures, for the benefit of broader civil society. In banking, the public interest would be served if the banking system allocated resources in a socially efficient

18

manner and performed well the other functions of finance.[1] In this case, socially efficient does not necessarily mean in a Pareto Optimal manner. Rather, socially efficient implies that the banking system allocates resources in a way that maximizes output, while minimizing variance, and is "distributionally preferred" (Mishan, 1969). National tastes determine the degree to which the specific focus is on output maximization, variance minimization, or broadening access to capital. But, regardless of the individual weights on these goals, when applied to banking, the public interest view clearly involves adopting bank regulatory practices that expand output and opportunities for the many, while minimizing unnecessary risks. Because banking crises, as further noted later, are expensive, and can reduce growth and worsen income distribution, their prevention often is an explicit goal, but one that derives from the more basic objectives noted earlier.

Within the public interest context, an active role for government is predicated on the existence of market failures. In a world with: (1) no information or transactions costs, (2) governments that maximize social welfare, and (3) well-defined and enforceable property rights, markets will achieve efficient outcomes (Coase, 1960). If the prerequisites for this laissez-faire "invisible hand" theory hold, government regulation of banks would be at best irrelevant and at worst potentially harmful to social welfare. Stated differently, the public interest in this case would be best served by a passive role for government because the prerequisites for active government interventions – significant market failures – do not exist. There are some examples in history of a relatively laissez-faire approach to banking, the best-known example being the Scottish free banking era, between 1695 and 1864 (Kroszner, 1997). The "free banking" era in the mid-1800s in the United States is another example of banking without much government regulation.[2] Still, as noted later, even when formal rules on banks were relatively light, governments had ways of grabbing available resources.

---

[1] As noted by Levine (1997), these other functions consist of facilitating payments, mobilizing savings, allocating capital, monitoring managers, and providing tools for the management and trading of a variety of risks.

[2] It would be incorrect to interpret these cases as free of government intervention. The Scottish free banking system depended both on the existence of large, limited-liability (and regulated) banks, as well as access in times of trouble to the Bank of England, so it was not free of regulation. And the U.S. "free" banks were not without regulation, and in fact usually were faced with significant portfolio requirements (Haber, 2004, and Bodenhorn, 2003). Also Hammond (1957) and White (1995).

The key role of banks in allocating scarce capital also motivates a very different view of regulation. The private interest view (or the economic, or political/regulatory capture view, Stigler, 1971), although it accepts the presence of market failures, instead conceives of regulation as a product, with various suppliers and demanders interacting to determine the exact shape and purpose it serves. Governments are usually the main supplier, and although consumers may demand regulation, industry itself is an important influence on the demand side both for and against certain types of regulation. Given that the benefits (and sometimes costs) of regulation are dispersed among many consumers, while the costs and benefits to industry are concentrated, many expect that industry will have a disproportionate role in determining the regulatory approach taken by the government.[3] Applied to banking, the private interest school would expect to see regulations that enhance the power or well-being of bankers and the politically well-connected. In fact, it is the central role of banks in allocating resources that makes them subject to and attracts the attention of various interest groups: bankers themselves (e.g., to engage in connected lending); politicians (to direct lending to family, friends, and supporters); and the interest of virtually everyone seeking money. Thus, different groups in society compete in attempting to manipulate national or subnational policies toward banks in ways that favor themselves even if these policies do not maximize social welfare. Accordingly, the private interest view supports greater reliance on market discipline, information disclosure, a light hand by the regulatory authorities, and significant oversight of the regulatory process itself (Shleifer, 2005).

After elaborating on these two broad approaches to bank regulation and noting that approaches to regulation can – and probably should be expected to – vary over time, the second part of the chapter then examines specific bank regulatory policies and discusses the pros and cons of these different policies from the perspectives of the public interest and private interest views. This section sets the stage for Chapter 3's description of how governments regulate banks, and Chapter 4's analysis of what works and what does not to promote social welfare.

Finally, the third section of the chapter considers the role of international forces and regulatory convergence. Regulation used to be overwhelmingly a domestic decision, but improved information and

---

[3] Readers will note the similarity to discussions of trade protection, in which the more concentrated benefits, relative to the dispersed costs, of protection bias the political process in this direction.

communications, the growth of global banking, the risk of international crises, pressures from international agencies, and the rise of international agreements for freer trade in services have coincided to bring about a narrowing of the choices being made by domestic regulators. Here we examine the most influential force molding bank regulation around the world: what we term the Basel approach, which is the approach to regulation and supervision espoused by the Basel Committee on Bank Supervision.[4] Virtually all governments today assert that they are following Basel, though the differences in implementation are huge. What constitutes this Basel approach and how it became the reigning "best practice" in bank regulation are addressed in the final section. Whether or not this "best practice" is best – or which elements of Basel recommendations enjoy empirical support – will be addressed in Chapter 4. The possibility that regulatory approaches may be a deeply endogenous variable – another way of restating the quotation at the start of this chapter – is an issue to which we return in Chapter 5.

2.A. TWO APPROACHES TO BANK REGULATION

2.A.1. Public Interest Approach

This section explains the public interest approach to bank regulation. We discuss broad public interest goals, such as boosting economic development, preventing or mitigating costly crises, and protecting consumers. We also review key market failures that provide an economic rationale for government interventions in banking and discuss how they have been encountered in practice. In this section, we take a very broad perspective and simply present an approach to bank regulation that focuses on improving social welfare. Individual policies are treated in more depth later in this chapter, after discussing the alternative private interest view.

We begin with the public interest approach, because it is the one that dominated thinking on regulation during much of the twentieth century and still is taken for granted in many international discussions of regulation. Indeed, it was only after the initial stages of our research, when we found that the public interest view did not seem consistent with the data, that we considered alternative views. We will first outline the theory behind the public interest view, cite some empirical evidence related to

---

[4] Chapter 3 addresses issues related to the World Trade Organization agreement on trade in financial services and the issue of regional financial systems.

the presence of market failures, and then review how this approach has played out in practice.

Pigou's (1938) classic treatment of regulation argues that where the market is imperfect, Adam Smith's invisible hand will not work. The imperfections that can impede the functioning of the market, and that create a potentially constructive role for government to enhance social welfare include monopolies, which will thwart competition; externalities (which induce markets to produce too many goods with negative social consequences, such as banks extending excessive credit, and too few goods with positive social consequences, such as information about borrowers); or information asymmetries or failures in property rights and contract enforcement, which will impede (make unnecessarily costly) the creation, verification, and enforcement of contracts to correct these market failures. This public interest or helping-hand (Shleifer and Vishny, 1998) view takes as given that (1) there are significant market failures and (2) government has the incentives and capabilities to ameliorate these market failures.

An extensive literature attests to information problems in finance, and most discussions of market failure in this area relate to imperfect information. Akerlof (1970) modeled the many consequences of information asymmetries – parties on one side of an actual or potential transaction knowing more than those on the other side. In financial markets, the party receiving funds (e.g., the borrower in a credit transaction) knows better what will be done with the funds, how much effort will be applied, and the intention to repay or the risks that will be taken once a contract has been signed. Although Akerlof applied this insightful idea to various sectors – most notably, used cars (inferior ones pejoratively termed the "lemons" in U.S. parlance) – his classic example was credit markets in developing countries, where local lenders (those having still imperfect, but better, information, compared with outsiders) charge seemingly exorbitant interest rates. Yet when outsiders enter this market to compete, they routinely suffer losses, being at a distinct information disadvantage. Those who enter such markets will be confronted by two serious problems: adverse selection (the riskier clients will be those most willing to pay the highest interest rates) and moral hazard (once the loan is dispersed, riskier than promised actions can be taken by borrowers). This situation clearly indicates why information asymmetries can explain a tendency in finance toward seemingly oligopolistic, or clublike, behavior: lenders tend to deal with those that they know, and information barriers tend to keep out other potential entrants.

Stiglitz and Weiss (1981) developed this idea further and showed how information imperfections can lead to rationing behavior in credit markets. Indeed, banks might not exist if there were no information asymmetries or contracting costs, for otherwise those with surplus funds and those seeking access to them could come together with equal information and sign contracts at no cost. Banks compile their own information sources on customers and economize on costs of verifying the conditions of borrowers (Townsend, 1979), monitoring them (Diamond, 1984) and enforcing contracts (Boyd and Prescott, 1986), and notwithstanding numerous competitors, provide a unique bundle of services (see also Calomiris and Kahn, 1991).

Intertemporal transactions (e.g., the provision of money today in exchange for its return, with the expectation of some positive gain in the future) exacerbate information asymmetries and may shorten credit terms. Relatively little risk may be associated with a loan to a company with payments coming due in the next month, especially where those making the payments are well known. However, when a loan stretches out over ten years, there is more time for shocks to occur, and also more time for the borrower to alter her behavior. Bankers' reaction in such situations is to keep borrowers on a short leash by relying on very short-term credit, at least until the borrower has proven her reliability, and by extending credit only to those with whom the bank has had an extended relationship.[5] Calomiris and Kahn (1991) argue that, notwithstanding its costs, depositors do the same to banks, using short-term and demandable debt as a way to curtail excessive risk-taking by bankers.

In addition to explaining the tendency toward relationship banking and short-term loans, information imperfections also can explain secrecy in lending and the dearth of secondary markets for banks loans. As banks lend to a wider array of borrowers, the latter acquire a credit history, the social value of which potentially exceeds that to the bank; bankers try to appropriate the gains from lending by keeping this information private.[6] Thus, studies (Barron and Staten, 2003) show that both negative

---

[5] These information failures do not mean that financial markets may not be reasonably efficient, in the sense of adjusting rapidly to take account of available information. However, financial markets nonetheless may be volatile, reflecting both that the information basis for contracts may not be accurate, and that intertemporal contracts are signed on the basis of assumptions about a variety of variables, the outcomes of which may differ from market expectations.

[6] Some regulations, however, restrict the use of information in credit scoring schemes used by banks. Yet, Barth, Cordes, and Yezer (1983) theoretically and empirically demonstrate that informational restrictions can produce undesirable credit supply responses.

information about borrowers (such as when they default, which tends to be public) and positive information (e.g., the number of times they pay on time, which in many countries is guarded by banks) have value in lending decisions and credit allocation. Even more evident, the main negative externality in banking resulting from imperfect information is a bank run or, even worse, a generalized banking crisis. Banks themselves are subject to severe informational asymmetries because bank managers have much more information about the quality of the bank's assets than depositors, other bank creditors, and small shareholders. If depositors and other creditors cannot readily verify the condition of banks, then once some begin withdrawing funds, others, not knowing the condition of the bank, may also withdraw their funds, thereby setting in motion a bank run. And if a run is going on at one bank, unless there is an explanation that is specific to that institution, it can spill over to neighboring banks (Diamond and Dybvig, 1983 – although note that their model of bank runs relies not on information asymmetries, but on random shocks). With literally perfect information (all eventualities in the world known with certainty), runs would tend not to occur, because fully informed depositors and creditors would begin demanding higher interest rates as a bank began increasing its risk. Consequently, risk-taking would be curtailed early on, before it could endanger the solvency of a bank. Short of perfect information, bank runs could happen when shocks occur, such as when there is a sharp drop in real estate prices and depositors lose confidence in banks with significant real estate exposure. Finally, runs could occur for strategic reasons, such as when competitors of a bank try to spread false information about their rival or otherwise encourage withdrawals. Note that with perfert information, this strategy would not work, as everyone would know the true state of the bank's exposure.

Information problems seem important in banking, but is there any evidence that they affect banks more than other sectors? Perhaps the most compelling evidence is provided by Morgan (2002), who shows that rating agencies disagree significantly more over banks (and insurance companies, another opaque intermediary) than they do over other types of firms. Although research by Flannery, Kwan, and Nimalendran (2002) do not confirm these findings using stock analysts reports, Santos (2004) finds that Moodys and Standard and Poors (S&P) disagreed about twice as often on the ratings of financial firms compared with nonfinancial firms. It is difficult to explain this finding unless banks are informationally more opaque than other firms. Morgan notes that banks "... hold very few assets that are physically fixed – bolted to the floor, in other words" (2002, p. 881), and "...may be the black holes at the center of the financial universe, powerful and influential, but are to some degree unfathomable" (2002, p. 888). Those banks with more fixed assets – capital and real estate holdings – tended to generate less disagreement among raters, although the significance of this last finding was shaky, reflecting the difficulty in understanding the true capital or real estate exposure of a bank. Morgan found that the only firms that generated more disagreements among raters than banks were insurance companies, the financial intermediary with even longer term liabilities than banks.

What are possible examples of the public interest approach to regulation over time? Given the goals of maximizing output, minimizing variance, and widespread access to capital, governments have intervened for a variety of reasons. For example, countries as diverse as China, Brazil, Egypt, Mexico, and Pakistan all have embarked on reforms in recent years with the stated goal of improving the financial system's contributions to economic development. More recently – Colombia in 2005 – the authorities were trying to modernize their financial sector with the stated objective being to improve its ability to support economic development. This interest goes back some years (and not just in Colombia): fostering economic development was an important consideration in the 1960s to such an extent that the Colombian central bank went beyond discounting to actually granting credit "to promote exports, eliminate bottlenecks in production, and substitute for imports" (White, 2005, p. 15). If markets had been perceived as doing an adequate job in these areas, presumably there would have been no reason for intervention. But the government did intervene: bank reserve requirements were lowered and the central bank was given the power to extend development credits – rising to over 80 percent of their loans and discounts (ibid, p. 16)! As White noted, the previous strictures of the long-accepted recommendations of the Kemmerer mission on monetary and supervisory policy were overturned in order to foster economic development.[7] The officials responsible in effect were acting in accordance with the model of Stiglitz and Weiss, noted earlier: they were attempting to alleviate credit rationing.

In addition to spurring economic development, the perceived fragility of fractional reserve banking also began to prompt calls for regulation,

---

[7] Professor Edwin Kemmerer promoted financial sector reforms in a variety of countries in Latin America and Asia in the early twentieth century. He and his team visited Colombia in 1922 and their recommendations, which included the establishment of a central bank and a superintendency of banks, were put into effect shortly thereafter. See Flandreau (2003) for more on the experience with international financial advisory work.

especially in the United States, where unit banking was a primary factor
behind this fragility until after the Great Depression.[8] Related to the
aforementioned goals, banking crises can reduce output, serve as a source
of economic volatility, and worsen income distribution, as clearly seen in
the Argentine crisis in 2002, where poverty rates soared to over 50% of
the population. The demand to be protected from bank failures arose
with economic development, as development was met by demands to
be protected from the negative consequences of industrialization, which
became more evident and more expensive (Glaeser and Shleifer, 2003).
For example:

Railroads brought with them some of the most dangerous conditions that mankind
had yet created, outside war. The loading of numerous passengers aboard wood
and metal cars weighing hundreds of tons, the movement of those cars at great
speed, propelled by huge portable furnaces generating high-pressure steam, and
the swift passage of the whole train along unfenced tracks that crossed numerous
horse and pedestrian rights of way – all this added up to a spectacular range of
hazards. From the very beginning, grisly accidents were the apparently inevitable
price of railroad development. With the official opening of the world's first commercial railroad – the Liverpool and Manchester (line), in 1830 – came tragedy.
A prominent member of Parliament found himself entangled in the train; and
before a stunned crowd in attendance at the celebration, he was dragged to his
death . . . the occasion of human error seemed to multiply wildly in the presence
of trains. In consequence whatever else governments might decide to do by way
of regulating this new industry, they obviously had to do something about safety.
(McCraw, 1984, pp. 26–27)

Banking crises are the train wrecks of finance. They are not necessarily
bloody, although the 1997 Indonesian and 2001 Argentine financial crises
saw significant violence, and in 1997 Albanian casualties totaled about
twenty-five hundred from rioting in the wake of the collapse of the large
Ponzi scheme that devastated the financial system. Thus, the pain and
turmoil created by a banking crisis can be horrific (World Bank, 2001).
Less visibly, banking crises often are followed by sharp reductions in
credit and an ensuing recession. Moreover, the fiscal pressure generated
by expensive banking crises can lead to reductions in vital expenditures,
such as for health or education.

Crises often are considered a manifestation of imperfect information,
coupled with externalities. As noted earlier, with better information

---

[8] The greater fragility of the unit banking states is similar to the greater fragility of financial
systems in very small developing countries, whose entire financial systems are smaller
than tiny U.S. banks today (Hanson, Honohan, and Majnoni, 2003). Thousands of unit
banks failed in the 1920s and 1930s in the United States.

about either exogenous shocks or the risk-taking behavior of banks, widespread withdrawals might not occur, except as noted below. Similarly, the gains to society of having safe and sound banks are dispersed, whereas the possible reduction in income from cautious lending is borne by bank owners. In fact, bank owners enjoy the upside from risk-taking but are largely protected from the downside by limited liability, giving them a particularly strong incentive to take on risk and conceal it. Indeed, the phenomenon that depositors can be lured to banks paying higher interest rates without regard to risk was amply seen in the Venezuelan banking crisis of the early 1990s, when one rogue bank (Banco Latino) bid real interest rates to 40–50 percent – forcing other banks to raise interest rates to retain their deposits. That banks could ever expect to earn real returns sufficient to pay such rates does not appear to have been a major concern to bankers or depositors. To be sure, it is possible that in fact depositors and bankers each knew exactly what they were doing: taking big risks in exchange for a substantial reward. Depositors and other creditors can take advantage of very high interest rates, with the expectation that they would get out in time before suffering losses. And bankers might rationally go after a high return, given the protection of limited liability. Thus, those who adhere to this view might go further and say that crises are not evidence of imperfect information but, rather, of excessive risk-taking. By contrast, adherents of the behavioral finance view (Kahneman and Tversky, 1979; Shleifer, 2000) would note that this very rational view of risk-taking is not borne out in experiments – in particular, people tend to give excessive weight to recent events, behaving in a myopic fashion. And although most bankers may escape with little damage given the protections they enjoy, depositors may be less fortunate, unless protected by deposit insurance. More generally, the belief in the ability to get out in time should be treated with skepticism, as some depositors have to be among those who fail to exit in time to receive anything.[9] This type of belief also characterizes asset market bubbles (see Box 2.1). Regardless of whether they are deemed rational or not, bubbles or any sharp movements in asset markets can destabilize banks to the extent that they are not well diversified. For example, during the boom in lending

---

[9] Depositors and creditors are not the only ones affected by information imperfections. Bank management in large international banks in the late 1970s and 1980s realized that the high returns in some of their profit centers might actually result from the enormous risks being assumed, and accordingly set out to measure these risks and allocate capital to them appropriately. In effect, this was an attempt to correct for information problems internal to banks.

Box 2.1 Asset Bubbles

Asset markets also can be characterized by relatively wide swings in prices, even when the fundamental determinants of those prices do not seem to have changed – "seem" because not all observers agree on the nature of these fundamentals. These wide swings in prices, in particular their decline, have often prompted calls for a regulatory response, not only but especially in cases in which the price movements have been associated with fraudulent activities. Sharp and sustained increases in asset prices occasionally are referred to as asset bubbles, or speculative bubbles, whose sudden decline or bursting can injure consumers and even indeed entire economies. In some events, such as the 1987 stock market crash, the impact on the economy was minimal, due in part to an accommodative monetary policy in the wake of the crisis, whereas others – the Japanese asset bubble of the 1980s – were followed by a long-lasting slowdown in economic growth. Some are skeptical of the existence of bubbles and the extent to which they may or may not be rational (Garber, 2000). Still, attempts to explain substantial swings in prices entirely by fundamentals strains credulity, as in the case of the 1987 crash, when stock indices in a number of countries plummeted by about 20 percent in one day with no evident new information.

Bubbles are more likely when, as is found in experiments, individuals are not fully rational in assessing risk, trade on noise rather than on fundamentals, exhibit positive feedback (buying because prices are rising, selling when they are declining), or as noted previously, behave myopically. The behavioral finance view (Kahneman and Tversky, 1979; Shleifer, 2000) that asset markets are prone to bubbles finds confirming evidence in countless episodes of sudden asset price collapses, typically with greater or lesser involvement by the banking sector. Although bankers might be expected, as businessmen in general, to behave more rationally than individuals, evidence is mixed. Kindleberger (1978) contains numerous examples of bankers behaving in a myopic fashion. By contrast, Temin and Voth (2004) show how Hoare's Bank made a killing (with profits from buying and selling stock equal to the bank's cumulative profit of the previous twenty years) by "riding" the South Sea bubble, and conclude that in addition to a number of myopic investors, bubbles are also characterized by a number of very sharp investors who understand the risks that they are taking. Regardless of which view is correct, and whether or not asset bubbles' bursting reduces economic growth, they are an example of the volatility from which the public likes to be protected.

to developing countries in the 1970s, many banks acquired such a large exposure to this area that a number of money center banks were technically insolvent when the debt crisis occurred in 1982; similar though less extreme problems were seen in the East Asian crisis (1997) and the Russian debt crisis of 1998, when some banks again took large unhedged positions in response to market movements.

In addition to the desire to spur economic development and to ensure systemic stability, some financial sector regulation has been based on the desire to protect consumers of (and investors in) financial services from fraud, manipulation, and other abuses. These interventions also can be justified as maximizing output, reducing volatility, and protecting the unsophisticated. For example, by making banks "safe and sound," people may be more willing to put their savings in banks, rather than putting them in less productive places, such as under their mattresses, with negative effects on economic development. In his "first fireside chat" in March 1933, after declaring a nationwide bank holiday closing the U.S banking system, President Roosevelt said "People will again be glad to have their money where it will be safely taken care of and where they can use it conveniently at any time. I can assure you that it is safer to keep your money in a reopened bank than under the mattress" (Roosevelt, 1933). Convincing citizens of the safety of the banking system was critical, as the recovery from the Depression depended on the functioning of the banks and the end of hoarding behavior by households.

The now widespread requirement to have "fit and proper" tests for potential entrants into banking can be viewed as reflecting a long history of fraud and swindles in finance (Kindleberger, 1996), which, if left unchecked, also can lead the public to avoid the formal banking sector. In the many recent banking crises in developing countries, fraud and outright looting have been cited as factors in the high cost of these crises (Caprio and Klingebiel, 1997). The cost to consumers when unscrupulous parties are allowed to enter banking was illustrated in the case of the Bank of Credit and Commerce International (BCCI), whose failure harmed governments and consumers in several countries, especially in Africa. Weak accounting practices and fraud, as seen in the Enron and Parmalat fiascos, can help inflate bubbles in individual asset prices but also may result from them as well. The fact that these major corporations could deceive banks, securities markets, workers, and pensioners attests to the strength of information problems in finance with or without a more generalized asset bubble, and in the wake of these episodes there was a prompt demand for a regulatory response, which in the case of the United

States resulted in the Sarbanes-Oxley Act of 2002 (Crockett et al., 2004; Benston et al., 2003).

Related to consumer protection, and one of the earliest features of Western banking systems, is the prohibition of usury, which is on the rise in Islamic countries today (Armstrong, 2003; LeGoff, 1990; and de Roover, 1966, all on the earlier experience with usury limitations). Originally, usury was defined as the payment of any form of fixed interest, with the intent being to protect consumers from sin – perhaps the ultimate consumer protection. Later, usury began to be defined as the payment of excessive rates of interest, with the goal being to protect consumers from falling into a vicious circle of borrowing at high rates of interest, followed by the need to borrow even more money to pay off earlier loans (Kohn, 1999; Homer and Sylla, 1996). Barth et al. (1983) analyze both theoretically and empirically the effect of various government regulations, including usury limits, on the personal loan market using statewide U.S. disaggregated data and find that such limits adversely affect credit extended.

Consumer protection also has been the driving force behind demands for legislative action following Ponzi or pyramid schemes, which in some cases were so large as to raise concerns about systemic stability. In these schemes, the investment manager usually has some complicated story of speculation that is guaranteed to yield a high return. Once initial investors are attracted, they are paid off with the funds invested by subsequent investors. In other words, the funds are not even invested! As noted in Kindleberger (1996), these schemes have been commonplace throughout history, and the casualties in Albania noted earlier resulted from the collapse of a very large Ponzi scheme. In fact, in contrast to the Akerlof (1970) "market for lemons" framework, in which markets with severe information asymmetries are expected to disappear, Ponzi schemes both recur and even grow in size (World Bank, 2001), as new groups or generations become available (Blanchard and Watson, 1982). Occasionally, these schemes are labeled "banks," even when not so licensed, to engender greater trust, and their failure can reduce trust in and even (when quite large) destabilize the banking system.

Given this experience with market failures in banking and related financial markets, was a role for government inevitable? Three factors suggest that the answer is no. First, failure and loss rates in banking were no greater than for nonbanks (Barth et al., 1985; Kaufman, 1994). Second, more recent studies in the United States (Kane, 1992; Benston and Kaufman, 1986; and Calomiris and Mason, 1994) and in several developing countries (Martínez Peria and Schmukler, 2001) provide evidence that depositors were to be able to distinguish between the risk characteristics of different banks. Third, before official regulation became important, markets were responding in some respects to many of the above demands for protection from costly market failures.

The vulnerability of banking, associated with a seizing up of the payment system and the curtailment of credit, led private banks to band together to form coalitions of various types, including (mostly) private clearinghouse associations.[10] Clearinghouses actually serve two purposes: as their name suggests, clearing bank notes more efficiently than would be possible by a series of bilateral exchanges, and helping banks provide liquidity to one another in times of trouble. In the United States, the latter purpose was important during the nineteenth and early twentieth centuries as result of a particularly fragile banking structure: not only were banks prohibited from diversifying by branching across state borders, but also the overwhelming majority of banks (about 96 percent of the twenty-one thousand banks in the early 1930s, according to Calomiris and White, 1994) were unit banks, meaning that they had no branch network at all.[11] This structure tended to make them highly specialized, reliant on local economic conditions, and accordingly highly susceptible to failure. Calomiris (1992) shows that states that permitted branching had significantly lower failure rates during the waves of banking crises that swept the United States in the nineteenth century. Also, as a result of higher failure rates, unit banking states enacted statewide deposit insurance schemes, which regularly failed, leading them to petition the federal government for nationwide deposit insurance. As the Federal Deposit Insurance corporation (1984) reports, 150 proposals for deposit insurance were made in the U.S. Congress beginning in 1886 before deposit insurance finally was adopted during the Great Depression.

In times of trouble, the clearinghouse association functioned as a single bank: it issued short-term certificates that were a liability of the clearinghouse association, so effectively healthy banks were extending their good credit status to weaker banks (Gorton, 1984, 1985; Gorton and Huang, 2001). In effect, the clearinghouse provided a combination of

---

[10] During the free banking period in Scotland, these coalitions constituted one response to the practice of the major banks of gathering up a bank's notes and presenting them suddenly for redemption, in an attempt to force the closure of that bank (Kroszner, 1997).

[11] Interestingly, U.S. President Grover Cleveland had recommended branches for national banks in 1895, but smaller banks successfully opposed his proposal. At the state level, moreover, only nine states permitted state-wide branching in 1909 (Barth et al., 1999).

lender of last resort and deposit insurer for member banks. Interestingly, the association would suppress information during panics, only providing information in aggregate form about the clearinghouse, and not about individual banks (Gorton, 1985, p. 280). However, the clearinghouse performed other functions later identified with central banks: "... by the early 20th century clearing houses look much like central banks. They admitted, expelled, and fined members; they imposed price ceilings, capital requirements, and reserve requirements; they audited members and required the regular submission of balance sheet reports. Finally, they issued money and provided a form of insurance during panics" (Gorton, 1985, p. 283). Similar coalitions of banks with almost unlimited mutual liability to one another, including explicit private deposit insurance, persisted in Germany throughout the twentieth century and to the present (Beck, 2002).

The point to be made is that private market solutions to one problem – bank fragility – seemed to work relatively well, especially where banks were allowed to branch.[12] Branched banks in a clearinghouse coalition represented a significant improvement in banking system stability. By contrast, clearinghouses may have restrained competition, as some also have claimed has been done by central banks, and Gorton and Huang (2001) argue that although they were more efficient in monitoring member banks, compared with central bank monitoring, being voluntary organizations clearinghouse associations depended on bank panics for their existence, which entailed costs to society.

In some cases, some or all of these functions performed by clearinghouses were organized around important banks, such as the Suffolk Bank in early-nineteenth-century New England. Beginning with the Dutch Wisselbank in 1609, the Swedish Riksbank in 1668, the Bank of England in 1694, the Bank of France in 1800, the Bank of the Netherlands in 1814, and the Reichsbank in 1875, what we now call "central" banks emerged gradually – over the course of several centuries – and took on the role of a lender of last resort in troubled times, as well as the task of smoothing credit or business cycles (Capie, 1997, Rousseau and Sylla, 2003). Only 18 central banks existed by the start of the twentieth century (but not all were lenders of last resort), rising to about 60 by 1950 and about 160 today as listed on the BIS Web site. The formation of the Federal Reserve System in the United States in 1913 reflected opinion, after the serious banking panic of 1907, that clearinghouses were insufficient,

---

[12] See Calomiris and Mason (2003), who find little evidence of contagion in the U.S. banking system during the Depression except when there was a run from the dollar.

and perhaps as well was a reaction to the influence exercised at the time by J. P. Morgan, who played a controversial role in deciding which banks survived and which failed. However, according to Gorton, the creation of the Federal Reserve System amounted to a nationalization of the clearinghouse system. As last resort lender, guardian of the economy, and often as bank regulator and supervisor, central banks, supplemented by finance ministries, in some cases by a separate bank regulatory agency, and even by separate subnational regulators, were endowed with regulatory powers by law and used their influence with banks, providing rules and guidelines as to what they could or could not do. Thus, industrial countries evolved from a system more reliant on private sector initiative to one in which government had a significant role. In Germany, the persistence of deposit insurance provided by private coalitions of banks attests to the strength of these private sector antecedents. Developing countries regularly copied the central banking model, often with the advice of industrial country experts, such as Kemmerer, noted earlier.

Before concluding the discussion of the public interest view, note that governments may be well intentioned but inept. This *ineffective-hand* view of regulation does not question the existence of market failures, or the incentives of the government. According to the ineffective-hand view, even if there are market failures and even if governments demonstrate exemplary integrity, official regulation might be generally ineffective at actually easing market failures.

It may be that the task assigned to the regulatory agency is just too difficult (Posner, 1974). For example, how would a bank regulator ensure the solvency of the banking system in a small economy subject to large economic shocks, and yet simultaneously encourage a positive developmental impact of the banking sector? Or how would a supervisor in an economy dominated by several large family groups and with undeveloped accounting and auditing really know the riskiness of a financial intermediary (unless he or she were a family member in good standing)? For instance, it is still true in many developing countries that on-site supervisory visits are rare – less frequent than annual – in part because of a shortage of skilled supervisors.[13] Bank regulatory agencies generally have great difficulty attracting and retaining skilled staff in developing countries; although this problem occurs in industrial countries, a

---

[13] This point takes on added meaning in light of findings mentioned below by Berger et al. (2000) that supervisory information in the United States (with all of its resources) is out of date (meaning that it predicts less well the condition of banks than the market) within months of an on-site investigation. Thus, reliance on supervision where resource constraints prevent ample on-site monitoring could pose significant risks.

number of the latter have broken the link between civil service pay and
the compensation for bank supervisors and other finance professionals,
whereas this link persists in many developing countries. Consequently,
supervisory salaries there appear to lag those in the private sector by
even more than in developed economies. Consider that in India in the
late 1990s, bank supervisors typically had a salary of $3,000 (some hous-
ing benefits were received as well), and the salary of the Governor of the
Reserve Bank of India was $5,000 plus housing. However, even an assis-
tant vice president at a private-sector bank there was earning $75,000
(twenty-five times higher than the supervisor's pay), and the head of
risk management received compensation about ten times still higher than
that. In contrast, competent bank supervisors in the United States who
moved to a private bank (after some cooling-off period) in the 1990s
might only have seen their income double or triple, at the very least until
they become quite successful in their new position.[14] The combination
of ambitious mandates (which the best regulatory agency in the world
could not satisfy), weak skills, and meager resources could result in a
regulatory environment that does not achieve its goals. In contrast to
the public interest view, which would predict that stronger official supervision will boost bank performance and stability, the ineffective-hand
view would expect no improvement at all, even in the absence of any
undermining of regulation by private interests, the view to which we now
turn.

2.A.2. Private Interest View of Regulation

Although the public interest view of regulation assumes that (1) there are
market failures, and (2) the government has the incentives and capabilities
to ameliorate these market failures, the latter condition may not hold.
Since the work of Stigler (1971), Posner (1974), and Peltzman (1986),
many economists have viewed regulation as a product and, like any other
product, therefore analyzed it by focusing on supply and demand forces.
This view could be described as the case of "regulatory capture" or "political capture" (or the "grabbing hand" of Shleifer and Vishny, 1998),
depending on where one sees the division of gains going. For example,

---

[14] Increased attention to a quantitative approach to risk management, in part as a result of
Basel II, is widening pay differentials for those with deep risk management skills, and
is making it more difficult for supervisory agencies to attract and maintain precisely the
skills needed to implement Basel. Given the long lead time to develop the necessary
mathematical skills, and the likelihood that the sophistication of these techniques will
increase, this shortage may persist for quite some time.

applied to banking, this view holds that governments regulate banks to facilitate the financing of government expenditures, to funnel credit to politically attractive ends, and more generally to maximize the welfare and influence of politicians and bureaucrats, even when loftier, public-interest objectives, are the ostensible goal. A proponent of regulatory capture might describe the same situation as one in which bankers enjoy large rents, in return for which they were willing to finance government expenditures, within certain constraints, and to do other favors for government officials. In terms of recent research on corruption and Figure 1.1, this would be an example of both venal and systematic corruption. As noted earlier, the fact that for broader society most regulatory benefits tend to be necessarily dispersed, whereas the effects on the industry being regulated typically are more concentrated, leads many economists to presume that industries' stake in regulatory outcomes is much greater. In any event, the key difference is that the private interests of some are given priority over the general public interest, hence the appellation.

Critically, we acknowledge that the public and private interest views are polar extremes, which can be used as caricatures that help in framing the complex motivations underlying regulatory policies (as in Kane, 1977, 1981, 1984, 1989, and 1997). Many regulatory systems, and indeed even individual government officials, might respond to different incentives at different points in time, in effect fluctuating between these extremes. We will return to this issue after discussing the private interest view and how it has functioned over time.

The private interest view of regulation – one in which banking policies are primarily shaped by the private interests of the regulator or regulatees (Kroszner and Strahan, 2001), rather than by the public interest – has deep historical roots. Kings first resorted to debasing their money when they needed resources:

In 476 the Roman Empire in the West went down, economically as well as militarily bankrupt. It had bled its subjects white through merciless taxation and discredited its coinage through reckless debasement, but . . . had not thought of borrowing what it needed from bankers against the collateral of its immense assets. There followed centuries of deep economic depression, sharp deflation of prices, and sluggish monetary circulation. (Center for Medieval and Renaissance Studies, 1979, p. 3)

Regardless of its success (the Roman method functioned well for several centuries), the process of creating currencies and their subsequent debasement when necessary was difficult to sustain. With the survival of the sovereign literally at stake and taxation difficult (plundering locals was tried but was subject to rapidly diminishing returns and eventually the plundered would revolt), the financial sector became critical. Starting with the rise of banking in thirteenth-century Europe, it did not take long for kings and princes to realize that bank resources could play a critical role in financing their armies. As Ehrenberg (1928) notes, during the feudal system, all freemen had to bear arms, but with economic development came greater specialization of labor and the rise of mercenary armies. Kings and princes were constrained in obtaining or retaining power by the absence of standing armies and by the lack of revenues to pay for them. Advancing technology – the development of firearms and cannons – led to the demands for more sophisticated and expensive defenses, in turn increasing the urgency of the demand for financing (Ferguson, 2001).

Early banks in Europe existed at the pleasure of the king or local ruler, and came with a heavy price: being ready to advance funds to the crown to support armies in times of conflict. This price was heavy, because kings regularly did not repay – even when they were victorious! And when banks tried to diversify by lending to foreign authorities, the relationship often ended up with the (foreign) crown grabbing their resources. Thus,

Lending to English kings proved disastrous to the Ricciardi of Lucca, who lent £400,000 between 1272 and 1310 and then failed when they could not collect their due. The Bardi and the Peruzzi of Florence helped finance the English side of the Hundred Years' War. They were bankrupted when Edward III defaulted to them in 1348. . . . The risk of lending to princes was high and known but the benefit might also be substantial. (Kindleberger, 1993, p. 45)[15]

Haber, Razo, and Maurer (2003), in their study of Mexico during the late nineteenth and early twentieth centuries, argue that despots will have a difficult time credibly committing that they will not appropriate resources; the shorter is the time horizon of the despot and the more liquid are the resources, the greater the incentive he or she will have to behave in a predatory fashion. Given the liquid forms in which banks hold their resources, relative to nonfinancial firms, they are an easy target for predation.

In view of these problems, why would banks voluntarily extend credit to the crown? First, they may estimate that the despot is benign (will repay). Second, they may reap enormous privileges from their relationship:

[15] In a somewhat different context, Kohn (1999) recalls Ecclesiastes: Lend not to him who is mightier than thou (VIII:13).

It is curious that the Italian companies should have lent so much to the crown when the financial returns were so poor, particularly when they may well have had to pay substantial charges to raise the money themselves . . . there were, however, advantages to be gained from royal favor. Under Edward II, the Frescobaldi were showered with grants. In 1309 Amerigo Frescobaldi received six manors for a nominal rent, and in the next year orders were issued to give preference to the firm's nominees for ecclesiastical offices. Exemptions from such burdens as jury service and taxation were also given. Court life seems to appeal to the Italians. (Center for Medieval and Renaissance Studies, 1979, p. 87)

Similarly, the Medici received substantial benefits during the times when they had a monopoly on the Vatican's banking business. These privileges included Lorenzo Medici's ability to make his son, Giovanni, a cardinal at the age of sixteen, who later became Pope Leo X, followed, two years later by Guilio Medici as Pope Clement VII (Hibbert, 2003). Whatever the initial investment, we suspect that the return was worth it!

In essence, lending to the sovereign was similar to a junk bond, potentially yielding a high return, but with a significant likelihood of default. When interest was explicitly charged, princes paid higher rates than merchants or even wealthy towns (Homer and Sylla, p. 99). This relationship between bankers and the crown could be described as the ultimate example of the "grabbing hand" – what better way to grab resources than to borrow and not repay! The tendency of kings and princes to behave in this fashion with impunity was fairly widespread.[16] Kohn (1999) also reports that although public banks were established in the fifteenth century partly in reaction to widespread failures of private banks, and even though these public banks seemed to do well for some time, most of them fell prey to "the Achilles' heel of public banks," namely, lending to the sovereign.

Government's relationship with banks was not driven by considerations of social welfare but, rather, the king's (or prince's) private welfare, namely his personal survival, and by the bankers' benefit – in cash or in kind – from the relationship. During an epoch when monarchs appealed to divine right (and Louis XIV could say, "*L'etat, c'est moi*"), putting the crown's private interest first seemed to be entirely routine, even divinely inspired.

The financing needs of government continued to motivate bank regulation in more modern times. First, in times of war, financial systems were harnessed to fund the needs of the state, as for example was seen

---

[16] Note the exception of the Dutch in the seventeenth century, where an active capital-market permitted the funding of short and long-term government paper (T'Hart et al., 1997).

in the 1930s in the case of Japan and Germany.[17] Second, government needs often come first even in times of peace. As Haber (2004) explains for the nineteenth-century United States, the inability of individual states to impose taxes on interstate trade or to issue money, combined with their rights to charter banks, encouraged them to use banks as a source of funding. States could sell charters or otherwise collect revenues, including equity participation in the bank, which would thereby provide a stream of dividends. Indeed, he cites research (Sylla, Legler, and Wallis, 1987) showing that revenues from dividends or taxes on banks were as high as 31 percent of state revenues in North Carolina and 61 percent in Massachusetts, not including some transfers![18] Bankers were willing to pay because they were acquiring a local monopoly that apparently was of great value. Over time, this monopoly broke down, in part because of the states' voracious appetite for funds (and consequent sale of additional bank charters). By the 1840s, a number of states were granting all requests for bank charters, a form of "free" banking. Then, with the onset of the Civil War, the federal government too came to be hard-pressed for revenues, resulting in a predictable attempt to grab these resources. Under the National Banking Acts of 1863 and 1864, banks were encouraged, if not forced, to apply for a federal charter, which allowed them to escape a new 10 percent tax on state-bank note issuance but then required that they hold government securities as collateral for national bank notes (Hammond, 1957). Although federally chartered banks predictably expanded at the expense of the states, the latter responded by easing their regulation, and the net result of this competition was about twenty-five thousand banks by 1914 (Robertson 1995, pp. 64–66). Interestingly, federal bank supervision in the United States only began in 1863 and from that point many banks became subject to the more stringent federal regulation (FDIC, 1984).

As Haber (2004) explains, the states fought back: some made it easier to obtain a banking charter by ending the requirement for double liability – which was required for national banks. Because double liability for owners would encourage more effective oversight (owners would have more to lose), the ending of this requirement not only stimulated an expansion in the number of banks but also likely undermined the safety

---

[17] The maintenance of low interest rates – well below market clearing levels – and the issuance and marketing of government bonds in the United States during World War II was a less confiscatory approach.

[18] Similarly, banks in India currently are among the largest taxpayers in the country.

of the system. There also were a series of reductions of reserve requirements by states in reaction to the National Banking Act (of 1864), the Gold Standard Act (1900), and the Federal Reserve Act (1913), as these acts tried to make federal charters more appealing, and thereby threatened the states' control over banks (White, 1982). Thus, beginning in 1863, there were two separate and independent banking systems in the United States – the state and federal systems – with banks being chartered and regulated by either regulatory authority without interference from the other. Starting with the Federate Reserve Act, federal regulatory involvement in the affairs of state-chartered banks began to grow and then accelerated with the establishment of the Federal Deposit Insurance Corporation in 1933. Thereafter, federal involvement in banking increasingly became more persuasive throughout the United States.

Of course, governments not inhibited by democracy had more direct means of seizing control of banks. As elaborated on in Chapter 5, when Porfirio Diaz came to power in 1876 in Mexico, he centralized much control with the federal government, including giving it sole authority on bank licensing, and limited the creation of banks to only one (additional) bank per state, with high capital requirements (Haber, 2004, pp. 48–50). His reign thus resembled more the extraction of rents from banks by kings and princes, noted earlier, rather than the competitive environment in the United States. It is also a clear example of systematic corruption, as discussed in Chapter 1, as Diaz used his influence with the banks to control the allocation of credit, favoring projects that would help him and his supporters maintain their positions of power.

What is the relevance of these historical events to developing countries today? With capital markets often vastly underdeveloped in low- and middle-income countries, the banking system is the main source of domestic financing for governments, and it would be surprising if regulation were not at least in part colored by government's own need for funding from banks. Many developing countries, before liberalization, had high reserve, liquidity, and portfolio requirements that necessitated significant holdings of cash and government bonds. For example, until the early 1990s, in India reserve and liquidity requirements totaled 53.5 percent and another 25 percent of credit was directed to various government priorities (Hanson, 2001). Figure 2.1 shows the ratio of credit to (claims on) government to total deposits for twenty-five large developing countries, both the average (in bold) as well as the individual ratios. What is striking is that on average, credit to government has been remarkably stable, so that developing country banks continue to hold substantial

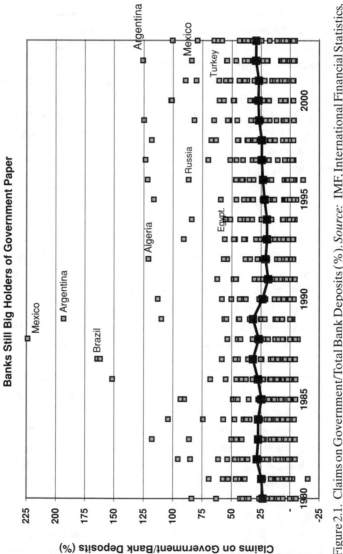

Figure 2.1. Claims on Government/Total Bank Deposits (%). *Source:* IMF, International Financial Statistics, 2004.

amounts of government paper, notwithstanding the ending or reduction of formal requirements. For example, in 2001, this ratio was exceptionally high in Argentina (100 percent), Mexico (79 percent), Algeria (65 percent), Brazil (61 percent), Turkey (58 percent), and India (44 percent), well above any required holdings, and for some time a number of countries have devoted 50 percent or more of their deposit base to government debt. Thus, one reason why liberalized financial sectors did not substantially increase credit to private sector firms is that they were still carrying substantial government financing burdens (Hanson, 2003). In effect, there was little choice, even after liberalization: in countries in which most of the financial sector assets are in the banking sector, and where there is a high level of domestic government debt, the banking system must hold a large share of these claims, with the main difference being that after liberalization the government must pay a higher interest rate. Note also that high debt burdens often are in part the result of difficulties in the financial sector, such as a prior banking crisis or underfunded pension liabilities. An added factor may be the zero risk weighting on government debt, applied in most developing countries, which makes lending to the government cheaper compared with lending to the private sector.[19]

In addition to using banks to finance government expenditures directly, as banks became more important for the overall success of the economy, controlling them through regulation became more important for the overall success and the political survival of governments. Although one could view this financing as being in the public interest, the term private interest remains more relevant to the extent that politicians are using banks either for easy financing of government (thereby sparing them the political risk of raising taxes or lowering expenditures) or are directing credit to preferred ends, which often include their own political supporters.

Thus, a later stage in the evolution of the private interest view of bank regulation holds that governments regulate banks to promote political constituencies (Shleifer and Vishny, 1998; Djankov, La Porta, Lopez-de-Silanes, and Shleifer, 2002), and we include this motivation in the private interest view, as in essence it addresses factors that influence the

---

[19] As discussed later, a key feature of the Basel capital standard of 1988 was that government debt held by banks did not require any capital (in comparison to commercial loans). This feature was justified by industrial country governments' reliability in servicing their debt, and ultimately because they could print the money needed to repay. Its emulation by developing country authorities may well have been motivated in part by the need for financing, even though developing countries typically have a larger share of their debt denominated in foreign currency.

demand for and supply of regulation. This is not a far cry from the origins of bank regulation: rather than directly grab resources for their armies, or other budgetary needs, government officials – still preoccupied with their own survival – use the resources of the banking sector to buy political support (systematic corruption), perhaps keeping some small amount for their own pockets (venal corruption). In effect, this view suggests that the main difference motivating bank regulation is a different form of political competition, with votes and influence replacing bullets.

However, it would be a mistake to think that government officials – especially in more democratic settings – necessarily are in the driver's seat of regulatory decisions and their enforcement: powerful banks or industrial interests may be able to capture bank regulators, usually through politicians, and use the regulatory agency to promote the interests of the banks, rather than social welfare. Kane (1997, in particular) has written extensively on the analytics of the influence of regulatees on financial sector regulation, including an agency view of lobbying and influence peddling. He argues that the latter behaviors will be the most pronounced where accountability is weak, and states that "In every country in the world, regulators produce a flow of clever disinformation that makes it hard for taxpayers to monitor regulatory performance and police agency costs" (1997, p. 61). Barth and Brumbaugh (1994a) also rely on an agency view to explain the record depository institution failures and failure costs during the 1980s in the United States. Kroszner (1998 and 2001) and Kroszner and Strahan (1999) describe the ways in which private interests use the political system to obtain a desired regulatory environment. For example, he notes that the pattern of branching deregulation in the United States occurred later in those states in which smaller banks had a more dominant position, suggesting that they used this position and their political influence to delay change. In contrast, he explains that had public interest theory been driving deregulation, these are precisely the states in which the regulation should have occurred first, because it is where the greatest gains from deregulation were expected (and later seen). Kroszner and Strahan (2001) also show that the timing of bank deregulation in the United States reflected not just industry developments but also the relative power of different interest groups: big versus small banks, banks versus insurance companies, and so on. Moreover, in an examination of congressional votes in this reform process, they find clear support for the importance of inter- and intra-industry rivalries in determining the outcomes, and little evidence that consumer interests mattered.

This interest group approach emphasizes how the costs and benefits of regulations can have a differential impact on various interest groups (whose power could shift over time) and helps to explain the evolution of bank regulation, as elaborated later. In a number of developing countries, a small group of families or conglomerates often controls a large portion of the economy and dominates the banking system as well (Claessens et al., 2000). In this setting, interest group competition is internalized among a few families or groups, and banking regulation will tend to be in line with those interests, absent some powerful outside forces. With family or group dominance, banks are even more likely to engage in related lending, as found in Mexico (LaPorta, Lopez-de-Silanes, and Zamarippa, 2003), Russia (Laeven, 2002a), and Pakistan (Khwaja and Mian, 2004). Although headline regulations may change in these settings, it is likely that these interest groups will oppose changes in implementation that might negatively affect their position. This theme will be taken up further in Chapter 5.

As noted earlier, it is plausible that at times a country's regulatory choices may be more consistent with the public interest view, and at other times private interests. Kane (1997) argues that officials will be subject to pressures to respond to both public and private interests, and that the outcome will depend not only on their personal characteristics but also importantly, on incentives. Indeed, he argues that the process is akin to a Hegelian dialectical struggle, suggesting that continual oscillation is to be expected. Kane also analyzes and describes mechanisms for aligning the incentives of the regulators with those of society.

The dynamics of the powerful pressures on regulators means that the "game" of regulation does not end. Society needs to be alert as to how a seemingly "best practice" regulatory framework can be gamed by the regulatees. This evolutionary view is consistent with greater reliance on market discipline, given that bureaucratic forces will encourage regulators, like generals, to fight the last war, rather than prepare for the next one.

If interest groups drive regulatory choices, it would be implausible to think that any one view dominates for all time, but, rather, that shifting power among these groups would lead to changes in the orientation of regulation. Within the private interest view it is plausible that the balance of power between government officials and private industry changes over time, or as Kroszner (1998, 2001) and Kroszner and Strahan (2001) suggest, that the power of different interest groups varies, leading to different political outcomes. In fact, the latter find that competition between interest groups explains well the pattern of deregulation seen in the United States in the 1980s and 1990s. Elections certainly could drive regulatory (and other) decisions. For example, Dinc and Brown (2004) show that bank bailouts are more likely after elections. This finding suggests that governments were exercising forbearance prior to elections, with the payoff coming afterward, and is a vivid example of the complicated web of possible relationships between regulator and regulatee.

The view that regulation will necessarily evolve over time is also related to the dialectical view of bank regulation (Kane, 1981), which notes that "Market institutions and politically imposed restraints reshape themselves in a Hegelian manner . . . the approach envisions repeating stages of regulatory avoidance (or 'loophole mining') and re-regulation, with stationary equilibrium virtually impossible." In other words, in addition to changes induced by exogenous developments (that is, exogenous to bank regulation), changes in bank regulation itself will set off a series of responses, in turn leading to further change in regulations. Kane uses this framework to explain the pattern of deregulation, which is also driven by changes in inflation and technological forces, and of reregulation.

In theory, these swings between the public and private interest approaches to regulation can take place with different frequencies, and conceivably last for a long time, especially if the factors driving change reshape political constituencies, as occurred with respect to the political consensus in Germany for low inflation following the hyperinflation of the 1920s. For example, Capie (2004, p. 85) argues strenuously that in the United Kingdom, the swings had a rather long life, as "Across at least two centuries (from the early 1800s) there was a relative absence of lobbying, rent seeking, of self-interest, and ultimately there were low levels of regulation." He attributes this to the revulsion against the corruption (we add, both systematic and venal) of the eighteenth century, although he notes that this reaction may be fading. In other words, a significant event can even swing the balance of interest group forces to give the upper hand to the public interest view.

Swings in the approach to regulation thus will reflect the interplay of industry and political forces or the occurrence of exogenous shocks, and at times it can be hard to discern whether public or private interests are dominant. For example, economic development appeared to be important in the regulatory choices made by a number of countries over time. In the United States, in addition to the reliance on unit banks, the large number of banks resulted in part from the states' powers to charter banks and the competition between states for economic development:

The fact that the United States had a federal system and a rapidly expanding frontier meant that population and business enterprises could easily relocate to other states. The fact that they also had an expanding frontier, with under populated frontier states especially eager to attract capital and labor meant that the pressures on state legislatures to hold their populations and businesses from emigrating were especially severe. Competition between states undermined the incentives of legislators to maintain the monopoly banks had earlier established. State legislators were under considerable pressure to provide public works projects, particularly canals, because powerful constituents (urban merchants and large farmers) stood to gain from the increase in commerce they would generate. (Haber, 2004, p. 24)

Perhaps because of information (and contract enforcement) problems, and at best monopolistic competition, banks were perceived to be under-supplying credit; small business often is the group that is rationed, and regularly presses for relief. Thus, White (1982, p. 34) reports that: "At the 1897 Indianapolis Monetary Convention, dominated by Midwestern businessmen, it was resolved that the lack of adequate banking facilities should be met by a diminution of the minimum capital required for banks in places of small population and authority for the establishment of branch banks." This same complaint of the undersupply of banking is widely heard in developing countries today. Although these political forces also clearly are responding to private, rather than public interests, the public benefit from the resulting economic development seems clear, even if private parties were allowed to appropriate a share of the gains.

The balance of power between private and public interests also can be influenced by exogenous shocks; in times of crisis, special interests might have less influence, or might change their views. For example, in the United States, after resisting for decades attempts to institute federal deposit insurance, the opposition to this safety net by money center banks was eroded in the wake of failures during the Great Depression (White, 1997).[20] And in developing countries, regulatory reforms have been observed in or shortly after banking crises, although these are not always long-lasting. Thus, after repealing deposit insurance in the wake of expensive crises in the 1980s, Argentine authorities reinstituted it in 1995,

---

[20] Or in explaining why limits on interstate banking in the United States finally came down only in the 1990s, Kane (1996) notes, "The answer lies in the sustained surges in failure rates and in organizational and service reengineering experienced in the deposit-institution industry during the prior decade and a half. High failure rates among geographically confined banks and S&Ls teach taxpayer-customers important lessons about the longer run dangers of doing business with under diversified institutions, especially at a time when advancing financial technology is fusing financial markets across the nation and around the globe" (p. 142).

months after the Tequila crisis began in December 1994. They also used that crisis, and the fiscal constraint associated with the Convertibility Law (or so-called currency board), to speed up the privatization of public sector banks. By contrast, following an equally large crisis in the early 1980s, the approach to increasing both supervisory powers and market monitoring in Chile proved to be relatively long-lasting, still in force twenty years later. We return to the link between political forces and bank regulatory choices in Chapter 5.

In sum, even though there may be significant market failures in banking, the private interest view casts a wary eye on an approach to regulation based on reliance on powerful official regulatory agencies. This view would suggest that some limits placed on banking earlier in the twentieth century did not just result from competitive forces and technological change but also were the result of the benefits to the industry, and to government officials as well, who imposed the limits. Thus, bankers began to press for deregulation only when they felt the competition from nonbanks and from foreign jurisdictions. And regulatory officials in some countries may have been positively influenced to support "modern prudential regulation and supervision" because it enhanced their budgets and other perquisites. In other words, they would have been failing to follow the advice of James Madison, in the quotation that opened Chapter 1, that government also must "govern itself."

As we have seen in this section, there are great differences in the polar views about the overall approach to bank regulation, both are plausible and have vigorous adherents, and there is wide scope for swings between the two. A number of studies cited have used historical examples within individual countries to make arguments for or against a certain broad approach. The next section will turn to specific government interventions in banking, examining the pros and cons of these interventions in the light of the broad approaches to bank regulation. Then after presenting the data on bank regulation and supervision around the world in Chapter 3, we will turn to our own empirical evaluation on the specifics of government intervention, as well as to assess the broader approaches.

2.B. BANK REGULATION: PROS AND CONS[21]

Governments typically intervene in the banking sector in a variety of ways, covering everything literally from the entry of banks to the manner

---

[21] This section draws on and amplifies on Barth, Caprio, and Levine (2004).

in which they exit the industry. Although not exhaustive, we review here, and link to the above debate, the pros and cons of regulations on bank activities, entry (both foreign and domestic), capital requirements, the powers given to supervisors, the safety net available for banking (deposit insurance), the regulations related to the ease with which the private sector can monitor banks, and finally, outright government ownership, the most pervasive form of government control. In the process, we also discuss the predictions of models that motivate these specific bank regulations based on particular market imperfections.

2.B.1. Restrictions on Banks, and on Links to Commerce

Activity restrictions are critical for banks, and in fact help define what observers mean by the term "bank." From the public interest view, there are five main theoretical reasons that have been advanced for restricting the degree to which banks can engage in securities, insurance, and real estate activities, or own nonfinancial firms:

- Conflicts of interest may arise when banks engage in these diverse activities. Banks, for example, may attempt to "dump" securities on or shift risk to ill-informed investors so as to assist firms with outstanding loans (Edwards, 1979; John, John, and Saunders, 1994; and Saunders, 1994).
- To the extent that moral hazard encourages riskier behavior by banks, they will have more opportunities to increase risk if allowed to engage in a broader range of activities (Boyd, Chang, and Smith, 1998).
- Broad financial activities and the mixing of banking and commerce may lead to the formation of extremely large and complex entities that are extraordinarily difficult to monitor (Laeven and Levine, 2005).
- Large institutions may become so politically and economically powerful that they become "too big to discipline."
- Finally, large financial conglomerates may reduce competition and hence efficiency in the financial sector.

According to all these public interest arguments, the government can ease such market failures and thereby enhance bank performance and stability and protect consumers by restricting activities.

By contrast, there are theoretical reasons for permitting banks to engage in a broad range of activities, so even the public interest argument about what to do is not clear. First, regulatory restrictions on the activities of banks can limit the exploitation of economies of scale and scope in gathering and processing information about firms, managing different types of risks for customers, advertising and distributing financial services, enforcing contracts, and building reputation capital with clients (Barth, Brumbaugh, and Wilcox, 2000; Claessens and Klingebiel, 1999; Santos, 1999; and Haubrich and Santos, 2005). Thus, regulatory restrictions may be inefficient. Second, such restrictions may reduce the franchise value of banks and thereby limit incentives for prudent behavior by banks. Third, by limiting banks' activities, regulatory restrictions could impede bankers' ability to diversify income streams, leading to greater instability. The private interest view would generally favor these arguments against restrictions, especially because restrictions can be structured so as to give discretion to the regulators, and thus the possibility of earning rents (Shleifer and Vishny, 1993). If activity restrictions were found to be associated with less financial sector depth, less efficient banks, or more financial crises, these findings could be consistent with either the public or private interest view. However, if restrictions on bank activities also were linked with greater corruption, then the evidence would be consistent only with the latter.

Although existing empirical studies provide mixed results regarding these theoretical debates, most of the literature suggests there are positive benefits from permitting broad-banking powers. For instance, studies of the U.S. case show that expanded banking powers are associated with a lower cost of capital and less stringent cash-flow constraints (Berger and Udell, 1996; DeLong, 1991; and Ramirez, 1999). Vennet (1999), moreover, finds that unrestricted banks have higher levels of operational efficiency than banks with more restricted powers. In terms of diversification, Eisenbeis and Wall (1984) and Kwan and Laderman (1999) argue that as profits from providing different financial services are not very highly correlated, there are diversification benefits from allowing broader powers. Notwithstanding allegations at the time, subsequent empirical studies show that broad or universal banks did not systematically abuse their powers in the pre-Glass-Steagall days of the United States (Ang and Richardson, 1994; Kroszner and Rajan, 1994; Puri, 1996; Ramirez, 1995; and Santos, 1998b) or fail more frequently (White, 1986). And Calomiris (1997a) showed that German firms enjoyed lower financing costs than in the United States, essentially because of the economies of scale and scope enjoyed by universal banks in Germany.

Using an earlier version of the cross-country data presented in Chapter 3, we found that greater regulatory restrictions are associated with a higher probability of a country suffering a major banking crisis and lower banking-sector efficiency after controlling for possible reverse causation (Barth, Caprio, and Levine, 2001a, and the discussion in Chapter 4). We found no positive effects from restricting banking-sector activities. Regulatory restrictions, for example, were not closely associated with less concentration and more competition in either the banking or industrial sector, and also were not closely linked with securities-market development.

2.B.2. Entry Restrictions

Governments typically influence banking by regulating the entry of new banks. Entry restrictions were an early intervention. In the Middle Ages, "Everywhere, entry into the banking was restricted" (Kohn, 1999, p. 19), by licensing or royal charters, guild membership, or an auctioning of a fixed number of banking tables (effectively, licenses) to the highest bidder. According to the public interest view, by effectively screening bank entry, governments can promote bank stability and protect the economy from the negative effects of bank failure. Bank entry could be destabilizing in two ways. First, the entry of "rogue" bankers (e.g., the aforementioned Banco Latino case in Venezuela) exposes consumers to the risk of fraud, and may set off a generalized run on other banks, to the extent that depositors then realize that they do not have good information about the risks being taken by banks. Second, to the extent that excessive entry leads banks to compete interest rates on loans down to a level below an appropriate, risk-adjusted return, instability would be the result (Hellmann, Murdoch, and Stiglitz, 2000, 2002).

Limits on bank entry also might be stressed from the view that banking itself is a natural monopoly, because of information asymmetries, and the particular information that individual banks possess. In fact, banks with some monopolistic power might have stronger incentives to incur the necessary costs associated with overcoming informational barriers, and thereby allocate credit more efficiently, as argued by Petersen and Rajan (1994). Also, entry limits can increase the franchise power of banks, which is the present value of their stream of future profits from banking. There is some expectation that banks with greater franchise value will behave more prudently, as the existence of significant future profits can motivate bank managers to ensure that their bank remains open and therefore able to enjoy these rewards (Keeley, 1990; Caprio and Summers, 1996).

The private interest view looks at barriers to entry quite differently: notwithstanding some possible justifications for entry limits, this view points out that industry – in this case, bankers – will tend to demand barriers to entry in order to limit competition. Regulators will be tempted to respond, both as a way to reward supporters, to help them maintain political control (again, an example of systematic corruption, noted in Chapter 1), and as a way to extract rents for their own benefit (the venal corruption described in Wallis, 2004, and Djankov, La Porta, Lopez-de-Silanes, and Shleifer, 2002). As just mentioned, an uncompetitive banking sector in fact could be instrumental in ensuring that both the rest of the economy as well as the political process remain uncompetitive, with incumbent politicians rewarding their supporters with a monopoly position in the banking industry, a position from which they can steer credit to other supporters of the government. In contrast, an open, competitive banking sector would erode the profits of those already in the industry, would limit the ability of regulators to extract bribes, and likely would allocate credit to a wider group. The study of the United States and Mexico by Haber, cited earlier, finds evidence exactly along these lines: the greater degree of political competition in the United States was associated with somewhat greater competition in the banking sector and in particular a wider distribution of credit, as the many local banks lent to a wider array of local businesses.[22] In sharp contrast, in late-nineteenth- and early-twentieth-century Mexico, the unification of power by Porfirio Diaz, at the expense of the states, was associated with a highly concentrated banking sector and a high degree of concentration in credit allocation. Haber, Razo, and Maurer (2004) then show that the Mexican textile industry was much more concentrated than that in United States, Brazil, or India, and link this to the lack of competition in the banking sector.

Other research, mostly on the United States, finds that competition is important for static and dynamic efficiency improvements (Berger and Humphrey, 1997; Claessens and Klingebiel, 1999). Swamy et al. (1996), in a time-series, cross-sectional study find that banking profits were significantly higher in those states within the United States with substantial barriers to entry. Jayaratne and Strahan (1998) provide evidence that when individual states within the United States created a more competitive (and diversified) banking sector by liberalizing their branching restrictions, the rate of economic growth within those states accelerated

---

[22] Notwithstanding the large number of U.S. banks at the time, the increase in competition was somewhat limited by the fact that most of the banks were unit banks. Competition was greater in states that permitted branching, other things equal.

and the quality of bank lending improved.[23] Furthermore, Shaffer (1993) finds evidence from an analysis of cross-sectional data for the United States that household income grows faster in markets where the banking sector is less concentrated. Greater bank competition in local U.S. markets is strongly associated with an increase in the number of nonfinancial sector establishments, and a greater presence of smaller firms (Cetorelli and Strahan, 2005). In other words, this evidence is consistent with the notion that limited competition in banking can help limit new entry in the rest of the economy. In contrast, in an earlier study Petersen and Rajan (1994) find that firms are less credit constrained and younger firms have access to cheaper credit in the more concentrated banking markets of the United States. One way to reconcile the two findings is that in the early 1990s, interstate branching barriers were still coming down, and it took a few years for the impact of increased competition to have an impact on the rest of the economy. It also may be the case that small firms need to form long-term relationships to get access to reasonably priced credit.

Evidence from around the globe further advertises the adverse effects of regulatory restrictions on competition in banking. Demirgüç-Kunt, Levine, and Min (1998) find that easier foreign entry improves bank performance, whereas in a cross-industry study, Cetorelli and Gambera (2001) show that greater banking-sector concentration exerts a depressing effect on overall economic growth, although it promotes the growth of industries that depend heavily on external finance. A particularly important study by Guiso, Sapienza, and Zingales (2004) examines the impact of different degrees of restrictions on bank competition across the regions of Italy. These differences date from a 1936 banking law, which restricted entry, the effects of which were found to be substantial. The study shows that, after controlling for possible reverse causation, in regions with less financial development (and less competition in banking), there was less access to credit and it was more difficult for younger people to start up firms. Interestingly, the effects of financial sector development and bank competition did not matter for large firms, who presumably have access to a national (and international) banking market, but was quite significant for small firms. The authors also find that these effects were highly significant in economic terms, so much so that they can explain over half of the difference in per-capita income levels between Milan and Rome. These real sector effects, and a

---

[23] This study is particularly important, because by comparing states within one country, it avoids problems associated with country specific factors in cross-country studies.

better appreciation of the importance of competition in banking, along with the role of international forces (more on this later), help explain the emphasis on financial liberalization since the 1990s and the move toward reforms of prudential regulation in Italy and around the world. In short, evidence is emerging that restricting competition in banking can have negative effects, but so far has been based on a narrow range of countries.

Even though restrictions on entry might hurt economic development generally, Calomiris and Ramírez (2002) provide theoretical and empirical evidence that some borrowers might favor restrictions because the barriers to entry will limit banks' options, to the benefit of some. Although borrowers with more mobile factors of production favored branch banking and more liberal entry, they find that landowners in a relatively high-wealth U.S. states preferred unit banking restrictions. The owners of the immobile factors of production gained in part from the implicit commitment that unit bankers make, that is, not to leave when the economy deteriorates, essentially when the price of the immobile factor falls. They note that this same logic might lead landowning elites in developing countries to favor barriers to entry for foreign banks. The industrial interests in these countries instead will favor and benefit from increased competition and superior banking services.

2.B.3. Capital Requirements

Once other entry criteria have been met, bank entrants need to comply with the initial minimum amount of capital that is required to enter a market, and the minimum prudential capital/asset ratio as banks grow. Capital regulation is a centerpiece of government intervention because it can affect risk-taking by bank owners and constitutes a buffer to absorb unexpected losses. With limited liability, owners may have an incentive to engage in riskier ventures, and minimum capital requirements become important in determining the amount that bank owners must have at risk (Lamoreaux, 1994). In the nineteenth and early twentieth centuries many countries had double, triple, or unlimited liability for bank owners, sometimes complemented with overall leverage ratios or minimum requirements for holding government paper. In the United States, national banks and those licensed by a number of states featured double liability in banking, which meant that in the event of insolvency, owners of banks not only would lose the amount of capital that they had paid in but also were liable for additional assessments (to cover losses) of an equal amount from their own investment. Saunders and Wilson (1999) document that states with these laws tended to see higher actual capital ratios than in states with limited liability, apparently because bank owners wanted to share the risk that they faced with other owners, and hence mobilized more capital. Also, banks funded themselves by issuing (uninsured) bank notes or other forms of marketable paper and those that held higher capital (relative to their assets) tended to be rewarded with a lower cost of funds. Saunders and Wilson also show that from the 1890s to the 1970s and 1980s, capital ratios fell from levels of about 30 percent in the United States (and even higher levels earlier) to about 5 percent; from 20 percent to about 3 percent in the United Kingdom; and from 25 percent to 5 percent in Canada following the ending of higher liability limits and the development of a safety net for banks.

Many approaches to the subject of bank regulation regularly assume the public interest view and emphasize the positive features of capital adequacy requirements in limiting risk-shifting behavior (Dewatripont and Tirole, 1993). With explicit deposit insurance, official capital adequacy regulations play a crucial role in aligning the incentives of bank owners with depositors and other creditors (Berger, Herring, and Szego, 1995; Kaufman, 1991; Kaufman and Kroszner, 1997; Stevens, 2000; Furlong and Keeley, 1989; and Keeley and Furlong, 1990). The reasoning is that if bank owners have more capital at risk, the upside gains that they would enjoy from risk-taking, in the form of higher profits and equity price appreciation, would be counterbalanced by the potential loss of their capital if their bank were to experience large losses. This effect will only be felt to the extent that the capital is real; if there have been large losses already, for which the bank has not yet set aside provisions, then its accounting capital will overstate true economic capital. When the latter is zero or negative, bank owners will have an incentive to lend to very high risk projects that might pay a high interest rate, as they will not be exposed to any downside loss.

Researchers, however, disagree over whether the imposition of capital requirements actually reduces risk-taking incentives. Allen and Gale (2003) argue that banks will choose an optimal capital structure without any government requirement, and that the theoretical rationale for capital requirements is lacking. To the extent that the rationale for capital requirements is to prevent financial contagion (one bank failure triggering another), they suggest that the cost of regulatory compliance needs to be taken into account.

Moreover, it is extraordinarily difficult – if not impossible – for regulators to set capital standards that mimic those that would be demanded by well-informed, undistorted private-market participants. Kahane (1977), Koehn and Santomero (1980), Lam and Chen (1985), Kim and Santomero (1988), Flannery (1989), Genotte and Pyle (1991), Rochet (1992), Besanko and Katanas (1996), Blum (1999), and Alexander and Baptista (2001) all note that higher capital requirements might increase risk-taking behavior, even though it could lead to a reduction in the size of the banks' overall balance sheet. This effect is expected to be greater with limited liability. In the framework of the models employed by these authors, the simple capital requirements do not vary with risk, but the result would be the same if the adjustment for risk in the determination of capital requirements lags behind the portfolio adjustments of banks. This line of research may account for the interest in moving away from Basel I, with fixed risk weights, to the advanced variants of Basel II, which take account of banks' own risk models.

Milne (2004) posits an inventory model, according to which bankers voluntarily maintain a buffer in excess of regulatory minima because of the illiquidity of their assets and the costs of raising capital, as well as of regulatory intervention. In his model, the impact of raising capital requirements are muted. However, his approach does not take into account any market reward for higher capital, meaning the possibility that funding costs could be lower for banks with more capital. The latter effect presumably would increase the size of the buffer, and as the buffer increases, the impact of capital requirements is muted still further.

In a more guarded assessment, Thakor (1996) demonstrates the conditions under which risk-based capital requirements increase credit rationing, with negative implications for economic growth. Also, Thakor and Wilson (1995) argue that higher capital requirements may induce borrowers to shift to capital markets and in the process impair capital allocation, whereas Gorton and Winton (1999) show that raising capital requirements can increase the cost of capital (raising the possibility of a conflict between prudential and developmental goals). Thus, there are conflicting predictions on whether capital requirements curtail or promote bank performance and stability (Santos, 2001).

Adherents of a private interest view tend to oppose regulations unless the benefits clearly exceed the costs and there is little hope of an alternative solution. Thus, they generally would oppose reliance on capital requirements in light of these mixed views because capital requirements both create an entry barrier and open another channel for possible rent extraction by government officials. It is quite difficult to make capital requirements effective because of the need to take account of banks' ability to alter their risk profiles, an ability that changing technology and financial engineering makes increasingly quick and easy. This means that the resulting requirement would then have to be evaluated with some discretion. Those inclined to the public interest approach, although also recognizing this difficulty, would nonetheless be more likely to endorse a reliance on official capital requirements, coupled with the discretion of the official supervisor, whereas the private interest approach would indicate that discretion should be supplied by the market, as discretion in the hands of officials is a recipe for either venal or systematic corruption.

2.B.4. Supervisory Powers

In addition to the assumption that market imperfections are important in financial markets, the public interest view takes as given that bank supervisors can overcome these failures, and, furthermore, that they have the incentive to do so. The combination of these assumptions leads to a particular approach to bank regulation, specifically one that provides the necessary powers to bank supervisors to ensure the safety and soundness of the banking system. In many countries for most of the twentieth century, bank supervision was a more compliance-oriented activity, as banks generally faced many detailed restrictions on what they could do, and the supervisor's job was to ensure that they followed these restrictions. Developing countries tended to have many directed credit programs, and also to have high reserve and liquidity requirements, which helped them remain more stable than otherwise might have been the case. As financial sectors began to be liberalized, first in industrial countries in the 1970s and 1980s, and then in developing countries in the 1980s and 1990s, reserve and liquidity requirements were significantly reduced, directed credit programs curtailed, interest rates were liberalized, and accordingly supervision began to be oriented to prudential issues. It was generally recognized that supervision became even more important in countries that had adopted explicit deposit insurance, because of its recognized potential to create incentives for excessive risk-taking behavior by banks, with a corresponding reduction in the incentives for depositors to monitor banks. Thus, strong, official supervision in the public interest view helps prevent banks from engaging in overly risky behavior and thus improve bank performance and stability. This view would call for independent supervisory agencies, in order to insulate regulators from political pressure from bankers.

As might be expected, the private interest view sees strong supervision in a different light. Governments with powerful supervisory agencies could use this power to benefit favored constituents, attract campaign donations, and extract bribes. Powerful regulators/supervisors, according to this view, will not focus on overcoming market failures and boosting social welfare; rather, they will focus on promoting their private interests. And even if supervisors attempt to behave in the public interest, they may be pressured by politicians motivated more by private concerns. According to this view, powerful supervision and regulation will be positively related to corruption and negatively associated with bank performance, with little or no benefit to stability. Abuses of supervisory powers would be more likely in countries in which the oversight of supervision, either from inside the government (e.g., by independent auditors, or by other supervisory agencies) or outside government (e.g., from an independent and educated media), is not highly developed. Indeed, both internal and external monitoring of supervision may be necessary to limit abuses of power or various forms of corruption. Independence may contribute to better supervisory outcomes, but only where it coincides with strong checks and balances on supervisory behavior. Thus, proponents of the private interest view would accept that in theory independence might be positive, but that in practice it could be used to conceal a variety of abuses, and would raise costs. True independence with effective oversight likely is a difficult combination to achieve.

There has been little empirical work on the effectiveness of bank supervision, and the only studies till now focused on its impact in the United States, a very particular institutional setting. Flannery et al. (2001) find evidence that government examinations of banks produce information that markets do not internalize for several months, whereas Berger et al. (2000) find that supervisory assessments normally are found to be less accurate than both bond and equity market assessments in predicting future changes in bank performance, and only have some added value when inspections are extremely recent. So if supervision contributes to bank monitoring, its "shelf life," appears to be quite limited, relative to the information that is available in the market, meaning that countries would need to invest substantial resources to ensure the ability to keep supervision current. Unfortunately, there have not been extensive studies of supervision's effectiveness in other countries, and in particular not in developing countries, with the exception of the cross-country research reported in Chapter 4.

2.B.5. Safety Net Support

A critical part of the regulatory framework is the safety net that is available to banks, in particular because it can affect the incentive of private monitors to oversee banks. To the extent that bank creditors believe themselves to be protected, they will have little incentive to oversee banks. The safety net has two key components: first, the lender of last resort, and second the existence of an explicit deposit insurance system. To the extent that the lender of last resort – usually, the central bank – adheres to the policy of providing unsubsidized support (or even at penalty rates) to illiquid but solvent banks, and, importantly, allows uninsured creditors to suffer losses, the impact on market discipline will be contained. Central banks can abuse their lender of last resort powers by providing essentially open-ended or subsidized discount window support to banks that are in difficulties, as appeared to have happened in recent banking crises in Indonesia and the Dominican Republic.[24] In practice, it is difficult to evaluate when central bank support is inappropriate, although Honohan and Klingebiel (2000) found a number of cases of banking crises in which liquidity support was provided for twelve months or longer and in excess of total banking system capital, which certainly would seem excessive. In these cases of "easy" intervention, which also included those in which blanket deposit guarantees were issued, insolvent banks were allowed to remain open (prudential regulations were suspended), or repeated bank recapitalizations or across-the-board debt relief occurred, the result was a very high fiscal cost. These policies are an important factor explaining why some developing country crises have been so expensive (World Bank, 2001). Moreover, they describe well the case of the savings and loan crisis during the 1980s in the United States, when hundreds of federally insured institutions were left open by the regulatory authorities despite publicly reporting their insolvency for years (Barth and Brumbaugh, 1994).

The other part of the safety net, and one that is growing rapidly, is the system of explicit (limited) deposit insurance. After the adoption of a national deposit insurance system in the United States in 1934, in other countries explicit systems grew slowly for the first thirty years, with only six being established. Then adoptions accelerated: twenty-two formal systems existed by the fiftieth anniversary of the U.S. system, and about

---

[24] Most central banks in industrial countries only provide liquidity support for a few days to a few months, and insist that the recipients be subject to strenuous supervisory oversight.

seventy-eight systems were in place by early 2004, with other countries studying the matter.[25] The public interest case for deposit insurance is twofold: to protect banking systems from bank runs, as well as to protect small depositors. Bhattacharya, Boot, and Thakor (1998), Calomiris and Kahn (1991), and Diamond (1984) observe that banking is particularly susceptible to runs due to information asymmetries, sequential service (first-come, first-served), and demandable debt. If too many depositors attempt to withdraw their funds at once (even if the only cause is a "sunspot"), an illiquid but solvent bank can fail from the forced sale of assets at fire-sale prices. Moreover, because monitoring banks is expensive and generates an externality, depositors will have a tendency to free ride on the monitoring efforts of others, leading to a socially suboptimal level of monitoring. It should be noted that there is much disagreement on the fragility of banking, as noted earlier. Also, there are other ways to protect small depositors (Calomiris, 1997).

Deposit insurance often is labeled as the source of the moral-hazard problem in banking. As suggested earlier in the discussion of limited liability, it is this feature, not deposit insurance, which allows bank owners to be protected from some of the large downside costs of excessive risk-taking. Deposit insurance instead facilitates risk-taking to the extent that it encourages depositors to relax their monitoring efforts and that it reduces or eliminates any risk premium in their cost of funds. In effect, limited liability allows bank owners to reduce the cost that they pay for taking risks, and deposit insurance helps them to raise funds and formalizes the process of how losses are covered. To protect banks depositors, a proponent of the public interest view would favor deposit insurance to protect payment and credit systems from contagious bank runs *plus* tight official oversight to augment private-sector monitoring of banks.

Potential gains from a deposit insurance scheme come at a cost, however. Even in the 1930s, there were concerns that deposit insurance would encourage excessive risk-taking behavior (Philipps, 1995; Barth, 1991), as noted earlier. More recently, Demirgüç-Kunt and Huizinga (2000) show that a reduction in market monitoring is not just theoretical. They find that rapidly growing banks in countries with explicit deposit insurance experienced little or no increase in their average cost of funds, whereas banks embarking on such a strategy without explicit deposit

---

[25] Recently, China and Namibia have rejected deposit insurance, at least for the present, whereas Russia, which had only adopted it in 2003, converted it to unlimited coverage when a run on a couple of banks was imminent in 2004.

insurance see a significant rise in their funding cost. Evidence in this and related research (see World Bank, 2001; Demirgüç-Kunt and Kane, 2002) suggests that deposit insurance is particularly costly in weak institutional settings, where the rule of law, the information environment, and bank regulation are underdeveloped. Barth (1991), Kane (1989), and White (1991), however, show that even in a country with a strong institutional setting such as the United States deposit insurance can be quite costly. Our earlier research (referenced in Chapter 4), using a previous version of our cross-country dataset, showed that explicit deposit insurance is strongly and negatively associated with banking sector stability, confirming the findings of Demirgüç-Kunt and Detragiache (1998). Thus, deposit insurance in this view may be a way to aid the small depositor or small banks but at the potential expense of taxpayers, who may be called to bail out the system.

The private interest view of deposit insurance is clearly at odds with the public interest view. Deposit insurance is a favorite of riskier banks, as it helps them to attract deposits without having to pay a premium – a finding confirmed by Laeven (2004) and Kroszner and Strahan (2001). A number of countries copied the feature of U.S. deposit insurance legislation, whereby a ceiling is established on the total size of the deposit insurance fund. As a result of this ceiling, no U.S. bank, regardless of its risk profile, has paid a deposit insurance premium in years. Even large banks might favor deposit insurance, to the extent that it is underpriced, and Laeven (2002) shows that deposit insurance is regularly underpriced in developing and emerging markets. Moreover, Kane and Wilson (1998) show how deposit insurance could and did help stockholders of large banks, using a model with asymmetric information and an agency-cost paradigm. Thus, the private interest view is that deposit insurance is a way to hand out subsidies and can undermine the market monitoring of banks. Thus, the private interest school would predict that deposit insurance would be associated with a less stable banking system.

2.B.6. Market Monitoring

In addition to or instead of focusing on directly regulating capital levels or asset allocation, supervisory agencies could focus on encouraging private monitoring of banks. For instance, supervisory agencies may require banks to obtain and publish certified audits or ratings from international rating firms. Many countries make bank directors legally liable if information disclosed is erroneous or misleading, but in about half of the countries in our sample, this liability either is not enforced or has never been enforced. Some supervisory agencies compel banks to produce reliable, comprehensive and consolidated information on the full range of bank activities and risk-management procedures. Furthermore, some countries credibly impose a "no deposit insurance" policy to stimulate private monitoring of banks.

Many economists over the years have advocated greater reliance on the private sector and expressed misgivings with official supervision of banks. Basel I did not really acknowledge private-sector monitoring, whereas Basel II includes it as one of three pillars, even if it has received less attention than the other two. The regulatory capture view holds that banks will pressure politicians who, in turn, can unduly influence supervisors and regulators, and that consequently greater reliance on market discipline is important. As noted earlier, in some countries supervisors are not well compensated and can quickly move into banking, resulting in a situation in which supervisors can face mixed incentives when it comes to enforcement. Also, because supervisors do not have their own wealth invested in banks, they have different incentives than private creditors when it comes to monitoring and disciplining banks. Because bank failures may be regarded (incorrectly, many would argue!) as supervisory failures, there may be a reluctance to close banks ("not on my watch"). Herring (2004) also argues that:

Market discipline is forward-looking and inherently flexible and adaptive. Market surveillance is continuous, impersonal, and nonbureaucratic.... In contrast, official oversight usually is rule-based, episodic, bureaucratic, and slow to change.... One of the principal merits of market discipline is that bank directors and managers are faced with the burden of proving to the market that the bank *is not* taking excessive risks rather than subjecting officials to the burden of proving, in a review process, that the bank *is* taking excessive risks. This surely places the burden where it belongs and facilitates better corporate governance by making clear that the directors and managers of a bank are responsible for its risk exposures and ability to bear loss, not the regulatory and supervisory authorities. (pp. 365–366)

Others, however, question placing excessive trust in private-sector monitoring, especially in countries with poorly developed capital markets, accounting standards, and legal systems. Viewed from the public interest perspective, countries with weak institutional environments will benefit more from official regulators containing excessive risk-taking behavior of banks and thereby instilling more confidence in depositors than would exist with private-sector monitoring. This view argues that, in weak institutional settings, increased reliance on private monitoring leads to exploitation of small savers and hence much less bank development. Of course, adherents of the private interest view retort that it is precisely in countries with a weak institutional setting in which supervisory powers are more likely to be abused or directed by narrow interest groups for their own benefit. Caprio and Honohan (2004) maintain that, despite weaknesses in disclosure and accounting, low-income countries may be better positioned to exercise market discipline: they tend not to offer deposit insurance, or if they do, fiscal difficulties may make it less credible, so market participants would still have a strong incentive to engage in oversight; increasingly, they have more foreign banks, on which information may be more available; their environment and banks are less complex, making monitoring easier; and the smaller size of the business and banking community also would facilitate monitoring. In fact, in low-income countries that are dominated by a few families, these family groups may possess significant information about much of the economy, partly offsetting the week formal information system. In short, it seems as though only empirical testing can resolve the debate over which approach better characterizes the regulatory polices countries make.

2.B.7. Government Ownership

The most complete form of government control of banks is outright ownership, an area in which there are sharp differences of views. Those who agree on the critical importance of banks may simultaneously hold the view that market failures are extremely severe, for example, because of very imperfect information or the difficulty of motivating private parties to behave in a socially optimal fashion. The public interest view would then reason that government ownership of banks would facilitate the mobilization of savings and the allocation of those savings toward strategic projects with long-term beneficial effects on an economy, whereas private banks would only allocate credit in line with potentially short-run private interests in mind. According to this view, governments have adequate information and sufficient incentives to ensure socially desirable investments. Consequently, government ownership of banks would help economies overcome capital market failures, exploit externalities, and invest in strategic sectors. Lewis (1950), Myrdal (1968), and Gerschenkron (1962) specifically advocated government ownership of banks to promote economic and financial development, especially in underdeveloped countries. Public-sector banks also might be endorsed because of the fear that privately owned banks would concentrate credit in the hands of the few, as well as the concern that excessive risk taking in private-sector banks could undermine the stability of the financial sector (World Bank, 2001).

The private interest view of government ownership, in contrast, argues that governments do not have sufficient incentives to ensure socially desirable investments (Kornai, 1979; and Shleifer and Vishny, 1993, 1994). Government ownership tends to politicize resource allocation, soften budget constraints, and otherwise hinder economic efficiency (Kaufman, 1999). Government banks tend to lend to state enterprises, which often are highly inefficient (World Bank, 1995). Thus, government ownership of banks facilitates the financing of politically attractive projects, but not necessarily economically efficient projects. Indeed, because the private sector would have no incentive to monitor public-sector banks, and because the public-sector would face a conflict in monitoring itself, the result may be that state banks would not be subject to monitoring, which would be conducive to a diversion of funds to satisfy a variety of interests (World Bank, 2001). Therefore, it would be surprising if a state-owned bank were *not* being used to further the interests of government, including its interest to strengthen its hold on power.

In an influential study, LaPorta, Lopez-de-Silanes, and Shleifer (2002) piece together data on government ownership of banks from an assortment of sources. They find that countries with higher initial levels of government ownership of banks tend to have both slower subsequent rates of financial-system development and slower economic growth. In a related paper, Barth, Caprio, and Levine (2001a) use data on bank ownership from Bankscope, and find that greater government ownership is generally associated with less efficient and less well-developed financial systems. Mian (2003) uses Bankscope data for about one hundred developing countries and finds evidence of the weak performance of state-owned banks, and suggests that this result is related to weak incentives and political corruption. The data used in these papers, however, do not cover all banks operating in an economy (La Porta et al. use only the ten largest banks, whereas the coverage of the Bankscope data varies from country to country).

Besides using our analysis of government banks in Chapter 4 to assess the two broad views on government's role, we make two specific improvements on existing studies of government-owned banks. First, we use data collected from each country's bank regulatory agency. Thus, the data cover all commercial banks and the definition of "government owned" is consistent across countries. Second, we control for differences in the regulatory, supervisory, and institutional environment in assessing the links between government ownership and bank development, performance, and stability. This framework permits us to examine, for example, whether government ownership in banking is better than private ownership with a weak regulatory environment.

To summarize, for all of the above aspects of regulation and supervision, there are contrasting views on whether or not they will serve public or private interests, and empirical evidence is limited generally to a few, mostly quite advanced countries, raising the question of how applicable the results are around the world. Moreover, even the few cross-country studies mostly investigate one aspect of regulation or supervision, omitting measures of other aspects. Thus, these issues are well suited to the type of empirical examination of Chapters 4 and 5 using a global database on bank regulation and supervision.

2.C. THE BASEL COMMITTEE AND REGULATORY CONVERGENCE

We now turn to the role of international forces and a specific example of regulatory convergence. Thus far, the discussion of the determinants of approaches to bank regulation and supervision ignored international influences. However, international forces can affect regulatory choices for four reasons. First, as foreign entry and cross-border banking increase, greater bank competition can lead to concerns about unfair competition and to lobbying for changes in regulation and supervision.[26] For example, if banks in one jurisdiction were permitted to hold lower capital, because of differences in explicit regulations or in supervisory practices, this could translate into a competitive advantage in world markets. Second, aside from competitive concerns, the cross-border operation of banks exposes economies – and their depositors and taxpayers – to the potential transmission of shocks and even loss, especially if there are gaps in regulation or supervision. Third, supervisors may learn from international practices, as in the earlier-cited example of the Kemmerer mission in Latin America.

---

[26] Foreign entry in banking is just what it says: it refers to the entry of foreign banks (banks whose headquarters/home office is licensed and regulated abroad). Cross-border banking can refer to this phenomenon, but it also can refer to the situation in which the residents of one country conduct banking transactions through banks in another country, by using the Internet, cell phones, or the older technology of telephone, fax, and telegraph. An example of cross-border banking in this second sense would be when residents of Mexico or Brazil do their banking with a Citibank office in Miami.

This type of learning is likely much greater now than in his era because of lower communication and transportation costs, as seen in the virtual explosion of meetings (physical and virtual) and conferences on bank supervision in recent years. Fourth, banks operating in a number of countries represent a force for harmonization, as it is less costly to have to comply with the one set of regulations, compared with the alternative of complying with as many regulatory systems as the number of countries in which a bank has branches or subsidiaries.

Although it can be difficult to distinguish the factors influencing policy decisions, all of these channels appeared to operate in the 1970s and 1980s as international competition in banking began to expand significantly. Almost immediately, the failure of an international bank (Herstatt Bank in 1974) and the uncertainty as to how different cross-border claims would be settled led the G-10 central banks to establish in 1974 the Basel Committee on Bank Supervision, and later to accelerate those efforts with the 1982 failure of Banco Ambrosiano.[27] The Basel Committee is composed of central bank and supervisory agency representatives of thirteen countries: Belgium, Canada, France, Germany, Italy, Japan, Luxembourg, the Netherlands, Spain, Sweden, Switzerland, the United Kingdom, and the United States. The Committee usually meets at the Bank for International Settlements (BIS) in Basel, where its permanent Secretariat is located. Although its initial focus was very much on the gaps in international regulation and supervision, specifically how branches and subsidiaries of foreign banks should be regulated and supervised, its area of responsibility and influence expanded with the increase in foreign bank entry and as the goal of establishing a level playing field became accepted.

Accordingly, the 1988 Basel Capital Accord (henceforth, Basel I) was devoted to producing an international standard for capital measurement. In 1987, U.K. and U.S. regulators agreed to implement a "risk-weighted" capital standard reflecting the riskiness of a bank's loan portfolio. This action was largely precipitated by the concern that Japanese banks were operating with substantially less capital than British and American banks

---

[27] In the latter case, a Luxemburg subsidiary of Banco Ambrosiano (an Italian bank that often did business with the Vatican) failed, and there was clear confusion over whether the subsidiary was a bank and who should have been supervising it. Somewhat colorfully, this case began with the discovery of the body of Roberto Calvi, the president of Banco Ambrosiano, hanging underneath the Blackfriars Bridge in London, weighed down with bricks and with his hands tied behind his back, and curiosity was no doubt heightened by the fact that his death was initially judged to be a suicide. See Cornwall (1983) for an interesting tale!

and thereby "unfairly" expanding into other countries' home markets.[28] In fact, Japanese banking assets in overseas branches expanded sharply in the 1980s; by 1988, more than 38 percent of the assets of Japanese banks were in their overseas branches and subsidiaries, especially in the United States and the United Kingdom. The later retrenchment of Japanese banks in the 1990s corroborated this concern, as the impact of crisis in Japan was felt both in selected financial markets in the United States (Peek and Rosengren, 2000) and possibly in East Asia. In any event, the impetus of the U.K. and U.S. authorities quickly led to negotiations among countries comprising the Basel Committee, and the result was Basel I in 1988.

It was understood that by changing its risk profile a bank could alter its economic capital, and Basel I was devised with a set of admittedly arbitrary risk weights (buckets) for several classes of risk (Powell, 2004). It defined a minimum capital requirement (8 percent of risk weighted assets) and stated the principle that the minimum should be higher for riskier banks (and presumably for riskier countries). Basel I gave greater prominence to capital ratios and may have promoted somewhat greater consistency in their measurement. However, such great differences remained regarding provisioning and other aspects of implementation that this improvement may have been rather limited. For example, it became known after the East Asian crisis that in Thailand a loan could be 365 days in arrears – four times or more the norm in most countries – and yet the bank that granted it was still allowed to accrue interest, as if the borrower were current on repayments. Although Basel I was intended for internationally active banks, it quickly became a de facto standard around the world. Developing country regulators, who were actively attempting to move away from direct controls to a more modern system of prudential regulation, began to follow the evident "best practice" in industrial countries embodied in Basel I. Also, following the recognition of weaknesses or outright crises in developing country banking systems, the World Bank and the International Monetary Fund began to encourage higher capital requirements, and Basel I was a convenient benchmark. Moreover, both organizations fostered communication of "good practices," and again Basel I was the only model available that enjoyed agreement by industrial country regulators.

---

[28] As Singer (2003, pp. 30–31) points out, "[i]n 1986, Citicorp and Barclays (U.K.) had capital-to-asset-ratios of 4.73 and 4.71, respectively, while Japan's Dai-Ichi Kangyo, Sumitomo, and Fuji had ratios of 2.38, 2.89, and 2.95."

Estimating the impact of Basel I is not straightforward, as other factors were changing. Beaty and Gron (2001) do not find systematic differences in capital ratios for U.S. commercial banks following the adoption of the risk-based capital standards of Basel I. In fact, banks with riskier assets tended to have smaller increases in capital and greater increases in their holdings of risky assets, the opposite of prior expectations – but in line with our earlier discussion. In seeming contrast, Lown et al. (2000) and Furfine (2001), also studying U.S. banks, show that regulatory factors played a role in the credit crunch (meaning a reduction in the availability of credit to the private sector) of the early 1990s. However, the latter finding is still consistent with the former: the regulatory regime pre-Basel I also could have led to a credit crunch, as supervisors could still be encouraged to tighten standards in any regime after fresh evidence that excessive risk-taking had occurred. Internationally, there were no data on bank capital that were comparable either across countries. Still, from the authors' experience, especially in developing countries, capital ratios in the 1990s rose, although this is not necessarily evidence that these increases were caused by Basel I, as a result of a number of other factors. For example, although capital ratios are difficult to define for government-owned banks, these banks generally held low-levels of capital in the 1980s – often 2–3 percent – and then the 1990s saw a significant move to bank privatization in developing countries. It is quite plausible therefore that regardless of Basel I, private-sector banks would have been encouraged, in order to get financing from markets, to hold capital ratios above those of the former state-owned entities. Moreover, it is likely that with the widespread occurrence of banking crises in industrial and developing countries, market pressures would have induced higher capital ratios. And large money-center banks in industrial countries have been holding capital ratios significantly above the Basel I minimum, so the impact of Basel I on these banks is difficult to discern.

Given that it was understood that capital requirements alone were not sufficient to ensure safe and sound banking, in 1997, in the wake of the Mexican crisis and as the Asian crisis was unfolding, the Basel Committee issued its Core Principles for Bank Supervision (the Basel Core Principles, or BCP), which became accepted as best practice for bank supervision around the world. The crises in East Asia also led to the creation in May 1999 by the IMF and the World Bank of the Financial Sector Assessment Program (FSAP), whose goal is to assess the primary stability and developmental issues in countries' financial sectors. As of February 2005, eighty-two FSAPs had been completed and another nineteen were in process, although, in a few cases, these were updates of earlier assessments. Virtually all FSAPs have included an assessment of countries' compliance with the BCP, which are recognized as one of the key international standards, and which are summarized in Appendix 4. The BCP represent the set of supervisory principles on which industrial countries reached agreement – although in this case there was consultation with developing countries – and they have become the de facto standard. It is important to add that the concept of developing best practice standards was characteristic of a number of areas related to the financial sector. Although there are even more, the Financial Stability Forum,[29] the World Bank, and the IMF recognize in addition to the BCP, standards in eleven other areas: accounting, auditing, anti-money laundering and combating the financing of terrorism, corporate governance, data dissemination, fiscal transparency, insolvency and creditor rights, insurance supervision, monetary and financial policy transparency, payment systems, and securities regulation.

Although many may see merit in the widespread adoption of common standards by countries, such uniformity could have weaknesses. For example, different national standards might offer the advantage that banks would be able to choose among countries in which to conduct operations, and the choices made will lead to differences in the performance of banking systems across countries from which one can obtain useful information. Different standards, moreover, may give rise to greater innovation in the type of financial products and services available in the global marketplace.[30] And uniform standards may be risky: Shin et al. (2001) argue that Basel II will encourage greater homogeneity in banks' approach to risk management, as was alleged at the time of the Russian default of 1998, and actually reduce the stability of the international financial system. However, it appears to be accepted wisdom in the regulatory community

---

[29] The Financial Stability Forum (FSF) was formed in 1999 regularly to gather senior representatives of national financial authorities, international financial institutions, international regulatory and supervisory groupings, and committees of central bank experts. Its only permanent component is a small secretariat at the Bank for International Settlements.

[30] In the United States, it has long been argued that a major advantage of a "dual banking" system (i.e., both state- and federally chartered financial institutions) is that it fosters greater financial innovation than a completely federally chartered system. For example, the adjustable-rate mortgage was an innovation of state-chartered institutions, not federally chartered institutions, which were severely restricted in their ability to offer such a product until the 1980s. As noted earlier, competition between state and federal regulators led to an easing of regulatory standards. See Kane (1997) on the benefits of public-public and public-private competition in regulation.

that the competition engendered by different standards will not promote well-functioning banking systems but, rather, may lead to a situation in which banks choose to operate in the least regulated countries, thereby inducing a "regulatory race to the bottom." Certainly there is some anecdotal evidence to this effect with the performance of offshore banks, but we hasten to add that there has been no formal empirical analysis of this issue.

Notwithstanding the consensus among regulators, shortly after its completion Basel I began to be criticized because of its narrow focus: originally, it dealt only with credit risk, the risk that loans might become nonperforming, and not with other important risks confronting banks, such as market risk (the risk that prices on its balance sheet, such as interest rates or exchange rates, could change) and operational risk.[31] The latter receives increased attention, following the September 11, 2001, terrorist act in New York City, and with the exponential rise in electronic security threats to financial intermediaries (Glaessner, Kellermann, and McNevin, 2004). In terms of the earlier discussion of the literature on capital requirements, it was recognized that banks could engage in "regulatory arbitrage," or change their risk profile, once any set of risk weights is announced. As mentioned earlier, at least one important factor behind the boom in securitization – the process of pooling similar assets and using them as collateral for newly issued securities – was Basel I, which provided an incentive for banks to shed assets that carried a high risk weight and acquire those with a lower risk coefficient (Shadow Financial Regulatory Committee, or SFRC, 1999).[32] This arbitrage lead to greater attention to the assignment of risk weights in calculating the minimum capital requirements.

A related set of criticisms of Basel I focused on the arbitrary assignment of risk weights: loans essentially were to be assigned to different risk categories, each with a different risk weight. In other words, it is important not just that the risk weight should be respected (and not evaded) but that the weights should be sensible. Government debt, for example,

---

[31] Subsequent amendments included some market risks. Operational risk is extremely broad-based, and it is defined by the Basel committee as "the risk of loss resulting from inadequate or failed internal processes, people and systems, more from external events. This definition includes legal risk, but excludes strategic and reputational risk" (Basel committee, 2003, p. 120). Operational risk was only incorporated recently in Basel II (see later).

[32] Other factors behind securitization included cheaper computing, improved information, and advances in financial technology, which permitted more accurate pricing of securities.

carried a zero credit risk weight, although not all governments repay in equal and timely fashion. Recall that this system was designed for industrial countries, and this requirement applied to their banks' holdings of OECD government paper. However, the requirement also came to be applied in developing countries, even though in some cases their own government paper carried considerable risk. Moreover, the risk weights did not differentiate between loans to small, risky firms and large, highly rated multinationals. In other words, "the degrees of risk exposure are not sufficiently calibrated as to adequately differentiate between borrowers' differing default risks" (Shadow Financial Regulatory Committee, 1999). A third set of critiques, by the SFRC and others, addressed the approach more broadly: rather than set minimum capital requirements on a loan by loan criterion, what matters for the riskiness of a bank is its diversification, or the covariation in its portfolio – yet Basel I made no adjustment for these factors, as the risk buckets were completely independent.

Both in response to these critiques, and in recognition of the changing financial markets (itself partly a response to Basel I), the Basel Committee devoted several years to revising the Capital Accord, and announced Basel II in June 2004, for implementation by the end of 2006 (or later, for its more complex aspects) in G-10 countries. Basel II, which consists of three pillars (capital, supervisory review process, and market discipline, as pillars I, II, and III, respectively), is extremely complex in some of its variations, and only its broad outlines will be discussed here.[33] The current revised framework (Basel Committee, 2004) consists of 239 pages – much shorter than earlier drafts – and pillar I receives the overwhelming majority of attention, as only seventeen pages are devoted to the supervisory review process (with many more pages associated with the BCP and other Basel documents), and fifteen pages to market discipline. This coverage reflects the overwhelming orientation of Basel II to addressing the many concerns with Basel I, and perhaps also the view that in the G-10 countries, supervisory powers and market discipline work reasonably well. Also, the committee plans to issue more guidance on pillar III. Powell (2004) notes, with respect to supervision, that compliance with the key core principles is significantly weaker in developing countries, and argues that the application of the Basel II there may be problematic.

Basel II is characterized by four options for determining minimum capital ratios, with the key difference being that in the simpler approaches,

---

[33] See Powell (2004) for a thorough description of its features, and *The Economist* (April 17, 2004) for a briefer account.

risk weights for credit risk are taken from those of export credit agencies or rating agencies, whereas in the more sophisticated variants, banks' internal models can be used to derive default probabilities and even the loss given default. Basel II essentially continues to analyze individual bank risks, but the more advanced methods take account of correlations with some ad hoc adjustments. As others have noted, markets would assess banks differently, focusing on the overall risk of the bank rather than its individual components.[34]

Importantly, a large part of the Basel II documentation is devoted to the use of banks' internal models. Interest in these models and their contribution to the supervisory process began with Kupiec and O'Brien (1995, 1997), who propose that banks be forced to disclose how they model risk and the capital needed given their knowledge of the risks of their business lines, and then be held accountable – even penalized, beyond limited liability, for violating the model. An attractive feature of this approach is that it addresses the concern that the Basel approach is too rigid and arbitrary. The more advanced variants of Basel II move in this direction, but at present only to the extent of taking some of the parameters from banks' internal models, and not wholly relying on these models and the disclosure process. According to some involved with the Basel committee, they are moving toward greater reliance on market discipline, and indeed see Basel II not as a final goal but as an evolving regulatory system.[35] A key part of the Kupiec-O'Brien approach, as interpreted, is a supporting role for bank supervision, and not the more intrusive one of Basel II, precisely because of the difficulty that supervisors have in keeping up with the way banks can change their risk profile. We will return to this discussion of the different approaches to supervision in Chapter 6.

Basel II puts more reliance on supervisors to determine minimum capital requirements than Pillar I. Pillar I provides a relatively formulaic, or model based approach, to establishing minimum capital requirements. Pillar II grants supervisors the ability to require banks to hold capital above the regulatory minimum, presumably depending on their own

---

[34] Powell (2004) makes a comparison of Basel I and II. Also, see von Thadden (2004), who summarized the special issue of the Journal of Financial Intermediation dedicated to an analysis of issues related to capital regulation under Basel II.

[35] In a recent talk, Jaime Caruana, the chairman of the Basel Committee, drew an analogy between the Basel standards and the Windows operating system, suggesting that there would be various releases of Basel II (2.0, 2.1, etc.). Moreover, he and others have said that the committee was not yet ready to put greater reliance on banks' internal models, though this is the direction in which they see future versions of Basel II moving.

assessment of banks' riskiness. There is no discussion of how greater discretion would be applied in an opaque environment, or indeed any concern that discretion in a weak institutional environment could lead to abuses and rent extraction by officials; in other words, the public interest view is taken for granted. In particular, although prompt action by supervisors is regarded as important in Pillar II, there is no attempt to mandate "prompt, corrective action," that is, automatic actions by supervisors as banks' conditions deteriorate, and this issue receives cursory attention in the BCP. Moreover, recall that an original goal of the Basel Committee was to harmonize capital and regulation more broadly so as to achieve a level playing field for banks competing internationally. How this will happen with so much discretion is not at all clear. Nor is it clear which countries practically speaking will be capable of adopting the more advanced features of Basel II in the next five to ten years, what the resource requirements will be, and whether for developing countries spending more on bank supervision would be the best use of scarce funds and human capital.

Basel II clearly was not written with developing countries as the primary target, but it has been proclaimed as an international standard. As of mid-2005, the position of the United States appears to be that only the ten to twenty largest U.S. banks will have to comply with Basel II by 2008, whereas the remaining banks, which have only a minimal amount of international activities, are being allowed to stay with Basel I. Some developing countries have announced that they will attempt to adhere to the more advanced parts of Basel II, some with the less advanced features, and some will stay with Basel I. However, there have already been changes by these countries, and by July 2004, just a few months after its finalization, over one hundred countries already indicated that they would adopt Basel II. As the position of industrial countries becomes clear regarding the extent, timing, method, and costs of adoption, developing countries may change their views on how they will proceed. The IMF and the World Bank have stated that in the FSAP they will evaluate developing countries by Basel I or by any of the above variations of Basel II, depending on the country's choice. Even though neither of these international organizations nor the Basel Committee are encouraging developing countries to adopt more advanced features of Basel II, at a June 2004 conference organized by the Federal Reserve Board, the IMF, and the World Bank, a number of developing country officials stated that they felt under pressure to adopt Basel II, with some pressure coming from international rating agencies. Also, the authorities were concerned that home-host issues (coordination problems between these two sets of supervisors) will arise for foreign banks following Basel II in their home countries, particularly to the extent that foreign banks may be employing more sophisticated features of Basel II. It is widely asserted that this will pose challenges for developing country supervisors, to the extent that they need to master the intricacies of advanced risk modeling techniques,[36] and also for their banks, to the extent that the advanced features of Basel II permit a lower capital ratio.

Regardless of the variant of the Basel standards, there are two overarching concerns.[37] First, many object that Basel attempts to replace the market with official supervisors or by complicated formulae (e.g., see the SFRC, Rochet (2003), Kane (1997, 2002, and 2004), Herring (2004), and others). Indeed, the SFRC notes that it is hardly surprising that Basel II is far more complex than Basel I, because taking the place of the market would require incredibly detailed formula. Even John (Jerry) Hawke, while in his role as U.S. Comptroller of the Currency, stated that "In my view, CP-3 (the third consultative paper on Basel II) is complex far beyond reason. Aspects of it – the formulas relating to securitizations, for example – are so complex that the mere visual depiction of them has been cause for ridicule, which serves only to undermine public regard for the [Basel] Committee" (Hawke, 2003). Complexity poses its own concerns: it can obfuscate the underlying risk positions (as seen in the 1998 Long Term Capital Management crisis); it places enormous burdens on the supervisory authorities to attract and maintain highly skilled staff capable of understanding complicated formulae; and it can raise regulatory costs, which can become especially burdensome for smaller and medium-sized banks.[38]

---

[36] Governments still have the option to impose a simpler capital regime in their own country (e.g., a simple leverage requirement) that would not entail significant compliance costs for domestic or international banks. If instead they attempt to impose a complex system that is different than Basel, internationally active banks may not find it worthwhile to operate within their borders.

[37] There are a variety of criticisms of detailed features of Basel II, such as that by Kashyup and Stein (2004) that the method of calculating default probabilities will make it more procyclical. However, as Basel II is still evolving, we will not discuss here its detailed advantages and disadvantages.

[38] Even in the absence of Basel recommendations, the intrusiveness of supervision and the cost of regulatory compliance may have been a concern in some countries. According to a 2005 survey of fifty-four countries by the Center for the Study of Financial Innovation and PriceWaterhouseCoopers, for the first time in the ten-year history of this survey, the high cost of regulation was perceived as the greatest threat to the financial sector (CSFI, 2005).

As an alternative to Basel II, the SFRC recommends a simple leverage ratio and a subordinated debt requirement, according to which banks
would be compelled to issue regularly relatively short-term, junior debt
that would be the first to take a loss after equity holders. Thus, holders
of subordinated debt would be exposed to a large downside risk, without
benefiting from the upside potential that equity holders enjoy, and therefore would have a powerful incentive to monitors banks and sell their
debt at the first sign of unwise risk taking (see also World Bank, 2001,
pp. 101–104 for a discussion). A bank encountering such pressure would
immediately be forced either to contract its balance sheet or pay a higher
cost of funding, either of which should curtail risk-taking and constitute
a highly visible signal. The SFRC also would require the institution of
prompt, corrective action, so that supervisors will be compelled to intervene early and with predetermined actions (so-called structured, early
intervention). In some respects, the SFRC's proposals are the opposite of
the Basel committee, with the former giving much more weight to market
discipline, reducing as much as possible the scope for supervisory discretion, and according relatively little importance to complex capital ratios.
Thus, the SFRC proposals rely on market discipline backed up by automatic supervisory action to ensure closure before a bank's net worth is
negative.

A second objection to the Basel standards is its status as "international
law," which may promote the importance of bureaucrats and technocrats
above democratically elected legislators within the realm of bank regulation. Both Basel I and II are regarded by legal experts as a form of "soft
law" and as Tarullo (forthcoming, Chapter 5, p. 31) points out,

In its idealized form, such an arrangement is a system of structured international activities carried on by national government officials with domestic regulatory responsibility, intended to make national laws and regulations more con-
gruent and to coordinate enforcement of similar laws. The arrangement is not
legally binding upon the participating nations – unlike trade agreements, for
example . . . enthusiasm for this new approach (including among banking officials)
arose partly from its promise as a means of managing a global financial system
in a world of nation states. Skepticism came from those who feared it was a way
for bureaucrats to protect their own interests in the face of regulatory competition (Macey, 2003) or a triumph of technocrats over democratically accountable
legislatures (Alston, 1997).

As will become clear in Chapter 4, bank regulatory systems can have significant consequences for economic growth, financial development, stability, access to credit, and even corruption. Thus, the decision as to the

type of system is important. Is Basel's emphasis on capital and supervision appropriate? Also, there is at least a question, which we think deserves more attention, as to how decisions about financial regulatory systems are made, and whether they need to be made in a more democratic, participatory fashion, with perhaps greater attention to the consequences of regulatory choices for economic development. We will return to this issue in Chapters 4 and 5.

2.D. CONCLUSION

Countries' approaches to regulation have varied considerably over time. The last thirty years have seen movements away from restrictions on interest rates, directed credit, and other crude measures of intervention, in favor of an approach to regulation based on prudential norms and supervisory oversight. Generally, the public discussion of the reform process proceeds as if it were taken for granted that reform is always motivated by a public-interest rationale. As we have seen in this chapter, there is a competing viewpoint that, whatever the superficial justification, financial regulation instead is driven by private interests. We have argued that regulators and systems may vary, both among themselves and over time in the extent to which they are dominated by public or private interests, and we have summarized the rationale and debates behind specific regulatory interventions.

The world is now at a critical juncture, apparently moving quickly to adopt a set of regulatory and supervisory practices based largely on the perception of what works in advanced markets. Consistent with the advice "look before you leap," the remainder of this volume takes stock of the different regulatory and supervisory systems around the world. We investigate empirically what works best, how the institutional environment affects the impact of regulatory choices, and also look at the effect of politics as a determinant of regulatory choices.

THREE

How Are Banks Regulated and Supervised Around the World?

When you can measure what you are speaking about, and express it in numbers, you know something about it; but when you cannot measure it, when you cannot express it in numbers, your knowledge is of a meager and unsatisfactory kind: it may be the beginning of knowledge, but you have scarcely, in your thoughts, advanced to the state of science.... If you can not measure it, you can not improve it.

William Thompson, Lord Kelvin[1]

3.A. OVERVIEW

How do countries regulate and supervise their banks? Until recently, there was no comprehensive and official database on which one could draw to assess (1) the extent to which bank regulatory and supervisory regimes differ across a wide spectrum of countries, (2) what works best with regard to bank supervision and regulation, and (3) the determinants of different bank supervisory and regulatory choices around the world. Moreover, regulatory officials, especially those from high-income countries, have often taken the view that their choice of how to regulate and supervise their own banks was best for banks everywhere. This "policy hubris" is aided and abetted by a lack of a sufficiently comprehensive and detailed database with which to compare the practices of individual countries. Most importantly, the absence of such data prevents one from

---

[1] The first part of the opening quote from Lord Kelvin is from his Popular Lectures and Addresses [1891–1894], as quoted in *Bartlett's Familiar Quotations*, Fourteenth Edition, 1968, p. 723a. The last sentence is from a Web site devoted to his wisdom, http://zapatopi.net/kelvin/quotes.html.

empirically testing any advice as to what a country should do to improve bank regulation and supervision and from assessing why countries adopt particular policies toward banks. Yet, this type of information is needed by government officials given the growing cross-border reach of ever more banks and the recent push for agreement on a common approach to regulation and supervision.

This chapter presents a new database that helps fill this void. The first version of this database was assembled for the late 1990s, whereas the current version, on which we draw in this chapter, updates and expands the earlier version. Specifically, the data that characterize regulations and supervisory practices are for year-end 2002, whereas the quantitative data are for year-end 2001. The first or earlier survey we assembled covers 107 countries, with 12 separate parts and about 180 questions, and another 10, mostly transitional, countries, were added; most of the observations from this first survey were for 1998–1999. The second survey, on which this chapter is based, covers 152 countries.[2] It, too, consists of 12 parts, but is expanded to include about 275 questions; Appendix 1 shows the shortened version of the survey, with the new questions identified.[3] In a number of cases there were consultations with the various authorities on the interpretation of questions in their particular regulatory and supervisory environment. The final questions selected for inclusion in our new survey reflect feedback from several banking experts who suggested both the elimination of questions from the first survey and the inclusion of new questions. In short, the completion of the survey was an iterative process that began in the spring of 2003 and ended in early 2004.

Figure 3.1 and Table 3.1 indicate the countries covered by both the "new" and "old" surveys. Although both surveys cover countries of different income levels, population sizes, stages of financial development, and parts of the world, the new survey includes nearly one-third more countries, many of which are African. A distinguishing feature of the entire dataset is the fact that it is based entirely on official government sources. Importantly, the dataset does not represent our own or any unofficial assessment of regulations and supervisory practices. Instead, it represents the official responses to a set of comprehensive and detailed

---

[2] In addition, China is included here based on the participation of one of the authors, James Barth, in an Asian Development Bank project on banking reform in that country. Depending on data availability, this means that the maximum number of countries mentioned at various places in this chapter will be 153.

[3] The detailed data are available both on the accompanying CD as well as at the World Bank Web site, http://econ.worldbank.org/programs/finance/topic/regulation/.

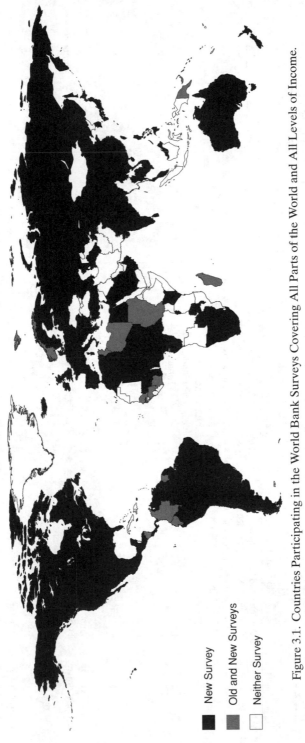

Figure 3.1. Countries Participating in the World Bank Surveys Covering All Parts of the World and All Levels of Income.

New Survey

Old and New Surveys

Neither Survey

Table 3.1. *World Bank Survey – Countries Classified by Income and Region (Total 152 Countries)*[1]

	High Income[2] (45 countries)	Upper Middle Income (32 countries)	Lower Middle Income (41 countries)	Low Income (34 countries)
Americas (35 countries)	Antigua and Barbuda* Aruba British Virgin Islands Canada Puerto Rico United States	Anguilla* Argentina Belize* Chile Commonwealth of Dominica Costa Rica* Grenada* Mexico Montserrat* Panama Saint Kitts and Nevis Saint Lucia* Trinidad and Tobago Turks and Caicos Islands Uruguay* Venezuela	Bolivia Brazil Colombia* Ecuador* El Salvador Guatemala Guyana Honduras Paraguay* Peru Saint Vincent and the Grenadines* Suriname*	Nicaragua*
Asia & Pacific (22 countries)	Australia Hong Kong, China* Japan Korea Macau, China New Zealand Singapore Taiwan	Malaysia	China Fiji* Philippines Samoa Sri Lanka Thailand Tonga Vanuatu	Bhutan Cambodia India Pakistan* Papua New Guinea*
Europe & Central Asia (50 countries)	Austria Belgium Cyprus Denmark Finland Italy Jersey* Liechtenstein Luxembourg Netherlands	Croatia Czech Republic Estonia Hungary Latvia Lithuania Poland Slovakia	Albania Armenia Belarus Bosnia and Herzegovina Bulgaria Romania Russia Serbia & Montenegro Turkey Turkmenistan	Azerbaijan Kyrgyzstan Moldova Tajikistan

Region					
	France, Germany, Gibraltar, Greece, Guernsey, Iceland, Ireland, Isle of Man*, Norway*, Portugal, Slovenia, Spain, Sweden, Switzerland, United Kingdom		Kazakhstan, Macedonia	Ukraine*	
Middle East and North Africa (14 countries)	Bahrain, Israel, Kuwait, Malta, Qatar, United Arab Emirates*, Lebanon, Oman	Saudi Arabia	Algeria*, Egypt, Jordan	Morocco, Tunisia*	Libya
Sub-Saharan Africa (31 countries)	Botswana, Gabon*	Mauritius, Seychelles	Namibia, South Africa	Swaziland*	Benin*, Burkina Faso*, Burundi, Cameroon*, Central African Republic*, Chad*, Congo*, Côte d'Ivoire*, Equatorial Guinea*, Gambia, Ghana, Guinea*, Guinea Bissau*, Kenya, Lesotho, Madagascar*, Mali*, Niger*, Nigeria, Rwanda, Senegal*, Sudan*, Togo*, Zimbabwe*

[1] In addition, China is included based on the participation of one of the authors, James Barth, in an Asian Development Bank project on banking system reform in that Country.

* Denotes additional countries in the new survey.

questions, both quantitative and descriptive.[4] The questions elicit a wide range of important information, including licensing and capital requirements, scope of allowable activities, official supervisory powers, liquidity, diversification, and provisioning requirements, and sources of market discipline and governance.

All the individual responses to the survey may be of interest in their own right, especially for governmental authorities who simply wish to compare particular features of their own banking systems with those in other countries. Those policy makers considering reforms, however, may want to know the general direction in which to proceed, such as whether to emphasize activity restrictions, capital requirements, supervisory surveillance, or market discipline. In this case, they will appreciate a greater degree of grouping and aggregation (and thus quantification) of some of the survey responses. This also will be the case for empirical researchers bound by degrees of freedom (and a need for quantifiable variables). Our approach to satisfy these types of needs is to construct indices based upon the survey responses, as we have previously done, to provide quantifiable and important dimensions of bank regulation and supervision (Barth, Caprio, and Levine, 2001, 2004).

The exact way in which the indices used in this chapter are constructed based upon the new survey is provided in Appendix 2. It is important to make clear, however, that there is no unique grouping or aggregation (or even quantification) of survey responses. Indeed, it should be noted at the outset that some of our variables are grouped under one heading when they could understandably be grouped elsewhere. A case in point is a certified audit variable, indicating whether or not an external audit by a licensed or certified auditor is a compulsory obligation of banks. We have included this particular variable with other related variables to construct a private monitoring index. Admittedly, however, to the extent that supervisory authorities require and rely on such audits, this variable also could be reasonably viewed as one of our official supervisory action variables. This example illustrates that one must not place undue emphasis on the specific headings under which all the different variables are listed. Nevertheless, the groupings discussed here reflect

---

[4] There are, of course, extremely useful sources of information on bank regulatory and supervisory regimes in countries, such as Courtis (2002) and especially the Institute of International Bankers (2003). These sources, however, do not report official responses to survey questionnaires, nor do they provide as comprehensive and detailed information for as many countries as our new survey.

our judgment of sensible ways in which to capture broader approaches to regulating and supervising banks, knowing full well that some variables may be used in more than one aggregate index. Indeed, we hope that researcher take our raw data and improve on our best efforts to construct informative indexes to address relevant questions in bank supervision and regulation.

This chapter uses our various indices, including several new ones introduced here, and individual survey responses to describe different dimensions of important ways in which countries regulate and supervise banks. In this regard, it is important to point out that what we do in this chapter has a direct relationship to some of the recent work of the Basel Committee. The reason is that, in addition to its specific focus on capital adequacy, the Basel Committee has identified standards of best practice for bank regulation and supervision. The most influential and recent standard it has disseminated is the Core Principles for Effective Banking Supervision (the "Core Principles") in 1997. This standard has taken place alongside, and in a number of cases has influenced the development of, other international standards of best practice for financial systems (listed in Appendix 3). The Core Principles comprise twenty-five basic principles that are deemed necessary for a supervisory system to be effective. These principles cover the fundamental authority bank supervisors need to effectively do their job, and emphasize the importance of supervisory independence from political pressure; licensing practices and supervisory powers; appropriate and effective methods of supervisors; and basic elements of prudential regulations for banks (see Appendix 5). In addition to the goal of helping policy makers design and improve bank regulation and supervision, the Core Principles are used in the joint International Monetary Fund-World Bank Financial Sector Assessment Program (FSAP) that began in 1999 (Sundararajan et al., 2001; Ingves and Carson, 2003). The core principles assessments, some of which are posted on the Web sites of the World Bank and the IMF, differ from our survey in that they represent the opinion of outside experts, rather than, as in our survey, the responses of official authorities. There are pros and cons to each approach. The key advantage of our dataset at this point is that is available for a wider range of countries, and that many of our survey questions were in a yes/no format, often with supporting documentation required. The core principles assessments are performed by supervisors from a very wide range of backgrounds, mostly but not exclusively from industrial countries, so that the "grading standards" may vary significantly. Also, country authorities who do not like the results can choose not to have them published, which creates a selection bias problem for researchers.[5]

Given the widespread attention paid to the Core Principles and the FSAP, our new database is particularly important because questions included in the survey overlap in many respects with essential elements of the Core Principles. The comprehensive and detailed nature of our data thus allows one to truly appreciate the range of differences in practices across countries. At the same time, it enables one to identify through empirical research those regulations and supervisory practices that work best to promote well-functioning and stable banking systems or, more generally, the broad approach to regulating and supervising banks that works best.[6]

The remainder of this chapter proceeds as follows. The next section discusses differences in the structure, scope, and independence of regulation and supervision, focusing on who regulates and supervises banks, the range of activities covered by the supervisory authorities, and the degree to which the authorities are free of undue pressure. The third section addresses the issue of what is meant by the term "bank," both from the standpoint of the range of activities in which banks are allowed to engage and the extent to which banks and nonbank firms are allowed to combine to form conglomerates. The fourth section discusses the extent to which competition may be restricted through entry requirements; the limitations on leveraging and risk-taking because of capital requirements; the degree to which supervisory authorities have powers to intervene – and, if so, are required to intervene – to promote a "safe and sound" banking industry. It also introduces a somewhat novel twist to bank regulation and supervision by discussing the extent to which the authorities may find their powers limited by actions of the courts. The fifth section examines whether or not countries have established explicit deposit insurance schemes and, if so, some of the features of those schemes.

---

[5] Neither approach can claim to measure the impact of bank supervision "on the ground," and in fact both approaches create a bias: both the promulgation of the Basel core principles and the publication of this survey in a sense teach authorities what are the right, or desired answers. Thus, as was the case with Basel I, when countries were far quicker to adopt the headline regulation of an 8 percent capital requirement than the underlying implementation framework to make this requirement truly meaningful, it is also possible that countries can change the regulatory framework to appear better on paper but not on the ground. In fact, the private interest view of regulation would predict this response.

[6] Summary information on differences across countries grouped in various ways is provided in Appendices 5–8.

Section six changes pace and focuses attention on the role of private monitoring and external governance, and the extent to which these factors are a source of market discipline in promoting viable and stable banking systems. The seventh section also provides a somewhat different perspective by examining the important issue of whether the mix of bank ownership (i.e., government, foreign, or private domestic) in a country is related to the types of regulations and supervisory practices it adopts. The last section discusses the extent to which the regulatory and supervisory regimes in various countries have become harmonized by virtue of their common membership in regional unions or international organizations. The member states of the European Union (EU), for example, agree to a minimum harmonization of rules for banks based on the principle of mutual recognition and home-country control. Countries that are members of the World Trade Organization (WTO), as another example, agree to a minimum harmonization with respect to the extent to which banks are allowed to enter and compete in each other's domestic banking markets. As will be discussed later, our indices may be used to examine the degree to which countries harmonize their regulations and supervisory practices in these types of situations. In sum, this chapter presents a picture of how countries around the world regulate and supervise their banks.

3.B. STRUCTURE, SCOPE, AND INDEPENDENCE OF REGULATION AND SUPERVISION[7]

Banking crises, rapid technological change, and the continuing globalization of banking have led national and multilateral policy makers to focus greater attention on the crucial role of bank regulation and supervision in recent years. This focus is reinforced by the fact that "... one of the important [international] trends has been, and continues to be, a move away from regulation and towards supervision" (Crockett, 2001). Policy discussions specifically focus on several issues that must be addressed in establishing and maintaining effective supervision, including who should supervise banks (i.e., the "structure" of supervision), should there be a single financial sector supervising authority (i.e., the "scope" of supervision), and how independent should the supervisory authority be of pressure and influence by politicians and banks (i.e., the independence of supervision)?

Three issues for policy makers to address with respect to the structure of bank supervision are whether there should be a single bank supervisory

---

[7] This section draws heavily on Barth et al., 2003.

authority, or multiple bank supervisors; and whether the central bank should play a role in bank supervision. Perhaps the "hottest" issue after Basel II in many countries is the scope of supervision: should there be a single authority for the entire financial services industry, with banks being just one part of that industry. Finally, the independence issue concerns the degree to which the supervisory authority can make decisions and take actions without undue political pressure. Indeed, a lack of independence has been identified in the FSAP as one of the major areas of concern in developing countries. In view of this fact, in the new survey an effort was made to enable one to more fully address these dimensions of regulation and supervision. How all these issues are addressed is important because policies that fail to provide for an appropriate bank regulatory and supervisory framework may undermine bank performance and even lead to full-scale banking crises.

3.B.1. Single Bank Supervisor or Multiple Bank Supervisors

A key policy decision in designing the structure of any bank supervisory system is whether there should be a single bank supervisory authority or multiple bank supervisors. Although the conceptual literature in this area covers a number of possible advantages and disadvantages to each option, one of the strongest reasons that some advocate a single bank supervisory authority is the fear of a "competition in laxity" between multiple bank supervisors, while those who favor a system with two or more bank supervisors stress the benefits of a "competition in innovation" among multiple bank supervisors (Barth et al., 2003, pp. 70–73 and Barth et al., 2002). Also, Rosen (2003) finds for the United States that bank regulators seem to specialize and this allows banks to switch regulators when they are switching business strategy, thereby improving performance.

One essential set of information from official sources missing from the existing literature on the issue of the structure of bank supervision is what different countries around the world have chosen to do. We therefore created a variable, *Multiple Supervisors*, to indicate whether there is a single official bank supervisory authority, or whether multiple supervisors share responsibility of supervising a nation's banks.[8] The following two questions were used to create this variable: What body/agency supervises banks? And is there more than one supervisory body? The first question

---

[8] For purposes of quantification in the empirical analysis, we assign a 1 when there are multiple supervisors and a 0 otherwise.

also enables us to determine whether the central bank is assigned supervisory responsibilities.

Table 3.2 provides information on the international "landscape" of bank supervisory structure. The vast majority of countries, 127 of 153, have a single bank supervisory authority. It should be noted at the outset that the maximum number of countries for which information is available is 153. However, not every country provided information for all questions covered by the survey. This fact should be kept in mind when reading this chapter. There are instances in which we will refer to differing country totals when discussing specific regulations and supervisory practices. That said, only twenty-six countries, including the United States, assign banking supervision to multiple supervisory authorities.[9] This preponderance in favor of a single over a multiple supervisory authority was also the case in the earlier survey. Of 107 countries, only 18 countries had a single supervisory authority. This situation may be reassuring to those who argue that the existence of a single authority makes sense in low-income countries with more limiter financial resources and a relative scarcity of skilled banking personnel.[10] Indeed, when countries are grouped by income level, only Nigeria among the low-income countries has multiple bank supervisory authorities. More generally, however, there is no significant correlation between GDP per capita (a measure of the level of economic development) and the existence of multiple supervisors. Yet, the existence of multiple supervisors is positively correlated with the total assets of all banks, or the size of a country's banking system, relative to GDP.

3.B.2. Bank Supervisory Role of the Central Bank

Countries also must decide on the contentious issue of whether to assign responsibility for bank supervision to the central bank in addition to its responsibility for monetary policy (Goodhart and Schoenmaker, 1995). As with the issue of single or multiple bank supervisors, the conceptual literature is split on the relative advantages and disadvantages of the central bank being a bank supervisor (Barth et al., 2003). Perhaps the most strongly emphasized argument in favor of assigning supervisory

---

[9] Briault (1999, pp. 15–16) briefly discusses the issue of a transnational financial services supervisor. See also the discussion in Biship (2002). Transnational issues also come into play in the debate over financial supervision in the EU. See, for example, Lannoo (2000), International Monetary Fund (2001), Goodhart (2002), and Schüler (2003).

[10] The survey does contain some limited information on the number, tenure, and budget for the bank supervisory authority (see Section 12 of Appendix 1).

Table 3.2. *Countries with Single vs. Multiple Bank Supervisory Authorities*

	Single Bank Supervisory Authority (127 countries)				Multiple Bank Supervisory Authorities (26 countries)
Africa (34 countries)	Algeria Benin Botswana Burkina Faso Burundi Cameroon Central African Republic Chad	Congo Côte d'Ivoire Egypt Equatorial Guinea Gabon Gambia Ghana Guinea	Guinea Bissau Kenya Lesotho Libya Madagascar Mali Namibia Niger	Rwanda Senegal South Africa Sudan Swaziland Togo Tunisia Zimbabwe	Morocco	Nigeria
Americas (21 countries)	Argentina Bolivia Brazil Canada Chile	Colombia Costa Rica Ecuador El Salvador Guatemala	Guyana Honduras Mexico Nicaragua Paraguay	Peru Suriname Trinidad and Tobago Uruguay Venezuela	United States	
Asia/Pacific (32 countries)	Australia Bhutan Cambodia Fiji	Japan Jordan Kuwait Kyrgyzstan	Pakistan Papua New Guinea Philippines Qatar	Singapore Sri Lanka Tajikistan Tonga	China Kazakhstan	Korea Taiwan, China Thailand

	Hong Kong, China	Lebanon	Russia	Turkmenistan			
	India	Malaysia	Samoa	United Arab			
	Israel	New Zealand	Saudi Arabia	Emirates			
Europe (39 countries)	Armenia	Estonia	Latvia	Serbia & Montenegro	Albania	Germany	Poland
	Austria	Finland	Lithuania	Slovenia	Czech Republic	Macedonia	Slovakia
	Azerbaijan	France	Luxembourg	Spain			
	Belarus	Greece	Moldova	Sweden			
	Belgium	Hungary	Netherlands	Switzerland			
	Bosnia and Herzegovina	Iceland	Norway	Turkey			
	Bulgaria	Ireland	Portugal	Ukraine			
	Croatia	Italy	Romania	United Kingdom			
	Denmark						
Offshore Centers (27 countries)	Aruba	Gibraltar	Macau, China	Panama	Anguilla	Grenada	Saint Kitts and Nevis
	Bahrain	Guernsey	Malta	Seychelles	Antigua and Barbuda	Liechtenstein	Saint Lucia
	Belize	Isle of Man	Mauritius	Turks and Caicos Islands	Commonwealth of Dominica	Montserrat	Saint Vincent and The Grenadines
	British Virgin Islands	Jersey	Oman		Cyprus	Puerto Rico	Vanuatu

responsibility to the central bank is that as a bank supervisor, the central bank will have direct and unimpeded access to pertinent information and thus readily available firsthand knowledge of the condition and performance of banks. This in turn can help it identify and respond to the emergence of a potential systemic problem in a timely manner. This may be even more important to the extent that monetary policy plays out through the credit channel and thus would be particularly useful during a credit crunch. Supervisory responsibility also may help the central bank implement the lender-of-last-result functions better, including distinguishing solvent but illiquid banks from simply insolvent banks.

Those pointing to the disadvantages of assigning bank supervision to the central bank stress the inherent conflict of interest between supervisory responsibilities and responsibility for monetary policy. The conflict could become particularly acute during an economic downturn, when the central bank might be tempted to pursue a too-loose monetary policy to contain adverse effects on bank earnings and credit quality. It also might encourage banks to extend credit more liberally than warranted based on credit quality conditions to complement an expansionary monetary policy. Although such a policy might initially be beneficial to the banking industry, it may ultimately be harmful to the overall economy. By contrast, many of those who favor taking supervision out of the central bank agree that the monetary authority should be appraised of the condition of banks because the central bank might implement a more expansionary monetary policy in downturns if the ability of the banking system to extend credit becomes seriously impeded, regardless of its role as bank supervisor.

As with the single versus multiple bank supervisor debate, a useful first step in addressing the debate over the bank supervisory role of the central bank is to ascertain basic facts. Table 3.3, which compares the supervisory role of the central bank in 153 countries, shows that about 60 percent of the countries assign the central bank some responsibility in banking supervision. This includes sixty-nine countries in which the central bank is the single bank supervisory authority. Interestingly, only two countries of the thirteen countries represented in the Basel Committee (Italy and the Netherlands) have the central bank as the only authority responsible for bank supervision. In any event, these are roughly the same percentages as those for the 107 countries in the earlier survey. In twenty-six countries that have a multiple-bank-supervisors system, twenty-one of them assign some bank supervisory responsibility to the central bank, including the United States. In the latter case, the central bank became an additional bank supervisory authority after multiple supervisory authorities had already been established. In early 2004, China established a new bank supervisory authority, but the central bank, which had been the sole authority, retained some limited supervisory responsibility (Barth, Koepp, and Zhou, 2004).

When viewed as regions, most countries in a region choose one of either two extremes; appoint the central bank as the sole supervisory authority or not an authority at all, with the exception of the offshore financial centers (OFCs). In the latter case, the central bank is one of the supervisory authorities in ten of the twenty-six OFCs. This mainly reflects the fact that eight of these ten countries are members of the Eastern Caribbean Currency Union (ECCU) and share a common central bank. In the Asia/Pacific region, twenty-seven of the thirty-one countries assign some supervisory responsibility to the central bank, with twenty-four of these countries assigning it sole responsibility. This is in contrast to the recent trend in Europe to assign the task of supervision to an authority different and independent from the central bank. Since the launch of the Euro in 1999, as will be discussed later, the European Central Bank (ECB) is in charge of monetary policy of countries participating in the European Monetary Union (EMU), but not bank regulation and supervision, which still resides in the individual countries of the EMU.

In all cases, however, the central bank and the supervisory authority are expected to share information and to cooperate. Indeed, this expectation is sometimes formalized by a Memorandum of Understanding (MoU). In the case of the United Kingdom, for instance, the MoU establishes a framework for sharing information and for the cooperation among the Treasury, the Bank of England, and the Financial Supervisory Authority.

The intense interest policy makers have recently shown in the issue of the appropriate structure of supervision has not yet been reflected in research. In particular, little systematic empirical evidence exists on how, or indeed whether, the structure of bank supervision affects the performance and stability of the banking industry. One recent study partially addressing this gap is Barth et al. (2003).[11] This study summarizes the

---

[11] Barth et al. (2003) also address the issues of the scope of supervision (i.e., whether the bank supervisory authorities also have responsibility beyond the banking industry, in particular for securities and insurance firms), and supervisory independence from political pressure. Also, see Organization for Economic Cooperation and Development (2002).

Table 3.3. *Countries with the Central Bank as a Supervisor Authority*

	Central Bank only (69 countries)	Central Bank Among Multiple Supervisors (21 countries)	Central Bank Not a Supervisory Authority (61 countries)
Africa (33 countries)	Botswana, Burundi, Egypt, Gambia, Ghana, Guinea, Lesotho, Libya, Namibia, Rwanda, South Africa, Sudan, Swaziland, Tunisia, Zimbabwe	Morocco, Nigeria	Algeria, Benin, Burkina Faso, Cameroon, Central African Republic, Chad, Congo, Côte d'Ivoire, Equatorial Guinea, Gabon, Guinea Bissau, Kenya, Madagascar, Mali, Niger, Senegal, Togo
Americas (21 countries)	Argentina, Brazil, Guyana, Suriname, Trinidad and Tobago, Uruguay	United States	Bolivia, Canada, Chile, Colombia, Costa Rica, Ecuador, El Salvador, Guatemala, Honduras, Mexico, Nicaragua, Paraguay, Peru, Venezuela
Asia/Pacific (31 countries)	Bhutan, Cambodia, Fiji, Hong Kong, China, India, Kyrgyzstan, Malaysia, New Zealand, Pakistan, Papua New Guinea, Samoa, Saudi Arabia, Singapore, Sri Lanka, Tajikistan	China, Taiwan, China, Thailand	Australia, Japan, Korea, Lebanon

	Israel Jordan Kuwait	Philippines Qatar Russia	Tonga Turkmenistan United Arab Emirates					
Europe (39 countries)	Armenia Azerbaijan Belarus Bulgaria Croatia Greece	Ireland Italy Lithuania Moldova Netherlands Portugal	Romania Serbia & Montenegro Slovenia Spain Ukraine	Albania Czech Republic Germany	Macedonia Slovakia	Austria Belgium Bosnia and Herzegovina Denmark Estonia Finland	France Hungary Iceland Latvia Luxembourg Norway	Poland Sweden Switzerland Turkey United Kingdom
Offshore Centers (26 countries)	Aruba Bahrain Belize	Macau, China Mauritius	Oman Seychelles	Anguilla Antigua and Barbuda Commonwealth of Dominica Cyprus Grenada	Montserrat Saint Kitts and Nevis Saint Lucia Saint Vincent and The Grenadines Vanuatu	British Virgin Islands Gibraltar Guernsey	Isle of Man Jersey Liechtenstein	Malta Panama Puerto Rico

policy debates surrounding the issue, drawing on a growing conceptual literature. It also examines whether and how the structure of banking supervision affects a key dimension of bank performance – bank profitability. The results indicate, at most, a weak influence for the structure of supervision on this particular dimension of bank performance. The study points out, however, that the key questions of whether and how supervision affects banking system safety and soundness remain to be empirically examined.

3.B.3. Scope of Supervisory Authority

Much of the discussion about consolidating financial services supervision takes as its starting point the observation that financial service companies are growing increasingly complex, by offering an ever widening array of financial products and services and by offering these products and services through a variety of delivery channels. Financial conglomerates, for example, that operate in the banking, securities, and insurance industries through various subsidiaries and affiliates are among the most complex and powerful corporations in many countries. Some have argued that a supervisor with broad scope to cover all financial services is necessary to supervise such entities effectively and, in particular, to ensure that supervisory oversight of risk management practices by such conglomerates is not fragmented, uncoordinated, or incomplete. The most significant argument against a supervisory authority with broad scope is that it would result in an undue concentration of power that would otherwise be dispersed among several agencies. This situation could increase the likelihood of regulatory capture and retard financial innovation (Barth et al., 2003; Quintyn and Taylor, 2004).

Despite the fact that empirical evidence bearing on this debate is scarce, a trend has emerged over the past two decades toward consolidating or "integrating" supervision of banking and other financial services into a single supervisory authority. Even though there may be an integrated financial supervisor, there still may be separate laws governing the activities of different financial institutions. Indeed, in most countries with an integrated supervisor there is no integrated legal framework to assure that similar financial products and services offered by different entities are subject to equal regulatory and supervisory treatment. The laws typically apply to financial institutions and not to specific products and services.

Table 3.4 illustrates this trend toward integrated supervision. It shows that 46 of 151 countries have assigned supervision over the financial sector to a single authority, and this includes countries in all parts of the world and at all levels of income. The one-third figure is based on official responses to a question included for the first time in the new survey. After checking with other unofficial sources, however, we believe that the classification of a few countries may be questionable. One must therefore be extra cautious in relying on the individual country responses to this particular question. Those seeking a high degree of precision in this area should consult the laws of individual countries. Even when doing so, however, researchers may disagree with one another in some instances. To illustrate, in the case of the United Kingdom, the regulation of corporate and group pension funds is the responsibility of the Occupational Pension Review Authority and the granting of consumer credit licenses, their issuances, and supervision is the responsibility of the Office of Fair Trading. Yet, most researchers consider the United Kingdom to have a single financial sector supervisory authority because bank and securities market supervision are conducted by one supervisory authority (Foot, 2004).

Among the early movers to a single financial supervisory authority were Singapore (1984), Norway (1986), and Sweden (1991), and more recent converts include the United Kingdom (1997), Japan (1998), South Korea (1998), and Austria (2002) (Martinez and Rose, 2003; Darlap and Grünbichler, 2004). In the case of Japan, the power to regulate banks, securities firms, and insurance companies was transferred from the Ministry of Finance to a new single supervisory authority, the Financial Supervisory Agency, excluding the central bank. In contrast, in the United Kingdom a new single financial supervisory authority was created by absorbing the responsibilities of a variety of different supervisory authorities, including those of the central bank. In 1997, Australia adopted what is known as the "Twin Peaks" model of bank regulation and supervision. The "twin peaks" are prudential regulation and supervision, under the Australian Prudential Regulation Authority (APRA), and consumer protection and market integrity, under the Australian Securities and Investments Commission (ASTC). In contrast to this type of consolidation, the United States has one of the most complex and multifaceted financial supervisory systems in the world. Not surprisingly, as Jackson (2004, p. 37) points out, "[t]otal U.S annual expenditures on financial regulation in the United States during 1998–2000 was in excess of $4.5 billion or 13.7 times the annual expenditures of the FSA [the Financial Services

Table 3.4. *Scope of Supervisory Authority*

	Single Financial Supervisory Authority for Financial Sector (46 countries)	Multiple Financial Supervisory Authority for Financial Sector (105 countries)
Africa (33 countries)	Algeria, Burundi, Gambia, Guinea, Lesotho, Rwanda, Swaziland	Benin, Botswana, Burkina Faso, Cameroon, Central African Republic, Chad, Congo, Côte d'Ivoire, Egypt, Equatorial Guinea, Gabon, Ghana, Guinea Bissau, Kenya, Libya, Mali, Morocco, Namibia, Niger, Nigeria, Senegal, South Africa, Sudan, Togo, Tunisia, Zimbabwe
Americas (20 countries)	Bolivia, Colombia, Ecuador, Guatemala, Honduras, Peru, Suriname, Venezuela	Argentina, Brazil, Canada, Chile, Costa Rica, El Salvador, Guyana, Mexico, Nicaragua, Paraguay, Trinidad and Tobago, United States
Asia/Pacific (32 countries)	Bhutan, Cambodia, Japan, Kazakhstan, South Korea, New Zealand, Papua New Guinea, Samoa, Singapore, Taiwan, China, Tonga	Australia, China, Fiji, Hong Kong, China, India, Israel, Jordan, Kuwait, Kyrgyzstan, Lebanon, Malaysia, Pakistan, Philippines, Qatar, Russia, Saudi Arabia, Sri Lanka, Tajikistan, Thailand, Turkmenistan, United Arab Emirates

Europe (39 countries)	Austria	Latvia	Norway	Albania	Czech	Italy	Serbia &
	Germany	Luxembourg	Sweden	Armenia	Republic	Lithuania	Montenegro
	Hungary	Moldova	United	Azerbaijan	Denmark	Macedonia	Slovakia
	Iceland		Kingdom	Belarus	Estonia	Netherlands	Slovenia
				Belgium	Finland	Poland	Spain
				Bosnia and	France	Portugal	Switzerland
				Herzegovina	Greece	Romania	Turkey
				Bulgaria	Ireland		Ukraine
				Croatia			
Offshore Centers (27 countries)	Aruba	Guernsey	Malta	Anguilla	Grenada	Montserrat	Saint Kitts and
	Bahrain	Jersey	Seychelles	Antigua and	Isle of Man	Oman	Nevis
	British Virgin	Macau, China	Turks and	Barbuda	Liechtenstein	Panama	Saint Vincent
	Islands		Caicos	Belize	Mauritius	Puerto Rico	and The
	Gibraltar		Islands	Commonwealth			Grenadines
				of Dominica			Vanuatu
				Cyprus			

Authority in the U.K.]. . . . Personnel levels of the U.S. (41,722) were more than 15 times higher than those of the FSA (2,765)." He adds that ". . . even if one normalized annual expenditures for the size of the economy or capital markets, substantial differences would remain." A relevant and as yet unexplored issue, however, is whether the additional expenditures and personnel result in a better functioning banking system.[12] The existence of a single authority is positively correlated with GDP per capita, but not correlated with the size of the banking system relative to GDP.

3.B.4. Independence of Supervision

The way in which the supervisory authorities supervise banks is quite important. Indeed, unless these authorities appropriately interpret and enforce the regulations governing banks, the regulations themselves become meaningless. Perhaps more important, it is the supervisors who have direct contact with the banks and therefore represent the main line of government defense against unsafe and unsound banking practices. Supervisory authorities therefore seek to detect, assess, and monitor activities and practices that expose banks to excessive risk relative to their levels of capital, and to require banks to appropriately manage their risk exposures. The authorities may even deem it necessary to ultimately liquidate banks when all other corrective actions fail. It therefore would appear to be extremely important that they are independent from undue pressure and influence exerted by politicians and banks. At the same time, however, it is not unreasonable to expect the supervisory authorities to be held accountable for their actions.

To address the issue of independence, we rely on the answers to several survey questions. In particular, we construct the following four variables to measure the degree of independence (for the exact construction of these variables, see Appendix 2):

---

[12] In a related vein, investment in bank regulation may be a partial substitute for private investment. For example, Udell (1989) points out that in the United States ". . .bank regulators have historically provided a free subsidy to banks by monitoring their loan officers through monitoring the loan officers' respective loan portfolios. Now banks have to pay for their own monitoring (i.e., loan review) because bank examinations no longer provide this subsidy." His argument is that bank examinations essentially provided banks with a highly subsidized good (i.e., loan officer monitoring), which when reduced forced banks to invest themselves in loan review. Bank regulations and supervisory practices may therefore generate externalities.

1) *Independence of Supervisory Authority – Political*: This variable measures the degree to which the supervisory authority is independent of the executive branch of government. This variable is based on the question: to whom are the supervisory bodies responsible or accountable? If the response to the question is a legislative body, a value of 1 is assigned and 0 otherwise.

The presumption is as follows: In a reasonably well-functioning democracy, the supervisory authority will enjoy greater independence from the political interest of the executive if it is instead accountable to a body of competitively elected individuals. In the nine countries in which the supervisory authority is responsible or accountable only to the prime minster, for example, we assign a value of zero.[13] As we discuss later, empirical analyses that use this variable should simultaneously use indicators of the degree to which the legislative body is competitively elected and independent of the executive.

2) *Independence of Supervisory Authority – Banks*: This variable indicates whether or not supervisors are legally liable for their actions, with an assigned a value of 1 if supervisors are not liable and 0 otherwise.

To allow supervisors to be sued or otherwise held legally liable for the actions they take against a bank must have a "chilling" effect on strong or tough enforcement actions. Yet in 55 of 150 countries this practice is allowed, including countries such as Argentina and Brazil. This practice occurs with about the same frequency in both industrial and developing countries. Of the 45 industrial countries, 15 allow supervisors to be sued and 40 of the 105 developing countries do the same. In the earlier survey, however, the situation was even more lopsided, with forty-two of ninety-eight countries allowing supervisors to be sued for their actions.

3) *Independence of Supervisory Authority – Fixed Term*: This variable is the term of service of the head of the supervisory agency. If the term of service is not fixed or is less than four years, a value of 0 is assigned. If the term of service is fixed at four years or greater, a value of 1 is assigned.

---

[13] It is for this reason that a country like the United Kingdom is assigned a relatively low independence value. The supervisory authorities are appointed and removable by the Treasury in this particular case. As better data become available, it will be possible to rate countries on the basis of how frequently, and even perhaps for what reasons, the head of supervision is removed.

The basis for this demarcation is the presumption that a fixed and relatively long term affords a greater degree of independence. In the survey, 96 of 151 countries set the term at four or more years.

4) *Independence of Supervisory Authority – Overall*: This variable is the sum of (1), (2), and (3). Higher values signify greater independence.

Table 3.5 provides information on the degree of overall supervisory independence. It may be seen that twenty-two countries have a high degree of independence, whereas sixty-eight countries have a low degree of independence. Yet, like the minimum capital requirements that countries set, the higher the level of independence does not necessarily imply that the supervisory authorities are tougher with respect to curtailing excessively risky or otherwise imprudent bank behavior.

Neither geographical region nor income level appears to be related to the degree of independence assigned to the bank supervisory authority. There is no correlation, moreover, between GDP per capita and the overall independence of the supervisory authority. There is, however, a tendency (with some exceptions) for more democratic countries to grant a greater degree of independence to the supervisory authority.

Admittedly, when reviewing the values for supervisory independence, there may be questions about those assigned some countries. In some cases, the values may seem too high (e.g., Cambodia, Egypt, Jordan, and Nigeria), whereas in other cases they may seem too low (e.g., Denmark, Italy, and Germany). This is a result of our straightforward approach to coding independence. Yet, as was indicated, the values are predicated on the existence of reasonably functioning democracies in countries. This assumption, however, clearly does not hold in all countries. To illustrate what effect the failure to account for this factor may have on our independence scores, we adjust several of them based upon the variable, Executive Constraints, from the Polity IV Project (Marshall and Jaggers, 2002). This variable captures the extent to which there are institutional constraints on the decision-making powers of chief executives like the head of the bank supervisory authority. It ranges in value from 1, reflecting unlimited authority of the executive's actions, to 7, reflecting executive parity or subordination with accountability groups (e.g., the legislature) having effective authority equal to or greater than the executive. If we add this variable to our index of supervisory independence, then Denmark, Italy, and Germany all move ahead of Cambodia, Egypt, Jordan, and Nigeria. These and other changes in the rankings resulting from this adjustment most likely accord better with one's a priori beliefs about the degree of independence of the supervisory authorities in our sample countries. The purpose of our survey, however, was not to assess how the strength of democracy interacts with supervisory independence in countries around the world. Nonetheless, it does have an important bearing on the independence of the supervisory authorities and therefore should be taken into account when assessing the impact of supervisory independence. The bottom line is that our independence variable is simply a "raw" indicator, which may be combined with information on national political institutions to construct a more accurate indicator of supervisory independence.

It is also useful before concluding this discussion to raise the issue of whether indeed the bank regulatory and supervisory authorities should be independent. The conventional wisdom, as embodied in the Core Principles, is that such independence is desirable. The presumption is that politicians are more likely to respond to banks' interests (e.g., engaging in forbearance), whereas independent supervisory officials are more likely to respond to the publics' interests. Based on these kinds of biases one would naturally consider higher scores for supervisory independence preferable to lower scores. This, in turn, would lead one to question the fact that countries such as Denmark and Germany score lower than countries such as Cambodia and Nigeria. However, depending on one's view of independence, lower scores might be preferable to higher scores and vice versa.

To put the independence issue into broader perspective, consider the situation in the United States as regards who formulates fiscal policy and who interprets the constitution. The public officials who formulate fiscal policy are elected, whereas the officials who interpret the constitution are appointed. The politicians responsible for fiscal policy are thus not independent but instead directly accountable to the electorate. The justices responsible for interpreting the constitution are appointed by politicians and, by virtue of their lifetime appointments, are independent of and unaccountable to the very politicians who appoint them. The public officials who head the bank regulatory and supervisory agencies are also appointed by politicians rather than elected. Yet, their terms vary among countries. In the United States, for example, the governors of the central bank are appointed to fourteen-year terms. But in Italy the governor of the central bank enjoys lifetime tenure, whereas in Brazil the governor serves at the pleasure of the president and thus may serve a week or less, as some governors have done in the recent past. Terms set longer than those of the elected officials appointing them, however, could

Table 3.5. *Degree of Supervisory Independence*

	Low Independence (68 countries)		Medium Independence (58 countries)	High Independence (22 countries)
	0	**1**	**2**	**3**
Africa (31 countries)	Madagascar Zimbabwe	Algeria Benin Burkina Faso Côte d'Ivoire Gambia Ghana · Guinea Bissau Mali Morocco Niger Senegal Togo · Botswana Burundi Cameroon Central African Republic Chad	Congo Equatorial Guinea Gabon Guinea Kenya · Namibia Rwanda South Africa Swaziland Tunisia	Egypt · Nigeria
Americas (20 countries)	Chile Colombia Costa Rica Mexico	Argentina Brazil El Salvador Guatemala · Suriname Uruguay Venezuela · Bolivia Canada Ecuador	Guyana Honduras Nicaragua · Peru Trinidad and Tobago United States	
Asia/Pacific (32 countries)	Bhutan Kyrgyzstan Thailand	China Fiji Hong Kong, China Israel · Philippines Samoa Saudi Arabia Singapore Sri Lanka · India Kuwait Malaysia	Qatar Russia · Tonga United Arab Emirates	Australia Cambodia Jordan · New Zealand Papua New Guinea

Europe (39 coutries)	Denmark Iceland Italy Poland	Japan Kazakhstan Korea Armenia Azerbaijan Belarus France Germany	Taiwan, China Tajikistan Spain Turkey Ukraine United Kingdom	Austria Belgium Bosnia and Herzegovina Croatia Estonia	Finland Greece Lithuania Luxembourg Macedonia	Moldova Netherlands Norway Slovakia Sweden	Albania Bulgaria Czech Republic Hungary Ireland Latvia	Portugal Romania Serbia & Montenegro Slovenia Switzerland
Offshore Centers (26 countries)	Aruba Liechtenstein	Bahrain Gibraltar Macau, China Mauritius	Oman Panama Puerto Rico Vanuatu	Anguilla Antigua and Barbuda Belize British Virgin Islands	Commonwealth of Dominica Grenada Isle of Man Montserrat	Saint Kitts and Nevis Saint Lucia Saint Vincent and The Grenadines Seychelles	Cyprus Guernsey	Jersey Malta

lessen political pressure. Terms set too short could provide an incentive for the supervisory authorities to perform corruptly, or at least create a potential conflict of interest if the authorities plan to enter the banking industry.

The issue that arises given this situation is whether the degree of independence and accountability for the bank regulatory and supervisory officials that exists in the United States, for example, assures the sort of decision making that best promotes a well-functioning banking system. More generally, our dataset shows that there are differences in the way in which banking officials are appointed, the extent to which they are held accountable, and in the length of their appointments. As a result, the same issue that arises in the case of the United States about the degree of independence and accountability arises for other countries around the globe. Not to be overlooked is the fact that the qualifications, skills, and motivation of the head of the supervisory agency, coupled with adequate financial and human resources, may be more important than supervisory independence per se. Furthermore, as we will discuss later, the supervisory authorities in some countries are required to take specific corrective actions against a bank as its solvency deteriorates, which in essence conveys a special type of independence. Absent guidance from a theoretical treatment of this issue, we remain agnostic as to the degree of independence/accountability that should be granted to the bank regulatory and supervisory officials (i.e., whether it should be as high as justices interpreting the constitution or as low as simply carrying out decisions of the heads of state).[14] Instead, we construct seemingly reasonable measures of independence, allowing others to construct alternative measures if they so wish, and then assess whether they matter for various banking-sector outcomes.

3.C. WHAT IS A "BANK"?

The banking industry is regulated and supervised in every country around the globe. Banks must be licensed and then are subjected to regulations specifying the activities in which they are permitted to engage. Countries may restrict banks to a narrow range of activities, or allow them to engage in a broad array. Because it is the scope of activities that essentially

---

[14] Of course, supervisory authorities never operate in a political vacuum. For example, politicians may hold hearings on actions taken or not taken by the supervisory authorities, publicly criticize the decisions of the supervisory authorities, or even enact laws that change the policy of the supervisory authorities.

defines the term "bank," a bank may therefore not be the same in every country around the world.[15] It is the regulatory authorities, moreover, who not only determine the extent to which the activities of banks differ across countries but also the extent to which they differ from nonbank firms within countries. Furthermore, these same authorities determine the extent to which banks and nonbank firms may combine to form financial (i.e., bank and nonbank financial) or mixed (i.e., bank and nonbank nonfinancial) conglomerates.

3.C.1. Scope of Bank Activities

There are three regulatory variables that importantly affect the activities in which banks may engage. The three variables involve securities, insurance, and real estate activities. We specifically measure the degree to which the national regulatory authorities in countries allow banks to engage in the following three fee-based, rather than more traditional interest spread-based, activities:

(a) *Securities*: the ability of banks to engage in the business of securities underwriting, brokering, dealing, and all aspects of the mutual fund industry.

(b) *Insurance*: the ability of banks to engage in insurance underwriting and selling.

(c) *Real Estate*: the ability of banks to engage in real estate investment, development, and management.

The survey provides information in response to a series of individual questions regarding each country's regulations concerning these activities.

---

[15] For an interesting discussion of the evolution of the legal definition of a bank in the United States, see Haubrich and Santos (2003, pp. 147–148). In a similar vein, there is the issue as to what is meant by the term "banking product." To a growing extent product convergence is occurring, in which similar financial products are offered by different financial service industries. The regulatory and supervisory issue that arises in this situation is that similar products may in effect receive different regulatory treatment because they are being offered from differently regulated industries. For example, there is a growing similarity between performance standby letters of credit typically issued by banks, and surety bonds typically issued by insurance firms. Also, there are "hybrid" or "complex" products that contain to varying degrees banking, securities, and insurance elements. The introduction of these newer types of financial products contributes to the push for a single regulator of the entire financial services sector or at least greater formal arrangements for information sharing and co-operation among multiple regulators of this sector. This situation also contributes to the push for a single law for the entire financial services sector rather than separate laws for each financial service industry.

Using this information, we quantified the degree of regulatory restrictiveness for each aggregate or composite activity on a scale from 1 to 4, with larger numbers representing greater restrictiveness. The definitions of the 1 through 4 designations are as follows:

1. Unrestricted – A full range of activities in the given category can be conducted directly in the bank.
2. Permitted – A full range of activities can be conducted, but all or some must be conducted in subsidiaries.
3. Restricted – Less than a full range of activities can be conducted in the bank or subsidiaries.
4. Prohibited – The activity cannot be conducted in either the bank or subsidiaries.

The difference between a 1 and 2 indicates only the locations in which the activity may be conducted, not whether the activity is restricted in any way. This type of difference, however, may matter for various measures of banking industry performance as well as for banking industry stability. Indeed, there has been considerable controversy over which organizational structure (i.e., a holding company or subsidiary structure) is most appropriate for conducting different activities to better ensure a safe and sound banking industry. In the United States, for example, the regulator of national banks, the Office of the Comptroller of the Currency, favored subsidiaries, whereas the regulator of holding companies, the Federal Reserve, favored holding companies. When the U.S. Congress enacted the Gramm-Leach-Bliley Act (GLBA) in late 1999, it sided with the Federal Reserve in mandating that the holding company organizational structure should be used when engaging in the widest range of activities allowed under the law (Barth, Brumbaugh, and Wilcox, 2000). More generally, these types of regulations determine the degree to which a bank may diversify its business operations as well as to attempt to capitalize on any synergies that may arise from complimentary activities.[16] We also construct an overall measure of activities restrictiveness, which combines the three aforementioned indices, that ranges in value from 3 to 12.

Figure 3.2 shows that securities activities are the least restricted in countries, while real estate activities are the most restricted. Indeed, only

---

[16] It should be noted that this particular quantification required judgment on our part taking into account information in the survey as well as information obtained from follow-up questions.

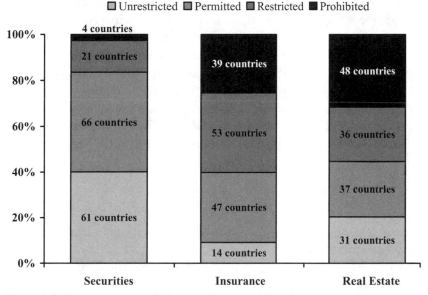

Figure 3.2. Regulatory Restrictions on Bank Activities by Degree of Restrictiveness.

4 of 152 countries actually prohibit banks from engaging in securities activities. In contrast, forty-eight countries prohibit them from engaging in real estate activities. Insurance activities are not far behind, with thirty-nine countries prohibiting banks from engaging in these activities. Gambia, Libya, and Nicaragua are the only countries that prohibit banks from engaging in securities, insurance, or real estate activities. However, fifteen other countries prohibit or restrict each of the three activities. Panama and Oman are interesting because they prohibit insurance and real estate activities for banks yet allow them unrestricted securities activities. At the other end of the restrictiveness spectrum, six countries grant banks unrestricted securities, insurance, and real estate powers – Estonia, Guinea, Luxembourg, New Zealand, Qatar, and Turkmenistan. All of these countries, moreover, have a single bank supervisory authority.

Recently, some countries have become more liberal in granting banks broader powers. The United States, for example, enacted GLBA to allow banks greater access to both securities and insurance activities. Barth, Brumbaugh, and Wilcox (2000) point out that GLBA was in part recognition of the fact that some banks had been granted broader securities powers years earlier. As a result of GLBA, however, the United

States in some respects tightened restrictions on the mixing of banking and commerce. Given the difficulty of regulating and supervising ever more complex organizations, it may well be that some countries use restrictions on activities as a crude tool to control risk-taking. The extent to which a narrower range of activities is actually associated with less risk is analyzed in Chapter 4. More generally, overall activities restrictiveness is negatively correlated with GDP per capita, but not correlated with total bank assets relative to GDP. Each of the individual components of overall activities restrictiveness is also negatively correlated with GDP per capita.

3.C.2. Formation of Financial Conglomerates

We constructed three aggregate variables to measure the degree of regulatory restrictiveness on the creation of financial conglomerates. We once again quantified the regulatory restrictiveness for each variable on a scale from 1 to 4. The specific variable definitions and the definitions of the 1–4 designations are as follows (for the exact construction of these variables, see Appendix 2):

(a) *Banks Owning Nonfinancial Firms*: the ability of banks to own nonfinancial firms.
  1. Unrestricted – A bank may own 100 percent of the equity in any nonfinancial firm.
  2. Permitted – A bank may own 100 percent of the equity in a nonfinancial firm, but ownership is limited based on a bank's equity capital.
  3. Restricted – A bank can only acquire less than 100 percent of the equity in a nonfinancial firm.
  4. Prohibited – A bank may not acquire any equity investment in a nonfinancial firm.

(b) *Nonfinancial Firms Owning Banks*: the ability of nonfinancial firms to own banks.
  1. Unrestricted – A nonfinancial firm may own 100 percent of the equity in a bank.
  2. Permitted – Unrestricted with prior authorization or approval.
  3. Restricted – Limits are placed on ownership, such as a maximum percentage of a bank's capital or shares.
  4. Prohibited – No equity investment in a bank.

(c) *Nonbank Financial Firms Owning Banks*: the ability of nonbank financial firms to own banks.

1. Unrestricted – A nonbank financial firm may own 100 percent of the equity in any bank.
2. Permitted – A nonbank financial firm may own 100 percent of the equity in a bank, but ownership is limited based on a firm's equity capital.
3. Restricted – A nonbank can only acquire less than 100 percent of the equity in a bank.
4. Prohibited – A nonbank may not acquire any equity investment in a bank.

We also constructed an overall measure of conglomerate restrictiveness, which combines the three aforementioned indices that ranges in value from 3 to 12.

These particular regulations are quite important and, needless to say, controversial. The regulation regarding the extent to which a bank may own shares in nonfinancial firms clearly affects the ability of a bank to diversify its revenue stream and is therefore similar in some ways to the regulatory restrictions on its activities as described above. We therefore also created a variable, Overall Activities and Bank Ownership Restrictiveness (OABOR), to capture the extent to which a bank could both engage in securities, insurance, and real estate activities and own nonfinancial firms. This particular "diversification" variable thus ranges in value from 4 to 16, with higher values indicating greater restrictiveness.

Figure 3.3 shows that the degree of restrictiveness on the creation of conglomerates displays substantial variation across countries. Bank ownership of nonfinancial firms is more restricted than nonfinancial firm ownership of banks. About 10 percent of the countries prohibit bank ownership of nonfinancial firms, whereas only 2 percent prohibit ownership of banks by nonfinancial firms. Twelve percent of the countries, including the United States, restrict the mixing of banking and commerce.[17] It is also the case that ten countries prohibit nonbank financial firms from owning banks. Based on overall restrictiveness, three countries are tied for being the least restrictive – Brazil, New Zealand, and the United Kingdom. Nine countries – El Salvador, Honduras, Jersey, Kenya, Lesotho, Nicaragua, Puerto Rico, Suriname, and Swaziland – by contrast, are tied

---

[17] Note that the new survey asks for responses at the bank level. The United States allows (financial) holding companies to own both bank and nonbank firms, subject to certain restrictions, with more restrictions on owning nonbank nonfinancial firms. See Barth, Brumbaugh, and Wilcox (2000) for a basic discussion of these possibilities under the Gramm-Leach-Bliley Act of 1999.

Rethinking Bank Regulation

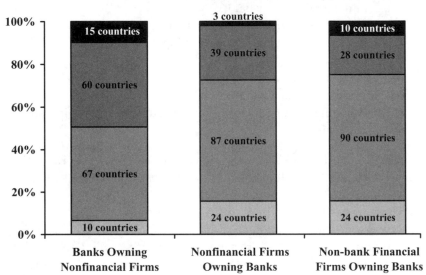

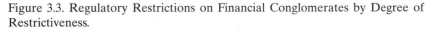

Figure 3.3. Regulatory Restrictions on Financial Conglomerates by Degree of Restrictiveness.

for being the most restrictive. More generally, there is no significant correlation between overall conglomerate restrictiveness and either GDP per capita or total bank assets relative to GDP. However, there is a negative correlation between banks owning nonfinancial firms and GDP per capita. OABOR is also negatively correlated with GDP per capita. As regards both allowable activities and the creation of conglomerates, Libya and Nicaragua are the most prohibitive among all countries. Overall, it seems that most countries allow some comingling of bank and nonbank firms.

Differences among countries in the regulatory treatment of permissible activities for banks and the formation of conglomerates are wide, but all countries share the ultimate regulatory and supervisory goal of promoting systemic stability. Additionally, regulation and supervision may also be aimed at promoting the development and efficiency of the banking sector. The important issue is what mix of permissible activities and degree of conglomeration is best for banks in each country to achieve these goals. At the theoretical level, there are arguments on both sides of the issue as discussed more fully in Chapter 2. As we saw there, restrictions on activities are often justified because of concerns about conflicts of interest, or fears of large conglomerates (which may be too complex to supervise [for an example of such a complex institution, see Figure 3.4], too big to

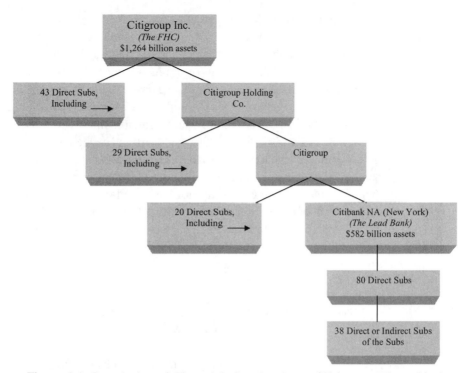

Figure 3.4. Complexity of Financial Conglomerates (Citigroup Hierarchical Organization). *Source:* Barth, Goldberg, Nolle, and Yago (2004).

fail, too willing to gamble with insured deposits, or just too inefficient and monopolistic).

Notwithstanding the arguments in favor of broadening the range of activities and ownership arrangements allowed, supervisors' concerns about conglomeration may be even more pronounced given the ever greater geographical spread of banking organizations. Consider, for example, the cases of Citigroup and Deutsche Bank. In 2003 Citigroup operated with more than one-third of its assets outside the United States and earned nearly 40 percent of its net income from abroad. Deutsche Bank operated with two-thirds of its assets outside Germany in 2002 and earned about 40 percent of its net income from foreign operations. As of early 2005, five other banks join these two in having balance sheets larger than $1 trillion, almost one-tenth the size of U.S. GDP. Such big global conglomerates – especially in a world with over one hundred countries with broad money less than $10 billion each – raise difficult but important issues regarding the sharing of responsibilities among the various

regulatory and supervisory authorities in countries in which these conglomerates operate. (In the new survey, of the sixty-five countries providing information, the average fraction of capital in the largest ten
banks owned by commercial/industrial or financial conglomerates is
40 percent). As Foot (2004) points out, "The largest UK-based bank
(HSBC)... operates in over 80 countries and sells somewhere in the world
every banking, securities and insurance product known to man. The FSA
has to maintain relationships with some 200 regulators and exchanges outside the UK in respect of a group like HSBC." He also adds that "... the
FSA is a member of well over 150 international regulatory committees."
Some countries, moreover, like China, do not yet have laws that specifically address the issue of conglomerates, even though they exist and thus
pose risks. In any event, the extent to which various restrictions on allowable activities, including bank ownership of nonfinancial firms, matter for
bank performance and stability are examined in Chapter 4.

3.D. ENTRY INTO BANKING, CAPITAL REQUIREMENTS, AND SUPERVISORY POWERS

3.D.1. How Liberal Are Entry Requirements into Banking?

The degree of competition in banking depends importantly on entry barriers, both domestic and foreign. The extent of barriers to foreign entry is
a separate and important indicator of the degree of competition or contestability in a country's domestic banking industry because as noted most
financial systems around the world are small. We rely on three variables
to qualitatively capture the extent to which competition within the banking industry is restricted. The variables all relate to the ability of existing
or new domestic and foreign banks to enter the banking business within
a country. More specifically, two of the three variables are defined and
quantified as follows:

1) *Entry into Banking Requirements*: this variable is based on whether
   or not the following information is required of applicants for a banking license:[18] (1) Draft by-laws; (2) Intended organizational chart;

---

[18] Each of these types of submissions was assigned a value of 1 if it was required and a
value of 0 otherwise. This means that the more information required by the regulatory
authorities of the type indicated when deciding upon whether or not to issue a license,
the more restrictive will be entry into banking. The Entry into Banking Requirements
variable is created by adding these eight variables together. It therefore may range in
value from 0 to 8, with higher values indicating more restrictiveness. The higher the score,

(3) Financial projections for first three years; (4) Financial information on main potential shareholders; (5) Background/experience of future directors; (6) Background/experience of future managers; (7) Sources of funds to be used to capitalize the new bank; and (8) Market differentiation intended for the new bank.

Regulators in most countries do not allow just anyone to enter the banking system, but rather screen entrants to better assure they are "fit and proper." By imposing the fairly basic requirements identified above before a banking license is accepted or rejected, those allowed to enter may be of higher quality and thereby enhance the overall performance of the banking industry. Our dataset indicates that more than 80 percent of all countries do indeed impose these basic requirements. This was also the case in the earlier survey. Table 3.6 identifies those countries that fail to comply with this seemingly universal best practice.[19] Even though each requirement may not be equally important, these types of differences raise questions about why some countries differ so much from this widely accepted practice, as well as whether it ultimately matters, an issue addressed in Chapter 4.

2) *Limitations on Foreign Entry/Ownership of Domestic Banks*: whether there are any limitations placed on the ability of foreign banks to enter the domestic banking industry. This variable is based on yes or no responses to the following questions:[20] Are foreign entities prohibited from entering through: (1) Acquisition?; (2) Subsidiary?; (3) Branch?

The key distinction between a branch and a subsidiary is that the latter is a separate legal entity, whereas a branch is not. The activities carried out in subsidiaries become important in the event of a bank failure. The independent legal status of a subsidiary allows for liquidation apart from the parent bank according to the laws of the country where the subsidiary

---

presumably the more entry into banking would be restricted because there are more grounds for rejecting a license request. The higher the score, moreover, presumably the quality of the new entrants would be better and therefore the less likely a banking crisis and the bigger the overall enhancement in bank performance.

[19] Although Ireland seems to stand out because it does not legally impose any of the eight requirements on individuals seeking a banking license, it does formally request them of all applicants, which in practice appears to have been equivalent to a legal requirement.

[20] Each of these questions was assigned a value of 1 if the answer was no and a value of 0 otherwise. These three values were then added together to create the Limitation on Foreign Bank Entry/Ownership variable. It therefore may range in value from 0 to 3, with lower values indicating more restrictiveness.

Table 3.6. *Common Requirements for a Banking License: Countries Responding "No" by Requirement*

Drafts by Law	Intended Organizational Chart	First 3 Year Financial Projections	Financial Information on Main Potential Shareholders	Background/ Experience of Future Directors	Background/ Experience of Future Managers	Sources of Funds to be Used to Capitalize the New Bank	Intended Differentiation of New Bank from Other Banks
China	Chile	Azerbaijan	Ireland	Chile	Belarus	Algeria	Argentina
Fiji	Guatemala	India	Israel	Croatia	Chile	Cyprus	Azerbaijan
Guernsey	Ireland	Ireland	Kuwait	Ireland	Finland	Finland	Belarus
Ireland	Israel	Serbia & Montenegro	Qatar	Qatar	France	Germany	Chile
Israel	Qatar	Trinidad and Tobago		Slovenia	Ireland	Gibraltar	China
Jersey	Trinidad and Tobago				Poland	Hong Kong, China	Cyprus
New Zealand					Portugal	Ireland	France
Seychelles						Israel	Greece
South Africa						Jordan	Guatemala
Swaziland						Kenya	Hong Kong, China
Trinidad and Tobago						Madagascar	India
						New Zealand	Ireland
						Peru	Israel
						Qatar	Japan
						South Africa	Libya
						Trinidad and Tobago	Kuwait
							Malaysia
							Mauritius
							Pakistan
							Paraguay
							Puerto Rico
							Russia
							Seychelles
							Trinidad and Tobago
							Turkey
							Uruguay

is located. The liquidation of a bank with branches is more complicated, however, because it may lead to either the liquidation of the entire bank or the liquidation of only those branches that are insolvent. This means that creditors in one case have claims on the entire bank, whereas in the other they may have claims only on a branch. This also may present problems with respect to the coverage of deposit insurance because of uncertainty of coverage by home country versus coverage by host country. Whether a bank chooses to enter a foreign country via a branch or subsidiary depends on such factors as the capital requirement imposed on and the allowable activities granted by the host country to each organizational form. In addition to entering through branches and subsidiaries, a bank may establish a foreign presence through correspondent banking, representative offices and agencies. However, these forms of foreign entry are subject to strong limitations on allowable banking activities, including not being allowed to accept deposits or make consumer loans. That said, all but 1 of 149 countries allows foreign entry through either acquisition or establishing a subsidiary. Turkmenistan prohibits entry through acquisitions, whereas Costa Rica prohibits entry through subsidiaries. Still another seventeen countries prohibit entry through the establishment of a branch, including Malaysia, Mexico, the Philippines, and Russia.

Countries may allow foreign banks to open branches but may impose limitations on the number of branches as well as require that branches be separately capitalized. In China, for example, foreign banks until recently could only open a single branch each year. That rule was eliminated effective September 2004, but each branch doing Yuan-dominated business with individual Chinese customers requires a minimum capitalization of approximately $60 million. As regards acquisitions, China has set the limit on foreign investment in a domestic bank at 20 percent for an individual investor and 25 percent for all investors. This degree of detail would be useful to include in future versions of our dataset.[21]

The variables relating to restrictions on domestic and foreign bank entry into the banking business within a country are quite important for capturing the competitive environment. The data indicate, however, that at least with respect to requirements or limitations on entry per se most countries are generally the same as regards this aspect of competition or contestability.

[21] However, eighteen of seventy-six countries in the earlier survey imposed limitations on foreign bank ownership of domestic banks. This less than one-fourth figure suggests limitations may not be widespread but also that better data are needed to answer some questions about foreign entry.

Rethinking Bank Regulation

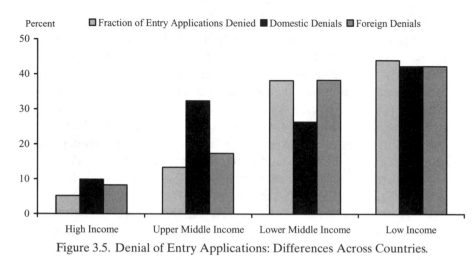

Figure 3.5. Denial of Entry Applications: Differences Across Countries.

The third measure of restrictions on bank entry consists of the fraction of domestic and foreign entry applications that are rejected by the regulatory authority. Denial rates provide information on the degree to which countries may simply engage in "cheap talk" – telling prospective applicants that entry is legally allowed but then rejecting those who apply. Indeed, countries like Ecuador, Egypt, Kenya, Namibia, Sudan, and Uruguay all state that there are no prohibitions to foreign bank entry, but deny all foreign bank entry applications. In this regard, Song (2004, p. 21) states that "[i]n emerging countries, the licensing policy for foreign banks is subject to political considerations. Political interference in the licensing process of foreign banks could appear on the basis of wider inter-governmental agreement rather than on strict prudential criteria." Some of these same countries (e.g., Ecuador and Sudan), however, at the same time do not reject any domestic entry applications, despite reporting high entry into banking requirements. Figure 3.5, moreover, shows that the denial rates progressively increase when one moves from high-to-low income countries. These figures indicate that some countries may say one thing but actually do something else.[22] Of course, it

---

[22] In Italy it was reported in 2005 that the central bank, to defend domestic control of Italian banks, would not allow a foreign entrant to hold a stake of more than 15 percent of any Italian bank. This has created concerns among some potential foreign purchasers, because even though EU law allows national regulators to vet potential buyers of a major stake in a bank, it does not give them the right to block a bid based on nationality. See Taylor (2005) and European Report (2005).

is possible that "predator" type banks (e.g., Bank of Credit and Commerce International (BCCI), which operated in about thirty countries when it was liquidated in 1992 amid allegations of fraud and other improper activities) try to get into low-income countries, which includes all the earlier-cited countries, where weaker rules of law allow them to victimize the public with less likelihood of legal action, inducing the authorities in such countries to deny entry applications with greater frequency.

3.D.2. How Stringent Are Capital Requirements?

It is widely agreed that regulatory requirements on the amount of capital that a bank should hold relative to its total assets is important in understanding bank performance and bank fragility as well as the overall development of the banking industry. There are, of course, different ways of measuring the importance of capital requirements to assess their effect on various banking outcomes deemed to be important. Here we present a few alternative quantitative measures of capital regulatory stringency based on the new survey information to examine differences across countries as well as to indicate the way in which our database may be used. Specifically, we present three alternative capital regulatory variables that capture different but complementary measures of the stringency of regulatory capital requirements. The first measure is as follows:

1) *Overall Capital Stringency*: whether there are explicit regulatory requirements regarding the amount of capital that a bank must have relative to various guidelines. We consider several guidelines to determine the degree to which the leverage potential for capital is limited. These are as follows:[23] (1) Is the minimum capital-to-asset ratio requirement risk weighted in line with the Basel I guidelines?; (2) Does the minimum ratio vary as a function of an individual bank's credit risk?; (3) Does the minimum ratio vary as a function of

---

[23] We assign a value of 1 to each of the questions if the answer is yes and a 0 otherwise. In addition, we assign a value of 1 if the fraction of revaluation gains that is allowed to count as regulatory capital is less than 0.75. Otherwise, we assign a value of 0. By adding together these variables, we create the variable Overall Capital Stringency. It ranges in value from 0 to 7, with higher values indicating greater stringency. Notice that this particular measure of capital stringency is to some degree capturing whether or not regulatory capital is solely an accounting concept or at least partially a market-value concept.

market risk?; (4) Before minimum capital adequacy is determined, is the market value of loan losses not realized on accounting books deducted from the book value of capital?; (5) Before minimum capital adequacy is determined, are unrealized losses in securities deducted from the book value of capital?; and (6) Before minimum capital adequacy is determined, are unrealized foreign exchange losses deducted from the book value of capital?

Figure 3.6 vividly shows the impact that Basel I, which is discussed more fully in Chapter 2, has had on banking systems around the globe. Of 151 countries that responded to the survey question about the capital requirement, only 9 countries have set the minimum risk-based capital requirement at less than 8 percent. Two of these, Costa Rica and Ghana, indicate that their requirements do not conform to Basel I. (In contrast, 7 of 107 countries in the earlier survey reported their requirements do not conform.) Of the remaining countries, eighty-one countries set the requirement at exactly 8 percent and sixty-two countries set it higher.[24] The overwhelming majority of countries are thus able to say that they technically comply with Basel I rules. To this extent, the Basel Committee achieved its goal of creating a more "level playing field" among banks by inducing 143 countries around the world to raise their capital ratios to a minimum of 8 percent. Yet concerns persisted since its adoption that banks may hold too little capital because of the simplicity of the risk-weighting scheme and the limited differentiation among degrees of risk in Basel I (see, for example, Palia and Porter, 2003 and Chapter 2). Although international standards may be widely adopted, the key question is whether such uniformity in standards actually promotes well-functioning and stable financial systems – that is, whether this "best practice" is actually good. We address this question in Chapter 4.

---

[24] There are, needless to say, caveats when it comes to being anything less than extremely detailed with respect to banking regulations and supervisory practices, especially in countries like the United States. To elaborate, in the United States under the Prompt Corrective Action Provisions of the Federal Deposit Corporation Improvement Act (FIDICIA) of 1991, banks are categorized as to whether they are well-capitalized, adequately capitalized, undercapitalized, or significantly undercapitalized to determine what, if any, mandatory actions are required to correct a deficiency in capital. Banks that have capital ratios above 10 or 8 percent are classified as well-capitalized or adequately capitalized, respectively. These banks are not subject to any mandatory actions. However, the other two categories of banks are subject to significant restrictions, including in the worst case being placed in receivership.

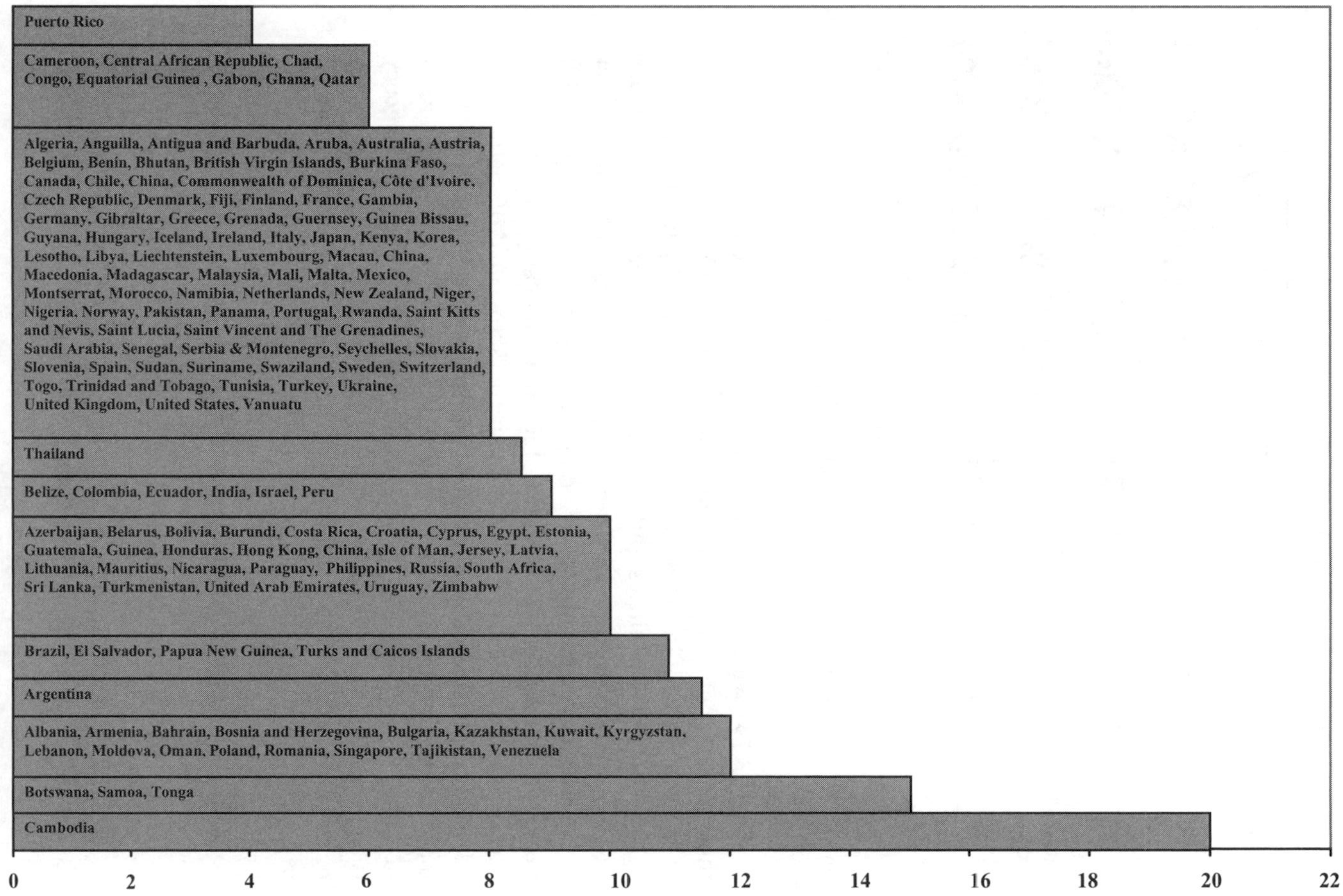

Figure 3.6. Minimum Risk-Based Capital Requirements Across Countries (151 Countries).

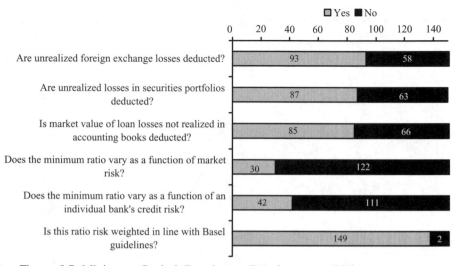

Figure 3.7. Minimum Capital Regulatory Requirements: Differences Across Countries.

Figure 3.7 provides important information on the extent to which, even though most countries set minimum risk-weighted capital requirements in line with Basel I, the ability of banks in these same countries to leverage capital may nevertheless differ significantly. The reason, as this figure shows, is that when calculating capital, countries differ both with respect to types of losses that are deducted and with respect to the type of risk that is taken into account in setting the minimum capital requirement. Thus, it may come as no surprise, as Figure 3.8 shows, that the actual risk-adjusted capital ratios for almost all countries exceed 8 percent, and in many cases by significant multiples of this widely observed standard of best practice. Figure 3.9, moreover, shows that overall capital stringency is significantly lower for the six of the seven countries setting the minimum capital requirement at less than 8 percent as compared to overall capital stringency for those countries setting higher requirements. Furthermore, overall capital stringency is not much greater for the three countries setting requirements greater than 15 percent as compared to the 124 countries setting requirements between 8 and 15 percent.

The second measure of the stringency of capital requirements is:

2) *Initial Capital Stringency*: whether the source of funds counted as regulatory capital can include assets other than cash or government securities as well as whether the sources are verified by the

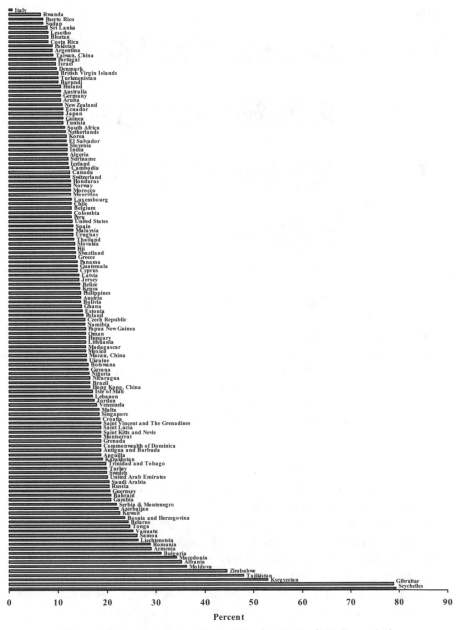

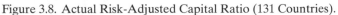

Figure 3.8. Actual Risk-Adjusted Capital Ratio (131 Countries).

Minimum Capital-to-Asset Ratio

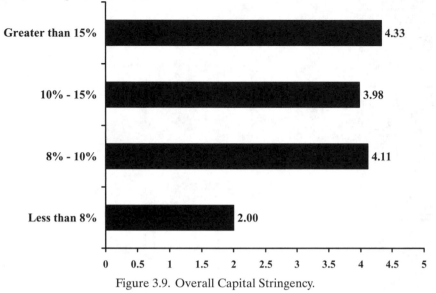

Figure 3.9. Overall Capital Stringency.

regulatory or supervisory authorities. More specifically, the following three questions were asked:[25] (1) Can initial disbursement or
subsequent injections of capital be done with assets other than cash
or government securities?; (2) Can the initial disbursement of capital be done with borrowed funds?; and (3) Are the sources of
funds to be used as capital verified by the regulatory/supervisory
authorities?

Figure 3.10 shows substantial variation across countries with respect
to what constitutes initial capital and whether the sources of capital are
verified by the authorities. This mix of responses as to what constitutes
initial capital is not much different from those provided in the earlier
survey. A relatively high percentage of countries in both surveys are not
particularly stringent when it comes to the source of funds used to initially
capitalize a bank. However, in the earlier survey, 19 of 105 countries
reported that the authorities do not verify the sources of funds to be used
as capital. In contrast, in the new survey, only 15 of 153 countries fail

[25] For questions (1) and (2) that are answered no, we assign a value of 1 and 0 otherwise.
We assign a value of 1 if the answer to question (3) is yes and 0 otherwise. This means
that when adding these three variables together our newly created variable may range
from a low of 0 to a high of 3, with a higher value indicating less stringency.

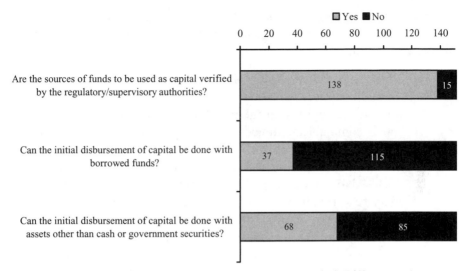

Figure 3.10. Initial Sources of Funds for Regulatory Capital: Differences Across Countries.

to verify the sources of capital. Nevertheless, such a practice seems so innocuous that it seems surprising that all countries would not adopt it.

The third and final capital stringency measure is:

3) *Capital Regulatory Index*: is simply the sum of overall capital stringency and initial capital stringency as discussed earlier. It therefore captures both the amount of capital and verifiable sources of capital that a bank is required to posses. This variable has a median value of 6 and ranges from a low of 3 to a high of 10, with a higher value indicating greater stringency.

The capital regulatory index is not correlated with GDP per capita or the size of the banking system relative to GDP.

3.D.3. What Powers Do the Supervisory Authorities Possess?

Do the supervisory authorities possess the power to take corrective action when confronted with violations of regulations or other imprudent behavior on the part of banks? In some cases, the authorities might even be required to take corrective action, whereas in others they may have the power to engage in forbearance. Courts, moreover, may intervene in some instances and thereby limit, delay, or even reverse actions taken by the supervisory authorities. We now consider the degree to which countries differ in these and other important respects. To start, we construct a measure of Official Supervisory Power based upon the following questions:[26]

1) *Official Supervisory Power*: (1) Does the supervisory agency have the right to meet with external auditors to discuss their reports without the approval of the bank?; (2) Are auditors required by law to communicate directly to the supervisory agency any presumed involvement of bank directors or senior managers in illicit activities, fraud, or insider abuse?; (3) Are off-balance sheet items disclosed to the supervisors?; Can supervisors: (4) take legal action against external auditors for negligence?; (5) force a bank to change its internal organizational structure?; (6) order a bank's directors or management to constitute provisions to cover actual or potential losses?; (7) suspend the directors' decision to distribute dividends?; (8) suspend the directors' decision to distribute bonuses?; (9) suspend the directors' decision to distribute management fees?; (10) Who can legally declare – such that this declaration supersedes some of the rights of shareholders – that a bank is insolvent?; (11) According to the Banking Law, who has authority to intervene – that is, suspend some or all ownership rights – a problem bank?; Regarding bank restructuring and reorganization, can the supervisory agency or any other government agency: (12) supersede shareholder rights?; (13) remove or replace management?; and (14) remove and replace directors?[27]

To better understand the importance of this variable, the responses to four of the fourteen questions used in its construction are indicated in Figure 3.11. Although the majority of countries give the supervisory authorities power in each of the four areas depicted, a significant number do not. Despite the importance of reliable and accurate financial statements, for instance, sixty-one countries do not grant supervisors the power to take legal action against external auditors for negligence. However, in the case of off-balance sheet items being disclosed to supervisors, all but

---

[26] The construction of this particular variable is relatively complex. For its exact construction, see Appendix 2. It ranges in value from 4 to 14.

[27] For questions 10–14, the responses may involve multiple agencies or authorities. More generally, the questions refer to whether the indicated power is possessed by each of the following: bank supervisor, court, deposit insurance agency, bank restructuring or asset management agency, and other.

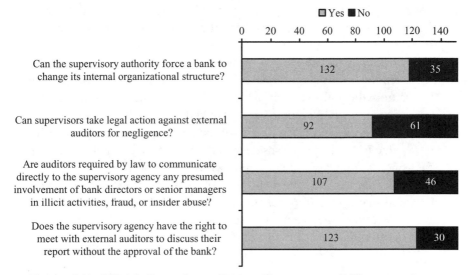

Figure 3.11. Official Supervisory Power Components: Differences Across Countries.

one of 151 countries responds that this is indeed the case. In the earlier survey, 2 of 106 countries reported this was not being done. Also, a relatively small number of countries, 11 of 153, including Finland, Germany, Italy, South Korea, and South Africa, fail to give the supervisory authorities the power to order a bank's directors or management to constitute provisions to cover actual or potential losses. Although even this small number may be troubling, it is an improvement, in both absolute and percentage terms, from the earlier survey in which 14 of 102 countries failed to provide this power to the supervisory authorities.

With respect to the last five questions, the supervisory authorities and the courts have the dominant power in the areas covered, with the supervisory authorities having a majority of power in every case but declaring a bank insolvent. Nevertheless, the courts clearly play an important role in the regulation and supervision of banks, as will be discussed more fully below. The official supervisory power variable is not correlated with either GDP per capita or the size of the banking system relative to GDP. It is, however, negatively correlated with a variable that equals 1 if a country is classified as an offshore financial center and 0 otherwise. In other words, official supervisory power is significantly lower in offshore financial centers than in other countries.

We also decompose the official supervisory variable into three constituent parts. The first of the resulting three variables is as follows:

1.1) *Prompt Corrective Action*: whether a law establishes predetermined levels of bank solvency deterioration, which forces automatic enforcement actions, such as intervention.[28] If the answer is yes, a value of 1 is assigned and multiplied by the sum of the answers to each of the following six questions (again with a value of 1 assigned to yes answers): (1) Are there any mechanisms of cease and desist-type orders, whose infraction leads to the automatic imposition of civil and penal sanctions on the bank's directors and managers? Can the supervisory agency (2) order the bank's directors or management to constitute provisions to cover actual or potential losses? or suspend the directors' decision to distribute: (3) dividends? (4) bonuses? (5) management fees? and/or (6) force a bank to change its internal organizational structure? The Prompt Corrective Action variable may range from 0 to 6, with a higher value indicating more promptness in responding to problems.

The prompt corrective action variable is quite interesting because it represents an attempt by governments to mandate the elimination of any discretionary power of the supervisory authorities to postpone or delay corrective actions to be taken against progressively deteriorating banks. This type of variable represents a substitution of "rules for discretion" on the part of the supervisory authorities. In this sense, prompt corrective action may be viewed as a component of independence insofar as it protects against political interference. Its creation was primarily an outcome of the U.S. savings and loan debacle in the 1980s. It was convincingly argued by many that the more than $150 billion it cost to resolve hundreds of failed savings and loans was excessively high because the relevant supervisory authorities granted forbearance to troubled institutions (Barth, 1991; Brumbaugh, 1988; Kane, 1989; and White, 1991). To prevent this situation from happening again, the Financial Deposit Insurance Corporation Improvement Act (FDICIA) was enacted in late 1991,

---

[28] The specific survey question asks: "Does the Law establish pre-determined levels of solvency deterioration which forces automatic actions (like intervention)?" This question is also used below in the Supervisory Forbearance Discretion variable, which some may view as a "negative" Prompt Corrective Action variable. It should also be noted that the labeling of the latter variable may be somewhat misleading because some of the variables employed in its construction are based upon the authority to engage in an action rather than the action being mandatory.

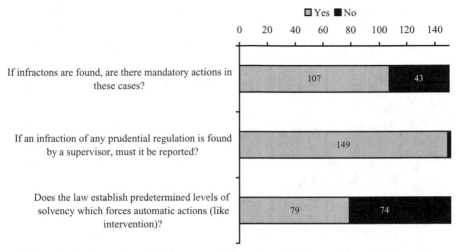

Figure 3.12. Supervisory Forbearance Discretion: Differences Across Countries.

which mandates specific and progressively more severe actions be taken against an institution as its capital deteriorates below specific thresholds.[29]

Even though the mere existence of such a law does not mean it will achieve its intended objective, proponents of prompt corrective action have nonetheless urged countries around the world to follow the lead of the United States in enacting laws that force supervisory authorities to take specific corrective actions against an institution as its capital progressively deteriorates. According to the new survey, there is a large split between countries, with seventy-nine having followed the lead of the United States in enacting such a law and with seventy-four not having done so (see Figure 3.12). There is also a relatively large split between countries as regards the existence of any mechanisms of cease and desist-type orders whose infraction leads to the automatic imposition of civil and penal sanctions on a bank's directors and managers, with ninety reporting yes and sixty-two reporting no. In some countries, such as Malaysia, supervisors have all the powers that one associates with prompt corrective action, but do not have an automatic trigger forcing specific actions. The issue, of course, that arises in these instances is whether the authorities

---

[29] See Benston and Kaufman (1988). Interestingly enough, when deposit insurance was being established in the United States, it was stated that "With the establishment of federal deposit insurance, the task of preventing banks from developing an unsound or embarrassed condition looms larger than ever before among the duties of the supervisory and examining authorities. They should, therefore, be given adequate powers, and be required to make full and effective use of them, in order that an incipient unhealthy condition may be immediately corrected, and that uneconomic banks may be closed before they reach a state where liquidation would involve losses." See Barth (1990).

with the power to take action will do so or must be required to do so by force of law. We should emphasize that the existence of prompt corrective action requirements does not necessarily mean that the system will work as intended.

The second and third variables derived from the official supervisory variable are as follows:

1.2) *Restructuring Power*: whether the supervisory authorities have the power to restructure and reorganize a troubled bank (for the exact construction of this variable, see Appendix 2). It may range in value from a low of 0 to a high of 3, with a higher value indicating more power.

1.3) *Declaring Insolvency Power*: whether the supervisory authorities have the power to declare a deeply troubled bank insolvent (for the exact construction of this variable, see Appendix 2). It may range in value from 0 to 2, with a higher value indicating greater power.

These two variables, restructuring power and declaring insolvency power, are particularly important because based on information in the new survey they reveal that courts intervene in banking matters far more frequently than perhaps many realize. Indeed, the courts have the power to declare that a bank is insolvent in more countries than the bank supervisory authorities (ninety-nine vs. eighty-six countries).[30] This situation, and the further elaboration on the role of courts that shortly follows, suggests more attention should be given to the role of the courts in assessing the overall development, performance, and stability of the banking sector in countries. More generally, these variables provide information on the extent to which the supervisory authorities, among others, have the power to resolve deeply troubled banks.

Instead of taking corrective action in response to troubled banks or otherwise imprudent behavior, the supervisory authorities may simply forbear when confronted with these types of situations. To measure this type of supervisory discretion, we construct the following variable:

2) *Supervisory Forbearance Discretion*: Supervisory authorities may engage in forbearance when confronted with violations of laws or regulations or with other imprudent behavior on the part of banks. To capture the degree to which this type of discretion is

[30] Traditionally, the courts have had this authority. Special legislation has been typically used to transfer it to the bank supervisory authorities.

allowed, we construct a variable based on the following questions:[31]
(1) Regarding bank restructuring and reorganization, can the supervisory authorities or any other government agency (i.e., bank supervisor, court, deposit insurance agency, bank restructuring or asset management agency, and other) forbear certain prudential regulations?; (2) Does the law establish predetermined levels of solvency deterioration that force automatic actions (like intervention)?; (3) If an infraction of any prudential regulation is found by a supervisor, must it be reported?; and (4) With respect to (3), are there any mandatory actions to be taken in these cases? (See Figure 3.12 for information on the variation among countries with respect to the last three questions.)

This particular variable may be viewed at first glance as the "negative" of prompt corrective action. Yet there is not a perfect overlap in the construction of these two variables. Indeed, the two variables have only one factor in common – whether the law establishes predetermined levels of insolvency deterioration which forces automatic actions. However, the variables are negatively correlated, with a correlation coefficient of 0.73.

As we have already indicated several times, the role of courts in banking matters is a relatively unexplored area of research. To stimulate more work in this area, we construct the following variable to measure the degree to which courts may critically affect various banking outcomes:

3) *Court Involvement.* This variable measures the degree to which the court dominates the supervisory authority. This variable was based on the following three questions:[32] (1) Is court approval required for supervisory actions, such as superseding shareholder rights, removing and replacing management, removing and replacing directors, or license revocation?; (2) Is a court order required to appoint a receiver/liquidator in the event of liquidation?

---

[31] We assign a value of 1 when the answer is no and a value of 0 otherwise, except for (1). We assign a value of 1 if the answer is bank supervisor, a value of 0.5 if the answer is deposit insurance agency or bank restructuring or asset management agency and a value of 0 otherwise. This variable is calculated as the sum of these assigned values. It may therefore range in value from 0 to 4, with a higher value indicating more discretion.

[32] We assign a value of 1 when the answer is yes and a value of 0 otherwise. The Court Involvement variable is calculated as the sum of these assigned values. It may therefore range from 0 to 3, with a higher value indicating less supervisory discretion.

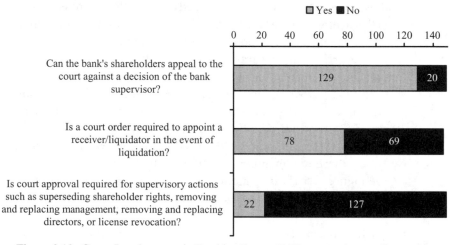

Figure 3.13. Court Involvement in Banking Issues: Differences Across Countries.

And (3) Can the bank shareholders appeal to the court against a decision of the bank supervisor?

The court involvement variable is included here for the first time and adds a relevant though often overlooked dimension to the study of bank regulation and supervision. Earlier in this chapter we discussed the structure, scope, and independence of the bank supervisory authorities but omitted a potentially critical player. In some countries, the courts are an additional bank oversight authority. They may have sole jurisdiction with respect to certain banking matters or have the power to supersede the authority of supervisors in other matters. The independence of the supervisory authorities may even become meaningless insofar as the courts succumb to political pressure when superseding the authority of supervisors. Alternatively, the lack of supervisory independence may become less important if an independent judiciary plays a powerful role in banking matters.

Figure 3.13 shows that the courts do have the power to approve or overturn key corrective actions taken by the bank supervisory authorities in some countries. Indeed, in 129 countries the shareholders of a bank may appeal to the court against a decision of the bank supervisor.[33] (See Table 3.7 for the list of the twenty countries that do not.) In the majority

---

[33] Of course, there is a distinction to be made between appealing a decision before and after it takes effect. In the United States, decisions can only be appealed ex post.

Table 3.7. *Court Involvement*

Is Court Approval Required for Supervisory Actions, such as Superseding Shareholder Rights, Removing and Replacing Management, Removing and Replacing Director, or License Revocation? Countries Responding "Yes"	Can the Bank Shareholders Appeal to the Court Against a Decision of the Bank Supervisor? Countries Responding "No"
Botswana	Bulgaria
Cambodia	Cambodia
Gibraltar	Chile
Guinea	Germany
Kenya	Japan
Libya	Poland
Netherlands	Qatar
Papua New Guinea	Slovakia
South Africa	Sweden
Suriname	United Arab Emirates
Swaziland	United States
Tonga	Benin
Vanuatu	Burkina Faso
Venezuela	Côte d'Ivoire
Anguilla	Guinea Bissau
Antigua and Barbuda	Mali
Commonwealth of Dominica	Niger
Grenada	Senegal
Montserrat	Slovakia
Saint Kitts and Nevis	Togo
Saint Lucia	
Saint Vincent and The Grenadines	

of countries (78 of 147), moreover, a court order is required to appoint a receiver or liquidator in the event of a bank insolvency. Even in the case of other supervisory actions, such as superseding shareholder rights, removing and replacing management, removing and replacing directors, or license revocation, court approval is required in twenty-two countries. (See Table 3.7 for a list of these countries.)

The role of the courts and their interaction with the bank supervisory authorities, and ultimately their affect on the banking sector, are largely unexplored issues. The impact of the courts on banks may depend, among other factors, on the (1) independence of the judiciary from the government, (2) the ability of the courts to adapt to changing financial conditions, and (3) the independence of the supervisory itself. We do not pursue this line of inquiry here, and leave this as a still unexplored but crucial issue.

The Court Involvement variable is positively correlated with bank assets relative to GDP.

Because banks are in the business of making risky loans, it is important to consider the way in which loans are treated in financial statements when borrowers fail to fulfill their contractual commitments. We therefore construct the following two variables:

4) *Loan Classification Stringency*. This variable measures the degree to which loans that are in arrears must be classified as substandard, doubtful, or loss. More specifically, we were provided with the actual number or a range of days beyond which a loan would be put into one of these three classifications. We simply summed the minimum numbers provided across the three classifications so that higher values of this variable indicate less stringency.[34]

5) *Provisioning Stringency*. This variable measures the degree to which a bank must provision as a loan is classified first as substandard, then as doubtful, and lastly as loss. We have been provided with the minimum percentage of the loan for which provisioning must be provided as a loan progresses through each of the three problem loan classifications. We therefore sum the minimum required provisioning percentages when a loan is successively classified as substandard, doubtful, and loss. This sum is then the value of our variable, Provisioning Stringency, with higher values indicating more stringency.

Loan classification and provisioning practices represent an attempt to reflect the fact that the market value of various assets may be less than the book value. These practices can be quite important given the opaqueness of loans in portraying more accurately the financial condition of institutions. In this respect, uniformity among countries in setting the standards for classifying and provisioning for loans would help promote greater transparency and facilitate cross-country comparisons. Yet, the new survey indicates that uniformity is far from universal. The median value for loan classification stringency is 630 days with a standard deviation of 209 days, while the comparable figures for loan provisioning stringency are 170 percent and 36 percent, respectively. In terms of correlations with GDP per capita and the size of the banking system relative

---

[34] It should be noted that countries may adopt forward-looking classification and provisioning models that are even more stringent, but this approach is relatively recent and not yet being used in many countries.

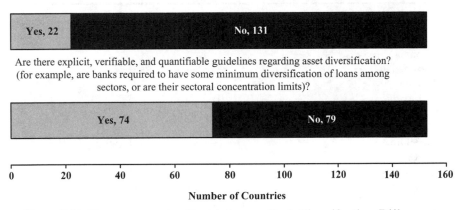

Figure 3.14. Encouragement or Restrictions on Bank Diversification: Differences Across Countries.

to GDP, the only significant correlation is a positive one between provisioning stringency and GDP per capita.

It was decided to include a variable to capture the degree to which banks are encouraged or restricted with respect to asset and geographical diversification. This variable is as follows:

6) *Diversification Index.* This index is based on the following two questions:[35] (1) Are there explicit, verifiable, and quantifiable guidelines regarding asset diversification?; and (2) Are banks prohibited from making loans abroad?

A way for banks to lower overall risk is to diversify their asset portfolios, including making loans abroad. Figure 3.14 shows about half of the 153 countries actually provide explicit, verifiable and quantifiable guidelines regarding asset diversification (e.g., requiring banks to have some minimum diversification of loans among sectors or to have some sectoral concentration limits). This is an improvement from the earlier survey, when only about one-third of the 107 countries had such requirements. Although perhaps it is surprising that an even greater percentage of countries do not encourage asset diversification, it is perhaps even

---

[35] On the basis of "yes or no" answers to these questions, we calculated a Diversification Index. A value of 1 was assigned to yes, except in the case of question (2), in which a 1 was assigned to no since this response is associated with greater diversification. These two values are summed and may range in value from 0 to 2, with a higher value indicating greater diversification.

Table 3.8. *Countries Prohibiting Banks from Making Loans Abroad*

Are Banks Prohibited from Making Loans Abroad? Countries Responding "Yes"	
Albania	Libya
Azerbaijan	Madagascar
Bolivia	Rwanda
Cambodia	Tunisia
Costa Rica	Zimbabwe
Fiji	Cameroon
Honduras	Central African Republic
Jordan	Chad
South Korea	Congo
Lebanon	Equatorial Guinea
Lesotho	Gabon

more surprising that twenty-two countries actually prohibit banks from making loans abroad. (These countries are listed in Table 3.8.) Interestingly, except for South Korea, all these economies are quite small – precisely the group for which diversification abroad could pay off. Indeed, Buch, Driscoll, and Ostergaard (2004, p. 2) find in the case of at least four countries that banks can "... improve their risk-return trade-off considerably by investing more internationally relative to investing purely in (risky) domestic assets." Lending abroad by banks in smaller economies, moreover, may be the most cost-effective way to diversify internationally when compared to establishing branches and subsidiaries abroad. Furthermore, it is somewhat ironic that a country would allow wealthy individuals to diversify by investing abroad but prohibit banks entrusted with the wealth of small depositors from similarly doing so. Yet, this is indeed the case in some of the countries listed in Table 3.8, including Bolivia, Honduras, Lebanon, and Lesotho. Some countries allow personal capital movements abroad but only with prior approval, including Albania, South Korea, Rwanda, Cameroon, and Chad (see International Monetary Fund, 2001, for detailed information on capital controls for countries). In the earlier survey, 15 of 106 countries prohibited banks from making loans abroad. The diversification variable, moreover, is positively correlated with GDP per capita.

3.E. EXPLICIT DEPOSIT INSURANCE SCHEMES

Regulations and supervisory practices clearly are important parts of a banking system. But they do not operate in a vacuum. Instead, their

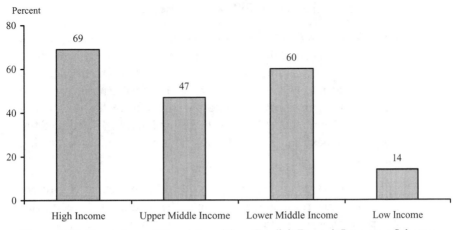

Figure 3.15. Percentage of Countries with an Explicit Deposit Insurance Scheme.

effect on various economic outcomes may depend importantly on whether or not a country has an explicit deposit insurance scheme and, if so, its features. We therefore construct several variables to address this issue. To start, in 75 of 152 countries there is no explicit deposit insurance scheme. In fourteen countries with schemes, however, depositors were not fully compensated (to the extent of protection legally specified) the last time a bank failed.[36] Deposit insurance was therefore not being provided in line with the law in these countries. We create the variable, No Explicit Deposit Insurance Scheme, to capture these two facts. The result is that eighty-nine countries are included in this variable and assigned a value of one, whereas the remaining sixty-three countries with an explicit deposit insurance scheme and that fully compensated depositors the last time a bank failed were assigned a value of zero. Figure 3.15 shows that an explicit deposit insurance scheme is most common among high-income countries, with almost 70 percent of these countries having established one. Such schemes are least common among low-income countries, with only about 14 percent of these countries having established one.[37]

We also construct or rely on four different quantitative variables to capture various features of the deposit insurance schemes countries have

---

[36] In addition to providing information as to whether depositors were fully compensated the last time a bank failed, our dataset provide information on how long it takes for depositors to be paid. See questions 8.4.1 and 8.4.2 in Appendix 1.

[37] To the extent that these countries declare banks insolvent and always protect all the depositors, an explicit deposit insurance scheme may not be needed.

chosen to adopt.[38] These are as follows:

1) *Deposit Insurer Power*: This variable is based on the assignment
   of 1 (yes) or 0 (no) values to four questions assessing whether the
   deposit insurance authority has the authority to make the decision
   to intervene in a bank, to cancel or revoke deposit insurance, to take
   legal action against bank directors or officials, or has ever taken
   any legal action against bank directors or officers. The sum of the
   assigned values ranges from 0 to 4, with higher values indicating
   more power.

The power of the deposit insurer is said to be important to protect
the deposit insurance fund. Less than half of the seventy-seven countries
with an explicit deposit insurance scheme, however, give the insurer the
three powers noted earlier. Of course, in the case of intervening in a bank
and taking legal action against bank directors or officials, this may not be
essential if the supervisory authorities have these powers and use them
to protect the insurance fund. Perhaps more questionable is the failure to
give the insurer the power to cancel or revoke deposit insurance. It is also
important to note that in thirty-two countries not only does the insurer
have the power to take legal action against bank directors or officials but
has actually done so in seventeen of these countries.

2) *Deposit Insurance Funds-to-Total Bank Assets*: This variable is the
   ratio of accumulated funds to total bank assets.

In the case of the U.S. savings and loan debacle during the 1980s, the
government insurance agency for these institutions itself reported insolvency and ultimately required taxpayer funds to clean up the mess. Until
sufficient funds were provided at the end of the decade, however, the
shortage severely limited the regulator's flexibility, if not ability, to effectively resolve failed savings and loans in a timely manner (Barth et al.,
1989). As this situation demonstrated, the lack of adequate funds to deal
with deeply troubled banks can actually enable such banks to engage in
excessively risky activities and hence result in greater failure costs. Con-
versely, in weak political systems with insufficient checks and balances on
government officials, funds may actually be looted or misappropriated,
or can encourage risk-taking, as in some countries the government's

---

[38] In some cases, a country would report that it has no explicit deposit insurance scheme, but
nonetheless answer questions about its features. We therefore conditioned all answers
about the features on whether a country reported that it indeed had a scheme in the
construction of the variables.

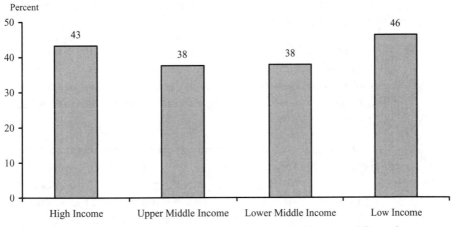

Figure 3.16. Percentage of Total Assets Funded with Insured Deposits.

guarantee may not be trusted without a fund. And research shows that prefunding in these cases is not recommended (World Bank, 2001; and Demirgüç-Kunt and Kane, 2002).

To address the issue of the extent to which banks actually depend on insured deposits to support their loans and other assets, we create the following variable:

3) *Funding with Insured Deposits:* This variable is the percentage of the banking system's assets that are actually funded with insured deposits.

Figure 3.16 shows the percentage of total assets that banks actually fund with insured deposits. It is interesting to note that the average insured-deposit funding percentages differ by no more than 8 percentage points across all four income categories, whereas the percentages of countries with explicit deposit insurance schemes differ by as much as 55 percentage points across these same categories (see Figure 3.15). This means banks in countries in all parts of the world and at all levels of income are, on average, able to fund the majority of their assets with uninsured deposits, even though they have explicit deposit insurance schemes.[39]

Even though countries may have established explicit deposit insurance schemes, the features of these schemes may differ in important respects.

[39] In the United States banks collectively funded 39 percent of their total assets with insured deposits, whereas two countries (Italy and Thailand) funded all their assets with insured deposits. It is also the case that the median value for total assets funded with total deposits is 40 percent with a minimum percentage of 2.7 percent (Turkmenistan) and a maximum percentage of 100 percent (Thailand).

To capture the extent to which some features may mitigate moral hazard, we construct the following variable:

4) *Various Factors Mitigating Moral Hazard*: This variable measures whether banks fund the deposit insurance scheme or pay risk-based premiums as well as whether there is a formal coinsurance component. It ranges in value from 0 to 3, with a higher value indicating greater risk-mitigating factors.

The issue of who funds a deposit insurance scheme is important because whoever pays has the greatest incentive to prevent losses covered by insurance. Some consider this to be especially the case when banks pay ex post the cost of a bailout, in contrast to fixed premia set ex ante. Because banks are in the best position to assess their financial condition, requiring them to fund the scheme should provide the most help in preventing losses borne by the insurer. Of sixty-seven countries, forty-three do indeed require the banks to bear the burden of funding the deposit insurance scheme. When it comes to levying charges, however, only twenty-three of seventy-four countries with schemes set risk-based premiums. As anyone who drives a car knows, co-insurance is a typical feature of automobile insurance policies. However, in only slightly more than half (thirty-seven vs. thirty-three) of the countries is there a co-insurance component in the deposit insurance schemes. Yet, including such a feature is a way to promote greater private monitoring of bank behavior. Some deposit insurance schemes provide 100 percent coverage up to a limit, and no, or little co-insurance, after that limit is reached. These types of schemes may be more effective insofar as they induce monitoring by large depositors.

The inclusion of all these variables is important because many countries around the world have established explicit deposit insurance schemes and the remaining countries are being urged to establish one. The existing schemes, however, differ in several important respects as discussed earlier. Some features may be better than others at reducing, if not eliminating, moral hazard. This is an issue we examine in Chapter 4. Of these deposit insurance variables, only the mitigating moral hazard variable is positively, albeit weakly, correlated with GDP per capita.

3.F. PRIVATE MONITORING AND EXTERNAL GOVERNANCE

3.F.1. Private Monitoring

Bank behavior clearly is circumscribed by various regulations and supervisory practices as indicated earlier. These actions taken by the official authorities essentially prejudge what is acceptable behavior and presume a single best way to transact business. But bank behavior is also affected by private market forces. It is therefore important to try to capture to some degree the extent to which market or private monitoring exists in different countries. To this end, we constructed and quantified five different measures of this type of variable using information from the survey and based essentially on information that is disclosed and thus available to the public. These measures are as follows:

1) *Certified Audit Required*: This variable captures whether an external audit is required of the financial statements of a bank and, if so, by a licensed or certified auditor. If both factors exist a 1 is assigned; 0 otherwise.

This type of audit would presumably indicate the presence or absence of an independent assessment of the accuracy of financial information released to the public. Only 2 of 152 countries, China and Italy, do not require a certified audit. In only three cases of those countries that do, moreover, are the auditors not licensed or certified (Bahrain, Burundi, and Jersey).

2) *Percentage of Ten Biggest Banks Rated by International Rating Agencies*: The percentage of the top ten banks that are rated by international credit rating agencies.

A high percentage of banks being rated indicates that more information is available to the public about the overall condition of the banking industry. This is especially important when the information is provided by an independent third party that operates globally and thus is less likely to be susceptible to pressure or influence from domestic sources.

3) *Percentage of Ten Biggest Banks Rated by Domestic Rating Agencies*: The percentage of the top ten banks that are rated by domestic credit rating agencies.

The greater the percentage, once again, the more the public has access to information about the overall condition of the banking industry as viewed by an independent third party. That said, the percentage of the biggest banks rated by international agencies is much higher than the percentage rated by domestic agencies – 48 versus 18 percent. However, this is not surprising given the skills and brand recognition of the international rating agencies. Figure 3.17 shows, moreover, that the percentage of the top ten biggest banks rated by both international and domestic rating agencies steadily increases as one moves from lower- to higher-income

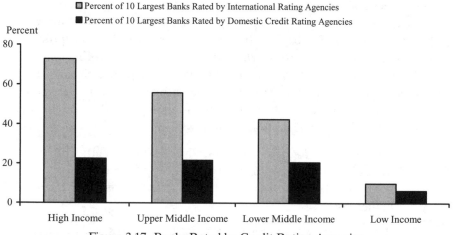

Figure 3.17. Banks Rated by Credit Rating Agencies.

levels. In terms of regions, the thirty-one countries of Sub-Saharan Africa have the lowest percentages of both international and domestic ratings at 7 and 6 percent, respectively. Finally, the percentage of the top ten banks rated by international, but not domestic, agencies is positively related to GDP per capita.

4) *No Explicit Deposit Insurance Scheme*: This variable takes a value of 1 if there is no explicit deposit insurance scheme and if depositors were not wholly compensated the last time a bank failed, and 0 otherwise. A higher value would indicate more private monitoring.

This variable is included here as a result of the evidence (see Chapter 2) that deposit insurance is associated with weaker market discipline. We find that the no explicit deposit insurance scheme variable is positively correlated with the percentage of total assets funded with total deposits but negatively correlated with the average size bank.

5) *Bank Accounting*: This variable indicates whether the income statement includes accrued though unpaid interest or principal on performing loans (10 of 150 countries report no) and nonperforming loans (135 of 149 countries report no), and whether banks are required to produce consolidated financial statements, including nonbank financial affiliates and subsidiaries (127 of 149 countries report yes). Also, it indicates whether bank directors are legally liable if information disclosed is erroneous or misleading. For each of the four factors, a value of 1 is assigned if the answer is yes;

0 otherwise. Ranging in value from 0 to 4, higher values indicate more informative bank financial statements.

The release of this type of information or its absence affects the ability of private agents to monitor and hence influence bank behavior.

6) *Private Monitoring Index:* the sum of (1), (2) [which equals 1 if the percentage is 100; 0 otherwise], (3) [which equals 1 if the percentage is 100; 0 otherwise], (4), and (5). In addition, four other measures are included in the index based on yes or no answers. Specifically, a 1 is assigned if off-balance sheet items are disclosed to the public; a 1 if banks must disclose risk management procedures to the public; a 1 if subordinated debt is allowable (required) as a part of regulatory capital; and a 1 if formal enforcement actions are made public. Higher values indicate more private oversight.

Private monitoring of firm behavior has always been widely recognized as an important factor in achieving an efficient allocation of scarce resources. This is no less true in regulated industries like banking and is part of Basel II. It is, therefore, essential in any study of bank development, performance, and stability to assess the role played by private monitoring. Our private monitoring variable is designed for just this purpose. Its construction is based on various types of information the public can rely on to influence bank behavior. In this regard, there is a substantial literature stressing the importance of subordinated debt as a component of capital for instilling market discipline (see Chapter 2). It therefore may be reassuring to many individuals that 146 of 152 countries do indeed allow such debt to count as capital. Less reassuring may be the fact that only seventeen countries require that subordinated debt be part of capital. Among the countries that score the highest with respect to private monitoring are Australia, Canada, Hong Kong, New Zealand, the United Kingdom, and the United States. More generally, private monitoring is positively correlated with GDP per capita but not correlated with the size of the banking system relative to GDP.

3.F.2. Does External Governance Play an Important Role?

Although all countries regulate and supervise banks, and many countries have instituted deposit insurance systems to promote banking system stability, a fundamental conflict remains between the owners of banks and the managers and directors of banks. The "principal-agent" problem as it has come to be known starts from the premise that the goals of owners (the principals) may be significantly different from the objectives of managers and directors (the agents), who may pursue policies inconsistent with share value-maximization. But the conflict does not stop here because the objectives of shareholders may differ from those of depositors, or in the case in which depositors are insured against losses, the interests of the deposit insurer. In short, all the interested parties may not agree in simply maximizing the overall risk-adjusted value of the bank. The various stakeholders may instead wish to maximize different components of that value. The result may be that, depending on which party dominates, investments that are too risky or that have negative net present values are undertaken. To some extent such conflicts of interest among the various stakeholders can be addressed by contractual agreements, augmented by a reliance on market discipline (Bliss, 2003). However, high transactions costs prohibit contracts from being written to cover all possible deviations from value-maximizing behavior, and the effective application of market discipline depends on the availability of accurate, relevant, and timely information. Hence, additional rules and practices – "corporate governance" procedures – have been instituted to address gaps in contractual specifications of rights and obligations of the various claimants on bank value, and to enhance the transparency of relevant information about the bank.

The issue of corporate governance for banks is particularly important, as Caprio and Levine (2002) and Macey and O'Hara (2003) argue. Banks and other financial intermediaries themselves exert corporate governance on firms, both as creditors of firms and, in many countries, as equity holders. Indeed, as Caprio and Levine (2002) point out, in many countries, especially developing ones, where banks dominate as providers of credit, banks are among the most important sources of external governance for firms. To the extent banks are well managed, the allocation of capital will occur efficiently in an economy. However, if there is poor corporate governance of banks, as Caprio and Levine (2002, p. 18) point out, "bank managers may actually induce firm managers to behave in ways that favor the interests of bank managers but hurt overall firm performance." This in turn can hurt the performance of an economy.[40] Indeed, Bushman and Smith (2003) make an explicit connection between corporate

---

[40] This is a particularly important issue in countries with both government owned banks and nonbank enterprises. In such cases, banks typically extend credit to many firms on terms that fail to reflect arm's-length transactions.

governance of financial intermediaries and the finance-and-economic-growth literature.

Despite the importance of this issue, according to Macey and O'Hara (2003, p. 91), "very little attention has been paid to the corporate governance of banks."[41] However, in the wake of recent well-publicized governance scandals at multinational firms headquartered in the United States and elsewhere, there has been a renewed interest in research on corporate governance, and this interest seems in part to have stimulated new interest in research on corporate governance for banking (Shleifer and Vishny, 1997). Conceptually, Macey and O'Hara (2003) argue that given the special nature of banking, it is worthwhile to consider as "stakeholders" constituents beyond shareholders. Because banks' liabilities, especially to depositors, play such a crucial role in the economy, they (2003, p. 102) argue that "bank directors should owe fiduciary duties to fixed claimants as well as to equity claimants." Adams and Mehran (2003, p. 124) add at least one more constituent. They argue that "the number of parties with a stake in [a financial] institution's activity complicates the governance of financial institutions. In addition to investors, depositors and regulators have a direct interest in bank performance." In a related vein, Caprio and Levine (2002, p. 19) explain that there are four sources of governance for banks: "equity holders, debt holders, the competitive discipline of output markets, and governments." Each of these constituents therefore has an interest in the way in which a bank functions.

An important dimension of corporate governance is the degree of comprehensive and reliable information that exists for the operations of a firm. The greater the transparency in how individual managers conduct a bank's business, the easier it is for stakeholders to be effective in monitoring and thereby influencing performance. We therefore introduce an external governance index here based upon accounting practices, external audits, financial statement transparency, and external ratings and creditor monitoring. We now discuss each of these four variables in turn.

---

[41] See also Caprio and Levine (2002, p. 18), and Adams and Mehran (2003, p. 123). Note also that in some countries the issue of corporate governance of banks and other financial institutions has recently captured renewed attention from policy makers and regulatory authorities. For example, in the United States, the Sarbanes-Oxley Act of 2002 deals extensively with legal requirements aimed at enhancing the quality of corporate governance in nonfinancial and financial firms. See also Office of the Comptroller of the Currency (2003) for a federal regulatory perspective on corporate governance practices for banks.

1) *Accounting Practices*: This variable indicates whether bank accounting practices are in accordance with International Accounting Standards (IAS) or U.S. Generally Accepted Accounting Principles and Standards (GAAP and GAAS). The adoption of either standard is assigned a value of 1; 0 otherwise.

One key to the provision of adequate and accurate information is the use of accurate accounting standards.[42] Currently, a major obstacle to the application of a single, well-recognized set of accounting practices is that there are several major alternatives employed across the globe (as well as a number of local, country-specific accounting standards that are difficult or impossible for stakeholders and potential investors to "translate" into terms similar to one of the major global standards). Table 3.9, which contains information new to this survey, illustrates the diversity in the application of accounting standards across countries. The majority of countries (118 of 152) apply International Accounting Standards (IAS) and 27 of these also apply U.S. Generally Accepted Accounting Principles and Standards (GAAP and GAAS).[43] However, two countries (Gibraltar and the United States) apply only GAAP/GAAS and thirty-two countries apply neither standard, including China, Russia, and many European countries.[44] The accounting standard that a country chooses is important because different standards may produce differences in the quality of financial statements, and thereby ultimately affect the ability to assess, monitor, and control the risk-taking behavior of banks. The push for a global accounting standard makes it all the more urgent to empirically assess which standard works best to promote well-functioning banking systems.

2) *Strength of External Audit*: This variable measures the effectiveness of external audits of banks (see Appendix 2 for the exact construction of these variables). It is based on the following questions: (1) Is an external audit a compulsory obligation for banks?; (2) Are specific requirements for the extent or nature of the audit spelled out?; (3) Are auditors licensed or certified?;

---

[42] For an empirical assessment of alternative book-value measures of bank capital and their effect on the costs of bank-failures, see Barth and Brumbaugh (1994b).

[43] There is a significantly negative correlation between the application of IAS and GDP per capita, but no significant correlation between GAAS and GDP per capita.

[44] However, the EU mandated that EU companies must use International Financial Reporting Standards (IFRS or, more formally, IAS) by June 2005, and non-EU companies must do so by 2006.

Table 3.9. *Bank Accounting Practices: An International Comparison*
(152 Countries)

Countries Applying International Accounting Standards (IAS)		Countries Applying U.S. Generally Accepted Accounting Standards (GAAS)	Countries Applying Both	Countries Applying Neither
Albania	Kyrgyzstan	Gibraltar	Australia	Argentina
Algeria	Latvia	United States	Bosnia and	Belgium
Anguilla	Lebanon		Herzegovina	Burundi
Antigua and	Libya		Brazil	Chile
Barbuda	Liechtenstein		British Virgin	China
Armenia	Lithuania		Islands	Colombia
Aruba	Macau, China		Costa Rica	Denmark
Austria	Madagascar		Ecuador	Finland
Azerbaijan	Malaysia		El Salvador	France
Bahrain	Mali		Gambia	Germany
Belarus	Malta		Honduras	Greece
Blize	Mauritius		Japan	Guatemala
Benin	Moldova		Kenya	Iceland
Bhutan	Montserrat		Korea	India
Bolivia	New Zealand		Lesotho	Israel
Botswana	Niger		Mexico	Italy
Bulgaria	Oman		Namibia	Kazakhstan
Burkina Faso	Pakistan		Nicaragua	Luxembourg
Cambodia	Papua New		Nigeria	Macedonia
Cameroon	Guinea		Panama	Morocco
Canada	Paraguay		Philippines	Peru
Central African	Peru		Puerto Rico	Netherlands
Republic	Qatar		Samoa	Norway
Chad	Romania		Sweden	Poland
Commonwealth	Rwanda		Switzerland	Portugal
of Dominica	Saint Kitts and		Taiwan, China	Russia
Congo	Nevis		Thailand	Saint Lucia
Côte d'Ivoire	Saint Vincent		Ukraine	Serbia &
Croatia	and The		Vanuatu	Montenegro
Cyprus	Grenadines			Slovenia
Czech Republic	Saudi Arabia			Spain
Egypt	Senegal			Suriname
Equatorial	Seychelles			Turkmenistan
Guinea	Singapore			United
Estonia	Slovakia			Kingdom
Fiji				Venezuela

(*continued*)

Table 3.9 *(continued)*

Countries Applying International Accounting Standards (IAS)		Countries Applying U.S. Generally Accepted Accounting Standards (GAAS)	Countries Applying Both	Countries Applying Neither
Gabon	South Africa			
Ghana	Sri Lanka			
Grenada	Sudan			
Guernsey	Swaziland			
Guinea	Tajikistan			
Guinea Bissau	Togo			
Guyana	Trinidad and			
Hong Kong,	Tobago			
China	Tunisia			
Hungary	Turkey			
Ireland	Turks and			
Isle of Man	Caicos Islands			
Jersey	United Arab			
Jordan	Emirates			
Kuwait	Uruguay			
	Zimbabwe			

(4) Do supervisors get a copy of the auditor's report?; (5) Does the supervisory agency have the right to meet with external auditors to discuss the report without the approval of the bank?; (6) Are auditors required by law to communicate directly to the supervisory agency any presumed involvement of bank directors or senior managers in illicit activities, fraud, or insider abuse?; and (7) Can supervisors take legal action against external auditors for negligence?

Figure 3.18 shows the variation in the seven different components of our strength of external audit variable. At last we find one supervisory practice that is universally found in all countries that responded to the new survey. In every country supervisors receive a copy of the auditor's report. Of course, the quality of the report and what is done with it is more important than simply its receipt by the supervisor. In this

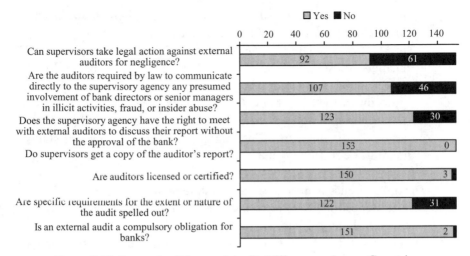

Figure 3.18. Strength of External Audit: Differences Across Countries.

regard, thirty-one countries do not specify the exact requirements of the extent and nature of the audit. More surprising is the fact that in thirty countries the supervisory authorities do not have the right to meet with the external auditors to discuss their report without the approval of the bank. Also surprising, and contrary to what would seem to be "best practice," is the situation in which auditors are not required to inform the supervisory authorities of illicit activities undertaken by the directors or senior management of a bank, or one in which the authorities cannot take legal action against external auditors for negligence. Yet, nearly 30 percent of the countries allow auditors to remain silent and an even greater 40 percent of countries do not allow supervisors to pursue auditor negligence in the courts. In the earlier survey, the corresponding percentages were 40 percent and 35 percent, respectively. This suggests that a serious issue is the failure to provide the supervisory authorities in a fairly large number of countries with the power to discipline auditors when they are negligent. Of course, determining when auditors have been negligent and their degree of negligence may not be an easy task, and the standards for doing so may vary from country to country.

3) *Financial Statement Transparency*: This variable captures the transparency and informativeness of bank financial statements. It is based on the following questions: (1) Does accrued, although

unpaid, interest/principal enter the income statement while the loan is still performing?; (2) Are financial institutions required to produce consolidated accounts covering all bank and any nonbank financial subsidiaries?; (3) Are off-balance sheet items disclosed to the public?; (4) Must banks disclose their risk management procedures to the public?; (5) Are bank directors legally liable if information disclosed is erroneous or misleading?; and (6) Does accrued, although unpaid, interest/principal enter the income statement while the loan is still nonperforming?

The transparency of a bank's financial statements is important because it enables depositors, creditors, and shareholders to better assess the bank's risk of default. By making it easier and less costly for these parties to observe that a bank is adequately monitoring and controlling its risk exposure, a bank can benefit from lower funding costs. The degree of transparency is therefore tied to a bank's funding costs by providing a clearer picture of its risk-taking behavior. Although there is relatively little research on this issue, Baumann and Nier (2003) do find that banks that disclose more information tend to have higher capital ratios, and hence more protection against unexpected losses, which should contribute to lower funding costs. That said, our measure of transparency captures both voluntary and required disclosure of information by banks. Furthermore, we take into account that transparency may be greater when bank directors are legally liable for disclosing erroneous or misleading information.

Figure 3.19 provides information on the variation in the practices of countries based upon the transparency of financial statements. Three things stand out in this figure. First, some may consider it striking that even 2 of 150 countries (Albania and Aruba) do not hold bank directors legally liable if information disclosed is erroneous and misleading. Nevertheless, there is essentially unanimity with respect to this practice given the importance of transparency to investors, though as mentioned in Chapter 2, there is much greater variability in the extent to which this has been enforced. Second, 141 of 151 countries allow accrued, although unpaid, interest/principal to enter the income statement while the loan is still performing. Finally, fourteen countries even allow this practice while the loan is nonperforming. Clearly countries do not agree on the importance of transparent financial statements. Yet, this variable is positively correlated with GDP per capita.

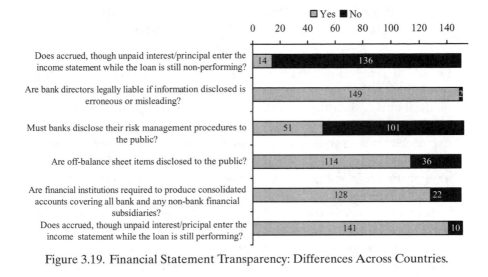

Figure 3.19. Financial Statement Transparency: Differences Across Countries.

4) *External Ratings and Creditor Monitoring*: This variable measures
   the extent to which subordinated debt is an allowable or required
   part of capital and credit ratings are used for all of the top ten banks.

As already noted, Figure 3.17 shows the percentages of a country's ten
largest banks rated by both international and domestic rating agencies.
These percentages are directly related to the income level of a country and
the relationship is especially strong for the share rated by international
rating agencies. The higher the income group, the greater the percentage
of large banks that are rated. But even in the high-income countries,
perhaps surprisingly, the ratings do not provide complete coverage of the
biggest banks.

The *External Governance Variable* is the sum of the four variables
described above. Higher values indicate a greater degree of external governance.

As already noted, the external governance variable is introduced here
for the first time. The inclusion of new questions in the survey allowed
the creation of such a variable. This variable is positively, but not perfectly, correlated with the private monitoring variable, with a correlation
coefficient of 0.64. More generally, the two variables may be viewed as
alternative ways to quantify and thus assess the role of external discipline on bank behavior. Both variables, moreover, are significantly and
positively correlated with GDP per capita.

3.G. DOES BANK OWNERSHIP TYPE AFFECT THE CHOICE OF REGULATIONS AND SUPERVISORY PRACTICES?

Within the banking system, there is an important "banking environment" factor that has a bearing, ceteris paribus, on the design and effectiveness of regulations and supervisory practices. This is the ownership composition of the banking industry. Banks may be government-owned, foreign-owned, or domestically (privately) owned. Chapter 2 discusses the incentive problems with government ownership; under such circumstances, it should be no surprise that the supervisory authorities are expected to play a supporting role and thus may overlook certain problems that develop in the banking sector.

Foreign ownership can be a double-edged sword. A foreign banking presence may provide host country supervisors with additional challenges in terms of developing a comprehensive understanding of foreign banks' operations and resolving any jurisdictional issues that may arise. Yet, foreign banks also may "import" effective supervision in cases in which the home country supervisor adheres to better practices in supervision. This situation may in effect "compete up" the overall level of supervision in the host country. Foreign banks may also be less susceptible to political pressure in the host country (but not necessarily in the home country). Even the potential for foreign banks to enter a country, moreover, may spur domestic banks to operate more efficiently. Finally, an ever-present concern about foreign banks is that they may "cherry pick" among customers, leaving domestic banks with lower-quality customers, and "exit" during bad times.

Table 3.10 shows the wide disparity in government ownership of banks.[45] Nearly two-thirds of the 136 countries for which data are available have some government ownership of banks. It ranges from a high of 98 percent in China to zero in fifty countries, including the United States. In only fifteen countries with some government ownership, however, does the figure exceed 50 percent.

Comparing the earlier and new surveys, one finds for the overlapping countries that in the majority of cases the government ownership percentage declined. Some examples of both increases and decreases in shares are shown in Table 3.11.

---

[45] Although ownership of banks is a means for a government to use banks to allocate credit, it is not the only means. As Banerjee, Cole, and Duflo (2004) point out in the case of India, the government for some time required both government and private banks to provide large portions of their funding to priority sectors.

Table 3.10. *Percentage of Bank Assets at Government-Owned Banks*

Country	Government-Owned Banks	Country	Government-Owned Banks	Country	Government-Owned Banks
China	98.10	Swaziland	14.20	Belgium	0.00
Turkmenistan	96.00	Switzerland	14.12	Belize	0.00
Algeria	95.78	Ecuador	14.00	Bolivia	0.00
Libya	89.00	Moldova	13.60	Botswana	0.00
India	75.27	Chile	13.30	Canada	0.00
Belarus	74.00	Slovenia	12.20	Denmark	0.00
Bhutan	70.00	Lithuania	12.16	Estonia	0.00
Egypt	64.70	Ghana	12.10	Finland	0.00
Costa Rica	62.26	Sudan	12.00	France	0.00
Montserrat	59.30	Ukraine	12.00	Gibraltar	0.00
Azerbaijan	58.30	Panama	11.80	Guernsey	0.00
Albania	54.00	Philippines	11.17	Guinea	0.00
Pakistan	53.79	Côte d'Ivoire	10.60	Honduras	0.00
Togo	51.00	Bosnia and	10.00	Hong Kong,	0.00
Saint Kitts	50.80	Herzegovina		China	
and Nevis		Italy	10.00	Iceland	0.00
Israel	46.10	Paraguay	9.15	Isle of Man	0.00
Qatar	46.00	Hungary	9.00	Japan	0.00
Tunisia	42.70	Venezuela	6.86	Jordan	0.00
Uruguay	42.50	Rwanda	6.60	Kuwait	0.00
Germany	42.20	Zimbabwe	6.09	Lesotho	0.00
Romania	41.80	Vanuatu	5.90	Malaysia	0.00
Korea	39.97	Luxembourg	5.05	Malta	0.00
Seychelles	39.76	Croatia	5.00	Mauritius	0.00
Commonwealth	38.80	Nigeria	4.65	Mexico	0.00
of Dominica		Tajikistan	4.60	Namibia	0.00
Russia	35.50	Slovakia	4.40	Norway	0.00
Morocco	35.00	El Salvador	4.24	Oman	0.00
United Arab	35.00	Cyprus	4.20	Peru	0.00
Emirates		Netherlands	3.90	Singapore	0.00
Saint Vincent	35.00	Czech	3.80	South	0.00
and The		Republic		Africa	
Grenadines		Serbia &	3.80	Spain	0.00
Brazil	32.00	Montenegro		Sweden	0.00
Liechtenstein	32.00	Latvia	3.80	Tonga	0.00
Argentina	31.90	Guatemala	3.20	Turks and	0.00
Turkey	31.82	British Virgin	1.70	Caicos	
Suriname	30.80	Macedonia	1.33	Islands	
Thailand	30.64	Islands		United	0.00
Taiwan, China	27.90	Fiji	1.10	Kingdom	
Poland	23.50	Kenya	1.10	United	0.00
Greece	22.80	Macau, China	0.78	States	

(continued)

Table 3.10 *(continued)*

Country	Government-Owned Banks	Country	Government-Owned Banks	Country	Government-Owned Banks
Portugal	22.80	Puerto Rico	0.72	Anguilla	0.00
Mali	21.80	Kazakhstan	0.50	Antigua and	0.00
Saudi Arabia	21.40	New Zealand	0.04	Barbuda	
Colombia	18.30	Armenia	0.00	Grenada	0.00
Bulgaria	17.60	Aruba	0.00	Saint Lucia	0.00
Kyrgyzstan	16.00	Australia	0.00	Benin	0.00
Guyana	15.00	Bahrain	0.00	Burkina	0.00
Trinidad and	14.53			Faso	
Tobago				Guinea	0.00
				Bissau	
				Niger	0.00
				Senegal	0.00

As may be seen, some of the declines in government ownership of banks are truly striking, especially when one realizes that the time that has elapsed between the two surveys is only two to four years. Despite the overall trend toward less government ownership, with populous countries such as China, India, Egypt (and, not in the current database, Indonesia)

Table 3.11. *Government Ownership Share of Assets in Surveys*

	New Survey (%)	Old Survey (%)	Percentage Change (%)
Decrease in Shares			
Mexico	0	25	100
Czech Republic	4	19	84
Russia	36	68	47
Poland	24	44	45
Romania	42	70	40
Brazil	32	52	38
Taiwan, China	28	43	35
India	75	80	6
Increase in Shares			
Morocco	35	24	46
South Korea	40	30	33
Bhutan	70	60	17
Belarus	74	67	10

being in this category, about 40 percent of the world's population lives in a country in which the majority of assets are in state-owned banks.

In the case of foreign ownership of banks, Table 3.12 shows there is also wide variation in this type of ownership. Only seven countries, Bhutan, Denmark, Iceland, Kuwait, Rwanda (where there was a significant foreign presence before the civil war), Taiwan, and Turkmenistan, have no foreign ownership among the 132 countries for which data are available. In the remaining 125 countries, the percentages range from a high of 100 percent in a country like Botswana to a low of 1 percent in Israel. Countries like Botswana, Estonia, and New Zealand, with extremely high percentages of foreign ownership, have essentially outsourced their entire banking sectors to banks in other countries. In many cases, the foreign-ownership percentages are quite high as a result of the privatization and subsequent foreign purchase of previously government-owned banks since 1990.

When one compares the foreign ownership percentages in the earlier and new surveys, in nearly every case the percentages increased. Some of the countries reporting the biggest increases are shown in Table 3.13. These are dramatic changes in the foreign ownership shares and, thus, the composition in many of these countries' banking systems in an extremely short time.[46] Given what has been happening, it is not surprising that the correlation between the government ownership share and the foreign ownership share is negative.[47] Both of these variables, moreover, are negatively correlated with GDP per capita. Also, the government ownership share is positively correlated with the percentage of bank assets in central government bonds, both for all countries and only those countries with populations exceeding one million people. Six countries have percentages of government bonds equal to or greater than 30 percent: Albania (52 percent), Lesotho (48 percent), Gambia (40 percent), Turkey (39 percent), Lebanon (33 percent), and Brazil (30 percent). (The percentage of bank assets at privately owned banks is presented

---

[46] For a recent summary of pros and cons of foreign bank presence in a country, see Song (2004, pp. 27–32). Also see Mathieson and Roldos (2001). The Basel Committee has issued standards for both home and host country regulation and supervision of cross-border banking.

[47] Table 3.14 shows the percentage of bank assets at privately owned banks. Three countries (Denmark, Ireland, and Kuwait) report figures of 100 percent, which means there are no assets at government- or foreign-owned banks. This variable is positively correlated with GDP per capita.

Table 3.12. *Percentage of Bank Assets at Foreign-Owned Banks*

Country	Foreign-Owned Banks	Country	Foreign-Owned Banks	Country	Foreign-Owned Banks
Botswana	100.00	Seychelles	60.24	Kazakhstan	17.90
Gibraltar	100.00	Malta	60.04	Portugal	17.70
Guernsey	100.00	Panama	59.30	Togo	17.50
Guinea Bissau	100.00	Armenia	59.00	Australia	17.00
Jersey	100.00	Antigua and	58.40	Lebanon	15.86
Lesotho	100.00	Barbuda		Tunisia	15.70
Tonga	100.00	Saint Lucia	58.00	Philippines	14.95
New Zealand	99.11	Burkina	56.00	Egypt	13.30
Estonia	98.90	Faso		Serbia &	13.20
Fiji	98.90	Ghana	53.50	Montenegro	
British Virgin	98.30	Macedonia	51.10	Cyprus	12.70
Islands		Tajikistan	50.00	El Salvador	12.34
Isle of Man	98.00	Romania	47.30	Oman	11.90
Gambia	95.81	Chile	46.80	Greece	10.80
Luxembourg	94.64	Albania	46.00	Switzerland	10.71
Belize	94.60	Saint Kitts	46.00	Ukraine	10.50
Vanuatu	94.10	and Nevis		Guatemala	9.00
Aruba	92.30	United	46.00	Russia	8.80
Benin	91.00	Kingdom		Spain	8.50
Czech	90.00	Uruguay	43.28	South Africa	7.70
Republic		Venezuela	43.22	India	7.30
Guinea	90.00	Peru	42.48	Ecuador	7.00
Croatia	89.30	Montserrat	40.70	Thailand	6.77
Hungary	88.80	Kenya	39.30	Japan	6.70
Grenada	88.70	Anguilla	38.50	Finland	6.20
Macau, China	87.66	Moldova	36.70	Italy	5.70
Samoa	87.00	Bolivia	36.30	Canada	4.80
Swaziland	85.80	Argentina	31.80	Azerbaijan	4.60
Slovakia	85.50	Puerto Rico	30.42	Germany	4.30
Côte d'Ivoire	84.20	Brazil	29.90	Sudan	4.00
Paraguay	83.47	Korea	29.54	Algeria	3.94
Mexico	82.70	Zimbabwe	28.02	Turkey	3.47
Senegal	78.70	United Arab	27.00	Liechtenstein	3.00
Lithuania	78.19	Emirates		Trinidad and	2.40
Bulgaria	74.56	Belarus	26.00	Tobago	
Niger	73.40	Suriname	25.50	Netherlands	2.20
Bosnia and	73.00	Kyrgyzstan	24.70	China	1.90
Herzegovina		Mauritius	24.50	Israel	1.20
Bahrain	72.00	Costa Rica	23.33	Bhutan	0.00

Country	Foreign-Owned Banks	Country	Foreign-Owned Banks	Country	Foreign-Owned Banks
Namibia	70.00	Colombia	21.50	Denmark	0.00
Poland	68.70	Morocco	20.80	Iceland	0.00
Madagascar	67.80	Saudi	20.70	Kuwait	0.00
Mali	67.00	Arabia		Rwanda	0.00
Latvia	65.20	Slovenia	20.60	Taiwan,	0.00
Saint Vincent	65.00	Pakistan	20.07	China	
and The		Norway	19.20	Turkmenistan	0.00
Grenadines		Guyana	19.00		
Jordan	64.30	Malaysia	19.00		
Commonwealth	61.20	United	19.00		
of Dominica		Honduras	18.50		

in Table 3.14, and is simply the residual category from Tables 3.12 and 3.14.)

We now examine the relationship between the type and degree of ownership and selected summary indicators of regulations and supervisory practices. To assist in this effort, we also have categorized our countries by the predominant type of bank ownership. For this purpose, we consider whether banks are mainly government owned, mainly privately owned, mainly foreign owned, mainly shared between foreign and private, and equally shared. Mainly government (foreign, private) means more than

Table 3.13. *Foreign Ownership Share of Assets in Surveys*

Increase in Shares	New Survey (%)	Old Survey (%)	Percentage Change
South Korea	30	0	–
Romania	47	8	488
Mexico	83	20	315
Czech Republic	90	26	246
Poland	69	26	165
Brazil	30	17	76
Lithuania	78	48	63
Chile	47	32	47
Hungary	89	62	44
Venezuela	43	34	26
Estonia	99	85	16

Table 3.14. *Percentage of Bank Assets at Privately Owned Banks*

Country	Privately Owned Banks	Country	Privately Owned Banks	Country	Privately Owned Banks
Denmark	100.00	Portugal	59.50	Macau, China	11.56
Iceland	100.00	Kyrgyzstan	59.30	Grenada	11.30
Kuwait	100.00	Saudi Arabia	57.90	Mali	11.20
Canada	95.20	Peru	57.52	Romania	10.90
Netherlands	93.90	Russia	55.70	Slovakia	10.10
Finland	93.80	United	54.00	Guinea	10.00
Rwanda	93.40	Kingdom		Lithuania	9.65
Japan	93.30	Germany	53.50	Benin	9.00
South Africa	92.30	Israel	52.70	Bulgaria	7.84
Spain	91.50	Venezuela	49.92	Poland	7.80
Oman	88.10	Moldova	49.70	Aruba	7.70
Guatemala	88.00	Macedonia	47.57	Paraguay	7.38
Italy	84.30	Tajikistan	45.40	Czech	6.20
Sudan	84.00	Morocco	44.20	Republic	
El Salvador	83.42	Burkina Faso	44.00	Croatia	5.70
Cyprus	83.10	Suriname	43.70	Belize	5.40
Trinidad and	83.07	Saint Lucia	42.00	Côte d'Ivoire	5.20
Tobago		Antigua and	41.60	Turkmenistan	4.00
Australia	83.00	Barbuda		Saint Kitts	3.20
Serbia &	83.00	Tunisia	41.60	and Nevis	
Montenegro		Armenia	41.00	Hungary	2.20
Kazakhstan	81.60	Malta	39.96	Isle of Man	2.00
Honduras	81.50	Chile	39.90	Estonia	1.10
Malaysia	81.00	Brazil	38.10	New Zealand	0.85
United States	81.00	United Arab	38.00	Luxembourg	0.31
Norway	80.80	Emirates		Algeria	0.28
Austria	80.20	Azerbaijan	37.10	China	0.00
Ecuador	79.00	Argentina	36.30	Albania	0.00
Ukraine	77.50	Jordan	35.70	Belarus	0.00
Mauritius	75.50	Ghana	34.40	Botswana	0.00
Switzerland	75.17	Latvia	31.60	British Virgin	0.00
Philippines	73.88	Togo	31.50	Islands	
Taiwan,	72.10	Korea	30.49	Commonwealth	0.00
China		Bhutan	30.00	of Dominica	
Puerto Rico	68.86	Namibia	30.00	Fiji	0.00
Slovenia	67.20	Panama	28.90	Gibraltar	0.00
Greece	66.40	Bahrain	28.00	Guernsey	0.00
Guyana	66.00	Niger	26.60	Guinea Bissau	0.00
Zimbabwe	65.89	Pakistan	26.14	Lesotho	0.00
Liechtenstein	65.00	Egypt	22.00	Montserrat	0.00
Turkey	64.71	Senegal	21.30	Saint Vincent	0.00
Bolivia	63.70	India	17.43	and The	
Thailand	62.59	Mexico	17.30	Grenadines	
Anguilla	61.50	Bosnia and	17.00	Seychelles	0.00
Colombia	60.20	Herzegovina		Swaziland	0.00
Kenya	59.60	Costa Rica	14.41	Tonga	0.00
		Uruguay	14.22	Vanuatu	0.00

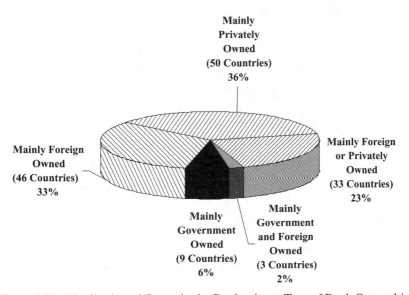

Figure 3.20. Distribution of Countries by Predominant Type of Bank Ownership.

60 percent of total assets are in banks with this form of ownership; foreign and private means these two types together hold more than 60 percent; and equally shared is a residual category (see Caprio and Honohan, 2003, for a more thorough discussion of this issue). Figure 3.20 shows the distribution of 138 countries according to these categories, with 3 countries that are equally shared (or government and foreign owned), whereas Table 3.15 indicates into which category the 141 individual countries for which we have data fall when grouped by income level.

Banks in about one-third of countries are mainly privately owned, and banks in another third are mainly foreign owned. Banks in only 6 percent of the countries, or nine countries, are mainly government owned, and not one of these is a high-income country. Interestingly, one of these (India) is the largest democracy in the world, while another (China) is the largest communist country. In the majority of the high-income countries, the banking industry is mainly privately owned. In the other three income categories, this is not the case. In the majority of the low-income countries, the banking industry is mainly foreign owned. Countries have been increasingly realizing, perhaps following losses in the banking system, that they do not need to rely primarily upon domestic ownership for banking services.

Table 3.15. *Distribution of Countries by Predominant Type of Bank Ownership and by Income Level*

	Mainly Government Owned	Mainly Foreign Owned	Mainly Privately Owned	Mainly Shared between Foreign and Private	Equally Shared
High Income (44 countries)		Aruba, Bahrain, British Virgin Islands, Gibraltar, Guernsey, Isle of Man, Jersey, Luxembourg, Macau, China, Malta, New Zealand	Australia, Austria, Belgium, Canada, Cyprus, Denmark, Finland, France, Greece, Hong Kong, China, Iceland, Italy, Japan, Kuwait, Liechtenstein, Netherlands, Norway, Puerto Rico, Singapore, Slovenia, Spain, Sweden, Switzerland, Taiwan, China, United States	Antigua and Barbuda, Germany, Korea, Portugal, United Arab Emirates, United Kingdom	Israel, Qatar
Upper-Middle Income (31 countries)	Costa Rica	Belize, Botswana, Commonwealth of Dominica, Croatia, Czech Republic, Estonia, Grenada, Hungary, Latvia, Lithuania, Mexico, Poland, Seychelles, Slovakia	Anguilla, Lebanon, Malaysia, Mauritius, Oman, Trinidad and Tobago, Turks and Caicos Islands	Argentina, Chile, Montserrat, Panama, Saint Kitts and Nevis, Saint Lucia, Saudi Arabia, Uruguay, Venezuela	

Lower-Middle Income (40 countries)	Algeria
	Belarus
	China
	Egypt
	Turkmenistan
		Bosnia and
		  Herzegovina
		Bulgaria
		Fiji
		Jordan
		Namibia
		Paraguay
			Saint Vincent
			  and The
			  Grenadines
			Samoa
			Swaziland
			Tonga
			Vanuatu
				Bolivia
				Colombia
				Ecuador
				El Salvador
				Guatemala
					Guyana
					Honduras
					Kazakhstan
					Philippines
					Serbia &
					  Montenegro
						South Africa
						Thailand
						Turkey
						Ukraine
							Albania
							Armenia
							Brazil
							Macedonia
							Morocco
							Peru
							Romania
							Russia
							Suriname
							Tunisia Azerbaijan

Low Income (25 countries)	Bhutan India Libya	Benin Côte d6Ivoire Gambia Guinea Guinea Bissau	Lesotho Madagascar Mali Niger Senegal		Nigeria Rwanda	Sudan Zimbabwe	Burkina Faso Ghana Kenya Kyrgyzstan Moldova Pakistan Tajikistan Togo

Note: mainly government (foreign, private) means more than 60 percent of total assets in this form of ownership; foreign and private means these two types together hold more than 60 percent; and equally shared is the residual category.

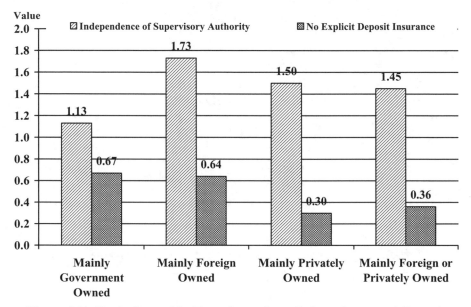

Figure 3.21. Bank Ownership Type, Supervisory Independence, and Deposit Insurance.

When one compares the type of bank ownership to the type of regulatory regime in countries, some interesting results emerge. For example, using our indices, Figures 3.21 to 3.25 show that governments differ with respect to how their banking systems are regulated and supervised depending on the ownership composition of banks. Figure 3.21 shows that in countries with mainly government-owned banks the supervisory authorities are less independent and the existence of explicit deposit insurance is quite low as compared to countries with either mainly privately owned banks or mainly foreign- and privately owned banks. Governments are also more restrictive in countries with mainly government-owned banks with respect to allowable bank activities and ownership combinations as compared to countries with mainly foreign-owned or privately owned banks, or a combination of the two (see Figure 3.22). When it comes to the percentage of the 10 biggest banks being rated by international credit rating agencies, as Figure 3.23 shows, this is a far more common practice in countries with mainly privately owned banks. Furthermore, Figures 3.24 and 3.25 show that external governance, private monitoring, and the minimum risk-based capital requirement

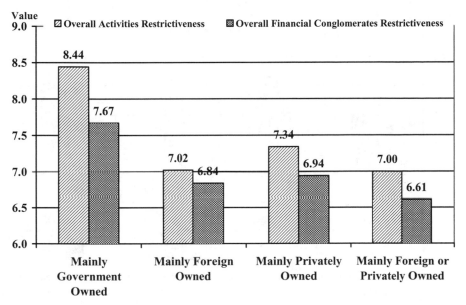

Figure 3.22. Bank Ownership Type and Degree of Restrictiveness.

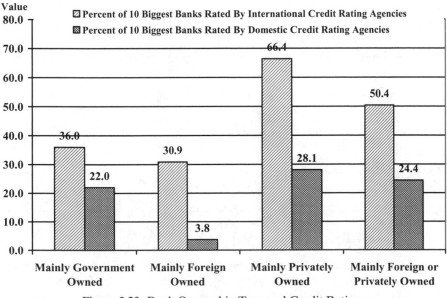

Figure 3.23. Bank Ownership Type and Credit Ratings.

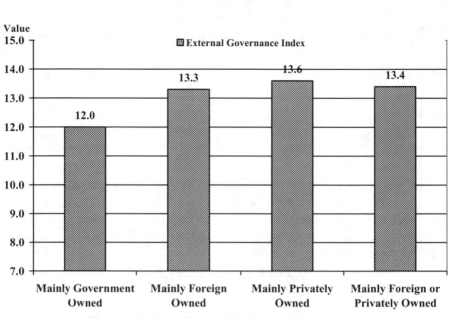

Figure 3.24. Bank Ownership Type and Governance.

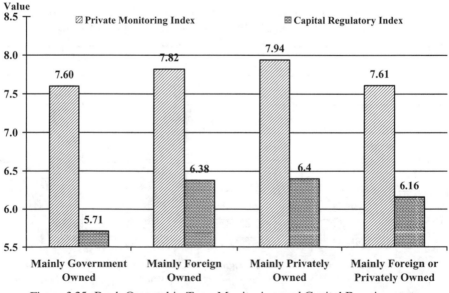

Figure 3.25. Bank Ownership Type, Monitoring, and Capital Requirements.

are lowest in countries with mainly government-owned banks. Thus, bank ownership and bank regulation and supervision seem to reflect broader social opinions about the role of government in the banking sector. Chapter 4 provides a more thorough and rigorous analysis of this issue.

3.H. FORCES FOR GREATER HARMONIZATION OF REGULATION AND SUPERVISION AMONG COUNTRIES

Earlier in this chapter, we discussed the issue of whether a country should create a single authority or multiple supervisory authorities for banks. A related issue is whether countries should adopt common or different standards for the regulation and supervision of banks. Both of these issues have received increased attention in recent years given the growing importance of financial conglomerates and the globalization of financial services. As discussed in Chapter 2, competition in regulatory standards may have advantages (encouraging innovation and improvements in banking policies) and disadvantages (a race to the bottom as countries adopt lenient policies to attract banks, which may also give rise to more money laundering, fraud, and other illegal activities).

Faced with this "regulatory and supervisory dilemma" between common standards that might stifle beneficial competition and diverse standards that may foster excessively risky international banking markets, some countries (and multinational organizations) have promoted a minimum harmonization of regulations and supervisory practices. Dale (1994) points out that "[u]ntil the mid-1970s there was no formal machinery for coordinating national regulation of international banks." One of the first efforts in this regard was the Basel Committee's Concordat issued in 1975 that set guidelines for cooperation between national authorities in the supervision of banks' foreign establishments.

Some countries, however, belong to regional unions or international organizations and thus are linked to one another in important ways by virtue of their common membership.[48] In these types of cases, the

---

[48] It might be noted that Islamic finance has recently been expanding throughout the world. This development has given rise to a push for greater harmonization of the regulation and supervision of Islamic financial institutions. For example, John Taylor (2004), former U.S. Under Secretary of the Treasury, states that "... regulators need to factor in the differences in these forms of finance and have at least minimal standards or benchmarks to gauge compliance or assess risks." He adds that "[t]here needs to be some form of consistency in regulatory treatment across the board...." This is a type of harmonization applied to financial institutions adhering to particular religious principles. In this

individual countries sharing common membership typically decide upon regulations and supervisory practices jointly. Indeed, membership itself requires some degree of minimum harmonization of practices among member countries to sustain cohesiveness. The adoption of international standards of best practice by countries is an interesting issue. As the number and importance of such countries grows, "holdout" countries are increasingly under pressure to be sure the benefits of "noncompliance" exceed the costs. Of course, even the universal adoption of a common standard does not imply uniform implementation or enforcement of that standard. We now examine using our new database three important groups of countries to assess the extent to which harmonization in bank regulations and supervisory practices exists. These are the European Union, the World Trade Organization, and Offshore Financial Centers. Each of these groups will now be discussed in turn.[49]

3.H.1. European Union[50]

An obvious and important group of countries is the EU, which is the culmination of the efforts of many countries over the past half century to establish a single market in Europe.[51] The 1973 directive on "The Abolition

---

regard, the Islamic Financial Services Board (IFSB) was established in 2002 to "... set and disseminate standards and core principles and adopt existing international standards for voluntary adoption by member countries..." In doing so, "[t]he harmonization ... should be conducive to effective prudential supervision of Islamic financial institutions in their home countries, and facilitate a sustained international expansion of Islamic banking." See Sundararajan and Errico (2002). For more on Islamic banking, see Kuran (2004).

[49] It should be noted that each of three groups of countries included in the new survey has uniform bank regulations and supervisory practices. The groups are the Eastern Caribbean Currency Union (ECCU) countries (Anguilla, Antigua and Barbuda, Commonwealth of Dominica, Grenada, Montserrat, St Kitts and Nevis, St Lucia, and St Vincent and the Grenadines), the West African Monetary Union (WAMU) countries (Benin, Burkina Faso, Côte d'Ivoire, Guinea Bissau, Mali, Niger, Senegal, and Togo), and the Central African Economic and Monetary Community (CAEMC) countries (Cameroon, Central African Republic, Chad, Congo, Equatorial Guinea, and Gabon). The countries in each of these groups have therefore achieved theoretically "perfect" regulatory and supervisory harmonization.

[50] This section draws heavily on the excellent paper by Dermine (2002).

[51] In 1957, the EU, or then the European Economic Community (EEC), consisted of just six countries: Belgium, Germany, France, Italy, Luxembourg, and the Netherlands. Denmark, Ireland, and the United Kingdom joined in 1973, Greece in 1981, Spain and Portugal in 1986, Austria, Finland, and Sweden in 1985. In 2004, ten new countries joined: Bulgaria, Czech Republic, Estonia, Hungary, Latvia, Lithuania, Poland, Romania, Slovakia, and Slovenia. All member countries of the EU, moreover, are members of the

of Restrictions on Freedom of Establishment and Freedom to Provide Services for self-employed Activities of Banks and other Financial Institutions" early on contributed to establishing a single banking market.[52] It required member countries to comply with the "national treatment" principle. This means member states are to provide equal regulatory and supervisory treatment for all banks, both domestic and foreign, from all member states. However, despite this effort toward harmonization, the existence of capital controls and a lack of coordination among the different bank regulatory and supervisory authorities meant that banks operating in different member countries remained subject to different rules.

This situation led to further attempts to achieve greater harmonization of bank regulations and supervisory practices among member countries. In particular, in 1977, the First Banking Directive was issued, which requires member states to comply with the principle of "home-country control." This means that the member state that licenses a bank is responsible for supervising its activities throughout the EU. This assures that all banks are supervised. Once again, however, despite further progress toward harmonization, obstacles to establishing a single banking market remained. For example, capital controls still impeded the cross-border supply of banking services, authorization was still required from the host countries for member countries' banks to operate in other member countries, and allowable activities were still determined by the host countries.

Perhaps the most significant single effort to eliminate remaining obstacles to a single banking market was provided in 1985 with the release of the European Commission's White Paper on "The Completion of the Internal Market." It spurred the member states into passing the Single European Act in 1986, which set out a timetable for completing a single market by 1993. This in turn led to the 1998 Second Banking Directive, which required member countries to comply with the principle of "mutual recognition." This means that banks in any member state are granted a

European Economic Area (EEA). Three countries are members of the EEA (Iceland, Liechtenstein, and Norway) but not members of the EU. However, because all members of the EEA agree to basically the same rules for banks, the effect is to create a larger single banking market. See European Freedom Trade Association (2004).

[52] The process of establishing a single market in the EU is based on a series of legislative measures, including both regulations and directives. Although both are legally binding, EC regulations take precedence over national laws, whereas EC directives generally require action on the part of the member countries to be implemented – which usually takes two to four years. See Zimmerman (1996).

"single passport" to offer services, either through cross-border provision of services or through the establishment of branches, in any other member state without seeking authorization from the host countries. This avoids the duplication of supervision. The single passport also allows a bank from one member country to conduct activities in another member country that that country's own domestic banks may not be allowed to conduct.[53] The reason is that the national law of the country in which a bank is licensed determines what that bank is allowed to do throughout the EU, not other countries' laws in which the bank operates. Furthermore, a bank from a non-EU country may establish a subsidiary in an EU country in order to secure the benefits of the single passport.

To ensure that the single passport does not lead to a situation in which the regulations and supervisory practices in a member country are so lax as to undermine the safety and soundness of the entire banking system in the EU, the Second Banking Directive also limits the scope for regulatory competition among countries. It does so by requiring a minimal harmonization (rather than full harmonization) of standards. This involves setting minimum capital adequacy standards, large exposure limits, and suitability requirements of bank shareholders. However, as Steil (1994) points out, the European "... Commission has never been explicit either about what sorts of rules do and do not require harmonization, or about how the 'minimum is to be determined.'" In the case of capital standards, the EU simply adopted Basel I as the minimal harmonization standard. This principle nevertheless clearly contributes to the harmonization of standards, but member states are nonetheless allowed to set more stringent standards, by virtue of the principle of mutual recognition. Subsequently, in 1994, a directive on Deposit Insurance Schemes was adopted to ensure a minimum harmonization of deposit protection in countries throughout the EU. The directive provides for mandatory deposit insurance for all banks and a minimum coverage per depositor, not deposit, of ECU 20,000. It does not mandate coinsurance or a particular funding scheme. Member countries, of course, are allowed to be more generous in protecting depositors than the directive mandates if they so

---

[53] This directive provides a list of bank activities or services that are subject to mutual recognition, including securities activities in addition to traditional banking activities. See Morner (1997). Also, the 1988 Directive on Liberalization of Capital Flows was important for the integration of the different financial markets in the EU countries. Heinemann and Jopp (2002) provide information on the dates of the final lifting of capital controls, interest deregulation, and the adoption of the First and Second Banking Directives in EU member states.

choose.[54] Indeed, Italy provides coverage for a depositor that is more than six times the minimum required by the directive.

As is clearly evident from the discussion thus far, substantial progress was made among the EU countries to establish a single banking market. Yet more work remained to be completed to achieve full integration.[55] This fact was acknowledged with the European Commission's launching of the Financial Services Action Plan (ECFSAP) in 1999, which consists of a series of initiatives taken to ensure a full integration of banking markets by 2005. The ECFSAP consists of forty-two measures intended to provide the complete regulatory and supervisory environment that will support the full integration of national financial markets. The goal of this effort is to finally create a single market for financial services across the EU. By the end of July 2004, thirty-nine out of the forty-two measures had been adopted in the EU (HM Treasury, 2004).

Thus, a substantial degree of harmonization has been achieved in the banking sector through the adoption of the various banking directives and the ECFSAP. The European Commission, moreover, established the Committee of European Banking Supervisors (CEBS) in 2004. Its role is to "[c]ontribute to the consistent implementation of Community Directives and to the convergence of Member States' supervisory practices throughout the community..." (see http://www.c-ebs.org/presslatest.htm). Given this objective, some information on the degree to which bank regulations and supervisory practices diverge in the EU countries is provided in Appendix 7, with countries divided into three groupings: old (fifteen countries), combined (twenty-five countries: old plus ten new members), and the twelve EU countries comprising the European Monetary Union (EMU). The appendix shows that there are indeed differences in the degree of restrictiveness of some practices in

---

[54] In a comparative study of the deposit insurance schemes in ten accession countries, Nenovsky and Dimitrova (2003, p. 16) argue that "meeting mechanically the requirements for nominal harmonization ... could have an adverse result-increasing probability of financial crisis and decreasing efficiency of the European banking system."

[55] Of course, in 1993, the ratification of the Treaty of Maastricht established the principle of a single European currency. On January 1, 1999, twelve EU countries became members of the European Monetary Union (EMU) by adopting the euro as their common currency. Of the "old" fifteen EU member countries, Denmark, Sweden, and the United Kingdom kept open their option to join at a later date. The Treaty reflected the effort of some countries to achieve the twin goals of a single market and a single currency throughout Europe. In the EMU countries, the European Central Bank (ECB) is responsible for monetary policy, whereas bank regulation and supervision remains the responsibility of the individual member nations, subject to the EU membership requirements already discussed.

EU countries as compared to non-EU countries as well as EMU countries as compared to non-EMU countries. Among the more important
differences are the following:

- Both old and new EU countries as well as European Monetary Union
  (EMU) countries are uniformly less restrictive with respect to allowing
  banks to engage in securities, insurance, and real estate activities than
  the countries comprising their counterparts.
- The EU and EMU countries are more tolerant when it comes to the formation of financial conglomerates than non-EU and non-EMU countries.
- The three groupings of European countries value prompt corrective
  power less than other countries, especially the old EU countries.
- Both private monitoring and external governance differ relatively little
  across the different groupings of countries, in part because the EU
  countries all have explicit deposit insurance schemes and have not yet
  uniformly adopted either IAS or GAAP/GAAS in contrast to many
  countries comprising their counterparts.
- All three groupings of EU countries score higher with respect to mitigating moral hazard than their counterparts.
- Both old and new EU countries as well as EMU countries have a far
  greater percentage of big banks rated by international credit rating
  agencies than the countries comprising their counterparts.

To further assess the degree of harmonization among the EU countries, we can compare dimensions of regulation and supervision for each
of the twenty-five member states. We can do this for the individual countries comprising each of two groups, the fifteen old and the ten new EU
countries, as well as compare differences across the two groups. There
obviously are cases in which the old EU countries will be identical. As
noted earlier, every member state is required to have an explicit deposit
insurance scheme and to adopt a minimum risk-adjusted capital adequacy
standard of 8 percent. All old member states meet these two requirements.
However, even though these countries have identical capital standards of
8 percent, some features of their insurance schemes are not identical.
There also are differences among these countries both with respect to
the restrictiveness of the activities in which banks may engage and the
restrictiveness of the formation of financial conglomerates. Overall, Italy
is the most restrictive with a score of 15, whereas the United Kingdom
is the least restrictive with a score of 7. The countries, moreover, differ
with respect to the stringency of the capital regulatory index, with Sweden

scoring a minimum value of 3 and both Austria and Spain scoring maximum values of 10. As a final example of differences among the EU countries, the strength of official supervisory power ranges from a low of 5 in the Netherlands to a high of 14 in Portugal. Given these and other types of differences, full harmonization of regulatory and supervisory regimes is still a goal to be achieved among the old EU countries.

The situation is no different for the new EU countries. Indeed, at the time of our data and before their accession into the EU in 2004, not all of these countries had an explicit deposit insurance scheme nor was the minimum capital adequacy standard the same across the countries. The capital requirement ranged from 8 to 12 percent. There were also differences in the other dimensions of regulation and supervision similar to those just discussed for the old EU countries. However, when one compares the old and new EU countries, one finds that the new members are on average more restrictive with respect to both the range of activities in which banks may engage and the formation of conglomerates than the old members. They also have more stringent entry into banking requirements, but at the same time provide the official supervisory authorities with greater powers. The bottom line, however, is that the 25 EU countries have not yet achieved full harmonization. The unresolved issues in this regard are twofold. First, is a single EU supervisory authority needed to achieve full harmonization? Second, and more important, if indeed full harmonization itself is appropriate, which common set of regulations and supervisory practices works best for every member state?

3.H.2. World Trade Organization[56]

The World Trade Organization (WTO) was established in 1995. In 2004 there were 148 member countries of the WTO, with around another 30 countries negotiating membership. It is a global international organization for liberalizing trade, a forum for governments to negotiate trade agreements, and a place for settling trade disputes. Before the establishment of the WTO, the major instrument used by countries from 1948 onward to negotiate agreements to reduce barriers to international trade in goods was the General Agreement on Tariffs and Trade (GATT). The GATT still remains the relevant vehicle for negotiating agreements

---

[56] This section draws heavily on the excellent studies by Alexander (2002), Key (2003), Marchetti (2003), and the University of Hong Kong (2004). Also, relevant materials can be found at http://www.wto.org.

covering trade in goods. But despite the growing trade in services, for a long time there was no vehicle similar to the GATT to negotiate agreements to reduce barriers to trade in services. Finally, along with the creation of the WTO, the General Agreement on Trade in Services (GATS) was agreed to in 1997 and took effect two years later.[57]

The GATS defines trade in services as the supply of services through four modes of supply: (1) cross border; (2) consumption abroad; (3) commercial presence; and (4) the temporary movement of natural persons. Given our focus on banks, the following examples may clarify what is meant by these different modes of supply for banking services. The cross-border supply of banking services occurs when consumers in one country are allowed to obtain loans from a bank in another country. Consumption of banking services abroad occurs when a country allows its citizens to purchase such services when traveling abroad. Commercial presence refers to a situation in which a bank in one country establishes a branch or a subsidiary to supply its services in another country. The temporary movement of natural persons occurs when a bank in one country sends executives or managers to the bank's branches or subsidiaries in another country. Countries may therefore negotiate agreements to reduce barriers to trade in banking services through these modes of supply.

The GATS clearly has important implications for the regulation and supervision of banks, especially foreign banks. The specific reason is that it contains both general principles – such as Most-Favored Nation (MFN) – and negotiable principles – such as Market Access and National Treatment. MFN requires that each WTO member country give foreign banks from any member country treatment no less favorable than foreign banks from any other member country. The purpose of this principle is to prevent a member from discriminating among banks from other members. This means, for example, that a member cannot condition the entry of foreign banks on reciprocity requirements with other members under the GATS. However, an exception to this general principle is that members have the right to enter into economic integration agreements, such as the EU, and accord preferences to other participants without extending those preferences to the entire WTO membership. Also, Key (2003, p. 34) points out that "[a]n MFN exemption allows a country to apply more favorable treatment than that guaranteed by its GATS commitments on a

---

[57] GATT and GATS cover two of the three main areas of trade handled by the WTO. The third is the Agreement on Trade-Related Aspects of Intellectual Property Rights (TRIPS), which covers trade in ideas and creativity or "intellectual property."

non-MFN basis, but it does not permit less favorable treatment." Under some circumstances, as she notes, this allows a country to pursue a unilateral reciprocity policy.

The other two key principles – Market Access and National Treatment – are negotiable principles, which means that WTO members decide voluntarily to what extent they will allow foreign participation in their markets and under what conditions with respect to the four modes of supply. National treatment requires, subject to any conditions or qualifications that are negotiated and become part of a schedule of commitments, that host regulators treat foreign banks no less favorable than they treat domestic banks. This means, for example, that member countries cannot erect barriers to entry or operation that discriminate against foreign banks as compared to domestic banks. However, as indicated, the host country may limit national treatment by stating as part of its commitments, for example, that special subsidies or tax benefits are granted to domestic banks only or that limitations on the location of branches apply only to branches of foreign banks.

Market access, in contrast to national treatment, is not defined in the GATS. Instead, a list of six measures restricting the free access to banking markets that may be applied to foreign banks is provided. A country that does not impose any of these restrictions is then regarded as providing full market access. The list includes numerical quotas on the number of foreign banks or their total assets, limitations on the type of foreign bank entry (e.g., requiring establishment of a subsidiary as opposed to a branch), limitations on the percentage of ownership in domestic banks, and limitations on the total number of natural persons that may be employed in the host country's banking sector or which the foreign bank itself may employ.

The way market access and national treatment work is that a member country would indicate in its negotiated schedule of commitments that it is granting market access and national treatment to foreign banks from other member countries. The country would then list in its schedule all restrictions on market access (i.e., based upon the six measures) and on national treatment that it is imposing on foreign banks. Table 3.16 provides examples of various types of limitations on market access and national treatment that may be imposed. Thus, agreements to eliminate or reduce limitations to market access or to provide national treatment are voluntary, applying only to those banking services included in a member country's schedule and to the extent specified therein. It should be emphasized that the GATS commitments are legally binding. In the event

Table 3.16. *Examples of Market Access and National Treatment Limitations*

Market Accesss	National Treatment
(a) Limitations on the number of services suppliers – Only a fixed number of bank licenses granted per year.	Nationality or residency requirements on the directors of a bank.
(b) Limitations on the value of transactions or assets – Only a fixed aggregate amount of loans can be made to residents by foreign banks. – Foreign bank subsidiaries limited to X percent of total domestic assets of all banks.	Requirements to invest certain amounts of assets in local currency.
(c) Limitations on the number of operations or on the total quantity of service output – Only a fixed number of bank branches.	Restrictions on the acquisition of land by foreign financial institutions.
(d) Limitations on the total number of natural persons that may be employed – Only X foreign personnel allowed for each establishment of a bank.	Special subsidy or tax privilege granted to domestic institutions only.
(e) Measures that restrict or require specific types of legal entity or joint venture – Only incorporated subsidiaries of banks allowed.	Special operational limits (limitations on the location of branches, prohibition of promotional activities, for example) applying only to branches or operations of foreign institutions.
(f) Limitations on the participation of foreign capital – Only X percent foreign ownership allowed in banks.	

Source: Marchetti (2003).

that there are differences among member countries regarding either the interpretation of any agreements or the compliance with any commitments, countries may resort to a dispute settlement mechanism that is provided as an integral part of the WTO.

Despite the obligations and commitments a country negotiates with WTO members as part of the GATS, it may nonetheless implement more stringent regulatory measures on foreign banks so long as they are taken "for prudential reasons, including the protection of depositors, policy holders or persons to whom a fiduciary duty is owed by a financial service supplier, or to ensure the integrity or stability of the financial system."[58] This so-called prudential carve-out, however, cannot, or perhaps more correctly, should not be used as a means to avoid a member country's obligations and commitments. Yet, the difference between a prudential and a protective measure, both of which restrict trade in financial services, may be difficult to determine because the GATS itself does not provide any specific guidance regarding the scope and extent of the prudential exception. Indeed, the GATS even prohibits member countries from listing prudential restrictions in their schedules of commitments. Instead, member countries retain the discretion to invoke prudential regulations to restrict cross-border trade in financial services at any time so long as the measures are taken for prudential reasons. According to Alexander (2002, p. 26), "Although no formal WTO complaints have yet been brought under the Financial Services Agreement, the ambiguity which exists in the Agreement regarding the type of regulatory measures that a state may take for prudential reasons to protect its banking and financial system will likely lead to much litigation at the WTO." The reason is that "broad regulatory discretion creates an incentive for states to adopt what are ostensibly prudential measures, but is in fact non-tariff, protectionists trade measures to protect their financial services market" (Alexander, 2002, p. 55). This situation thus raises the question as to what criteria or standards can be used to determine the prudential validity of regulatory and supervisory restrictions on cross-border trade in banking and other financial services.

Given the potential for disputes among countries as to what constitutes a prudential basis for restricting cross-border trade in financial services, it seems imperative that some agreement be reached regarding this issue before serious disputes actually arise. For as Alexander (2002, p. 23) points out,

Because of the lack of guidance in defining the concept of prudential regulation or supervision, it is a strong possibility that this will be defined by panelists in WTO dispute resolution, and that panels could potentially defer to the principles and standards adopted by international standard setting bodies, such as the Basel Committee on Banking Supervision and possibly look to the regulatory practices

---

[58] See Article 2(a) of the Annex on Financial Services (WTO Analytical Index) at http://www.wto.org/english/res_e/booksp_e/analytic_index_e/gats_e.htm.

of major states, such as the United States and EU member states. It is questionable whether this will be a good result for the many developing countries and emerging market economies that may need differential standards of prudential regulation to address the different economic and legal structures of their financial markets.

The importance of financial markets for economic growth, development, and stability necessitates that much more effort be devoted to determining more precisely what indeed does constitute defensible and prudential restrictions on cross-border trade in financial services. This is especially important for all the WTO member countries around the world that differ in so many important respects. A full harmonization or one-size-fits-all approach to financial regulation and supervision certainly is not the way to resolve the prudential issue. Instead, the information on the regulation and supervision of banks in countries around the globe that we have been describing in this chapter may prove valuable in this respect. Countries that encounter disputes may defend their practices with such information by pointing to other countries acting in a similar manner. Also, the analysis of such data, as is done in subsequent chapters, may assist in determining how best to measure the "prudential exception" and thereby ward off any disputes that might otherwise occur among WTO member countries.

The WTO obviously is considered to be an important organization as evidenced by the fact that its membership has increased over time to nearly 150 countries in 2004. The fact that such a large number of countries have become members has led to fewer restrictions on cross-border banking throughout the world. The reason for this is that members, as part of their negotiation for membership, are pressured to lessen, if not eliminate, restrictions on foreign bank entry. Existing members have every incentive to negotiate for as few restrictions as possible with those countries seeking membership. China, for example, became a member in December 2001 and, as a result of negotiations committed by December 2006, at the end of a five-year phase-in period, to grant relatively free access to its domestic banking industry by foreign banks. Specifically, it agreed to impose no limitations on the ability of foreign banks to operate in China, whether by geographic location, currency (foreign or Renminbi), type of customer (foreign or domestic, institutional or individual), or type of entity (branch or subsidiary) that do not apply to domestic banks. The WTO negotiation process thus contributes to greater liberalization and more harmonization of regulations and supervisory practices. (See Appendix 8 for information on the degree to which the restrictiveness of various regulations and supervisory practices differs between WTO countries and non-WTO countries.)

3.H.3. Offshore Financial Centers

Offshore financial centers (OFCs) play an important role in the structure of international banking markets. They effectively represent a third tier in the structure of these markets, with the first two being domestic banking markets and traditional foreign banking markets, respectively. We have already discussed differences in the composition of the banking systems in countries with respect to government-, domestic-, and foreign-owned banks. The OFCs merit special attention because their existence is primarily, if not entirely, dependent on legal frameworks that typically provide anonymity to beneficial owners, low or zero taxes, and a lenient regulatory and supervisory environment. They therefore deliberately diverge from the standards of bigger and more powerful countries as a means to attract foreign business.

Ever since their emergence and growth in the 1960s and 1970s, OFCs have posed special regulatory and supervisory challenges. Although OFCs predominately provide services to legitimate banks, some cater to more dubious banks by facilitating tax evasion, money laundering, and terrorist financing. The number of OFCs can vary significantly depending on the definition used (see IMF, 2000, p. 5, which indicates there are as few as fourteen and as many as sixty-nine OFCs). A relatively high figure is obtained if one defines an OFC as any financial center where offshore activity takes place, as all the major financial centers of the world would be included. Instead, the IMF (2000) suggests a "practical definition" of an OFC, with which most observers would agree, based on the following three characteristics (IMF, 2000, p. 5):

(1) Financial systems with external assets and liabilities out of proportion to domestic intermediation;
(2) Relatively large numbers of financial institutions engaged primarily in business with nonresidents; and
(3) Provision of some or all of the following services: low or zero taxation, moderate or light financial regulation, banking secrecy and anonymity.

Relying on this definition, the Financial Stability Forum (FSF), which was convened in 1999 to promote international financial stability and brings together international financial institutions, national regulators and supervisors, and central bank experts for this purpose, has identified forty-two jurisdictions that it considers to have significant offshore activities (IMF, 2000, Table 3.2).

The number of banks in OFCs is significant and the magnitude of cross-border financial activity taking place in OFCs is substantial, even if the number of banks is not available for all OFCs and the level of activity is somewhat difficult to measure. To illustrate this point, consider the following. The Cayman Islands alone is reported to have 580 banks, with a population of only about forty-three thousand people.[59] Guernsey, the Isle of Man, Jersey, and Vanuatu, collectively, with a population of only about 430 thousand people, have more banking assets than India with a population of more than one billion people. Vanuatu by itself has a bank asset-to-GDP ratio that is more than 2,250 times as great as that of the United States. Finally, each of these four OFCs has a foreign-share of total bank assets that ranges from a low of 94 percent to a high of 100 percent (see Table 3.12).

Apart from the legitimacy of the banking activities conducted in OFCs, a major concern among banking authorities is that lenient or inadequate regulation and supervision can increase potential financial vulnerabilities in the OFCs that, in a worst-case scenario, can spread throughout the international financial system. As cross-border financial activity has increased over time and OFCs have proliferated, greater international pressure has been put on the OFCs to improve their regulations and supervisory practices, primarily by pressuring them to comply with the Basel Core Principles. Indeed, the IMF launched the offshore financial center (OFC) program in July 2000, which included an assessment program concerned with assessing financial regulation and supervision in the OFCs.[60] At that time, the FSF considered twenty-five OFCs ". . . as having a low quality of supervision, and/or being non-co-operative with onshore supervisors, and with little or no attempt being made to adhere to international standards" (IMF, 2000, p. 6).

---

[59] See U.S. Department of State (2004) and CIA World Factbook (2004).

[60] In 1980, the Offshore Group of Banking Supervisors (OGBS) was established. The members of this group commit to the Core Principles as well as to preventing money laundering and terrorist financing. In early 2005, there were nineteen members: Aruba, Bahamas, Bahrain, Barbados, Bermuda, Cayman Islands, Cyprus, Gibraltar, Guernsey, Hong Kong, Isle of Man, Jersey, Labuan, Macao, Mauritius, Netherlands Antilles, Panama, Singapore, and Vanuatu.

Offshore financial centers emerged in importance in the 1960s and the 1970s as a response to distortionary regulations in developed countries. Such measures included interest rate ceilings, restrictions on the range of products and services banks could offer, capital controls, and high effective tax rates. Subsequently, as onshore banking restrictions have been eased in major developed countries, and as the principle of consolidated supervision encompassing all subsidiaries and affiliates, domestic and foreign, of banking organizations began to be widely observed, OFCs have lost significant ground in offshore banking from the mid-1990s on. The fact that many OFCs have been raising their standards to improve their reputations has contributed to this erosion.[61] Yet, it has been reported by the IMF (2000, p. 9) that "[t]here are some recent entrants to the OFC market who have deliberately sought to fill the gap at the bottom left by those that have sought to raise standards."

Information on some of the differences in regulation and supervisory practices between OFCs and non-OFC countries is presented in Figures 3.26, 3.27, and Appendix 8. Figure 3.26 shows that OFCs score lower than non-OFC countries in five different dimensions: official supervisory power, prompt corrective power, supervisory forbearance discretion, the strength of external audits, and external governance. Figure 3.27 shows that OFCs have almost twenty-two times as many banks per capita as non-OFC countries and a minimum capital entry requirement that is about one-fourth that of the non-OFC countries. Also, the figures show that the OFCs also have a far lower percentage of the ten biggest banks rated by domestic credit rating agencies and a lower minimum capital adequacy ratio. Appendix 8 shows the extent to which OFCs differ in many more dimensions of regulation and supervision from the non-OFC countries. Although based on averages for relatively large numbers of countries, two major differences worth pointing out are the larger fraction of domestic entry applications denied by OFCs and the smaller fraction of foreign applications denied as compared to the non-OFC countries.

Despite the fact that some OFCs are indeed more lenient with respect to some regulations and supervisory practices, not to mention imposing

---

[61] Also, the U.S. Department of State (2004, p. 1) reports that "[t]he USA Patriot Act provision that prohibits transactions (directly or indirectly) between U.S. financial institutions and foreign shell banks [i.e., banks with very limited physical presence and the business decisions taken elsewhere] played a key role in Nauru's decision to cancel the licenses of nearly 400 shell banks in its jurisdiction and, undoubtedly, was a major factor contributing to the decrease noted globally in the number of offshore banks."

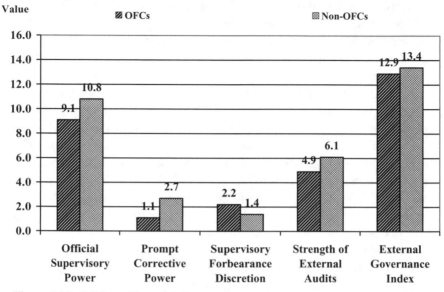

Figure 3.26. Offshore Financial Centers, Regulations, and Supervisory Practices.

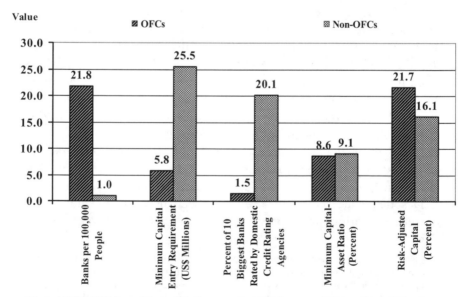

Figure 3.27. Offshore Financial Centers, Regulations, and Supervisory Practices.

lower tax rates, than many non-OFC countries, it is important to point out that OFCs nevertheless continue to be attractive to banks operating in more highly regulated and more heavily taxed economies. For these very reasons, OFCs may actually play a constructive role by promoting less restrictive regulatory and supervisory regimes, and perhaps even lower tax rates, in non-OFC countries.

FOUR

What Works Best?

The more extensive a man's knowledge of what has been done, the greater will be his power of knowing what to do.

Disraeli

It ain't what you don't know that gets you into trouble. It's what you know for sure that just ain't so.

Mark Twain[1]

4.A. GOALS AND BOUNDARIES

4.A.1. Goals

This chapter assesses the book's central question: which bank regulatory and supervisory strategies work best? As stressed in Chapter 1, three inter-related motivations drive this chapter's analyses. First, because banks importantly influence economic growth, poverty alleviation, and economic volatility (Levine, 2005a), it is critical to identify those policies that encourage efficient bank operations. Consequently, this chapter provides the first broad, cross-country assessment of a variety of regulations to determine which ones enhance bank development, stability, efficiency, performance, and the degree of corruption in bank lending. Second, the Basel Committee routinely makes influential recommendations for countries to adopt regarding bank regulatory and supervisory strategies.

[1] The Disraeli quotation is at http://www.quotationspage.com/quote/28708.html; that by Mark Twain is found at http://www.brainyquote.com/quotes/quotes/m/marktwain109624.html and other Web sites.

As described in Chapter 2, it most recently recommended Basel II, which is based on three pillars: capital standards, official supervision, and market discipline, respectively. This chapter provides the first cross-country assessment of the relative merits of these three "pillars." Third, our inquiry about what works best in bank regulation and supervision bears directly on the epic debate on the proper role of government in an economy. From before the *Federalist Papers*, philosophers, political scientists, and economists have warned about the adverse repercussions of unchecked power of any branch of government. At the same time, many economists (e.g., Atkinson and Stiglitz, 1980) stress that, in the presence of information and transaction costs, governments can improve social welfare by ameliorating these market imperfections through coordinating the activities of many of society's actors. Thus, some stress that a powerful government is the only mechanism for easing severe market imperfections, while others emphasize the dangers associated with powerful government agencies.

In our examination of banking policies, we take account of and assess competing visions of the proper role of government. To elaborate, recommendations of the Basel Committee assume: (i) significant market imperfections exist in financial markets, (ii) the ability of bank supervisors to overcome, at least partially, those imperfections, and (iii) the beneficent incentives of bank supervisors to ameliorate market imperfections and hence improve the operation of banks. In contrast to this **public interest view**, the **private interest view** stresses that powerful supervisors will act in their self interest and will not necessarily ameliorate market imperfections. Rather, the private interest view emphasizes that: (1) politicians will attempt to use a powerful supervisory agency to pressure banks to lend to politically connected firms; (2) powerful banks will seek to "capture" bank regulators and induce regulators to act in the best interest of banks, not the interest of society at large; and (3) political and legal institutions are generally unable to contain these forces. Thus, a private interest view highlights political failures: the inability of political systems to eliminate the rent seeking behavior of politicians or to protect bank supervisors from the corrupting influence of powerful bankers. From this perspective, political imperfections are a bigger risk for developing an efficient banking system than market imperfections. Indeed, strengthening the authority of bank supervisors in the absence of well-functioning political institutions could very well reduce social welfare rather than address the problems arising from information and transactions costs. In essence, just as the regulations and supervisory practices of a country make more explicit what a bank is, the role of a government in a country makes more explicit what is meant by bank regulation and supervision. The recognition of this fact underlines the analysis in this and the following chapter.

We provide new empirical evidence bearing on this classic debate by using the multicountry laboratory of bank regulation and supervision. Obviously, we do not attempt to resolve this historic feud! Rather, we more modestly assess the merits of these competing views within the narrow context of bank regulation and supervision.

4.A.2. Boundaries

In examining which bank regulatory and supervisory policies work best, we need to inject empirical shape and substance into the terms "work best" and "bank regulation and supervision." In deciding how to make these concepts more concrete, we naturally and necessarily rely on certain definitions and approaches while forgoing still others. The choices we make create boundaries for our analyses with corresponding costs and benefits. In this brief subsection, we explain our choices, advertise the advantages, and discuss the disadvantages.

In defining "work best," we take a broad, inclusive approach that encompasses a variety of outcomes. In particular, we examine the impact of bank regulation and supervision on a range of empirical indicators of overall bank development, bank stability, bank efficiency, bank performance, and integrity (lack of corruption) in bank lending. Thus, we do not choose a single definition of "work best."

This expansive approach has both advantages and disadvantages. The main disadvantage is that we do not select one measure of working best. We do not construct or rely on a single metric for assessing whether a particular policy improves or worsens bank operations. Rather than judge each of the different bank regulatory and supervisory policies along a single yardstick, we assess whether some approaches to bank regulation and supervision are better than others along a spectrum of measures of outcomes reflecting bank development, stability, efficiency, performance, and integrity. This tactic may produce ambiguous results regarding the relative merits of different policies. Some policies may improve bank operations along some dimensions, while adversely affecting bank operations along others. Nevertheless, complex tradeoffs may exist across the different bank regulatory and supervisory policies that this expansive approach will identify and highlight. In doing so, however, this expansive approach will be unable to resolve any ambiguities that arise across the different dimensions of "working best" because we are unwilling to impose weights on the comparative importance of bank development, stability, efficiency, performance, and the degree of corruption in bank lending. This means that we do not provide a single metric of working best.

The advantages to proceeding in this way derive from the same factors that underlay the disadvantages. Any particular policy can influence bank operations in complex, ambiguous ways. A policy can enhance stability and yet reduce efficiency. A regulation may increase the market value of a bank, but undermine the integrity of bank lending (i.e., increase corruption in bank lending). This is the type of information we wish to uncover. We do not wish to bury this information in an aggregate indicator constructed by selecting arbitrary weights for each of the different outcomes reflecting bank development, stability, efficiency, performance, and lending integrity. Moreover, this expansive approach has the potential to yield a very revealing conclusion. If a specific approach to bank regulation and supervision consistently ranks better than other approaches across the entire spectrum of measures of bank development, stability, efficiency, performance, and integrity, then this consistency provides a particularly powerful message about what works best in bank regulation and supervision.

A second boundary that shapes our examination of "What Works Best?" involves the construction of useful empirical proxies of bank regulation and supervision from the enormous dataset presented in Chapter 3. We literally have collected hundreds of rules regarding bank regulation and supervision. Given the scope and detail of information, we had to decide how to proceed to accomplish our goals.

Although we could have examined each of these rules individually, there are considerable limitations and shortcomings with such an approach and corresponding advantages to constructing and analyzing broader indices of key bank regulatory and supervisory policies. First and foremost, an "examine-every-rule" approach does not focus on achieving this chapter's goals: providing the first cross-country empirical evidence on the efficacy of: (1) major banking sector policies, (2) Basel II's three pillars, and (3) the strategic role of government in supervising and regulating banks. In seeking to provide evidence bearing on these broad issues, it is not particularly useful to focus on extremely detailed rules. For example, one could consider the rule for how many days in arrears before a loan is classified as "substandard" versus the rule for how many days before a loan is considered "nonperforming." However, rather than examining an individual rule associated with the classification of loans, we believe one can obtain more useful information by constructing an aggregate index of the stringency of loan classification. As a second example, consider the numerous rules prospective banks are required to comply with to obtain a license. Rather than examine each filing requirement, we can, arguably, obtain more practical and useful policy advice by constructing and analyzing a general index reflecting the many impediments to obtaining a banking license. Although this broad approach might limit guidance on the most efficacious way to reform entry barriers, such an index nevertheless sheds empirical light on the strategic question of whether lowering or raising entry barriers increases bank development, reduces bank fragility, boosts bank efficiency, fosters improved bank performance, and promotes greater integrity in bank lending practices. This type of information should serve to focus any debate over reform where it belongs, first on the need for and general direction of reform, and only after this has been done on the exact details of reform.

Statistical and theoretical issues also provide reasons for using broader indices rather than focusing on an examine-every-rule approach. Many of the individual rules are extremely highly correlated. It is impossible to identify the independent impact of very narrowly defined regulatory rules on bank operations when controlling for numerous other features of the regulatory and supervisory environment. Finally, theory provides guidance on only a few broad concepts of bank regulation and supervision, not on the hundreds of bank regulatory and supervisory rules in our dataset. Theory does not, for example, provide guidance on the optimal loan classification system or on the optimal screening system to be used in granting a banking license. Thus, in seeking to use theory to guide our empirical work, this, too, suggests focusing on a relatively few key measures of bank regulation and supervision.

Abandoning the examine-every-rule approach is not without its costs, however. From a practical perspective, policy makers around the world must choose a combination of bank regulatory and supervisory rules whether theory provides specific guidance on each and every rule or not. This suggests examining all of the rules in our dataset. But this chapter's goal is not to produce a comprehensive checklist of best practice rules. To the contrary, we ultimately argue that such a goal is inadvisable. Instead, this chapter's goal is to provide strategic guidance to policymakers – for example, to inform them about whether they should seek to limit the degree to which banks engage in nonlending financial services. The goal is not to write the country-specific rules associated with implementing this strategy. Given that currently no broad cross-country information exists on bank regulation and supervision, we believe this is a useful initial contribution. At this stage, any guidance beyond this would be presumptuous and, as we show in Chapter 5, potentially nugatory. We thus recognize that our contribution is limited insofar as country-specific analyses will have to bolster, refine, and tailor these findings to national circumstances.

A second weakness with abandoning the examine-every-rule approach is that we are necessarily forced to construct indices. Yet, there is an inherent arbitrariness in constructing indices and in weighting the different components of the indices. For instance, in constructing an index of regulatory restrictions on bank activities, which is composed of rules on banks engaging in securities, insurance, and real estate activities, should the components be given equal weights? Or, should regulatory restrictions on securities activities be treated more importantly than restrictions on real estate? Or, should one use a principal components procedure that constructs a single index that best explains the individual components? The principal component index is objective, but the weights do not reflect conceptual and practical arguments about the comparative importance of the individual components. Although recognizing the problems associated with constructing indices, we confirm this chapter's results using both equally weighted and principal component indices. Moreover, as argued earlier, we believe that constructing indices that measure broad bank regulatory and supervisory policies is a far better way to proceed to achieve this chapter's three objectives than an examine-every-rule approach.

Thus, to examine which bank regulatory and supervisory policies work best, we proceed at four levels. First, we use the key indices developed and discussed in Chapter 3. Specifically, we analyze a broad array of bank regulatory and supervisory policies, including regulatory restrictions on bank activities, regulatory restrictions on the entry of new banks, capital regulations, the power of the supervisory agency to discipline, restructure, and obtain information from banks, the degree to which regulations force banks to disclose reliable, comparable data to the public, the generosity of the deposit insurance scheme, and the degree of government ownership of the banking industry.

Second, we investigate whether specific bank regulatory and supervisory choices work differently in distinct policy, political, and institutional settings. For example, we consider whether a powerful supervisory agency alleviates market imperfections and improves bank operations in an open, competitive political environment, whereas a similarly powerful supervisory agency fosters corruption, inefficient intermediation, and political/regulatory capture under autocratic political institutions. As another example, supervisory strategies designed to improve market discipline of banks through greater information disclosure may need sound political and legal institutions, too. Specifically, private investors may need both information and effective legal mechanisms to exert sound governance over banks. To derive sound inferences about what works best in banking policies, one should consider the possibility that the impact of policies may differ across alternative political and institutional environments.

Third, we focus on Basel II's three pillars. In this regard, we aim the analytical spotlight on assessing the impact of capital regulations, official supervisory power, and market discipline on bank development, stability, efficiency, performance, and integrity. Although we examine an array of bank regulatory and supervisory policies, we focus comparatively greater effort on those indicators of Basel II's three pillars because of the importance of Basel II in the bank supervisory community.

Finally, and at the most general level, we examine supervisory strategies. Here, to repeat, we use the term "strategies" to mean an approach, a guiding principle, or a paradigm. Thus, a bank supervisory strategy represents an overarching philosophy toward bank regulation and supervision. It does not represent an individual rule or policy. To compare empirically different philosophies toward bank regulation and supervision, we assess the relationship between bank development and operations and (1) regulatory and supervisory policies that stress official oversight of and government restrictions on banks and (2) policies that stress private-sector monitoring of banks through information disclosure. In practice, countries do not fall along a simple spectrum from those that focus on private monitoring to those that focus on direct official oversight. For instance, the United States and Japan have both strong bank disclosure rules and official supervisors with ample powers to discipline and monitor banks, whereas Belarus and Guatemala have weak disclosure rules and weak official supervision. Thus, rather than including an index indicating where countries fall along an artificial spectrum from private to official monitoring, we simultaneously include measures of both official supervisory power and private monitoring in assessing which bank supervisory strategies are more effective at boosting bank development, stability, efficiency, performance, and lending integrity.

4.B. BANK REGULATION AND SUPERVISION AND
BANK DEVELOPMENT

4.B.1. Data and Correlations

This section examines the impact of bank regulation and supervision on bank development. We do not begin our investigation by assessing the linkages between bank regulatory and supervisory policies and bank-level measures of efficiency, or firm-level indicators of corporate access to bank credit. Our introductory assessment of what works best starts at the aggregate level by examining the connection between bank regulatory and supervisory policies and a countrywide measure of bank development. Although not without its limitations, this aggregate indicator is designed as a proxy for the functioning of the banking system. Except where noted, the data on bank regulation and supervision are based upon our earlier survey (mostly 1998–1999), rather than the more recent data analyzed in Chapter 3 in order to reduce some of the econometric problems discussed below.

We measure **Bank Development** with a commonly used, country-level indicator that equals credit issued by banks to private sector firms as a share of GDP in 2001.[2] Admittedly, Bank Development has shortcomings. Most important, it does not directly measure what theory and practice suggest that well-functioning banks provide to an economy. Specifically, this banking development indicator does not directly measure the ability of banks to overcome informational asymmetries and hence identify good projects, offer risk management services, lower transactions costs, or exert sound corporate governance over the firms they fund. Nevertheless, Bank Development improves on many existing cross-country measures of financial development. Specifically, unlike many indicators of financial development, Bank Development excludes credit issued to governments, government agencies, and state-owned enterprises. Thus, it measures the

---

[2] Bank Development is computed using data from the International Monetary Fund (International Financial Statistics) using the following formula: $\{(0.5)^*[F(t)/P\_e(t) + F(t-1)/P\_e(t-1)]\}/[GDP(t)/P\_a(t)]$, where F is credit by deposit money banks to the private sector (lines 22d). GDP is line 99b, P_e is end-of period CPI (line 64) and P_a is the average annual CPI. This method carefully deflates the data. The banking data are measured at the end of the period, so we use end of period price indices to deflate them. However, GDP is computed over the period, so we use a separate price index to deflate GDP. After deflating appropriately, we take the average of the real credit variable in period 2001 and 2000 and relate this to real GDP in 2001. This reduces mismeasurement that is common in past studies of banking development.

intermediation of society's savings to private firms. We believe this is a better, albeit still limited, proxy of the degree to which banks ameliorate information and transactions costs than alternative indicators that simply measure the size of the banking industry. Furthermore, past research shows that this specific Bank Development variable is a good predictor of long-run economic growth, which suggests that it exerts a causal impact on growth (Levine, Loayza, and Beck, 2000). Thus, we examine the impact of bank regulatory and supervisory policies on an indicator that significantly helps explain national economic performance. Finally, although it is crucial to examine the linkages between bank regulation and supervision and more microeconomic measures of bank performance, it is natural to start with an aggregate, cross-country study. Thus, we assess which bank regulatory and supervisory policies are associated with higher levels of Bank Development while controlling for potential reverse causality running from bank development to regulatory and supervisory policies.

There are five key observations that emerge from simple correlations of various bank regulatory indicators with (1) Bank Development and (2) Absence of Graft. Absence of Graft measures freedom from official corruption (i.e., the absence of the use of public power for private gain [Table 4.1]), as obtained from Kaufman, Kraay, and Zoido-Lobaton's (1999) database on the functioning of public institutions. The correlations suggest that specific bank regulatory and supervisory policies reflect national approaches to the role of government in the financial sector. Since Chapter 3 extensively defines and discusses the bank regulatory and supervisory indicators, we provide only a brief definition here.

First, greater government ownership of banks is positively associated with policies that reduce competition and restrict international financial integration, and negatively associated with policies that promote transparency and private-sector monitoring of banks. In terms of the specific variables in Table 4.1, Government-Owned Banks is the fraction of the banking systems asset's that are in banks that are 50 percent or more government owned. Entry Applications Denied equals the fraction of applications for commercial banking licenses that have been denied. No Foreign Loans equals one if the regulatory authorities prohibit banks from making loans abroad. The Private Monitoring Index measures the degree to which the regulatory authorities require reliable information disclosure. Specifically, the Private Monitoring Index includes information on whether there is a compulsory external audit, the percentage of large banks that are rated by international credit rating agencies, the reliability of bank financial statements, the transparency of risk management

Table 4.1. *Bank Supervision: Correlations*

	Entry Into Banking Requirements Index	Entry Applications Denied	Capital Regulatory Index	Activities Restrictions	Private Monitoring Index	Moral Hazard Index	Official Supervisory Power	Limitations on Foreign Bank Entry/Ownership	Government Owned Banks	Bank Development
Entry Applications Denied	-0.06 (0.592)	1								
Capital Regulatory Index	0.01 (0.889)	-0.49*** (0.000)	1							
Activities Restrictions	0.07 (0.567)	0.27* (0.051)	-0.20 (0.119)	1						
Private Monitoring Index	-0.17 (0.113)	-0.55*** (0.000)	0.24** (0.022)	0.22* (0.081)	1					
Moral Hazard Index	-0.22 (0.120)	-0.17 (0.269)	0.32** (0.020)	-0.18 (0.222)	0.18 (0.195)	1				
Official Supervisory Power	0.12 (0.238)	0.12 (0.305)	-0.07 (0.524)	-0.05 (0.711)	-0.11 (0.295)	-0.02 (0.896)	1.00			
Limitations on Foreign Bank Entry/Ownership	0.02 (0.824)	0.30*** (0.009)	-0.06 (0.593)	-0.01 (0.942)	-0.23** (0.029)	-0.18 (0.193)	0.08 (0.452)	1.00		
Government Owned Banks	-0.11 (0.321)	0.40*** (0.001)	-0.20* (0.075)	-0.03 (0.850)	-0.39*** (0.000)	-0.03 (0.840)	-0.01 (0.918)	0.28** (0.013)	1.00	
Bank Development	-0.03 (0.808)	-0.34*** (0.007)	0.32*** (0.005)	-0.36*** (0.005)	0.47*** (0.000)	0.04 (0.816)	-0.11 (0.345)	-0.22* (0.050)	-0.40*** (0.001)	1.00
Absence of Graft	-0.19* (0.078)	-0.41*** (0.001)	0.28*** (0.010)	-0.36*** (0.005)	0.45*** (0.000)	0.09 (0.548)	-0.27*** (0.014)	-0.22* (0.048)	-0.29*** (0.013)	0.69*** (0.000)

Notes: P-values are in parentheses.

*, **, *** indicate significance levels of 10, 5, and 1 percent, respectively.

procedures, and whether bank directors are legally liable if information disclosed is erroneous or misleading. As shown in Table 4.1, Government-Owned Banks is positively associated with Entry Applications Denied, positively associated with No Foreign Loans, and negatively associated with Private Monitoring Index. Thus, countries with more government ownership of banks also tend to impose greater restrictions on both competition and international financial integration but develop fewer policies for fostering transparency and private-sector oversight of banks.

Second, we do not observe the complex regulatory tradeoffs stressed by the theoretical models reviewed in Chapter 2. For instance, consider the generosity of the deposit insurance regime, which is measured with the Moral Hazard Index assembled by Demirgüç-Kunt and Detragiache (2002). The Moral Hazard Index is a principal components indicator that is large when there is explicit deposit insurance and even larger when there is no coinsurance, foreign currency deposits are covered, interbank deposits are covered, it is government funded, premiums are not risk-based, membership is voluntary, the government manages the fund, and the coverage limits are great. Thus, the Moral Hazard Index is designed so that higher values imply greater incentives for banks to assume greater risks. From the perspective of a welfare maximizing government, we expected to find that countries that adopt generous deposit insurance regimes (high values of the Moral Hazard Index) would also have powerful official supervisors, extensive private monitoring, and perhaps greater restrictions on bank activities to ameliorate the risk-inducing incentives associated with generous deposit insurance. We did not find this to be the case. Although the generosity of the deposit insurance regime is significantly and positively correlated with the stringency of capital regulations (Capital Regulatory Index), it is not significantly correlated with indices of Private Monitoring or Official Supervisory Power, in which Official Supervisory Power measures the degree to which the supervisory agency has the authority to take a wide array of actions to prevent problems, discipline banks, and correct perceived weaknesses in banks, including the authority to meet with, demand information from, and punish external bank auditors, force banks to disclose information to the supervisor, order the bank's directors to change its organizational structure, constitute loan provisions, suspend dividends, bonuses, fees, declare a bank insolvent, or intervene in a problem bank.

As another example, we did not find that countries with more generous deposit insurance schemes restrict banks from engaging in nonlending activities, where Activities Restrictions measures the degree to which regulations limit banks from conducting securities, insurance, real estate, or nonfinancial sector activities. Thus, we found no evidence of tradeoffs between policies that tend to increase incentives for risk, like generous deposit insurance, and policies that might be expected to curtail excessive risk-taking, such as more intense private and public monitoring or restrictions on the scope of bank activities.

As a final example, we did not find that countries with higher levels of the Private Monitoring Index had significantly lower levels of Official Supervisory Power. Thus, there is not a simple tradeoff between powerful official supervision and private monitoring. Rather, some countries rely almost exclusively on official oversight, whereas others put a correspondingly greater weight on private monitoring without necessarily reducing official supervision.

Third, although not uniform, the correlations suggest that countries tend to fall along a spectrum from those with governments that take a more hands-on approach to bank regulation to those that foster private-sector monitoring of banks. For instance, governments that restrict the entry of new banks (Entry Applications Denied) also tend to limit the range of bank activities (Restrictions on Bank Activity), prohibit banks from making foreign loans (No Foreign Loans), and have a high level of government ownership of banks (Government Ownership). Governments with these "hands-on" policies, however, tend to lack regulations that force information disclosure by banks (Private Monitoring Index).

Fourth, the correlations indicate that countries with more open, private-sector-oriented approaches to regulation and supervision tend to have greater bank development. Specifically, better-developed banks (Bank Development) are associated with higher levels of the Private Monitoring Index, fewer Activity Restrictions, and lower levels of Government Ownership, less stringent restrictions on banks making loans abroad (No Foreign Loans), and lower barriers to new banks entering the domestic market (Entry Applications Denied).

Fifth, the correlations show that government corruption (lower levels of Absence of Graft) tends to be higher in countries where the government plays a large role in supervising, regulating, and owning banks. In particular, Absence of Graft is negatively associated with Entry Applications Denied, Activity Restrictions, Official Supervisory Power, No Foreign Loans, and Government Ownership, whereas Absence of Graft is positively associated with Private Monitoring and Capital Regulations.[3]

---

[3] We find a very strong, positive relationship between corruption and countries with powerful supervisory agencies, tight Activity Restrictions, and entry barriers that limit

These correlations are consistent with, although clearly not a proof of, the private interest view.

Although illustrative, these correlation results do not control for other aspects of regulation and supervision, nor do they control for other country-specific traits, and nor do they control for potential endogeneity. Thus, we turn to the regression results to address these types of issues.

4.B.2. Bank Development and Regulations: Regression Methodology

As a first step, we examine the relationship between bank regulations and bank development using simple cross-country, reduced form analyses. We control for: (a) exogenous determinants of bank development, (b) potential reverse causality running from Bank Development to bank regulations and supervisory practices, and (c) include many bank regulatory and supervisory indicators simultaneously, so we can evaluate the independent relationship between each indicator and bank development conditional on other features of the regulatory regime. We do this in two steps.

First, we examine key bank regulatory and supervisory variables one-at-a-time. We use existing research to identify exogenous determinants of banking development and include these controls in the bank development regressions along with the bank regulatory and supervisory variables. Furthermore, we use instrumental variables to control both for endogeneity and biases due to errors in measuring bank regulation and supervision. We obtain the same results using simple ordinary least squares regressions that do not use instruments, and the results are robust to controlling for a wide array of exogenous determinants of bank development. Thus, Table 4.2 contains regressions based on the following system:

$$\text{Bank Development} = \alpha + \beta s + \gamma X + u \qquad (4.1)$$
$$s = \delta Z + \varepsilon,$$

where s is one of the bank regulatory and supervisory indicators, X is a matrix of exogenous determinants of Bank Development, Z is a set of instrumental variables for the bank supervision/regulation variables,

competition and a negative relationship between corruption and countries that promote private-sector monitoring of banks when (1) controlling for many other country characteristics and (2) using instrumental variables. Rather than pursue this line of investigation here using aggregate data, we examine the supervision-corruption link below using firm-level data so that we can directly examine corruption in lending, not aggregate corruption.

both u and ε are error terms, and where α, β, γ, and δ are the estimated parameters. The system is estimated using two-stage least squares with standard errors that are robust to heteroskedasticity. Because we use more instrumental variables (Z) than endogenous regressors (s), we test the validity of the instruments using a test of the overidentifying restrictions (OIR-test). The OIR-tests assesses whether the instrumental variables are uncorrelated with the error term (u). The economic meaning of these conditions is that the instrumental variables only affect the dependent variable through the explanatory variables. Under the null hypothesis that the instruments are uncorrelated with the error term, the test is distributed as χ^2 with degrees of freedom equal to the number instruments minus the number of regressors. If the data do not reject the null hypothesis – if the specification passes the OIR-test – then the data do not reject the validity of the instrumental variables.

In selecting X, the matrix of exogenous determinants of Bank Development, we include dummy variables for each country's legal origin. La Porta, Lopez-de-Silanes, Shleifer, and Vishny (1998) argue that (1) legal origins differ in terms of the priority they attach to the rights of private investors and (2) the protection of these rights form the basis of financial contracting and hence financial development. From this perspective, historically determined differences in legal origin help explain international differences in financial development today. According to this view, the English common law evolved to protect private property owners against the crown. This facilitated the ability of private property owners to transact confidently, with positive repercussions on financial development. In contrast, the French and German civil codes in the nineteenth century were designed to solidify state power. Over time, state dominance produced legal traditions that focused more on the power of the state and less on the rights of individual investors. According to this law and finance hypothesis, these legal traditions spread throughout the world through conquest, colonization, and imitation, so that much of the international differences in financial development today can be traced back to different legal traditions. Empirical evidence confirms these predictions.[4] In the data, legal origin is the source of each country's Company Law or Commercial Code. For each country in their sample, La Porta, Lopez-de-Silanes, Shleifer, and Vishny (1999) indicate whether the national

---

[4] For empirical evidence, see La Porta, Lopez-de-Silanes, Shleifer, and Vishny (1997, 1999), along with Levine (1998, 1999) and Beck, Demirgüç-Kunt, and Levine (2001, 2003a, 2004a, 2005a). For reviews of the literature on legal origins and finance, see Beck and Levine (2005) and Levine (2005b).

legal system derives from one of five possible legal origins: English Common Law, French Civil Law, German Civil Law, Scandinavian Civil Code, and Socialist Law. To assess the independent link between bank development and bank regulatory and supervisory practices, therefore, we include dummy variables for each legal origin in the bank development regressions.[5]

We base our selection of the instrumental variables, Z, on both theory and recent empirical work. First, religious composition may shape governmental approaches to regulation and supervision. Specifically, Landes (1998), Putnam (1993), and Weber (1958) argue that the Catholic and Muslim religions tend to produce comparatively centralized, hierarchical, and powerful governments. In turn, these centralized, strong governments may exert a powerful influence on the banking sector through tight regulations and powerful official supervisory agencies. According to this view, Catholic and Muslim countries will tend to use regulatory restrictions and powerful supervisory agencies to guide credit allocation decisions. This is what we find when examining the relationship between the instrumental variables and the regulatory indicators. Countries where a higher fraction of the population is Catholic or Muslim tend to have greater restrictions on bank activities and more powerful official supervisory agencies. Thus, we include measures of religious composition as instrumental variables.

---

[5] Scandinavian legal origin is the omitted dummy variable. Because of data limitations, there are some regressions in which there are no Socialist legal origin countries. We also considered a wide array of other control variables to assess the robustness of the results. For instance, Stulz and Williamson (2003) find that a country's dominant religion influences financial development. They argue that the Muslim and Catholic religions foster vertical bonds of authority that concentrate power in the hands of small political elite and this centralized command thwarts the development of competitive financial systems. Similarly, Easterly and Levine (1997) argue that ethnic diversity makes it difficult for the different groups in a society to agree on the provision of public goods, including the rule of law and the protection of private property rights that underlie financial development. Finally, as discussed later, tropical climates were frequently not conducive to European settlers. Consequently, there was a greater tendency in tropical environments for Europeans to establish extractive regimes (Acemoglu, Johnson, and Robinson, 2001). These extractive regimes frequently involved a small European elite that used indigenous or slave labor to enrich the Europeans. These extractive regimes fostered the creation of institutions that protected the elite and were antithetical to broad-based property rights enforcement, competition, and private contracting. According to this view, these institutions endured well after colonization ended, so that tropical climates are still plagued by institutions that do not support financial development and entrepreneurship. When we include measures of each country's religious composition, ethnic diversity, and distance from the equator as proxy for the absence of a tropical environment, these additional controls do not alter the results.

To measure religious composition, we use La Porta, Lopez-de-Silanes, Shleifer, and Vishny's (1999) measure of the percentage of the population in each country that is Roman Catholic, Protestant, Muslim, or belongs to "other denominations." The numbers are in percent and sum to 100 (so we omit Protestant from the regressions).

Second, economists, historians, and biogeographers emphasize the impact of geography on economic institutions that influence banking development through a number of channels. Diamond (1997) emphasizes that lands with poor agricultural yields – such as the tropics – do not support large-scale farming. Because the surpluses generated from efficient farming permit some individuals to specialize in nonsubsistence activities, rich geographical environments are particularly conducive to the development of complex institutions. Thus, countries close to the equator may be less likely to develop a wide array of institutions associated with supporting private property and economic interactions. Similarly, Engerman and Sokoloff (1997), Acemoglu, Johnson, and Robinson (2001), and Easterly and Levine (2003) stress that geographical endowments encountered by Europeans as they conquered much of the world influenced the creation of institutions that endured long after the fall of colonization. For instance, tropical climates were frequently not conducive to European settlers. Consequently, there was a greater tendency in tropical environments for Europeans to establish extractive regimes (Acemoglu, Johnson, and Robinson, 2001), which frequently involved a small elite using indigenous or slave labor to extract natural resources or grow crops for export. These extractive regimes fostered the creation of institutions that protected the elite from the general population and were antithetical to broad-based property rights enforcement, competition, private contracting, and representative government. From this perspective, these institutions endured well after colonization ended, so that tropical climates are still plagued by institutions that do not support competitive financial development. Beck, Demirgüç-Kunt, and Levine (2003a) provide empirical confirmation of this theory. Thus, as an instrument for bank regulation and supervision, we use latitudinal distance from the equator. From these theories and past empirical work, we expect that countries in a tropical environment will rely less on regulatory policies that promote transparent information disclosure and more on policies that rely on powerful official supervisors with close ties to the ruling elite. Consistent with these theories, the first-stage regression results indicate that countries farther away from the equator tend to have fewer regulatory restrictions on bank activities or bank entry, more regulations designed to facilitate private monitoring, and less powerful official supervisory agencies.

Finally, the other explanatory variables in the equation – the legal origin variables – are naturally included as instruments for the endogenous variables (the regulatory/supervisory variables).[6] As noted, La Porta, Lopez-de-Silanes, Shleifer, and Vishny (1998) argue that civil law and socialist law countries will tend to support stronger governments relative to private property to a greater degree than common law countries. Thus, legal origin also may influence approaches to bank regulation and supervision.[7]

For the instruments to be valid, they must (1) explain cross-country differences in bank regulation and supervision and (2) pass the OIR-test described above. As noted throughout the regressions, the instruments pass the OIR-test in all of the Bank Development regressions. Furthermore, the instruments explain cross-country variation in bank regulation. In all cases, we reject the null hypothesis that the excluded instruments (the instruments not included in the second stage regression) do not explain the bank regulation variable. Thus, although we do not present a theory linking these instruments directly to bank regulatory decisions, the instrumental variables pass the standard validity tests.

Readers may wonder why we do not control for economic development in these analyses. These instrumental variable regressions are designed to illustrate the relationship between the exogenous component of bank regulation and bank development. They are reduced form specifications in that we focus on controlling for potential exogenous determinants of bank development. Therefore, we do not control for economic development. Past work shows that bank development exerts a causal impact on economic development (Beck, Levine, and Loayza, 2000). Thus, if we want to control for economic development in the bank development regressions below, we would need to build a structural model

---

[6] For a discussion of both the endowment and law views on the development of financial and property rights systems, see Levine (2005b).

[7] The results hold when using an alternative set of instrumental variables that measures the percentage of years since 1776 that the country has been independent instead of the religious composition variables. As noted, European colonizers may have strongly influenced the formation of national institutions around the world. This influence, however, may wane over time. Thus, we use the percentage of years since 1776 that the country had been independent as an empirical measure of the country's ability to form its own independent institutions.

and use valid instrumental variables to extract the exogenous component of economic development. Rather than pursue this route, we simply use instrumental variables to extract the exogenous component of bank regulation and evaluate the relationship between this exogenous component of bank regulation and bank development while controlling for exogenous determinants of bank development. Thus, these cross-country regressions must be interpreted cautiously. In the microeconomic-based regressions later, we control for many country characteristics, including the level of economic development.

The second step in assessing the impact of bank regulation and supervision on bank development involves the simultaneous inclusion of numerous bank regulation and supervision indices. Rather than examine the bank regulation and supervision indicators one at a time, we include them together in the Bank Development regression. Unfortunately, we do not have a sufficient number of powerful instrumental variables to conduct this multivariate analysis using instrumental variables. Similarly, if we had a time-series on the bank regulatory and supervisory variables, we could use panel techniques that would allow us to examine many banking policy variables simultaneously while controlling for endogeneity. Although we have started the process of collecting bank supervision and regulatory variables over time, we do not yet have sufficient time-series information to move to panel estimation of the impact of banking policies on Bank Development. Thus, this second step in the analysis involves running the following ordinary least squares regression:

$$\text{Bank Development} = \alpha + \beta S + \gamma X + u, \tag{4.2}$$

where S is a matrix of bank supervision/regulation indicators and now β represents a vector of parameter estimates on these bank regulation and supervision variables. We use the same exogenous controls, X, as before. For simplicity, equation 4.2 uses similar Greek symbols to represent parameter estimates as equation 4.1, but the estimates will obviously take on different values in the two equations.

4.B.3. Bank Development and Regulations: Regression Results

The results from the instrumental variables regressions in Table 4.2 communicate a clear message about the: (1) proper role of government in the banking industry, (2) the Basel II recommendations, and (3) specific

Table 4.2. *Part A: Bank Development and Supervision: Controlling for Endogeneity*

	(1)	(2)	(3)	(4)	(5)	(6)
Legal Origin – Common	0.425 (0.719)	0.302 (0.261)	0.179 (0.471)	0.098 (0.730)	0.032 (0.871)	−0.087 (0.786)
Legal Origin – French	0.331 (0.766)	0.071 (0.756)	−0.007 (0.975)	0.018 (0.950)	0.088 (0.674)	−0.259 (0.416)
Legal Origin – German	0.745 (0.428)	0.611 (0.011)**	0.493 (0.043)**	0.491 (0.115)	0.421 (0.085)*	−0.093 (0.845)
Legal Origin – Socialist	0.291 (0.826)	−0.371 (0.065)*	−0.250 (0.310)	−0.010 (0.974)	−0.237 (0.245)	−0.302 (0.449)
Entry Into Banking Requirements Index	−0.485 (0.485)					
Limitations on Foreign Bank Entry/Ownership		−0.504 (0.026)**				
Entry Applications Denied			−1.535 (0.008)***			
Private Monitoring Index				0.340 (0.003)***		
Activities Restrictions					−0.282 (0.001)***	
Capital Regulatory Index						0.720 (0.096)*
Constant	0.119 (0.918)	0.687 (0.001)***	0.766 (0.001)***	0.411 (0.143)	0.468 (0.017)**	0.639 (0.030)**
Observations	70	55	55	70	69	69
O.I.R. P-value	0.2168	0.3325	0.4392	0.2496	0.2133	0.9173

Notes: The dependent variable is Bank Development.
Estimated using Two Stage Least Squares.
Instruments used are (a) Latitude and (b) the fraction of the population that is Catholic, (c) the fraction that is Muslim, and (d) the fraction that is Non-Protestant. The omitted category is the fraction of the population that is Protestant.
P-values are in parentheses.
*, **, *** indicate significance levels of 10, 5, and 1 percent, respectively.
O.I.R.: Test of overidentifying restrictions, that is, it assesses whether the instrumental variables are correlated with Bank Development beyond their association with the supervisory strategy variables. Thus, a low reported P-value rejects the validity of the instrumental variables.

bank regulatory and supervisory policies in terms of their relationship with aggregate Bank Development.

First and foremost, supervisory policies that strengthen the rights of private sector monitors of banks are associated with higher levels of bank development. We find a positive relationship between bank

Table 4.2. *Part B: Bank Development and Supervision: Controlling for Endogeneity*

	(1)	(2)	(3)	(4)	(5)	(6)
Legal Origin – Common	0.360 (0.470)	0.546 (0.193)	0.730 (0.528)	−0.628 (0.362)	−0.178 (0.491)	0.271 (0.397)
Legal Origin – French	0.062 (0.881)	0.555 (0.158)	0.706 (0.534)	−0.590 (0.323)	−0.196 (0.358)	0.135 (0.625)
Legal Origin – German	0.144 (0.747)	1.403 (0.006)***	2.200 (0.301)	−1.073 (0.636)	0.440 (0.103)	0.818 (0.034)**
Legal Origin – Socialist		0.407 (0.372)	1.290 (0.538)	−2.140 (0.370)	−0.430 (0.042)**	0.163 (0.706)
Moral Hazard Index	0.244 (0.274)					
Official Supervisory Power		−0.429 (0.032)**				
Prompt Corrective Power Index			−1.839 (0.395)			
Multiple Supervisory Agencies				3.857 (0.456)		
Supervisory Independence Banks					0.065 (0.823)	
Government Owned Banks						−3.142 (0.027)**
Constant	0.450 (0.230)	−0.041 (0.912)	−0.076 (0.940)	0.687 (0.000)***	0.252 (0.474)	0.916 (0.000)***
Observations	46	70	68	70	69	61
O.I.R P-value	0.5503	0.3167	0.7271	0.9737	0.1103	0.8434

Note: The dependent variable is Bank Development.
Estimated using Two Stage Least Squares.
Instruments used are (a) Latitude and (b) the fraction of the population that is Catholic, (c) the fraction that is Muslim, and (d) the fraction that is Non-Protestant. The omitted category is the fraction of the population that is Protestant.
P-values are in parentheses.
*, **, *** indicate significance levels of 10, 5, and 1 percent, respectively.
O.I.R.: Test of over-identifying restrictions, that is, it assesses whether the instrumental variables are correlated with Bank development beyond their association with the supervisory strategy variables. Thus, a low reported P-value rejects the validity of the instrumental variables.

development and regulations that boost private monitoring when controlling for simultaneity bias (Table 4.2), and when controlling for other features of the regulatory and supervisory regime (Table 4.3). Although many fear that countries with poorly developed capital markets, accounting

Table 4.3. *Bank Development and Supervision – Multivariate Analysis*

	(1)	(2)
Capital Regulatory Index	0.058	0.022
	(0.114)	(0.598)
Private Monitoring	0.110	0.102
	(0.001)***	(0.003)***
Official Supervisory Power	−0.022	0.003
	(0.503)	(0.941)
Entry Into Banking Requirements Index	0.018	0.011
	(0.527)	(0.683)
Activities Restrictions	−0.134	−0.151
	(0.001)***	(0.002)***
Government Owned Banks		−0.175
		(0.287)
Legal Origin – Common	0.054	−0.000
	(0.780)	(1.000)
Legal Origin – French	0.029	0.024
	(0.883)	(0.912)
Legal Origin – German	0.446	0.440
	(0.051)*	(0.075)*
Legal Origin – Socialist	−0.203	−0.249
	(0.305)	(0.262)
Constant	0.473	0.515
	(0.013)**	(0.018)**
Observations	69	61
R-squared	0.552	0.588

Notes: The dependent variable is Bank Development.
Estimated using Ordinary Least Squares with robust standard errors.
P-values are in parentheses.
*, **, *** indicate significance levels of 10, 5, and 1 percent, respectively.

standards, and legal systems will be unable to rely on private monitoring, our results emphasize that the exogenous component of Private Monitoring is positively associated with Bank Development. The positive connection between Bank Development and regulations that force reliable, comparable information disclosure moreover holds even when accounting for a wide array of other banking sector policies. In complementary research, La Porta et al. (2005) find that securities market regulations that induce information disclosure promote stock market development. Our results on strengthening private sector monitoring of banks emphasize the importance of regulations that make it easier for private investors to

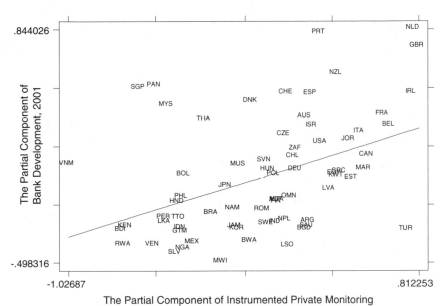

Figure 4.1. Bank Development and the Exogenous Component of Private Monitoring. *Notes:* This is the partial scatter plot of regression 4 in Table 4.2, Part A, which is a two-stage least squares regression of Bank Development in 2001 against Private Monitoring in 1999. The included exogenous variables in the second stage are the dummy variables for legal origin. The excluded instrumental variables are Latitude and the percentage of the population that is Catholic, Muslim, or another non-Protestant religion.

acquire reliable information about banks and exert discipline over banks.[8] This finding underscores Basel II's third pillar.

Figures 4.1 and 4.2 illustrate the robust, positive relationship between Private Monitoring and Bank Development while controlling for endogeneity and the potential impact of outliers.[9] Figure 4.1 projects the second stage of Table 4.2's two-stage least squares regression with Private Monitoring into the two-dimensional space spanned by Bank Development and Private Monitoring. Specifically, to construct this figure, first compute the predicted value of Private Monitoring from the first stage

---

[8] We do not find a robust relationship between the generousity of the deposit insurance regime and Bank Development, but see Cull et al. (2005).

[9] The construction of Figures 4.1 to 4.8 is somewhat complicated. We include the step-by-step guidance for Figure 4.1 in the text but not in the notes to Figure 4.1 so that the reader will have a sense of how to interpret these figures, but the precise instructions for Figures 4.2 to 4.8 will only be found in the notes to each figure.

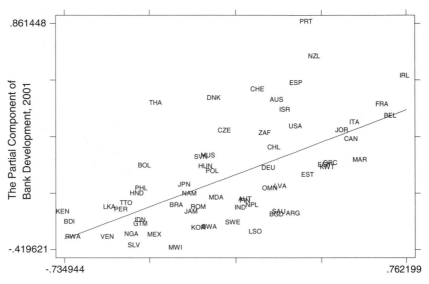

The Partial Component of Instrumented Private Monitoring

Figure 4.2. Bank Development and the Exogenous Component of Private Monitoring, Outliers Removed. *Notes:* After removing Malaysia, The Netherlands, Panama, Singapore, Turkey, the United Kingdom, and Vietnam, this is the partial scatter plot of Bank Development in 2001 against Private Monitoring in 1999. The included exogenous variables in the second stage are the dummy variables for legal origin. The excluded instrumental variables are Latitude and the percentage of the population that is Catholic, Muslim, or another non-Protestant religion. To construct this figure, first compute the predicted value of Private Monitoring from the first stage regression. Second, regress Bank Development on the included exogenous variables and collect the residuals. This is called the partial component of Bank Development. Third, regress predicted values of Private Monitoring from the first stage regression on the included exogenous variables and collect the residuals. This is called the partial component of the instrumented Private Monitoring. Finally, plot the partial component of Bank Development against the partial component of Instrumented Private Monitoring. This represents the two-dimensional representation of the regression plane in Bank Development – Private Monitoring space while controlling for the endogeneity of Private Monitoring.

regression. Second, regress these predicted values of Private Monitoring from the first stage regression on the included exogenous variables and collect the residuals. This is called the partial component of instrumented Private Monitoring. Third, regress Bank Development on the included exogenous variables and collect the residuals. This is called the partial component of Bank Development. Finally, plot the partial component of Bank Development against the partial component of instrumented

Private Monitoring. For each observation, the figures provide the three-letter country code (Appendix 9 gives the country names and codes). Thus, Figure 4.1 presents the two-dimensional representation of the regression plane in Bank Development–Private Monitoring space while controlling for the endogeneity of Private Monitoring.

After controlling for the impact of particularly influential observations, we confirm the positive impact of regulations that enhance private monitoring of banks on overall bank development. To control for potential outliers, we redo Figure 4.1 after eliminating particularly influential observations. Specifically, we run the regression excluding each country one at a time and compute the change in the estimated coefficient on Private Monitoring. Using the standard metric of "particularly influential," which tests whether the absolute value of the change in the estimated coefficient is greater than two divided by the square root of the number of observations, we eliminate particularly influential countries. The procedure identifies Malaysia, the Netherlands, Panama, Singapore, Turkey, the United Kingdom, and Vietnam as outliers. After eliminating these outliers, Figure 4.2 again provides the two-dimensional regression relationship between Private Monitoring and Bank Development. Again, the analyses suggest a positive relationship between the exogenous component of Private Monitoring and Bank Development. Private Monitoring enters significantly at the 5 percent significance level.

The second finding from these introductory cross-country regressions is that there is no support for the view that official supervisory power exerts a positive impact on overall banking sector development (Table 4.2). Rather, official supervisory power enters negatively in the instrumental variable regressions. These instrumental variable results are consistent with the view that powerful supervisors exert a negative influence on bank development. Indeed, Kane (1990), Boot and Thakor (1993), Shleifer and Vishny (1998), and Djankov et al. (2002) all stress that powerful supervisors may use their powers to benefit specific constituencies, with deleterious implications for overall banking development.

Figures 4.3 and 4.4 illustrate the negative relationship between official supervisory power and Bank Development while controlling for endogeneity and outliers. Figure 4.3 graphs the negative relationship between official supervisory power and bank development documented in Table 4.2. Figure 4.4 shows that this negative relationship is robust to controlling for particularly influential observations.

However, we must be cautious in interpreting the negative relationship between official supervisory power and bank development.

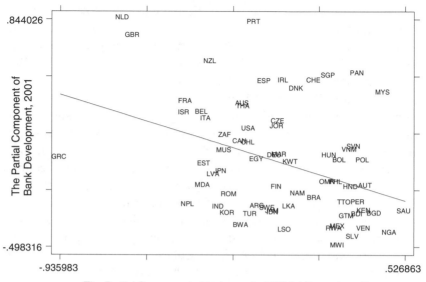

The Partial Component of Instrumented Official Supervisory Power

Figure 4.3. Bank Development and the Exogenous Component of Official Supervisory Power. *Notes:* This is the partial scatter plot of regression 2 in Table 4.2, Part A, Part B, which is a two-stage least squares regression of Bank Development in 2001 against Official Supervisory Power in 1999. The included exogenous variables in the second stage are the dummy variables for legal origin. The excluded instrumental variables are Latitude and the percentage of the population that is Catholic, Muslim, or another non-Protestant religion. To construct this figure, first compute the predicted value of Official Supervisory Power from the first stage regression. Second, regress Bank Development on the included exogenous variables and collect the residuals. This is called the partial component of Bank Development. Third, regress predicted values of Official Supervisory Power from the first stage regression on the included exogenous variables and collect the residuals. This is called the partial component of the instrumented Official Supervisory Power. Finally, plot the partial component of Bank Development against the partial component of Instrumented Official Supervisory Power. This represents the two-dimensional representation of the regression plane in Bank Development – Official Supervisory Power space while controlling for the endogeneity of Official Supervisory Power.

Official supervisory power is sufficiently correlated with other features of the regulatory and supervisory regime, so that the significance of the Bank Development-Official Supervisory Power relationship vanishes in the multivariate framework (Table 4.3). Thus, although it is difficult to argue from these regressions that strengthening official supervisors impedes bank development, these simple cross-country comparisons

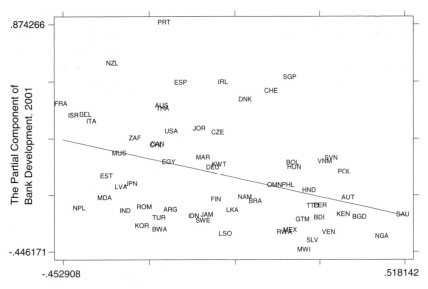

The Partial Component of Instrumented Official Supervisory Power

Figure 4.4. Bank Development and the Exogenous Component of Official Supervisory Power, Outliers Removed. *Notes:* After removing Greece, Malaysia, the Netherlands, Panama, and the United Kingdom, this is the partial scatter plot of Bank Development in 2001 against Official Supervisory Power in 1999. The included exogenous variables in the second stage are the dummy variables for legal origin. The excluded instrumental variables are Latitude and the percentage of the population that is Catholic, Muslim, or another non-Protestant religion. To construct this figure, first compute the predicted value of Official Supervisory Power from the first stage regression. Second, regress Bank Development on the included exogenous variables and collect the residuals. This is called the partial component of Bank Development. Third, regress predicted values of Official Supervisory Power from the first stage regression on the included exogenous variables and collect the residuals. This is called the partial component of the instrumented Official Supervisory Power. Finally, plot the partial component of Bank Development against the partial component of Instrumented Official Supervisory Power. This represents the two-dimensional representation of the regression plane in Bank Development – Official Supervisory Power space while controlling for the endogeneity of Official Supervisory Power.

clearly do not support the contention that official supervisory power improves banking sector development by overcoming informational barriers and improving the governance of banks. These findings therefore do not provide empirical support for Basel II's second pillar.

We also examine whether an increase in official supervisory power has a positive – or less of a negative – impact in certain political and institutional environments. Specifically, if countries develop mechanisms that constrain politicians from inducing bank supervisors to behave in politically expedient ways, then this will increase the likelihood that strengthening official supervision will improve the governance of banks and hence boost overall banking sector development. Thus, we present ordinary least squares regressions of the following form:

$$\text{Bank Development} = \alpha + \beta s + \gamma X + \delta s^* p + \lambda p + u, \qquad (4.3)$$

where p is a proxy measure for political constraints on the government.

We experiment with numerous interaction terms, that is, we use many different variables for p. Table 4.4 report the results with five of these, including measures from the Polity IV database (Marshal and Jaggers) on: (1) Executive Constraints, which measures the degree to which institutional constraints limit executive authority; (2) Executive Openness, which measures the degree to which hereditary succession is important; (3) Executive Competition, which measures the degree of competition in executive elections; and (4) Democratic-Autocracy, which measures the degree of democracy, relative to autocracy. We also examine Voice and Accountability, which measures the degree to which average citizens have a voice in the political process and the degree of accountability on the part of politicians (Kaufmann, Kraay, and Zoido-Lobaton, 1999). In unreported robustness checks, we also examined two measures of the openness of the media, as an independent media may reduce political/regulatory capture by exposing illegal or inappropriate behavior. Specifically, we considered (a) the degree to which the media is privately owned and (b) the degree to which the government represses the media (Djankov, McLiesh, Nenova, and Shleifer, 2003). In additional, unreported tests, we included the interaction of official supervisory power with private monitoring to assess whether official supervisory power facilitates private monitoring and vice versa. Although each of these eight measures is imperfect, we use them collectively to test whether official supervision works well in certain political/institutional contexts.

We find mixed evidence for the proposition that official supervisory power boosts bank development in specific political, media, and regulatory contexts (Table 4.4). For the cases of (a) Constraints on the Executive and (b) Democracy-Autocracy, official supervision exerts less of a negative impact on Bank Development in countries where there are sufficiently effective constraints on executive power and a sufficiently high

Table 4.4. *Bank Development and Supervision with Interaction Terms*

	(1)	(2)	(3)	(4)	(5)
Legal Origin – Common	−0.078 (0.711)	−0.089 (0.674)	0.075 (0.730)	−0.055 (0.793)	−0.045 (0.826)
Legal Origin – French	−0.083 (0.699)	−0.100 (0.644)	0.083 (0.718)	−0.062 (0.773)	−0.055 (0.795)
Legal Origin – German	0.494 (0.044)**	0.528 (0.028)**	0.520 (0.031)**	0.588 (0.013)**	0.617 (0.009)***
Legal Origin – Socialist	−0.296 (0.209)	−0.282 (0.224)	−0.123 (0.624)	−0.237 (0.309)	−0.271 (0.236)
Official Supervisory Power	−0.228 (0.004)***	−0.105 (0.005)***	−0.056 (0.314)	−0.160 (0.073)*	−0.099 (0.337)
Executive Constraints	0.040 (0.122)				
Official Supervisory Power* Executive Constraints	0.031 (0.036)**				
Democracy-Autocracy		0.008 (0.324)			
Official Supervisory Power* Democracy-Autocracy		0.009 (0.073)*			
Voice & Accountability			0.193 (0.004)***		
Official Supervisory Power* Voice & Accountability			0.036 (0.510)		
Executive Competition				0.067 (0.126)	
Official Supervisory Power* Executive Competition				0.040 (0.266)	
Executive Openness					0.081 (0.002)***
Official Supervisory Power* Executive Openness					0.014 (0.647)
Constant	0.387 (0.139)	0.578 (0.009)***	0.379 (0.104)	0.419 (0.079)*	0.289 (0.194)
Observations	71	71	72	71	71
R-squared	0.302	0.283	0.420	0.281	0.298

Notes: The dependent variable is Bank Development.
Estimated using Ordinary Least Squares with robust standard errors.
P-values are in parentheses.
*, **, *** indicate significance levels of 10, 5, and 1 percent, respectively.

degree of democracy.[10] For instance, even in countries with the highest level of constraints on the executive (i.e., a value of seven), such as the United States, Germany, the United Kingdom, Japan, Italy, Canada, and Spain, the combined effect of the direct negative impact of official supervisory power, (β), and the positive interactive effect with constraints on the executive, (δ), is still negative. Thus, the inflection point is higher than the maximum possible value of constraints on the executive. The evidence suggests that constraints on the executive mitigate the adverse effects of official supervisory power but does not eliminate it. Moreover, we classify these findings as mixed because none of the other interaction terms, including the results on media ownership and repression and private monitoring, enters significantly.

A third result from these exploratory cross-country regressions relates to Basel II's first pillar. The data provide mixed results on the relationship between capital regulations and bank development, as shown in Tables 4.2 and 4.3. The capital regulatory index enters positively and significantly at the 10 percent level in Table 4.2. This is illustrated in Figure 4.5. Furthermore, when removing particularly influential observations, the capital regulatory index enters significantly at the 5 percent level in the instrumental variables regression. This is graphed in Figure 4.6. However, the capital regulatory index does not enter significantly in the multivariate setting, as reported in Table 4.3. This suggests that the capital regulatory index does not enjoy an independent link with Bank Development after controlling for other features of the bank regulatory and supervisory environment. Although traditional approaches to bank regulation and supervision emphasize the positive role of capital adequacy requirements in promoting bank stability, we included capital regulations in this initial assessment of the determinants of overall bank development for completeness. We examine the connections between capital regulations and bank stability later.

Fourth, we examine the contentious issue of government ownership of banks. On the one hand, government ownership may ameliorate a number of market failures. In the presence of market distortions, private banks may invest in socially suboptimal ways. In contrast, government-owned banks focused on maximizing social welfare may not respond to market distortions and therefore will improve the allocation of capital above what it would be with only privately owned banks. Similarly, if the government

---

[10] Specifically, the interaction term (s * p) enters with a positive and significant coefficient (δ), but the effect is limited.

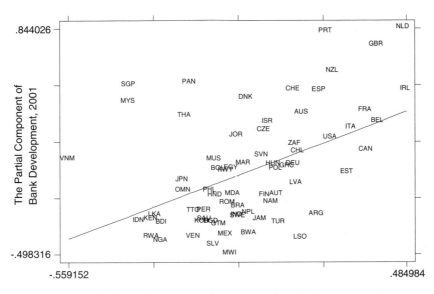

The Partial Component of Instrumented Capital Regulatory Index

Figure 4.5. Bank Development and the Exogenous Component of Capital Regulatory Index. *Notes:* This is the partial scatter plot of regression 6 in Table 4.2, Part A, which is a two-stage least squares regression of Bank Development in 2001 against Capital Regulatory Index in 1999. The included exogenous variables in the second stage are the dummy variables for legal origin. The excluded instrumental variables are Latitude and the percentage of the population that is Catholic, Muslim, or another non-Protestant religion. To construct this figure, first compute the predicted value of Capital Regulatory Index from the first stage regression. Second, regress Bank Development on the included exogenous variables and collect the residuals. This is called the partial component of Bank Development. Third, regress predicted values of Capital Regulatory Index from the first stage regression on the included exogenous variables and collect the residuals. This is called the partial component of the instrumented Capital Regulatory Index. Finally, plot the partial component of Bank Development against the partial component of Instrumented Capital Regulatory Index. This represents the two-dimensional representation of the regression plane in Bank Development – Capital Regulatory Index space while controlling for the endogeneity of the Capital Regulatory Index.

has better information about investment opportunities, it can improve the allocation of resources through government-owned banks. Furthermore, government-owned banks may hold a unique position in terms of coordinating externality-rich activities that a private bank would not undertake because of its inability to identify or internalize the benefits. On the other hand, governments may not have superior information. Moreover, even

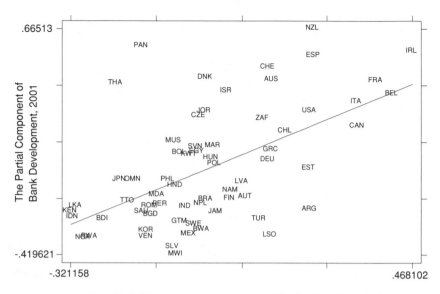

The Partial Component of Instrumented Capital Regulatory Index

Figure 4.6. Bank Development and the Exogenous Component of Capital Regulatory Index, Outliers Removed. *Notes:* After removing Malaysia, the Netherlands, Portugal, Singapore, the United Kingdom, and Vietnam, this is the partial scatter plot of Bank Development in 2001 against the Capital Regulatory Index in 1999. The included exogenous variables in the second stage are the dummy variables for legal origin. The excluded instrumental variables are Latitude and the percentage of the population that is Catholic, Muslim, or another non-Protestant religion. To construct this figure, first compute the predicted value of Capital Regulatory Index from the first stage regression. Second, regress Bank Development on the included exogenous variables and collect the residuals. This is called the partial component of Bank Development. Third, regress predicted values of Capital Regulatory Index from the first stage regression on the included exogenous variables and collect the residuals. This is called the partial component of the instrumented Capital Regulatory Index. Finally, plot the partial component of Bank Development against the partial component of Instrumented Capital Regulatory Index. This represents the two-dimensional representation of the regression plane in Bank Development–Capital Regulatory Index space while controlling for the endogeneity of the Capital Regulatory Index.

if they have better information, governments may not use the information in a socially productive manner. Government ownership of banks may politicize capital allocation and facilitate the financing of politically attractive projects without taking full account of risk-return factors.

The data do not support the view that government ownership of banks boosts banking sector development (Tables 4.2 and 4.3). The regression results indicate that the degree of government ownership of the banking industry lowers Bank Development, as exemplified in the instrumental variable regressions. However, the fraction of bank assets held by government controlled banks (Government Owned Banks) is so correlated with other characteristics of the policy environment that it does not enter significantly when controlling for other bank regulatory and supervisory policies. Thus, governments taking a hands-on approach to the banking sector, which includes government ownership as well as powerful official supervision, limits on entry, and restrictions on bank activities, do not foster greater banking development.

Fifth, we examine regulatory restrictions on the ability of banks to own nonfinancial firms and engage in securities market, insurance industry, and real estate activities (Activity Restrictions). Some theories emphasize that fewer regulatory restrictions permit banks to exploit economies of scale and scope in providing a wide array of financial services to clients (Claessens and Klingelbiel, 2000). Others disagree and instead emphasize that large financial conglomerates: (1) reduce competition and hence efficiency, (2) exert a distorting political influence that reduces the effectiveness of bank supervision, and (3) are complex and more difficult to monitor, so that allowing banks to engage in a diverse set of nonlending activities adversely affects the governance of banks.

The results indicate that regulatory restrictions on bank activities retard Bank Development. Figure 4.7 illustrates the instrumental variable results from Table 4.2. Furthermore, Figure 4.8 shows that this relationship is robust to controlling for potential outliers. Moreover, the negative relationship between regulatory restrictions on bank activities and overall banking sector development also holds in the instrumental variables regressions and the multivariable setup.

Sixth, we examine regulatory restrictions on the entrance of new banks. Some argue that effective screening of potential new bank entrants can promote the safety and soundness of the banking sector by reducing the entry of low quality bankers and by keeping the number of banks aligned with official supervisory capabilities. Others hold that monopolistic profits in banking are beneficial insofar as they reduce incentives for banks to engage in excessively risky behavior (Keeley, 1990). In contrast, regulatory restrictions on entry can protect inefficient banks and may reflect a broader set of policies designed to safeguard the interests of the few against the forces of competition.

The instrumental variable regression indicates that both (1) restrictions on foreign banks entering the domestic market or purchasing domestic

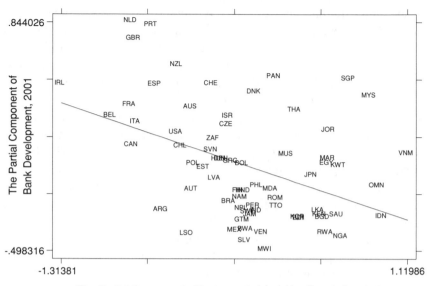

The Partial Component of Instrumented Activities Restrictions Index

Figure 4.7. Bank Development and the Exogenous Component of Activities Restrictions. *Notes:* This is the partial scatter plot of regression 5 in Table 4.2, Part A, which is a two-stage least squares regression of Bank Development in 2001 against Activities Restrictions in 1999. The included exogenous variables in the second stage are the dummy variables for legal origin. The excluded instrumental variables are Latitude and the percentage of the population that is Catholic, Muslim, or another non-Protestant religion. To construct this figure, first compute the predicted value of Activities Restrictions from the first stage regression. Second, regress Bank Development on the included exogenous variables and collect the residuals. This is called the partial component of Bank Development. Third, regress predicted values of Activities Restrictions from the first stage regression on the included exogenous variables and collect the residuals. This is called the partial component of the instrumented Activities Restrictions. Finally, plot the partial component of Bank Development against the partial component of Instrumented Activities Restrictions. This represents the two-dimensional representation of the regression plane in Bank Development–Activities Restrictions space while controlling for the endogeneity of Activities Restrictions.

banks and (2) a high rate of denial of bank entry applications reduce the level of overall bank development. The number of procedures for obtaining a banking license (Entry into Banking Requirements Index), however, is not significantly associated with bank development.

The sizes of the coefficients are economically large. For instance, the coefficients suggest that in a country such as Egypt that imposes tight Activity Restrictions (i.e., its value is a little more than one standard

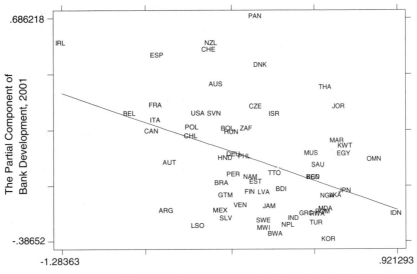

The Partial Component of Instrumented Activities Restrictions Index

Figure 4.8. Bank Development and the Exogenous Component of Activities Restrictions, Outliers Removed. *Notes:* After removing Malaysia, the Netherlands, Portugal, Singapore, the United Kingdom, and Vietnam, this is the partial scatter plot of Bank Development in 2001 against Activities Restrictions in 1999. The included exogenous variables in the second stage are the dummy variables for legal origin. The excluded instrumental variables are Latitude and the percentage of the population that is Catholic, Muslim, or another non-Protestant religion. To construct this figure, first compute the predicted value of Activities Restrictions from the first stage regression. Second, regress Bank Development on the included exogenous variables and collect the residuals. This is called the partial component of Bank Development. Third, regress predicted values of Activities Restrictions from the first stage regression on the included exogenous variables and collect the residuals. This is called the partial component of the instrumented Activities Restrictions. Finally, plot the partial component of Bank Development against the partial component of Instrumented Activities Restrictions. This represents the two-dimensional representation of the regression plane in Bank Development–Activities Restrictions space while controlling for the endogeneity of Activities Restrictions.

deviation above the mean, 1.2), a loosening of regulatory restrictions on bank activities to the sample mean (0) would boost bank development by 0.12 (= 1.2 * 0.13) when using the coefficient from regression 1 in Table 4.3. This means Egypt's bank development increases from 0.51 to 0.67, which is about the level in Canada. Next consider a change in the Private Monitoring Index using the estimates from regression 1, Table 4.3. The estimated coefficients indicate that a one standard deviation increase in the Private Monitoring Index (an increase of one) in Bangladesh would produce an increase in Bank Development of about 43 percent, pushing it from its current low level of 0.23 to 0.33. This would give it a higher value of Bank Development than India and approach the level in the Philippines. We do not present these examples as exploitable policy experiments but, rather, as indicative of the potential economic importance of bank regulation and supervision.

Finally, Table 4.2 also presents regressions using information on the degree of supervisory independence and whether there are multiple supervisory agencies that monitor banks. Chapter 3 discusses the potential impact of the degree to which supervisors are protected from pressures by politicians or banks. Table 4.2 captures one part of this: We have information on the independence of supervisors from banks, that is, are supervisors legally liable for their actions. If rich banks can sue individual supervisors, then this might jeopardize the alacrity with which supervisors monitor banks. The results presented in Table 4.2, and those in Barth, Caprio, and Levine (2004), however, indicate that the independence of the supervisory agency does not affect banking system development. As discussed in Chapter 3, our second survey contains more questions about supervisory independence from the government and the structure of the supervisory agency in general. We do not use those data here because, as stated earlier, we use measures of bank regulation and supervision in 1998–1999 to explain bank development in 2001 in order to minimize reverse causality concerns (along with the use of instrumental variables). As more data on the functioning of banks after 2005 become available, we believe that future research should examine the impact of supervisory independence and the structure of the supervisory agency on the functioning of the banking system. Besides the direct effect, the degree of supervisory independence may affect the impact of other regulatory policies on the banking system as suggested by Beck, Demirgüç-Kunt, and Levine (2003b). In Table 4.2, we also examine the relationship between bank development and whether multiple supervisory agencies monitor the nation's banks (or whether supervision is conducted by a single official agency). Again, we find no relationship between bank development and whether the country has more than one bank supervisory agency.

There are a number of shortcomings, however, with these initial results. First, these aggregate cross-country results do not shed light on the impact of bank regulation and supervision at the microeconomic level. They do not tell us what is happening to the behavior of individual banks or how banking sector policies influence the ability of firms to access bank credit.

Second, these results on bank development do not consider issues of stability. Many bank regulatory and supervisory policies are designed to reduce stability, not boost bank development. Thus, some bank regulatory and supervisory policies should be assessed on criteria other than their effects on Bank Development. We next examine stability and later turn to microeconomic analyses.

4.C. BANK SUPERVISION, REGULATION, AND STABILITY

One objective of bank regulation and supervision is to reduce bank fragility and thereby avoid systemic banking failures. This subsection reports the results of tests of the relationship between bank regulatory and supervisory policies and the probability of suffering a systemic banking crisis.

4.C.1. Definitions and Methodology: Systemic Crises

To define a systemic crisis, we rely on Demirgüç-Kunt and Detragiache's (2002) influential study. We identify and date episodes of banking sector distress during the period 1988–1999 using the primary source data from Lindgren, Garcia, and Saal (1996) and Caprio and Klingebiel (1999). Then, these episodes of distress are classified as systemic if emergency measures were taken to assist the banking system (such as bank holidays, deposit freezes, blanket guarantees to depositors or other bank creditors), or if large-scale nationalizations took place. Episodes were also classified as systemic if nonperforming assets reached at least 10 percent of total assets at the peak of the crisis, or if the cost of the rescue operations was at least 2 percent of GDP. There is an inherent arbitrariness in distinguishing a "systemic crisis" from a "large" crisis, or from a situation where a well-known bank fails. Nevertheless, in assessing different bank regulatory and supervisory policies, it is crucial to provide some evidence on crises as stability is a major – if not the major – objective of public policy. Thus, although imperfect, these data on banking crises are the best available and provide a useful input into assessing different banking policies.

To assess the relationship between banking sector policies and systemic crises, we use a logit probability model that is robust to heteroskedasticity. The dependent variable, Banking Crisis, takes the value one if the country experienced a systemic crisis at some point during the period 1988–1999 and zero otherwise. Because many studies find that macroeconomic instability induces banking sector distress, we also include the average inflation rate during the five years before the crisis in countries that experienced a banking crisis. In countries that did not, we include the average inflation rate during the five years before the survey of bank regulatory and supervisory indicators (1993–1997). The regressors of focus are the bank regulatory and supervisory indicators. When interpreting the regression results, the estimated coefficients do not indicate an increase in the probability of a crisis given a one-unit increase in the corresponding explanatory variables because the one-unit increase will have different effects on the probability of a crisis depending on the country's initial conditions.

There are methodological shortcomings with examining systemic crises. Critically, the regulatory and supervisory variables are measured primarily in 1999, but the crises, if any, occur at some point over the preceding eleven years. Thus, the explanatory variables are measured *after* the dependent variable. We still conduct this analysis for three reasons. First, there is no choice. Nobody conducted a large-scale international survey of bank regulation and supervision before our collection of these data. Second, small pieces of information suggest that bank regulation and supervision has not changed much over time. For instance, Carkovic and Levine (2004) show that bank regulation and supervision changed very little in Chile from 1990 to the present. More important, Barth, Caprio and Levine (2001a) show that regulatory restrictions on bank activities have not changed much over the last ten years across countries. If anything, countries reduce their Activity Restrictions following crises, which biases the results against the findings reported below. Third, we are able to complement the work by Demirgüç-Kunt and Detragiache (2002). They examine the impact of deposit insurance on banking crises using time-series data. But, they do not control for other features of the bank regulatory and supervisory regime because our data were not yet available. We complement their research by simultaneously assessing the impact of a broad array of bank regulatory and supervisory policies on banking system fragility. Although these comments may provide some comfort, readers should be particularly wary of these systemic crises results.

4.C.2. Bank Supervision, Regulation, and Stability: Results

There are two sets of results on banking crises reported in Table 4.5 in which we are comparatively confident. We first present these results and then turn to the remaining results on banking system fragility.

Table 4.5. *Banking Crises Regressions*

	(1)	(2)	(3)	(4)	(5)
Activity Restrictions	0.631	1.158	0.647	1.709	0.918
	(0.076)*	(0.017)**	(0.179)	(0.036)**	(0.035)**
Entry Into Banking	−0.183	−0.279	0.125	−0.704	−0.162
Requirements Index	(0.499)	(0.387)	(0.618)	(0.147)	(0.614)
Capital Regulatory	−0.264	−0.749	−1.035	−0.107	−0.216
Index	(0.475)	(0.178)	(0.073)*	(0.887)	(0.636)
Private Monitoring	0.391	−0.016		1.168	0.219
	(0.435)	(0.980)		(0.126)	(0.632)
Official Supervisory	−0.270	−0.224	−0.243	−0.655	
Power	(0.393)	(0.497)	(0.570)	(0.322)	
Government-Owned	2.312	5.269	2.846	3.414	0.792
Banks	(0.200)	(0.090)*	(0.190)	(0.262)	(0.697)
Inflation	0.051	0.064	0.031	0.138	0.055
	(0.087)*	(0.010)***	(0.173)	(0.011)**	(0.041)**
Moral Hazard Index			0.719		
			(0.000)***		
Limitations on Foreign				1.911	
Bank Entry/Ownership				(0.055)*	
Diversification Index					−13.328
					(0.020)**
Diversification					0.484
Index*LnGNP					(0.022)**
Constant	−0.566	−0.210	−0.314	−2.732	0.755
	(0.327)	(0.801)	(0.630)	(0.012)**	(0.517)
Observations	52	46	43	40	52

Note: The dependent variable is Banking Crises.
Estimated using Logit analysis. Column (2) restricts the sample to countries with data on stock market trading.
P-values are in parentheses.
*, **, *** indicate significance levels of 10, 5, and 1 percent, respectively.

First, the systemic banking crises regressions provide powerful results on a long-standing debate regarding regulatory restrictions on bank activities. Some theories suggest restricting the ability of banks to engage in nonlending services to promote bank stability. For instance, Boyd, Chang, and Smith (1998) argue that to the extent that moral hazard encourages riskier behavior, banks will have more opportunities to increase risk if allowed to engage in a broader range of activities. Also, complex banks are difficult to monitor, so restricting the range of bank activities may facilitate the oversight of banks and thus reduce bank fragility. Moreover, from a political economy perspective, financial conglomerates may become so politically and economically powerful that they become "too big to discipline" and thus destabilize the entire financial system. In contrast to these arguments, others hold that restricting bank activities will actually increase bank fragility. Fewer regulatory restrictions may increase the franchise value of banks and thereby augment incentives for more prudent behavior. Furthermore, when banks engage in a broad array of activities, this may enable banks to diversify income streams and thereby become more resilient to shocks with positive implications for banking system stability.

We find that regulatory restrictions on bank activities are associated with an increase in the likelihood of suffering a major crisis.[11] In the full sample, we find a weak, positive relationship between the likelihood of a crisis and restricting bank activities (Table 4.5: Regression 1). As noted, however, banks may only obtain the stabilizing effects from fewer regulatory restrictions when they are able to diversify their income streams through a broad array of nonlending activities. Banks may only have the ability to stabilize income flows by diversifying activities, however, if they operate in countries with a sufficiently high level of securities market development. To proxy for this, we restrict the sample to countries with some stock market activity. When restricting the sample to countries for which the World Bank has been able to collect at least some data on stock market transactions, we find that greater regulatory restrictions are indeed strongly, positively associated with the likelihood of suffering a crisis (Table 4.5: Regression 2). Thus, consistent with some theoretical predictions, the data indicate that restricting bank activities is negatively associated with bank stability primarily when banks can diversify income sources through nonlending activities.

We have a comparatively high degree of confidence in the finding that regulatory restrictions on bank activities increase systemic fragility because these particular analyses avoid many of methodological issues plaguing most systemic banking crisis regressions. Specifically, the results on regulatory restrictions on bank activities are not a result of the timing problem that we measure bank regulation and supervision after some of the crises. Although we do not have historical data on all of the bank regulatory and supervisory variables, we have constructed historical data on regulatory restrictions on bank activities. When we repeat the

---

[11] For more on regulations and crises, see Claessens, Demirgüç-Kunt, and Huizinga (2001), Levine (2004), and Beck, Demirgüç-Kunt, and Levine (2006a, 2006b). For a discussion of resolving crises, see Honohan and Laeven (2005).

analysis using regulatory restriction indicators measured *before* the crisis, we confirm these results (Barth, Caprio, and Levine, 2001a). Thus, the regulatory restriction indicator does not suffer from the timing issue discussed earlier and therefore does not appear to be a result of reverse causality. Also, because we control for official supervisory practices, capital regulations, regulations on competition, government ownership of banks, and the moral hazard generated by the generosity of the deposit insurance regime, the negative relationship between regulatory restrictions on bank activities and bank stability does not appear to be a result of an obvious omitted variable.

In Table 4.6, we also examine whether restricting bank activities has stabilizing effects under specific policy environments. For example, Boyd, Chang, and Smith's (1998) model predicts that restricting bank activities may reduce financial fragility in the presence of generous deposit insurance. Thus, in unreported regressions, we entered an interaction term into the systemic crises analyses. The interaction term equals Activity Restrictions * Moral Hazard Index, where Moral Hazard Index is the Demirgüç-Kunt and Detragiache (2002) measure of deposit insurance generosity. This aggregate index of moral hazard equals the first principal component of the following deposit insurance design features: the existence of coinsurance, coverage of foreign currency, coverage of interbank deposits, the type of funding, source of funding, who manages the deposit insurance fund, membership, and the level of explicit coverage. The index varies over time since different countries adopted deposit insurance or revised its design features at different points in time. We use the value of the index before the crisis, if the country experienced a crisis, and the value in 1998 if the country did not experience a crisis.

We do not find any support for more subtle theories regarding the efficacy of restricting bank activities under particular conditions. For instance, the conclusions do not change when including the interaction between regulatory restrictions on bank activities and deposit insurance generosity (Activity Restrictions * Moral Hazard Index). The variable, Activity Restrictions, retains its positive association with the likelihood of a crisis, whereas the interaction term is not significant.

Similarly, we assess whether in supervisory regimes with weak Official Supervisory Power, the absence of Prompt Corrective Powers, or low Capital Regulations, regulatory restrictions on bank activities have a stabilizing effect. When we include interaction terms for these variables, we again find no support for the contention that Activity Restrictions promotes stability in some institutional contexts.

Table 4.6. *Banking Crises Regressions*

	(1)	(2)	(3)	(4)
Activity Restrictions	1.880	0.735	0.656	0.627
	(0.046)**	(0.271)	(0.173)	(0.199)
Entry Into Banking	0.398	0.249	0.127	0.164
Requirements Index	(0.285)	(0.437)	(0.617)	(0.603)
Capital Regulatory Index	−1.268	−1.075	−1.026	−1.201
	(0.346)	(0.035)**	(0.084)*	(0.057)*
Official Supervisory Power	−1.191	−0.222	−0.246	−0.241
	(0.230)	(0.602)	(0.571)	(0.586)
Government-Owned Banks	9.480	3.963	2.761	2.869
	(0.119)	(0.197)	(0.228)	(0.177)
Inflation	0.025	0.023	0.031	0.030
	(0.313)	(0.237)	(0.181)	(0.184)
Moral Hazard Index	1.442	2.132	0.716	0.769
	(0.010)***	(0.002)***	(0.000)***	(0.001)***
Moral Hazard Index*	−0.513			
Political Openness	(0.014)**			
Political Openness	0.762			
	(0.146)			
Moral Hazard Index*		−0.288		
Rule of Law		(0.037)**		
Rule of Law		−0.295		
		(0.540)		
Moral Hazard Index*			−0.031	
Official Supervisory Power			(0.844)	
Moral Hazard Index*				−0.131
Capital Regulatory Index				(0.605)
Constant	−1.410	1.761	−0.308	−0.094
	(0.351)	(0.456)	(0.641)	(0.906)
Observations	40	41	43	43

Note: The dependent variable is Banking Crises.
Estimated using Logit analysis.
P-values are in parentheses.
*, **, *** indicate significance levels of 10, 5, and 1 percent, respectively.

We also experimented with an interaction term that equals Activity
Restrictions * Absence of Graft to test whether limiting the range of
permissible bank activities stabilizes the financial system in corrupt environments. Our results do not support this suspicion. We continue to find
a negative association between Activity Restrictions and stability when
including Activity Restrictions * Absence of Graft, and this interaction
term enters insignificantly. Thus, the bank fragility results remain broadly

consistent with the argument that there are diversification benefits from allowing banks to engage in nontraditional activities.

Besides the positive link between regulatory restrictions on bank activities and systemic banking failures, a second finding in which we have comparatively strong confidence regards an equally contentious public policy issue: deposit insurance. Theory provides conflicting predictions about the impact of deposit insurance on bank stability.[12] The core arguments in favor of deposit insurance derive from the view that depositors have a difficult time assessing the quality of bank assets. Thus, if depositors become suspicious about the quality of a bank's assets and attempt to withdraw their funds all at once ("bank run"), illiquid but solvent banks may be forced into insolvency. Similarly, problems in one bank may elicit fears about the quality of other banks and induce depositors to withdraw their funds from banks that have no problems because of the difficulties associated with distinguishing the quality of individual bank assets. This "contagion" can induce a situation in which a problem in one bank causes insolvency in otherwise sound banks. Thus, to prevent these types of instability, many countries (about eighty by early 2004) adopted deposit insurance. By contrast, many models emphasize that deposit insurance schemes come at a cost. Deposit insurance intensifies the moral hazard problem in banking because bank owners collect most of the benefits from making risky investments that succeed but share the losses with the deposit insurance fund if the investments fail. With deposit insurance, depositors no longer face the risk of losing their savings, which diminishes the resources and time they will devote to preventing banks from undertaking excessively risk investments. Thus, generous deposit insurance may encourage excessive risk-taking behavior that overwhelms any stabilization benefits.

Nevertheless, many policy makers hold that bank regulation and supervision and capital standards can sufficiently mitigate the moral hazard incentives engendered by deposit insurance so that deposit insurance in conjunction with strong official regulation and supervision will boost bank stability. Thus, the impact of deposit insurance on bank fragility is an empirical question.

The Table 4.5 results indicate a positive relationship between the generosity of the deposit insurance regime and the incidence of a systemic banking crisis. Furthermore, the positive relationship between the

[12] For research on the determinants of deposit insurance, see Demirgüç-Kunt, Kane, and Laeven (2005).

generosity of the deposit insurance regime (Moral Hazard) and bank fragility is robust to alterations in the control variables. This result is consistent with the view that deposit insurance aggravates moral hazard with deleterious effects on bank stability. Although not necessarily refuting the public interest view, the finding that deposit insurance generosity is positively linked with the probability of suffering a systemic crisis certainly does not support the public interest prediction that countries adopt deposit insurance to promote the stability of banking systems. Along these lines, Laeven (2004) finds that deposit insurance coverage is more generous in countries where poorly capitalized banks dominate the market, which is consistent with the private interest view that "weak parties" – such as risky, failing banks – will favor deposit insurance.

One reason we feel relatively confident about the positive relationship between deposit insurance generosity and bank fragility is that our results confirm those by Demirgüç-Kunt and Detragiache (2002), who show that deposit insurance generosity *predicts* future banking crises when using annual data. Thus, their methodology does not suffer from the same timing issues that plague our analyses. They, however, were unable to control for other features of the regulatory/supervisory environment because these data were unavailable to them. We find that deposit insurance generosity is positively associated with the likelihood of a crisis while controlling for many features of regulation and supervision. Thus, although our methods have weaknesses and the Demirgüç-Kunt and Detragiache (2002) approach has weaknesses, the weaknesses are different and the findings are the same: more generous deposit insurance is associated with a higher probability of suffering a systemic banking crisis.

The relationship between deposit insurance and bank fragility is economically large. For instance, using regression 3 (Table 4.5) we can compute the drop in the probability of a banking crisis for Mexico. If Mexico's quite generous deposit insurance scheme (3.9) were reduced to the sample mean of 0, then Mexico's probability of a crisis would fall by 12 percentage points, using Mexico's values for all the variables in regression 3. Again, we stress that our study does not identify an exploitable relationship and this may not represent a marginal change. Nonetheless, this illustrative example confirms the Demirgüç-Kunt and Detragiache (2002) conclusion that the adverse incentive effects created by generous schemes may be economically substantial.

Besides controlling for other features of the bank regulatory and supervisory environment, one additional contribution that we make to

Demirgüç-Kunt and Detragiache's (2002) research is that we examine whether specific bank regulatory and supervisory policies reduce the destabilizing effects of generous deposit insurance. Thus, we examine whether official supervisory power or tighter capital regulations mitigate the negative relationship between generous deposit insurance and bank fragility (Table 4.6).

Contrary to substantial theoretical work, we find no support for the view that more powerful official supervisors or more stringent capital requirements reduce the destabilizing effects of generous deposit insurance. However, better-developed private property rights – as proxied by greater adherence to the rule of law (Rule of Law) – and greater political openness (Political Openness) do mitigate the negative association between moral hazard and bank fragility.[13] It is worth noting, however, that the generosity of deposit insurance is positively associated with the probability of suffering a crisis even in countries with the highest Rule of Law values (e.g., the cross-over point is Rule of Law $= 7.4$, but the maximum Rule of Law value is 6). Thus, although greater Rule of Law reduces the negative association of generous deposit insurance, it does not eliminate it. Furthermore, although many stress tighter official supervision and more stringent capital requirements as the antidote to generous deposit insurance, these regressions do not support this position.

In terms of the remaining results on banking system fragility, consider first capital regulation, which forms the basis of international efforts to enhance banking system stability. As discussed in Chapter 2, capital serves as a buffer against loses and may reduce the inclination for bank owners to invest in highly risky ventures. Thus, capital regulations may help align the incentives of bank owners with depositors and other creditors, including the deposit insurance agency. However, research questions whether official capital regulatory requirements actually reduce incentives for risk-taking (e.g., see Santos, 2001; Koehn and Santomero, 1980; Kim and Santomero, 1988; Besanko and Kanatas, 1996; and Blum, 1999).

Empirically, there are specifications in which capital stringency is negatively associated with banking crises (Table 4.5) but the relationship between capital stringency and systemic banking crise is not robust to

---

[13] The Rule of Law is an indicator of the degree to which the country adheres to the rule of law. It ranges from 0 to 6 with higher values indicating greater confidence in the legal system to settle disputes. It is obtained from the International Country Risk Guide and is averaged over 1990–1999.

changes in specification (Table 4.6). Also, capital regulations do not reduce the destabilizing effects of deposit insurance. Furthermore, one might expect capital regulations to be especially important in countries with weak official supervisory systems or with a regulatory environment that does not spur private monitoring. However, when we included these interaction terms in the analyses, we found no evidence for these more subtle notions of when capital regulations foster stability. Thus, although recognizing that capital regulations are negatively correlated with the level of nonperforming loans in each country's banking system, the links with crises are nonrobust and do not follow predictable patterns.

One should not draw overly confident conclusions from the inability to identify a robust relationship between capital regulations and banking system stability. The investigation is handicapped by the harmonization of capital adequacy standards internationally. In 1988, the Basel Committee on Banking Supervision introduced the Basel Capital Accord, which has influenced capital regulations around the world. The harmonization of capital regulatory policies has, as documented in Chapter 3, reduced cross-country variation in capital regulations. This comparative lack of international differences in capital standards makes it difficult to explain cross-country differences in bank fragility – or any other measure of bank performance – with cross-country differences in capital regulatory policies. Thus, the weak link between capital regulations and banking system fragility may simply reflect insufficient variation in the explanatory variable. We are unable to reject or confirm the view that the Basel Capital Accords reduced bank fragility below what it would have been in the absence of these Accords.

Next, consider Basel II's second major pillar for promoting the safety and soundness of the banking system: official supervision. As discussed in Chapter 2, those with a Pigouvian/public interest view hold that strong official supervision of banks will help overcome a number of market failures. For instance, small depositors in banks may lack the incentives and ability to monitor complex banks, especially in the presence of deposit insurance. Official supervision can help fill this gap. The contrasting view holds that the objectives of official supervisors may differ from those of society at large and instead stresses that if the problem is too little private monitoring, then the solution is to facilitate private monitoring.

The results do not lend support to the view that stronger official supervisory power enhances bank stability either by reducing the incidence of systemic banking crises, or by reducing the destabilizing effects of generous deposit insurance. In fact, Official Supervisory Power is positively correlated with the level of nonperforming loans as a share of total loans in a country. We could not find a robust relationship between the likelihood of suffering a systemic crisis and a broad array of official supervisory indicators, with one exception. The one exception involves the diversification index (which aggregates diversification guidelines and the absence of restrictions on making loans abroad). There is a negative relationship between the diversification index and the likelihood of suffering a major crisis in small economies. Specifically, we include the interaction between the diversification index and the logarithm of real per capita GDP in 1995 (these are Purchasing Power Parity adjusted figures from the Penn World Tables). As shown in Table 4.5, diversification is negatively associated with the likelihood of a crisis but diversification guidelines have less of a stabilizing effect in bigger countries. The cut-off is high; diversification guidelines have stabilizing effects in all but the nine largest countries. While confirming the intuition, "don't put all your eggs in one basket," we emphasize the tentative nature of these pure cross-country crisis regressions.

The regression analyses do not indicate a confident relationship between regulations designed to enhance private sector monitoring of banks and banking system fragility. Confirming findings in Barth et al. (2004), Private Monitoring does not enter significantly in any of the systemic banking crises regressions (Table 4.5). Thus, although Private Monitoring tends to boost overall banking system development (Tables 4.2 and 4.3), there is no evidence that it reduces banking system fragility. In a recent extension of this line of work, Tadesse (2004) uses individual components of the private monitoring variable along with other data and constructs a measure that focuses only on information disclosure. His findings support the view that more transparent, timelier, and more comprehensive information disclosure enhances banking system stability.

The results in Table 4.5 also indicate in several regressions that the likelihood of a major banking crisis is positively associated with greater Limitations on Foreign Bank Entry/Ownership. We find that foreign-bank ownership per se is not associated with the likelihood of a crisis. Rather, it is limitations on foreign-bank entry and ownership that are positively associated with banking system fragility. Moreover, we assessed whether restrictions on bank entry – both domestic and foreign bank entry – boost stability when countries have weak official supervisory powers. But, again, we find no evidence of a stabilizing effect of bank entry restrictions.

In sum, although subject to the variety of methodological qualifications noted earlier, we draw the following tentative conclusions on banking system fragility and bank regulations. Regulatory restrictions on banking activities and generous deposit insurance do not have a stabilizing effect on banks; rather, they tend to increase banking system fragility. Furthermore, our analyses do not provide cross-country empirical support for the views that: (1) more stringent capital regulations, (2) official supervisory agencies with greater disciplinary powers, or (3) regulations that force accurate information disclosure increase banking system stability. We now assess the implications of bank regulatory and supervisory policies on the behavior of individual banks.

4.D. BANK SUPERVISION, REGULATION, AND BANK EFFICIENCY

4.D.1. Bank Supervision, Regulation, and Bank Efficiency: Issues, Data, and Methods

This section examines the connections between measures of national bank regulatory strategies and the efficiency of individual banks.[14] Thus, we shift from the pure cross-country methodology to the use of bank-level data. This disaggregated focus has important methodological and conceptual advantages.

Rather than providing a broad international perspective on those regulatory policies that are associated with better-developed banks, a microeconomic approach focuses on mechanisms through which banking sector policies influence the "real economy." Do national approaches to bank regulation and supervision influence how individual banks behave in terms of (1) the interest margins that they charge and (2) the overhead costs that they incur? The goal is to assess whether bank regulatory and supervisory policies influence the efficiency of intermediation.

We examine two indicators of bank efficiency: the net interest margin and overhead expenditures.

Net Interest Margin equals interest income minus interest expense divided by interest-bearing assets and is averaged over 1995–1999.[15]

---

[14] This section draws on Demirgüç-Kunt, Laeven, and Levine (2004) and Levine (2004).

[15] We use both net interest margin and overhead cost averaged over the period 1995–1999 to reduce the impact of business-cycle fluctuations that could unduly influence these cost variables in a single year. However, we obtain the same results when we restrict ourselves

Because the net interest margin focuses on the conventional borrowing and lending operations of banks, we normalize by interest-bearing assets rather than total bank assets. High net interest margins can signal inefficient intermediation and greater market power that allows banks to charge high margins.

Overhead Costs equals overhead costs divided by total assets averaged over the period 1995–1999. We use this variable to capture cross-bank differences in the efficiency with which banks are managed. High overhead costs can signal unwarranted managerial perquisites and market power that contradict the notions of sound governance of banks and efficient intermediation.

In the tortured terminology of economists, there are "nontrivial problems" with using net interest margins and overhead costs to gauge bank efficiency that we attempt to mitigate. Many factors besides weak governance, inefficiencies, and market power may influence bank interest margins and overhead costs. For instance, banks engaging in fee income generating activities may have different net interest margins because of cross-subsidization of activities and different overhead cost structures because of the different product mixes. In this case, cross-bank differences in net interest margins or overhead costs may reflect differences in bank activity, rather than differences in efficiency, governance, or competition. Also, bank margins and costs may reflect different asset allocations and risk preferences. We want to hold sufficient other factors constant such that we can interpret greater overhead costs and larger net interest values as reflecting managerial perquisites, operational inefficiency, or market power. Thus, to evaluate the independent relationships between bank regulatory and supervisory policies and individual bank net interest margin and overhead costs, we need to control for an array of bank-specific characteristics.

Well-structured bank regulatory and supervisory policies may keep overhead costs and interest margins from becoming excessive by fostering competition and by encouraging effective governance of bank managers. Contentious debates exist, however, about which regulatory and supervisory practices will boost bank efficiency. The public interest approach holds that a powerful supervisory agency that monitors and disciplines banks directly can improve bank operations, reduce collusion among

to net interest margin and overhead cost data for the period 1999, which is the year of the first bank regulation and supervision survey.

banks, and foster greater competition and efficiency. In contrast, the private interest approach contends that official supervisors will not remedy market failures. According to the private monitoring corollary of the private interest view, the most efficacious approach to bank supervision relies on encouraging private monitoring of banks through information disclosure rules and improved contract enforcement mechanisms. We subject these competing views to empirical testing.

To assess the impact of bank regulatory and supervisory approaches on bank efficiency while controlling for bank-specific and country-specific factors, the following equation is used:

$$\text{Bank Efficiency}_{i,k} = \alpha + \beta_1 S_i + \beta_2 B_{i,k} + \beta_3 C_i + \varepsilon_{i,k}, \qquad (4.5)$$

where the subscript i indicates country i, and the subscript k indicates bank k; S_i represents bank regulatory and supervisory indicators, where we focus on Official Supervisory Power, Private Monitoring, and Activity Restrictions; $B_{i,k}$ is a vector of bank-specific characteristics for bank k in country i; C_i is a vector of country-specific control variables; and $\varepsilon_{i,k}$ is the residual. Because the model includes country-specific variables, we use a generalized least squares estimator with random effects.[16] We use bank-level data from Demirgüç-Kunt, Laeven, and Levine (2004), who examine the impact of bank concentration on bank efficiency while controlling for regulatory and institutional characteristics.

For the vector of bank-specific control variables, $B_{i,k}$, we include the following variables. **Market Share** equals the bank's assets divided by total bank assets in the economy. A bank that dominates the national market and faces little competition may enjoy larger overhead costs than

---

[16] Because the dependent variable in the regressions is an individual bank's Net Interest Margin or its Overhead Costs, it seems unlikely that an individual bank's efficiency drives national approaches to bank supervision. Nevertheless, as a robustness check, we used instrumental variables and confirmed the findings. For instruments, we used the same instruments as in the Bank Development regressions, which included the latitudinal distance from the equator and the percentage of the population that is Catholic, Muslim, or a non-Protestant religion. Furthermore, we also included instruments the number of years since 1776 that the country has been independent and the political openness of the country in 1800 or the first year of independence. As discussed earlier, we included years of independence since independence allows countries to reform the institutions left by colonial powers. We include initial political openness because the initial political regime may continue to shape bank regulatory and supervisory policies today. Specifically, more authoritarian and less democratic regimes may tend to favor strong official supervision and shed a wary eye on supervisory practices that emphasize transparent dissemination of information. The results are robust to many combinations of instruments.

a bank that does not control much of the market. **Bank Size** equals the logarithm of total bank assets in millions of U.S. dollars. Size may be an important determinant of overhead costs if there are increasing returns to scale in banking. In particular, larger banks may require lower overhead expenditures as a share of total assets. **Liquidity** equals the liquid assets of the bank divided by total assets. We use this indicator to control for differences in bank assets. In some cases, banks with considerable market power may hold a high ratio of liquid government assets and also enjoy high overhead costs. **Bank Equity** equals the book value of equity divided by total assets. Some theories suggest that well-capitalized banks face lower expected bankruptcy costs and hence lower funding costs. Thus, higher bank equity implies greater opportunities for larger overhead costs when loan rates do not vary much with bank equity. **Fee Income** equals non-interest-operating income divided by total assets. Banks have different product mixes. These differences may influence the pricing of loan products. For instance, banks with well-developed fee income sources may have lower interest margins due to cross-subsidization of bank activities.

For the vector of country-specific controls, we include a variety of country traits. **Growth** equals the growth rate of the economy over the period 1995–1999. GDP Growth is included to control for business-cycle forces. **Voice and Accountability** is an indicator of the degree to which the average citizen has a voice in the political process and the extent to which politicians can be held accountable for their actions through elections. This variable is from Kaufman, Kraay, and Zoido-Lobaton (1999), who compile the index from numerous surveys. When using an alternative indicator of the political environment that focuses on political violence, also from Kaufman et al. (1999), we confirm the results. **Absence of Graft** is an index of the overall level of corruption in the country's government, where larger values imply that government officials are less likely to demand illegal payments. This variable is also taken from the Kaufman et al. dataset on institutional development. We want to control for the overall level of country corruption to assess the strength of the independent link between bank regulatory and supervisory policies on bank efficiency. **Government-owned Banks** equals the fraction of the banking system's assets that is held by banks that are more than 50 percent owned by the government, which is taken from our bank regulatory and supervisory survey. Because government ownership may distort the application of different supervisory approaches, it is important to control for the degree of state-owned banks. **Political Openness** measures the openness, competitiveness, and level of democracy of the country.[17] Controlling for national institutions permits us to assess whether bank regulation and supervision influence bank margins and overhead costs beyond broad national approaches to competition. If bank regulatory and supervisory policies reflect national approaches to competition in general and our data comprehensively measure institutions, then any association between regulations and bank efficiency should disappear when we control for the institutional development indicators.

4.D.2. Bank Supervision, Regulation, Efficiency: Regression Results

Tables 4.7 and 4.8 present the bank-level regressions of the net interest margins and overhead costs, respectively. Each table presents six regressions. The first column presents the basic regression that includes bank-specific controls, overall economic growth, and the bank regulatory and supervisory variables. The next four columns include country-specific control variables one at a time. The last column includes all of the regressors simultaneously. Three important results emerge from the bank-level regressions.

First, neither Official Supervisory Power nor Capital Regulatory Index exerts a statistically significant and robust impact on Net Interest Margin or Overhead Costs. Although Official Supervisory Power always enters with a negative coefficient, the relationship is not statistically robust. From these analyses, it is difficult to argue that strengthening the power of supervisory agencies (or tightening capital regulations) will improve bank efficiency by reducing agency problems, lowering market power, or minimizing operational inefficiencies. Thus, the major two pillars of Basel II are not associated with greater bank efficiency.

---

[17] The political openness variable is the first principal component of five indicators from the Polity IV database (Marshall and Jaggers, 2002): (1) Polity measures the degree of democracy-autocracy, for example, institutions through which citizens express preferences, constraints on executive, the guarantee of civil liberties, the lack of suppression of political participation, the openness to nonelites (-10 to $+10$). (2) XROPEN measures the openness of executive recruitment and ranges from hereditary succession (0) to competitive election (4). (3) XRCOMP measures the degree of competitiveness of executive recruitment and ranges from unopposed elections (0) to multiparty, competitive elections (3). (4) XCONST measures institutional constraints on executive decisions and ranges from unlimited authority (1) to institutional arrangements where a legislature has equal/greater authority (7). (5) PARCOMP measures the competitiveness of political groups and ranges from (a) repressed (no significant opposition outside ruling party) (1) to (b) highly competitive (enduring groups regularly compete for influence).

Second, Private Monitoring is associated with greater bank efficiency, as measured by lower levels of Net Interest Margin and Overhead Costs. As shown in Table 4.7, Private Monitoring enters negatively and significantly in all of the Net Interest Margin regressions. This includes regressions that control for an array of both country-specific and bank-specific factors. Thus, the results imply an independent impact of Private Monitoring on bank efficiency. The Overhead Cost regressions in Table 4.8 are similarly strong with one exception. Private Monitoring enters negatively and significantly in all of the regressions except when all of the bank-level and country-level variables are included simultaneously in column six. Thus, there is multicollinearity across the various country-level indicators of bank regulation and supervision, economic growth, government ownership of banks, and the broad political/institutional environment. Taken together, these results suggest a strong link between bank regulatory and supervisory policies that foster private sector monitoring and bank efficiency.

Third, tighter regulatory restrictions on bank activities boost bank net interest margins when controlling for bank-specific characteristics, and the rate of economic growth. Furthermore, complementary research by Demirgüç-Kunt, Laeven, and Levine (2004) finds that restrictions on bank entry and general impediments to the freedom of bankers to conduct their business (as measured by the Heritage Foundation) boost interest margins.[18] The overriding message that emerges from these analyses is that regulatory restrictions on bank activities and competition reduces the efficiency of bank operations without a corresponding benefit in terms of stability or other measures of bank performance.

There is an important caveat to the finding that bank regulations explain net interest margin: regulatory restrictions on bank activities (and bank entry) cannot be viewed in isolation from the overall/political

---

[18] Laeven and Levine (2005) investigate whether the diversity of activities conducted by financial institutions influences their market valuations. They find that there is a diversification discount: The market values financial conglomerates that engage in multiple activities, for example, lending, securities operations, insurance, etc. lower than if those financial conglomerates were broken into financial intermediaries that specialize in the individual activities. The results are consistent with theories that stress intensified agency problems in financial conglomerates that engage in multiple activities and indicate that economies of scope are not sufficiently large to produce a diversification premium. Future research needs to reconcile and clarify why financial conglomeration induces potential equity purchasers to demand a price discount, but at the same time, the ability to diversify activities – lower regulatory restrictions on bank activities – boosts bank efficiency.

Table 4.7. *Net Interest Margin and Supervision*

	(1)	(2)	(3)	(4)	(5)	(6)
Market Share	1.211	1.123	1.179	0.888	1.090	0.757
	(0.037)**	(0.052)*	(0.044)**	(0.127)	(0.063)*	(0.201)
Bank Size	−0.201	−0.198	−0.198	−0.179	−0.203	−0.177
	(0.000)***	(0.000)***	(0.000)***	(0.000)***	(0.000)***	(0.000)***
Liquidity	−0.019	−0.019	−0.019	−0.020	−0.021	−0.022
	(0.000)***	(0.000)***	(0.000)***	(0.000)***	(0.000)***	(0.000)***
Bank Equity	0.024	0.024	0.024	0.025	0.021	0.022
	(0.000)***	(0.000)***	(0.000)***	(0.000)***	(0.001)***	(0.000)***
Fee Income	−0.032	−0.031	−0.031	0.005	−0.028	0.014
	(0.216)	(0.219)	(0.229)	(0.853)	(0.283)	(0.615)
Activity Restrictions	0.728	0.384	0.195	0.817	0.608	0.274
	(0.003)***	(0.144)	(0.484)	(0.002)***	(0.023)**	(0.397)
Growth	−0.278	−0.232	−0.124	−0.305	−0.271	−0.159
	(0.003)***	(0.013)**	(0.288)	(0.002)***	(0.005)***	(0.238)
Official Supervisory Power	−0.156	−0.230	−0.345	−0.171	−0.152	−0.357
	(0.448)	(0.255)	(0.099)*	(0.419)	(0.474)	(0.126)
Private Monitoring	−1.230	−0.873	−0.935	−1.100	−1.143	−0.801
	(0.000)***	(0.002)***	(0.006)***	(0.000)***	(0.000)***	(0.058)*

	(1)	(2)	(3)	(4)	(5)	(6)
Capital Regulatory Index	0.208	0.278	0.279	0.410	0.193	0.489
	(0.383)	(0.237)	(0.231)	(0.113)	(0.439)	(0.078)*
Voice & Accountability		−1.025				−0.416
		(0.002)***				(0.642)
Absence of Graft			−1.070			−0.867
			(0.001)***			(0.102)
Government- Owned Banks				0.352		−0.346
				(0.759)		(0.783)
Political Openness					−0.475	0.088
					(0.086)*	(0.875)
Constant	7.327	7.671	7.194	7.146	7.526	7.483
	(0.000)***	(0.000)***	(0.000)***	(0.000)***	(0.000)***	(0.000)***
Observations	1362	1362	1355	1201	1284	1116
Number of Countries	68	68	65	61	64	54

Notes: The dependent variable is Net Interest Margin.
Estimated using Generalized Least Squares with random country effects.
P-values are in parentheses.
*, **, *** indicate significance levels of 10, 5, and 1 percent, respectively.

Table 4.8. *Overhead Costs and Supervision*

	(1)	(2)	(3)	(4)	(5)	(6)
Market Share	0.687	0.629	0.751	0.612	0.665	0.645
	(0.201)	(0.243)	(0.165)	(0.266)	(0.228)	(0.261)
Bank Size	−0.135	−0.132	−0.134	−0.114	−0.131	−0.108
	(0.000)***	(0.000)***	(0.000)***	(0.000)***	(0.000)***	(0.000)***
Liquidity	0.006	0.006	0.006	0.005	0.006	0.005
	(0.031)**	(0.040)**	(0.041)**	(0.080)*	(0.041)**	(0.121)
Bank Equity	0.026	0.026	0.026	0.029	0.025	0.028
	(0.000)***	(0.000)***	(0.000)***	(0.000)***	(0.000)***	(0.000)***
Activity Restrictions	0.143	0.017	−0.184	0.165	0.142	−0.154
	(0.453)	(0.935)	(0.389)	(0.429)	(0.486)	(0.535)
Growth	−0.160	−0.143	−0.116	−0.171	−0.150	−0.128
	(0.035)**	(0.064)*	(0.203)	(0.036)**	(0.050)*	(0.225)
Official Supervisory Power	−0.112	−0.139	−0.262	−0.071	−0.072	−0.192
	(0.487)	(0.396)	(0.105)	(0.672)	(0.660)	(0.288)
Private Monitoring	−0.703	−0.577	−0.640	−0.586	−0.656	−0.377
	(0.001)***	(0.014)**	(0.015)**	(0.013)**	(0.004)***	(0.257)

	(1)	(2)	(3)	(4)	(5)	(6)
Capital Regulatory Index	0.082	0.110	0.137	0.254	0.084	0.335
	(0.664)	(0.565)	(0.450)	(0.220)	(0.662)	(0.119)
Voice & Accountability		−0.380				−0.501
		(0.152)				(0.466)
Absence of Graft			−0.650			−0.578
			(0.010)***			(0.159)
Government-Owned Banks				0.757		0.521
				(0.408)		(0.595)
Political Openness					−0.078	0.406
					(0.713)	(0.351)
Constant	4.654	4.785	4.805	4.298	4.695	4.722
	(0.000)***	(0.000)***	(0.000)***	(0.000)***	(0.000)***	(0.000)***
Observations	1362	1362	1355	1201	1284	1116
Number of Countries	68	68	65	61	64	54

Notes: The dependent variable is Bank Overhead Costs.
Estimated using Generalized Least Squares with random country effects.
P-values are in parentheses.
*, **, *** indicate significance levels of 10, 5, and 1 percent, respectively.

233

institutional framework. As shown in Table 4.7, Activity Restrictions becomes insignificant when controlling for Voice & Accountability and the Absence of Graft. Thus, when controlling for these broader, national characteristics, bank regulations do not provide additional explanatory power of cross-bank net interest margin. As shown, these broad indicators of the operation of national political systems explain cross-bank differences in net interest margin. We do not interpret these results as suggesting that bank regulations are unimportant for explaining bank margins. Rather, we interpret the findings as consistent with the idea that the functioning of national political systems affects the selection and implementation of banking sector policies and regulations.

Some may raise concerns that the core question involves country-level regulatory and supervisory policies, but we are examining bank-level data across countries. Because there are multiple banks for each bank regulatory and supervisory system, this methodology may lower the coefficient standard errors artificially by boosting the number of observations. When possible, we endeavor to gauge the channels through which bank regulatory and supervisory policies influence banks. This requires an examination of individual banks while controlling for each bank's characteristics. Moreover, we repeated the analyses examining banking systems, rather than individual banks, so that we had one observation per country. Thus, we compute the average value of Net Interest Margin and Overhead Costs for each country's banking system. Then, following exactly the same methodology that we employed when studying Bank Development, we regressed Net Interest Margin and Overhead Costs on the bank regulatory and supervisory variables using instrumental variables on a purely cross-country approach. We confirm the core bank-level results: Private Monitoring exerts a negative impact on both systemwide interest margin and overhead costs, but Official Supervisory Power does not.

The move to bank-level data permitted the examination of particular channels through which bank regulation and supervision influence the operation of banks. The results broadly confirm the pure cross-country analyses of bank development: bank supervisory strategies that focus on facilitating private monitoring tend to be more successful around the world than strategies that rely on strengthening official supervisory powers, capital regulations, or other regulatory rules governing bank entry or activities. This supports Basel II's third pillar.

The bank-level results go further than the pure cross-county findings, however. The regression results indicate that: (1) supervisory practices and regulations that facilitate private monitoring boost bank efficiency, as measured by a lower net interest margin and overhead costs; (2) strengthening official supervision does not improve bank efficiency; and (3) bank regulations that restrict bank activities, reflecting broad national political/institutions, tend to lower bank efficiency. Nevertheless, these results are also problematic because: (i) although we attempt to control for bank-specific factors, net interest margin and overhead costs are conceptually imprecise measures of bank efficiency; (ii) there are other mechanisms through which bank policies may influence the economy; (iii) bank efficiency is only an indirect indicator of what ultimately is our interest: the efficiency with which banks allocate capital; and (iv) we have not directly studied the private interest view of bank regulation and supervision.

4.E. BANK SUPERVISION, REGULATION, AND BANK LENDING

4.E.1. Bank Policies and Lending Integrity: Concepts, Data, and Methods

This section turns from examining the linkages between bank regulation and banks to studying the linkages between bank regulation and firms. We have presented evidence on the impact of bank regulation on bank development, bank stability, and bank efficiency using pure cross-country comparisons and pooled cross-country, cross-bank panels of data. Although it is useful to understand how bank regulation and supervision influence bank development, stability, and efficiency because past work suggests that operations of banks influence the overall economy (Levine, 2005a), we also seek to provide direct information on how banking sector policies influence the allocation of capital. These analyses will also provide more direct evidence on the private and public interest theories.

Based on research by Beck, Demirgüç-Kunt, and Levine (2005b), this section assesses the impact of bank supervisory policies on corruption in bank lending. We examine the degree to which corruption in lending impedes the ability of firms to raise external finance. To the extent that firms face large obstacles to obtaining a loan because they need corrupt ties with bankers, this suggests that banks are not allocating capital in a socially optimal manner. Using newly available firm-level data on more than twenty-five hundred firms across thirty-seven countries from the World Business Environment Survey (WBES), we study whether specific bank supervisory strategies lower – or increase – corruption in lending.

Theory provides conflicting predictions about the impact of specific bank supervisory strategies on the extent to which corruption of bank officials impedes the efficient allocation of bank credit. The public interest view holds that a powerful supervisory agency that directly monitors and disciplines banks can enhance the corporate governance of banks, reduce corruption in bank lending, and thereby boost the efficiency with which banks intermediate society's savings. In contrast, the private interest view argues that politicians and supervisors may induce banks to divert the flow of credit to politically connected firms, or banks may "capture" supervisors and induce them to act in the best interests of banks rather than in the best interests of society. This theory suggests that strengthening official supervisory powers – in the absence of political and legal institutions that induce politicians and regulators to act in the best interests of society – may actually reduce the integrity of bank lending with adverse implications on the efficiency of credit allocation. Finally, as a corollary to the private interest view, the private monitoring view contends that bank supervisory policies should focus on enhancing the ability and incentives of private agents to overcome information and transaction costs, so that private investors can exert effective governance over banks. From this perspective, corruption of bank officials will be a smaller obstacle to firms raising capital in countries that foster public information disclosure than in countries where powerful official supervisors have the power to influence bank credit decisions.

To examine the relationship between bank supervisory strategies and corporate financing obstacles, we use firm-level survey data. The WBES surveyed firms of all sizes; small firms (between five and fifty employees) represent 40 percent of the sample, medium-sized (between fifty-one and five hundred employees) firms are 40 percent of the sample, and the remaining 20 percent are large firms (more than five hundred employees). The survey comprises mostly firms of the manufacturing, construction, and services sectors. We have information on whether these are government-owned, foreign-owned, or privately owned firms. The data indicate whether the firm is an exporter and provide information on firm employment, sales, industry, growth, financing patterns, and the number of competitors.

Bank Corruption equals the response to the question: "Is the corruption of bank officials an obstacle for the operation and growth of your business?" Answers vary between 1 (no obstacle), 2 (a minor obstacle), 3 (a moderate obstacle), or 4 (a major obstacle). Thus, bigger numbers imply the corruption of bank officials is a bigger obstacle to obtaining financing. Overall, 7.7 percent of the firms in our sample report bank corruption as a major obstacle, 7.8 percent rate bank corruption as a moderate obstacle, 19.5 percent respond that corruption is a minor obstacle, whereas 65 percent report that the corruption of bank officials is not an obstacle to firm growth. The perceived degree to which the corruption of bank officials is an obstacle to efficient corporate finance not only varies across firms within countries but also across countries.[19] For instance, the average firm in Thailand reports that the corruption of bank officials is a substantial obstacle to obtaining external finance (3.14), whereas the average firm in Canada or the United Kingdom reports a very high degree of integrity in bank lending (1.03).

The WBES survey is unique in providing information on the degree to which corruption in lending represents an obstacle to firms. The WBES survey provides direct information from firms about specific perceived obstacles and therefore does not infer the existence of general financing constraints from other information. Furthermore, the WBES database has excellent coverage of small and medium-sized firms (as well as large firms), whereas other cross-country studies of corporate finance that focus almost exclusively on large, listed corporations. Finally, the WBES has very broad country coverage that is important for linking the firm-level data with the bank supervision data.

Although there are potential problems with using self-reported data, because a firm facing the same obstacle may respond to questions differently in different institutional, cultural, or economic settings, we do not believe the data bias our conclusions for the following reasons. First, if reporting anomalies represent pure measurement error, this would bias the results *against* finding a significant relationship between bank supervision and firm financing obstacles. Second, to the extent that reporting anomalies represent institutional, cultural, or economic factors, we control for many country-specific traits and obtain consistent results. Third, additional work suggests that the survey data are closely associated with other measurable outcomes. Hellman et al. (2000) show that in a subsample of twenty countries there is a close connection between responses and measurable outcomes, and they find no systematic bias in

---

[19] The overall standard deviation of the bank corruption variable is 0.93, whereas the between-country standard deviation is 0.49, and the within-country standard deviation is 0.82.

the survey responses. Furthermore, Beck, Demirgüç-Kunt, and Levine (2003b) (a) find a negative relationships between corruption in lending and Wurgler's (2000) measure of the efficiency of investment flows and (b) note that industries that are technologically heavy users of external finance grow faster in countries where firms report the corruption of bank official is less of an obstacle to firm growth. Thus, firms' responses to the survey are associated with measurable outcomes.

As an additional robustness check on the usefulness of firm responses to the question regarding the degree to which corruption of bank officials is an obstacle, we redo all of the analyses controlling for *each* firm's response to the following question regarding **Financing Obstacles**: "How problematic is financing for the operation and growth or your business?" If a particular firm is particularly pessimistic or is simply blaming other factors on its performance, this should be reflected in both its response to this general financing obstacle question as well as its response to the more specific question on the corruption of bank officials. By incorporating this Financing Obstacle variable in the regressions, we lower the likelihood that idiosyncratic firm responses are biasing the results. Thus, if we obtain the same results even when controlling for each firm's response to this general financing obstacle question, this strengthens the interpretation of an independent relationship between the bank supervision indicators and the degree to which the corruption of bank officials is an obstacle to firms obtaining external finance.

To assess the impact of bank supervisory approaches on the degree of corruption in bank-firm relations while controlling for bank-specific and country-specific factors, we estimate regressions of the following form:

$$\text{Bank Corruption}_{j,k} = \alpha + \beta_1 S_i + \beta_2 F_{j,i} + \beta_3 C_i + \varepsilon_{j,k}, \qquad (4.6)$$

where the j and i subscripts indicate firm and country respectively. S_i represents bank regulatory and supervisory indicators in country i; $F_{j,i}$ is a vector of firm-specific control variables; C_i is a vector of country-specific control variables; and $\varepsilon_{i,k}$ is the residual.

Because the dependent variable, Bank Corruption, takes discrete values of 1, 2, 3, or 4, we use a standard maximum likelihood ordered probit estimator with heteroskedasticity-robust standard errors.[20] The

---

[20] Questions exist about whether this type of equation should be estimated using clustering or not. When allowing for clustering within countries, this does not restrict observations to be independent within countries; rather, it requires that observations are independent across countries. Although boosting efficiency, it may induce biases. Beck, Demirgüç-Kunt, and Levine (2005b) show that the results hold with or without clustering.

coefficients, however, cannot be interpreted as marginal effects of a one-unit increase in the independent variable on the dependent variable, given the nonlinear structure of the model. Rather, the marginal effect is calculated as $\varphi(\beta'x)\beta$, where φ is the standard normal density at $\beta'x$.

The analyses control for several firm-specific attributes ($F_{j,i}$). In terms of ownership, **Government Firm** takes on the value one if the government owns any percentage of the firm, and **Foreign Firm** takes on the value one if foreign entities own any fraction of the firm.[21] Our sample includes 6 percent government-owned firms and 25 percent foreign firms. In terms of each firm's line of business, competitive environment, and size, the regressions include dummy variables for whether the firm is an exporting firm (**Exporter**), whether it is a manufacturing firm (**Manufacturing Sector**), and whether it is a service sector firm (**Services Sector**). The analyses also include the log of the number of competitors that each firm faces (**Number of Competitors**). In sum, 38 percent of the firms in our sample are in manufacturing and 47 percent in service, and on average they face 2.1 competitors. Also, the regressions include the log of sales in U.S. dollars as an indicator of size (**Sales**). Finally, as noted earlier, we also control for each firm's response to the **Financing Obstacle** question ("How problematic is financing for the operation and growth or your business?").

The analyses of the impact of bank supervisory strategies on bank corruption also controls for various country-specific traits (C_i), which we have defined earlier. We include: (1) the growth rate of GDP per capita, **Growth,** since firms in faster growing countries may face lower obstacles; (2) **Political Voice and Accountability** to control for the political environment; (3) **Absence of Graft** since we want to assess the independent relationships between bank supervisory indicators and corruption in bank lending in particular even when controlling for the aggregate level of corruption in the country's government; (4) **Government-owned Banks** to control for the degree of state-owned banks; and (5) the logarithm of the gross domestic product per capita of the country (**GDP per Capita**) to control for the overall level of institutional development.

---

[21] Although these simple zero-one indicators of ownership may not capture the varying degrees of influence that arise from different levels of government or foreign ownership, information on the percentage of ownership is available for less than 10 percent of the sample. However, among the firms for which we have data on the percentage of foreign and government ownership, more than two-thirds of firms with foreign ownership are majority foreign-owned and more than 60 percent of firms with government ownership are majority state-owned.

In order to examine the conflicting theories regarding the impact of bank supervisory strategies on corruption in lending, we focus most of our attention on the Official Supervisory Power and Private Monitoring indices. Nevertheless, we also include the degree of generosity of the deposit insurance regime (Moral Hazard) as higher values may reduce governance of banks and therefore decrease the integrity of bank lending. We want to evaluate whether Official Supervisory Power and Private Monitoring are not proxying for this potential effect.

These firm-level analyses require an additional caveat to the data problems mentioned earlier. We are examining the responses of individual firms to questions regarding the corruption of bank officials, but the explanatory variables are country-level measures of bank regulation and supervision. Thus, we are explaining cross-firm responses with a cross-country explanatory variable, which some may view as artificially inflating the degrees of freedom in the analyses. Clustering the residuals at the country level, as in Beck, Demirgüç-Kunt, and Levine (2005b), will partially alleviate the problem because it allows the errors to be correlated across firms within a country. We cannot, however, collapse the data to run a pure cross-country regression because (1) we have a limited dependent firm-level variable and firm level regressors besides the country level regressors and (2) we want to assess the impact of bank regulation and supervision on the nature of firm-bank lending relationships while controlling for other firm-level (and country-level) characteristics. Thus, although arguably problematic, this methodology provides a vehicle for studying the mechanisms through which bank regulation and supervision may influence real activity in economies.

As a final caveat before presenting the results, these regressions do not distinguish between the view that politicians use powerful supervisory agencies to achieve political objectives and the view that powerful supervisory agencies simply use their power for private gain. In short, we do not distinguish political from regulatory capture. These analyses simply examine the relationship between the bank regulatory regime and the degree of corruption in bank lending perceived by firms.

4.E.2. Bank Policies and Lending Integrity: Results

Table 4.9 presents the firm-level regression results of Bank Corruption. The table provides six regressions with different conditioning information sets. The first column uses a very limited set of control variables.

Then we include additional variables individually. Finally, column six includes everything simultaneously.

Three results emerge.

First, the results contradict the public interest view, which predicts that powerful supervisory agencies will reduce market failures with positive implications for the integrity of bank-firm relations. Rather, we observe that Official Power never enters the Bank Corruption regressions with a significant and negative coefficient.

Second, the results are broadly consistent with the private interest view. Official Power enters positively and significantly in all six regressions. These results are consistent with fears that governments with powerful supervisors further their own interests by inducing banks to lend to politically connected firms, so that strengthening official supervisors accommodates increased corruption in bank lending.[22] Importantly, these results hold even when controlling for the overall level of corruption in society (Absence of Graft). Thus, this suggests that there is a strong, positive, independent link between official supervisory power and bank corruption. This finding suggests further caution in implementing Basel II's second pillar, which gives greater discretion to supervisors.

The positive relationship between corruption in lending and Official Supervisory Power is robust to (1) controlling for nationwide corruption and (2) allowing for clustering of errors within countries (Beck, Demirgüç-Kunt, and Levine, 2005b). These robustness tests reduce, although do not eliminate, concerns that some third factor – associated with nationwide corruption – drives both the adoption of a high level of Official Supervisory Power and a high degree of corruption in lending. Even if this "third factor" is not captured by the corruption index or clustering, however, it does not resurrect Basel II's second pillar. If nationwide corruption induces countries to (1) adopt powerful official supervisory agencies and (2) have high levels of corruption in lending, this certainly does not imply that countries will improve the integrity of bank-firm relationships by empowering official supervisors.

Beck, Demirgüç-Kunt, and Levine (2005b) go on to test whether the positive impact of Official Supervisory Power on corruption in lending is a result of reverse causality or whether Official Supervisory Power

[22] We recognize that politicians who are determined to intervene in the allocation of credit will likely find another channel besides bank regulation and supervision if supervisory powers are weakened. Still, these results suggest that powerful supervision can be abused and that it would be best to understand the institutional factors at work before recommending "strengthening" official supervision.

Table 4.9. Corruption and Lending

	(1)	(2)	(3)	(4)	(5)	(6)
Government firm	-0.044	-0.046	-0.005	-0.031	-0.079	0.005
	(0.747)	(0.737)	(0.967)	(0.831)	(0.615)	(0.975)
Foreign firm	-0.192	-0.190	-0.121	-0.207	-0.188	-0.132
	(0.000)***	(0.000)***	(0.031)**	(0.000)***	(0.001)***	(0.046)**
Exporter	-0.085	-0.082	-0.092	-0.046	-0.079	-0.036
	(0.272)	(0.282)	(0.267)	(0.568)	(0.284)	(0.674)
Manufacturing Sector	0.075	0.078	0.127	0.022	0.100	0.077
	(0.332)	(0.307)	(0.107)	(0.771)	(0.184)	(0.370)
Services Sector	0.148	0.151	0.221	0.117	0.179	0.175
	(0.139)	(0.137)	(0.018)**	(0.267)	(0.064)*	(0.087)*
Sales	-0.039	-0.041	-0.031	-0.037	-0.017	-0.018
	(0.011)**	(0.011)**	(0.037)**	(0.033)**	(0.089)*	(0.071)*
Number of Competitors	0.241	0.226	0.234	0.220	0.113	0.204
	(0.139)	(0.118)	(0.160)	(0.224)	(0.399)	(0.151)
Growth	-12.052	-11.809	-9.854	-13.104	-0.582	3.455
	(0.042)**	(0.043)**	(0.090)*	(0.029)**	(0.928)	(0.605)
Official Supervisory Power	0.144	0.150	0.143	0.172	0.161	0.262
	(0.026)**	(0.020)**	(0.047)**	(0.031)**	(0.011)**	(0.005)***

	(1)	(2)	(3)	(4)	(5)	(6)
Private Monitoring	−0.271 (0.020)**	−0.266 (0.026)**	−0.232 (0.053)*	−0.298 (0.022)**	−0.106 (0.413)	−0.230 (0.189)
Moral Hazard Index		−0.013 (0.703)				−0.017 (0.653)
Financing Obstacle			0.262 (0.000)***			0.218 (0.000)***
Government-Owned Banks				0.226 (0.618)		0.004 (0.992)
Voice & Accountability					−0.403 (0.002)***	−0.486 (0.001)***
Absence of Graft						−0.023 (0.911)
Log GDP Per Capita						0.172 (0.324)
Number of Observations	2259	2259	2259	2124	2259	2032

Notes: The dependent variable is Corruption.
Estimated using ordered probit analysis with clustering.
P-values are in parentheses.

243

reduces corruption in countries with well-functioning political and legal institutions. Using instrumental variables to control for simultaneity bias, they confirm the results reported earlier. Furthermore, Official Supervisory Power may only work well when a country has sound political and legal institutions that induce politicians and regulators to promote public welfare, not private interest. Beck, Demirgüç-Kunt, and Levine (2005b), therefore, allow the effect of Official Supervisory Power on corruption in lending to vary with the level of development of political and legal institutions. Although sufficiently sound political and legal systems reduce the pernicious effects of official supervisory power, they never find that empowering official supervisors significantly reduces corruption in lending.

Third, the results support the private monitoring corollary. Private Monitoring enters negatively and significantly in all of the regressions. Thus, firms in countries with stronger private monitoring tend to have less of a need for corrupt ties to obtain bank loans. This is consistent with the assertion that laws that enhance private monitoring will improve corporate governance of banks with positive implications for the integrity of bank-firm relations. Again, these results hold when controlling for: (1) firm-specific traits and a range of country-level controls, including GDP per capita; (2) aggregate corruption; and (3) the firm's answer to the question regarding how hard it is to obtain financing. Thus, even when controlling for general financing obstacles, the aggregate level of corruption, the level of economic development, the political system, and firm traits, the data still indicate a strong, negative link between Private Monitoring and Bank Corruption. This result advertises the importance of Basel II's third pillar on information disclosure and private monitoring.

The economic magnitudes of these results are not inconsequential. We computed the impact of a change in Official Power from one standard deviation below the sample mean to one standard deviation above the mean. The estimates from regression (6) in Table 4.9 indicate that this would almost double the probability that a firm reports that the corruption of bank officials is a major obstacle for the operation of the business (i.e., it almost doubles the probability that a firm reports a value of Bank Corruption of four). In terms of private monitoring, we calculated the impact of a change in Private Monitoring from one standard deviation below the sample mean to one standard deviation above the mean using the estimates from regression (6) in Table 4.9. The results indicate that this would cut in half the probability that a firm reports that the corruption of bank officials is a major obstacle for the operation of the business (i.e., it reduces by 50 percent the probability that a firm reports a value of Bank Corruption of four). To give a specific country example, the estimates suggest that if Mexico had the same level of Private Monitoring as the United States, this would reduce by 40 percent the probability that a firm reports that the corruption of bank officials is a major obstacle in Mexico.

Beck, Demirgüç-Kunt, and Levine (2005b) also test whether the impact of Private Monitoring depends on political and legal system characteristics. Specifically, the private interest view holds that when supervisory agencies force banks to disclose accurate information to the public, then private investors can use this information to exert effective governance over banks with positive implications for the integrity of bank lending. This view, however, assumes that private investors have a well-functioning legal system at their disposal so that they can use this information to improve bank operations. Furthermore, this view assumes that the government is effective at forcing banks to disclose accurate information. That is, the government not only has statutes requiring banks to disclose accurate information, but it also successfully induces banks to disclose this information to the public. From this perspective, improvements in information disclosure rules will only improve the quality of bank lending when the legal system and government work effectively.

The evidence indicates that Private Monitoring increases the integrity of bank lending in countries with sufficiently well-developed legal and government institutions (about two-thirds of the sample), but it has no significant effect in countries with poor institutions. Beck, Demirgüç-Kunt, and Levine (2005b) find no cases in which Private Monitoring significantly increases corruption in lending.

4.F. SUPERVISION, REGULATION, AND BANK GOVERNANCE

4.F.1. Supervision, Regulation, Laws, and Ownership: Concepts, Data, and Methods

To assess which public policies improve the operation of banks, we now examine the impact of bank regulation and supervision, shareholder protection laws, and the ownership structure of banks on the governance of banks. If bank managers face well-functioning governance mechanisms, then this increases the probability that banks will allocate society's savings efficiently and exert sound governance over the firms to which they lend. Furthermore, if the legal system and private sector provide effective mechanisms for overseeing banks, then this may reduce the need for official regulation and supervision. Yet, very little is known about which laws and regulations enhance the governance of banks.

To measure the quality of corporate governance of corporations, researchers frequently use Tobin's Q, which equals the ratio of the market value of the firm's equity plus the book value of its liabilities to the book value of the firm's assets. Intuitively, investors are willing to pay more for equity when sound corporate governance mechanisms effectively protect their rights and reduce expropriation by corporate insiders. Here, expropriation is defined broadly to include theft, inappropriate transfer pricing, asset stripping, the hiring of family members, the allocation of capital in a manner that enriches insiders but hurts the firm as a whole, and any other "perquisites" that benefit insiders at the expense of all shareholders. In sum, higher values of Tobin's Q are frequently interpreted as indicating better corporate governance.

Substantial research examines how shareholder protection laws and ownership influence the corporate governance of non-financial corporations. In terms of shareholder protection laws, Claessens et al. (2000) and La Porta, Lopez-de-Silanes, Shleifer, and Vishny (2002) show that countries with laws that protect the rights of minority shareholders tend to have more highly valued firms, as measured by Tobin's Q, than countries with weaker investor protection laws. The evidence is consistent with the view that investor protection laws provide tools for small shareholders to stop large shareholders from expropriating corporate resources.

Researchers have also devoted considerable efforts to examining the relationship between ownership structure and the value of nonfinancial corporations. A substantial theoretical literature examines a crucial agency problem: the ability of controlling owners to expropriate – often legally – corporate resources.[23] The incentives of the controlling owners to expropriate resources from the firm, however, depend on their cash-flow rights. As their cash-flow rights rise, expropriation involves a greater reduction in their own cash flows. Because expropriation is costly, increases in the cash-flow rights of the controlling shareholders will reduce incentives to expropriate corporate resources and, therefore, boost the market value of the corporation. Research on corporate valuations has also examined the interactions between ownership structure, shareholder protection laws, and firm valuation (Shleifer and Wolfenzon, 2002). This work makes two inextricably linked predictions. First,

[23] See Jensen and Meckling, 1976; Grossman and Hart, 1988; Stulz, 1988; Burkart, Gromb, and Panunzi, 1998; and Bennedsen and Wolfenzon, 2000.

in a firm with a controlling owner that has substantial cash-flow rights, a marginal improvement in the legal protection of small shareholders will have less of a positive impact on corporate valuations than in a firm without a controlling owner, or where the controlling owner has smaller cash-flow rights. Put simply, shareholder protection will exert less of an impact on corporate valuations in firms with a larger controlling owner exerting corporate governance. Second, in a country with a high degree of effective legal protection of minority shareholders, a marginal increase in the level of cash-flow rights of the controlling owner is less important for limiting expropriation of minority shareholders' wealth. If the law is already limiting expropriation, concentrated ownership is less important. For nonfinancial firms, La Porta, Lopez-de-Silanes, Shleifer, and Vishny (2002) empirically verify these predictions.

But are banks different? Many argue that banks are different because they are extraordinarily complex and opaque (Morgan, 2003). Thus, investor protection laws may not provide a sufficiently powerful mechanism for protecting small shareholders, reducing expropriation of bank resources, and boosting bank valuations. Others argue that banks are different because they are heavily regulated and supervised by the government. Thus, extensive bank regulations may render shareholder protection laws superfluous, or bank regulatory and supervisory policies may supersede standard investor protection laws. In sum, although cash-flow rights concentration and shareholder protection laws tend to reduce expropriation and boost corporate valuations in nonfinancial firms, will these same mechanisms work equally well in opaque, heavily regulated banks?

This subsection reviews recent evidence by Caprio, Laeven, and Levine (2004) on the impact of bank regulation and supervision, shareholder protection laws, and ownership structure on the valuation of banks. Information on bank valuations provides direct evidence on banks' cost of capital and indirect information on the market's assessment of the governance of banks. Holding other things constant, effective governance mechanisms that reduce the ability of insiders to expropriate bank resources, promote bank efficiency, and improve the allocation of credit will boost the market value of banks.

Following Caprio et al. (2004), we consider two measures of bank valuation. **Tobin's Q** is the traditional measure of valuation and equals the ratio of the market value of equity plus the book value of liabilities divided by the book value of assets. **Market-to-Book** equals the ratio of the market value of equity to the book value of equity. These data are computed from the Bankscope database in 2003, which is maintained by Bureau Van Dijk. We only present results using the Market-to-Book measure because banks are extraordinarily heavily leveraged corporations. All of the results hold using the traditional Tobin's Q measure of valuation.

To measure shareholder protection laws, we use **Rights** from La Porta, Lopez-de-Silanes, Shleifer, and Vishny (1998). Rights is an index that is formed by adding one when: (1) the country allows shareholders to mail their proxy vote, (2) shareholders are not required to deposit their shares prior to the General Shareholders' Meeting, (3) cumulative voting or proportional representation of minorities on the board of directors is allowed, (4) an oppressed minorities mechanism is in place, (5) the minimum percentage of share capital that entitles a shareholder to call for an Extraordinary Shareholders' Meeting is less than or equal to 10 percent (the sample median), or (6) when shareholders have preemptive rights that can only be waived by a shareholders meeting. The range for the index is from zero to six, with larger values indicating greater protection of minority shareholder rights.

Caprio et al. (2004) measure ownership concentration by computing the cash-flow rights of the shareholder with the largest direct and indirect voting rights. This computation involves the following complex process. First, identify all major shareholders who directly control over 5 percent of the votes.[24] Second, if these major shareholders are themselves (financial or nonfinancial) corporations, find the major shareholders of these corporations. Third, continue to search down this indirect ownership chain until one finds the ultimate owners of voting rights. For example, a shareholder has $x + y$ percent total voting rights of Bank A if she directly owns y percent of the votes and indirectly owns x percent of the votes of Bank A by controlling directly firm C that, in turn, controls directly firm B that, in turn, controls x percent of the votes of Bank A. In practice, these control chains can be quite long. Fourth, divide banks into (a) those without a controlling shareholder and (b) those with a controlling shareholder. Widely held banks do not have a controlling shareholder (i.e., no legal entity owns more than 10 percent of the voting rights).[25] Fifth, compute

---

[24] Most countries do not require disclosure of ownership shares below 5 percent.

[25] There are five categories of controlling shareholders who own more than 10 percent of the voting rights: a family, the state, a voting trust/foundation, a widely held nonfinancial corporation, and a widely held financial institution. As discussed in Caprio et al. (2004), it is not clear whether banks controlled by a widely held corporation should be categorized as widely held or as having a controlling owner. On the one hand, there is a legal entity with more than 10 percent of the voting rights of the bank. On the

the direct and indirect cash-flow rights of the controlling shareholder. For instance, if the controlling owner of Bank A holds the fraction y of cash-flow rights of firm B and firm B in turn holds the fraction z of the cash-flow rights of firm C and firm C in turn holds the fraction x of the cash-flow rights in Bank A, then the controlling owner's indirect cash-flow rights through this chain equals the product of x and y and z (x^*y^*z). **Cash-Flow** equals the fraction of the bank's cash-flow rights owned directly and indirectly by the bank's controlling shareholder and equals zero if the bank is widely held.[26]

Using these data, Caprio et al. (2004) estimate regressions of the following form:

$$\text{Market-to-Book}_{b,i} = a + b\text{Cash-Flow}_{b,i}) + c(\text{Rights}_i)$$
$$+ \cdots d(\text{Rights}_i{}^*\text{Cash-Flow}_{b,i}) + e(S_i)$$
$$+ f(C_i) + (B_{b,i}) + u_{b,I}, \quad (4.7)$$

where the subscript "b" indicates that the variable is available at the bank level, and the subscript "i" indicates that the variable is available across countries. Thus, Rights_i is the shareholder rights index that is available across countries, while $\text{Cash-Flow}_{b,i}$ is the cash-flow rights of the controlling owner available at the bank level across countries. In terms of the other variables, S_i includes the many regulatory and supervisory indicators discussed earlier; C_i is a country-level control variable, such as the level of institutional development, corruption, and political openness; and $B_{b,i}$ represents bank-level control variables, such as the size of the bank, asset growth, and whether the State is the controlling owner of the bank. The equation is estimated using random effects because tests reject the

---

other hand, the management of the bank is not accountable to an ultimate individual owner. Caprio et al. (2004) show that the results are robust to either classification. They show that the most important distinction is whether a person/family is the controlling owner.

[26] As demonstrated and discussed by Caprio et al. (2004), there can be important differences between cash-flow rights and the voting rights of the controlling owner. For example, consider a shareholder who owns 10 percent of the voting rights and cash-flow rights of firm A, and firm A in turn holds 20 percent of the voting rights and cash-flow rights of bank B. Assume that this shareholder (i) does not own direct shares in bank B and does not have control or cash-flow rights of bank B through other indirect chains of control and (ii) is the largest equity holder of firm A. In our calculations, this shareholder has 20 percent voting rights of bank B because the shareholder controls firm A and firm A has 20 percent of the voting rights of the bank. This shareholder's cash-flow rights, however, equals 2 percent because the shareholder only receives 2 percent of the bank's dividends (20% * 10%).

null hypothesis that the errors are independent within countries, so we do not treat banks within a country as independent observations and the random effects estimator adjusts the standard errors accordingly.[27] The analyses cover 244 banks across 44 countries and include the 10 largest publicly listed banks (data permitting) in each country.

4.F.2. Supervision, Regulation, Laws, and Ownership: Results

First, on ownership, banks are generally not widely held. In the average country, only 25 percent of the banks are widely held in our sample of the largest banks. Indeed, in only seven of the forty-four countries are more than half of the banks widely held (United States, United Kingdom, Norway, Japan, Ireland, Canada, and Australia). In contrast, twenty-one of forty-four countries do not have a single widely held bank. In terms of voting rights, 73 percent of the countries have banks where, on average, the control rights of the largest shareholder exceed 20 percent of total voting rights. Thus, banks do not adhere to the typical textbook model of diffuse ownership. Rather, the typical large bank has a large, controlling owner, as La Porta, Lopez-de-Silanes, Shleifer, and Vishny (2002) found for nonbank firms.

Second, rather than being widely held, banks are generally controlled by a family, and to a lesser degree by the state. In the average country in our sample, a family is the controlling owner in 52 percent of those banks with a controlling owner and the state is the controlling owner in 19 percent of banks with a controlling owner. In some cases, the state plays a dominant role. For instance, the state controls more than half of the sampled banks in Egypt, Greece, India, Indonesia, and Thailand. Again, these observations emphasize that it is important to pay considerable attention to the importance of family and state ownership of banks, rather than primarily viewing banks as widely held corporations.

Third, laws concerning shareholder protection are importantly associated with the degree of ownership concentration. Countries with low levels of shareholder protection tend to have fewer widely held banks and greater cash-flow rights concentrated in the hands of the controlling owner. For example, the fifteen countries with rights equal to one or two

---

[27] Furthermore, Caprio et al. (2004) confirm the results using instrumental variables to control for the potential endogenous determination of cash-flow rights and market valuations.

have banks with cash-flow rights that on average equal 33 percent. In contrast, the sixteen countries with rights equal to four or above have banks with average cash-flow rights of 20 percent. Caprio et al. (2004) provide formal statistical tests that are consistent with the prediction that strong protection of minority shareholder rights makes potential small investors more confident that insiders will not exploit them.

Fourth, Caprio et al. (2004) find that bank valuations respond to the same corporate control mechanisms as nonfinancial corporations. Thus, a representative regression from Caprio et al. (2004) yields the following result:

$$\text{Market-to-Book}_{b,i} = 1.929^{***}(\text{Cash-Flow}_{b,i}) + 0.296^{***}(\text{Rights}_i)$$
$$- .689^{***}(\text{Rights}_i{}^*\text{Cash-Flow}_{b,i})$$
$$+ 0.018(\text{Official Supervision})$$
$$- 0.197(\text{State}_{b,i}) - 0.113(\text{Loan Growth}_{b,i}),$$

where *** indicates significance at the one-percent level, State is a dummy variable that equals one if bank b, in country i has the State as the controlling owner and zero otherwise, and Loan Growth is the growth rate of each bank's loan portfolio over the last three years. There are three major results on cash-flow rights and shareholder protection laws:

- Larger cash-flow rights by the controlling owner boost valuations.
- Weaker shareholder protection laws lower bank valuations.
- Greater cash-flow rights mitigate the adverse effects of weak shareholder protection laws on bank valuations.

These findings support the contention that expropriation of minority shareholders in banks is an important consideration in the determining the market value of banks, that shareholder protection laws can restrain expropriation, and concentrated cash-flow rights are a frequently used mechanism for reducing expropriation and governing banks. Thus, in contrast to some policy advice to restrict ownership concentration of banks, these results suggest that concentrated cash-flow rights are an efficient and effective response in countries with weak shareholder protection laws. These results are robust to controlling for a vast array of country-specific control variables, including bank regulatory and supervisory policies, as well as bank-specific characteristics and different estimation procedures that control for potential simultaneity bias.

Fifth, official supervisory practices, capital regulations, and regulatory restrictions on bank activities do not influence bank valuations. Specifically, there is no evidence that the stringency of capital requirements, official supervisory power, or regulatory restrictions on bank activities boost bank valuations by reducing fears of expropriation. These findings do not support Basel II's first two pillars.[28] At the same time, these results are inconsistent with fears that (1) powerful supervisory agencies, stringent capital requirements, and regulatory restrictions on bank activities provide mechanisms for governments to expropriate bank resources with negative repercussions on bank valuations and (2) extensive supervisory power represents a large tax on banks with negative implications for bank valuations. Rather, consistent with the general thrust of Basel II's third pillar on market monitoring, the results emphasize the importance of shareholder protection laws in explaining bank valuations.

4.G. SUMMARY OF RESULTS

We preface this concluding section by emphasizing three limitations with our analyses. First, given the novelty of the bank regulation and supervision data, future researchers may discover more informative ways of using the raw data to construct useful indices of bank regulation and supervision around the world. To be sure, we believe that there are good reasons for the choices we made in constructing these indices, but they are not unique. Similarly, we have merged these regulatory data with country-level, bank-level, and firm-level datasets and employed a battery of methodological

---

[28] Caprio, Laeven, and Levine (2004) were concerned that these results may reflect the net impact of two countervailing forces. First, effective supervision/regulation may reduce fears of expropriation and thereby exert a positive influence on bank valuations. Second, especially in the presence of deposit insurance, supervision/regulation may reduce bank risk below the level desired by shareholders and thereby exert a negative influence on bank valuations. Put differently, with government sponsored deposit insurance, bank shareholders will tend to want banks to assume greater risk than official supervisors do, so that effective supervision/regulation will push bank risk below the level sought by shareholders. The net results may hide the separate impacts of supervision/regulation on expropriation and risk-taking. To address this concern, they examine an alternative econometric specification that allows supervision/regulation to exert a direct positive impact on valuations (to capture the expropriation channel) and an indirect negative impact on bank valuations (to capture the risk-reducing channel). To allow for the risk-reducing channel, they include the interaction term of Moral Hazard (from Demirgüç-Kunt and Detragiache, 2003) with the supervision/regulation variables. If the risk-reducing channel is important, then the interaction term should enter negatively. This interaction term never enters significantly.

procedures to assess what works best. Again, future researchers may use better datasets and more effective statistical methods. Thus, our efforts are a start, not an end. We trust that others will extend and improve upon our initial efforts.

Second, inextricable latent factors and endogeneity biases may underlie many of our findings and cloud the interpretation of the results. Banking sector policies almost certainly reflect historically fashioned attitudes toward the financial sector and the role of government regulation, political interest groups, colonial heritage, and the influence of international institutions. In short, these policies are "path dependent," an issue explored further in Chapter 5. Similarly, some may note that there is a positive correlation between policemen and crime. This does not imply that policemen cause crime. Rather, it implies that societies engage policemen to curb crime. In the case of bank regulation, inefficient, unstable, and corrupt banking systems may attract regulators to address these ills. From this perspective, it is wrong to attribute poor banking to regulatory restrictions on bank activities and competition, official supervisory power, and government ownership of banks.

In this chapter, we have attempted to control for potential statistical and interpretational biases that may arise from either the endogenous determination of bank regulatory and supervisory policies or the influence of a decisive third factor by using instrumental variable methods, microeconomic datasets, and by controlling for many country-specific traits. Based on these robustness tests, the results suggest that bank regulatory and supervisory strategies that focus on empowering private sector monitoring of banks work better than strategies that rely excessively on official supervision. That said, we do not believe that a country's approach to bank regulation and supervision can be easily changed from one that emphasizes official regulatory limitations on bank entry and activities combined with hands-on official oversight to one that relies on forcing banks to disclose reliable, comparable information to the public. A checklist approach to improving private monitoring will not work! As discussed in the next chapter, bank regulatory and supervisory strategies reflect deeply rooted national institutions and attitudes toward the role of government in society. Indeed, it is the role the government plays in a society that sets the tone for regulation and supervision. To better understand both the determinants of bank regulatory and supervisory policies and effective strategies for reforming those policies, future research should use country case studies to trace the forces shaping the evolution of bank regulation and supervision.

The third category of limitations with our analyses involves the methodological problems associated with each part of this chapter's investigation. For example, the pure cross-country analyses do not examine the channels through which bank regulation and supervision may influence the operation of banks and the allocation of capital in an economy. Bank-level analyses focus on net interest margin and overhead costs, which may not accurately capture interbank differences in efficiency. The stability results are based on indicators of systemic crises that generally involve timing problems when matched with existing bank regulatory and supervisory indicators. The analyses of corruption in lending provide insights into a particular mechanism through which banking sector policies influence firms' access to bank credit, but the data involve subjective self-reporting by firms. Finally, the examination of the impact of laws and regulations on the corporate governance of banks supports the conclusion that strengthening official oversight of banks is less efficacious than strengthening the legal rights of private claimants on the bank in boosting bank valuations, but questions remain about the accuracy of market-to-book value type measures as proxies for the effectiveness of corporate governance. Each of these approaches to examining what works best has problems. But, these problems are unlikely to be perfectly correlated. Thus, the fact that each of the examinations of what works best provides a consistent "big picture" answer to the question, what works best in bank regulation and supervision, increases our confidence in the overall results.

In summarizing the findings regarding which bank regulatory and supervisory policies work best, we focus on two of the three goals articulated at the start of this chapter: assessing the validity of the Basel II recommendations and providing evidence on the public interest versus the private interest debate in banking policies. This chapter's third objective involved providing a cross-country assessment of the relationship between a broad array of bank regulatory and supervisory policies and bank development, stability, efficiency, lending integrity, and the governance of banks. Besides Basel II's three pillars, capital regulations, official supervision, and private monitoring, we examined additional bank regulatory and supervisory policies. These included regulatory restrictions on the entry of foreign and domestic banks, regulatory restrictions an the nonlending activities of banks, the generosity of the deposit insurance regime, government ownership of the banking industry, regulatory restrictions on banks making foreign loans, and independence and structure of the supervisory authority. Because we summarized the results on each of these policies when discussing the empirical results on bank development stability, efficiency, lending integrity, and governance, this concluding section focuses on Basel II and overall strategies regarding the role of government in regulating banks.

This chapter's analyses advertise the importance of Basel II's least developed pillar: effective use of information disclosure to strengthen market discipline of banks. The results indicate that countries that adopt regulations forcing the disclosure of accurate, comparable information about banks to the private sector tend to have better developed banks. Also, countries with pro-private monitoring regulations enjoy lower bank interest rate margins and lower bank overhead costs, which suggests greater bank efficiency. Moreover, countries that facilitate private sector governance of banks through regulations that require banks to disclose relevant information to the public tend to have a higher degree of integrity in lending; that is, firms report that corruption in bank lending is less of an impediment to obtaining bank credit in countries with pro-private monitoring policies. Finally, although not a direct measure of bank regulation and supervision, we examine the impact of investor protection laws on the governance of banks. We find that laws that strengthen the legal rights of shareholders boost the market value of banks. Again, this stresses the importance of private discipline rather than public oversight. Although the results on the linkages between bank stability and information disclosure regulations are weak, the bulk of the evidence emphasizes the importance of regulatory and supervisory policies that facilitate market discipline of banks.

In contrast, the results question the merit and desirability of Basel II's second pillar: increasing the authority of the official supervisory agency to discipline and influence banks. Critically, we never find that boosting official supervisory power has significant and robust positive effects. Boosting official supervisory power does not boost bank development, efficiency, stability, lending integrity, or the governance of banks. Indeed, if anything, empowering official supervisory agencies makes banks work worse. Countries with stronger official supervisory agencies have firms that report bank corruption as a more important obstacle to obtaining bank credit than countries with less powerful official supervisory agencies. This is consistent with fears of political/regulatory capture. Furthermore, some evidence suggests that official supervisory power lowers the overall level of bank development, although this effect is small in countries with well-developed political institutions that may reduce political/regulatory capture. In sum, although the evidence does not permit the overarching conclusion that strengthening official supervisory power makes banks work worse, the results provide no support for the view that official supervisory power makes banks work better based on any criteria. There is weak support that the impact of supervision is more positive, or not quite as negative, on financial sector development in countries with a very strong institutional environment, but the bad news is that this only applies to a country whose institutions place it in the "top ten."

In terms of Basel II's first pillar, our analyses do not provide much support for the view that capital regulations exert a reliably positive impact on either bank stability or performance. In terms of bank development, efficiency, and governance, we find no evidence that capital regulations improve the functioning of banks. There is some evidence that countries with more stringent capital requirements have a lower probability of systemic banking crises. But the capital regulation results are plagued by a comparatively large number of problems that lower our confidence in them. Specifically, the systemic banking crisis results are not robust to controlling for other features of the regulatory and supervisory regime. Also, measurement issues plague the crisis findings because the information on capital regulations was collected *after* many of the systemic crises. As emphasized, our inability to identify a robust link between capital regulations and bank operations may derive from the harmonization of capital standards internationally since Basel I in 1988. There may be insufficient cross-country variation in measured capital regulatory standards today to assess the impact of capital standards on bank stability and performance.

Finally, in terms of the epic debate on the proper role of government in the economy, the chapter's analyses: (1) provide no support for the public interest view, (2) support for the private interest view, (3) do not reject the view that governments are ineffective at designing and implementing welfare improving policies, and (4) bolster the corollary of the private interest view that stresses the efficacy of "sunshine" regulations that force information disclosure and strengthen market discipline of banks. As noted, we do not find official supervisory power, regulatory restrictions on bank activities or the entry of new banks, government ownership of banks, or generous deposit insurance have positive effects, so the analyses do not bolster the public interest view of bank regulation and supervision. Rather, official supervisory power is associated with greater corruption in lending – a prediction of the private interest view. Moreover, in contrast to the public interest view but consistent with the private interest view, regulatory restrictions on bank activities reduce bank development, increase bank fragility, and decrease bank efficiency. Similarly, quite the opposite from the public interest view but fully consistent with private interest arguments, barriers to new bank entry and restrictions on international banking tend to reduce bank development and stability. Rather, the results support an approach to bank regulation and supervision that seeks to facilitate private monitoring of banks through effective information disclosure. Even if the findings on corruption are driven by an omitted variable, so that supervision is merely ineffective, the results still emphasize the benefits of private monitoring.

These findings undoubtedly confront strong prejudices. The types of prejudices that exist are reflected in the common language of the financial sector policy community. Official reports typically use the phrase "strengthening official regulation and supervision" as synonymous with adopting regulatory and supervisory policies that enhance the operations and stability of banks. This chapter's results make this conventional usage more precise. We believe that adopting regulatory and supervisory policies that improve bank performance and stability is crucial for economic welfare. Our empirical results identify regulatory and supervisory practices for achieving these goals. Critically, we find that care is required in using the phrase "strengthening official regulation and supervision." The results suggest that "strengthening official regulation and supervision" does not mean increasing the power of the official supervisory agency. Rather, the findings imply that "strengthening official regulation and supervision," means adopting policies that facilitate private monitoring of banks because these policies enhance the operations of banks and therefore improve the impact of banking on the economy.

FIVE

Choosing Bank Regulations

"... my aim will not be to provide a detailed program of policy but rather to state the criteria by which particular measures must be judged if they are to fit into a regime of freedom. It would be contrary to the whole spirit of this book if I were to consider myself competent to design a comprehensive program of policy. Such a program, after all, must grow out of the application of a common philosophy to the problems of the day."

(Hayek, 1960, p. 5)

5.A. RECAP AND MOTIVATION

As discussed in Chapter 4, the empirical results are broadly consistent with the private interest view of bank supervisory and regulatory policies and generally inconsistent with the public interest view. For instance, the public interest view suggests that supervisory agencies adopt regulatory restrictions on bank activities and limit the entry of new banks to promote the safety and soundness of the banking system. Yet, we find that these policies do not lower the probability of banking crises. Rather, they increase both net interest margins and bank overhead costs, which is more consistent with the private interest hypothesis that narrow interests will use bank regulations to enrich and protect special interests in society. Similarly, the public interest view suggests that countries will empower official supervisory agencies so that they can more effectively monitor banks and induce banks to behave in a socially efficient manner. Yet, we find that official supervisory power boosts the degree of corruption in lending and reduces the efficiency of financial intermediation, without inducing a corresponding reduction in banking system fragility. Consistent with the private interest theory of regulation, we find that countries that force banks to provide accurate information to the private sector have less corruption in bank lending and better developed banking systems, with no offsetting negative ramifications from strengthening and relying on private sector monitoring of banks.[1]

As emphasized earlier, our findings on the private and public interest theories fit into an extensive literature that examines whether and how narrow groups in society use the coercive power of the government to extract rents from others in the economy (Stigler, 1971; Peltzman, 1976, 1989; Becker, 1983).[2] The public choice literature holds that special interest groups with a significant stake resting on particular policies are better able to organize politically to support those policies than society at large is able to organize to defeat socially inefficient policies.[3] Furthermore, Baron (1994) and Grossman and Helpman (2001) stress that when the general voting public has incomplete information about public policies, this increases the effectiveness of well-organized special interests. Other research focuses on how narrow groups exploit lobbying, the legislative bargaining process, electoral procedures, corruption, the inability of politicians to commit credibly to future policies, and other mechanisms to exert a disproportionately large impact on public policies.[4]

---

[1] The decision to implement an approach more oriented to supporting private monitoring may partially reflect a government's beliefs that (1) direct, hands-on government supervision and regulation alone will not achieve socially efficient bank operations and (2) private interest incentives may lead to socially inefficient regulatory actions. Some may, therefore, classify the private monitoring approach as the government acting in a "public interest" manner. That is, the government acts in the best interest of the public by not relying on official regulators to monitor and discipline banks directly but instead strengthening private sector oversight of banks. This is valid. Nevertheless, we classify evidence that supports the private monitoring approach as consistent with the private interest view of regulation because such evidence emphasizes the advantages, from a social welfare perspective, of adopting bank regulations that minimize the adverse effects stemming from private interest incentives in policy making.

[2] For helpful discussions, see Persson and Tabellini (2000, 2003a, 2003b) and Grossman and Helpman (2001).

[3] See Tullock (1959), Olson (1965), Weingast, Sheplsle, and Johnsen (1981), and Becker (1983, 1985).

[4] On the legislative bargaining process (including decision-making rules, agenda-setting, amendment rights, and the control over the sequencing of decisions), see, for example, Baron and Ferejohn (1989), Baron (1991, 1993), and Persson, Roland, and Tabellini (1997). On lobbying (including campaign contributions and strategic, information gathering and dissemination to politicians), see Grossman and Helpman (1994, 1995), Dixit, Grossman, and Helpman (1997), and Potters and van Winden (1992). On interactions between lobbying, elections, and government formation (including the conditions under which politicians focus on competing for the support of particular lobbies), see Baron (1993, 1994), Besley and Coate (1996), and Austen-Smith and Banks (1988).

Our findings also fit into a growing body of evidence from the history of banking in the United States that finds that the private interest theory of regulation explains both the enactment and elimination of bank regulations better than the public interest view. As discussed in Chapter 2, researchers document that the comparative political power of small banks relative to large banks – rather than public interest considerations – has shaped regulatory restrictions on branching.[5] Other research notes that some regulations influence small firms differently from large firms and stresses that the comparative power of these different groups influences regulatory policies (Kroszner and Strahan, 1999). These analyses provide a rich and detailed picture of bank regulation in the United States.[6] We add to this work by providing cross-country evidence on the supervision and regulation of banks. Our research confirms that a private interest view of regulation provides a more accurate and useful depiction of bank regulation around the world than a public interest view.

In this chapter, we address related, although broader, questions: Do differences in political systems influence the choice of bank regulatory policies? Do political systems influence the degree to which small groups exert a disproportionately large impact on bank regulations? What is the role of new data and new evidence in reforming bank regulations if political systems shape regulatory choices? Thus, this chapter uses a political economy framework to assess the determinants of bank supervision and regulation around the world.

The premise is that the ability of a narrow group to control policy and promote its own interests depends on the political system. Some political systems discourage transparency, participation, and competition. Indeed, some political systems are controlled by entrenched elites and remain secretive about the exact nature of public policies. These political systems may be less successful in creating socially efficient banking regulations than open, competitive, democratic systems that encourage transparency and penalize corruption. Thus, even if one accepts that special interests influence the choice and operation of bank regulations in an open democracy such as the United States, the degree to which private interests can

---

[5] See White (1983), Flannery (1984), Abrams and Settle (1993), Economides, Hubbard, and Palia (1996), Kane (1996), Jayaratne and Strahan (1998), and Kroszner and Strahan (1999).

[6] Laeven (2004) shows that deposit insurance policies around the world are more consistent with private interest theories of regulation than public interest explanations. Furthermore, see Demirgüç-Kunt and Kane (2002), who examine the operation of deposit insurance in different countries.

easily manipulate public policies for their own gain may depend on the organization and operation of political institutions. Elites have greater control over bank regulations in an autocracy than a democracy.

Although some may argue that the connection between politics and regulatory choices is so obvious that it is not worth empirically exploring or testing, others disagree. As noted, even within the context of democratic political systems, a considerable body of research argues that small – but exceptionally powerful – segments of society frequently exert a disproportionately large impact on the choice of public policies. Thus, special interest groups may be so effective at achieving their objectives (even within democracies) that competitive elections are unlikely to yield socially efficient policies (Buchanan and Tullock, 1962). Others may cling to a public interest view and argue that bank regulation, when it does not function well, primarily reflects ignorance and mistakes about what works best. From this perspective, path dependency and miscalculations matter more than politics in explaining international variation in regulatory choices. Still others express greater optimism that electoral competition will induce opportunistic politicians to enact efficient policies (Stigler, 1971). Furthermore, rather than focusing on political system differences or the strategies employed by special interest groups, Poole and Rosenthal (1991) highlight the importance of ideological differences across political parties in accounting for voting patterns in the U.S. Congress. This divergence of views motivates our empirical assessment of the connection between regulation and the organization and operation of political systems.

The first part of this chapter provides motivation for the importance of the role of policies in banking by comparing the evolution of bank regulations in Mexico and the United States. The experiences of these two countries suggest that differences in the operation and organization of political systems shape banking sector policies.

The second part provides a conceptual framework for considering how political systems shape banking sector policies. It is, of course, not the only way to link politics and regulations. Indeed, the discussion in Chapter 2 on the private and public interest views of bank regulation reviews ways in which bankers and other groups use political levers to obtain advantageous policies. The conceptual framework presented in this chapter focuses on broad political system traits and therefore motivates the cross-country regressions that we use to assess the importance of political system traits in shaping bank regulations. Critically, the framework considers alternatives to focusing on political determinants of banking sector policies. In particular, policies may reflect historical accidents and ignorance, or special interest groups may be so effective in achieving their ends that broad political institutions are unimportant in accounting for cross-country differences in bank regulation and supervision.

Finally, we provide empirical results on the impact of the organization and operation of political systems on bank regulations and also discuss the implications of these findings for actualizing bank regulatory reform. We find that measures of the degree of political system openness, competition, and transparency help explain cross-country differences in bank supervision and regulation in very predictable ways. Given these results, identifying sound policies is a necessary condition for formulating efficacious reform strategies, but successful reform recommendations also would need to consider the political forces at work in each country. Specifically, making policy recommendations that actually induce socially efficient reforms will require a keen understanding of national, and perhaps even subnational, political institutions and almost certainly involve custom-designing bank regulatory reform based on these institutions.

5.B. MOTIVATING EXAMPLE: MEXICO AND THE UNITED STATES[7]

5.B.1. Mexico

Between independence in 1821 and the first Porfirio Diaz presidency in 1876, Mexico had seventy-five presidents, suffered a 20 percent drop in GNP per capita, and fragmented into regional fiefdoms ruled by political and military bosses. To avoid the plight of his predecessors, Diaz faced considerable challenges. Unification and stability were expensive since "[a]rmies had to be paid, a bureaucracy had to be created, and regional transport barriers had to be overcome by subsidizing the construction of a national railroad network (Haber, et al., 2003). Yet, Mexico could not access international capital markets to finance these expenditures because of past defaults. Nor could the federal government raise more taxes because provincial leaders thwarted tax collection.

To centralize control and secure his leadership, Diaz established a political-economic system that provided secure property rights, supportive banking policies, and other advantageous policies for small elites in

---

[7] This subsection is based on Haber (2004). We augment the discussion with insights from Bodenhorn (2003), Haber, Razo, and Maurer (2003, pp. 41–123), Haber (1997), Maurer (2002a), Hammond (1957), Federal Reserve Staff (1941), Robertson (1995), and others.

return for political support and funding (Haber, Razo, and Maurer, 2003). In terms of politics, Diaz centralized power. From the states, the federal government assumed the powers to regulate and tax both natural resources and interstate trade and the right to grant bank charters (Haber, 2004). As Diaz centralized power, there were no effective political institutions to check his control. In theory, Mexico was democratic and had a bicameral legislature to balance executive power. In practice, Diaz's political machine, not competitive elections, chose the candidates and hence the outcomes. Diaz handpicked the governors of Mexico's states, many of whom were not even from the states that they governed. Indeed, virtually all Senate votes after Diaz took power were unanimous (Haber, Razo, and Maurer, 2003).

In terms of banking, Diaz demanded loans that allowed him to centralize control, establish security, build a bureaucracy, and finance a national railroad. In effect, Diaz gambled that the government could use loans from domestic banks to establish political stability and foster economic development and the resultant stability and growth would produce sufficient extra tax revenues to service the loans.

In return for loans and political support, the government let Mexico's bankers write the banking laws, which generated large rents for bankers and reinforced the political regime.[8] Given the authors, the banking policies drafted by Mexico's bankers are not surprising. In 1884, Diaz merged two existing banks and formed a huge bank, Banco Nacional de Mexico (Banamex). Banamex was allowed to increase its uncalled capital by eight million pesos whereas the government received a loan for the same amount. In return for providing credit to the government, Banamex was given: (1) a monopoly on providing financial services to the government, including underwriting government debt issuances, holding federal deposits, and collecting taxes; (2) a monopoly on international financial transactions; (3) lower reserve requirements than other banks; (4) lower taxes than other banks; and (5) extremely high protective barriers, including (a) the legal requirement that a new bank would need the approval of both the Secretary of the Treasury and the Federal Congress and (b) extraordinarily high minimum capital requirements. Furthermore, Banamex and Banco de Londres y Mexico were the only two banks permitted to branch nationally. Thus, in return for financing

---

[8] As suggested in Chapter 2, it can be difficult to determine who has the upper hand, or whether it is more a case of political capture (by politicians) or regulatory capture (by those being regulated).

Federal and state projects, Diaz facilitated the creation of a very secure and closely controlled banking environment.

To make the arrangement between the banking and political systems credible and hence successful, Diaz needed to assure bankers and firms that the government would not confiscate property and extort funds. To accomplish this task, Diaz engineered a merger of bankers and politicians. As Haber (2004, p. 42) notes, "The board of directors of Banamex, for example was populated by members of Diaz coterie, including the President of Congress, the Under-Secretary of the Treasury, the Senator for the Federal District, the President's Chief of Staff, and the brother of the Secretary of the Treasury." Being on the board entitled directors to director's fees, stock distributions, and most importantly influence over the flow of capital. The board of directors of the Banco de Londres was also composed of political all-stars, with the chairman being the Secretary of War (Haber, 2004, p. 42). The boards of directors of regional banks looked very similar. Indeed,

The only difference was that state governors, rather than cabinet ministers, sat on their boards and received directors' fees, stock distributions, dividends, and in some cases loans made with no expectation of repayment. In some cases, the governor himself received the bank concession. In fact, the system was deliberately conceived to distribute benefits to the state governors, and give them a stake in the maintenance of Porfirio Diaz's rule. (Haber, 2004, pp. 42–43)

The merger between banking and politics created a concentrated, inefficient banking system that primarily lent money to businesses with close ties to the directors of the banks. Others were shut out of the formal credit market. Not only did Banamex and Banco de Londres control 60 percent of all banking assets, but they were also devastatingly effective in allocating this capital: "From 1886 to 1901 *all* of the private (non-governmental) loans made by Banamex went to its own directors" (Haber, 2004, p. 45). This control over the flow of society's savings had enormous ramifications on industrial efficiency. In a series of studies, Haber (1991, 1997), Maurer and Haber (2004), and Maurer (2002) show that Mexico's industries were considerably less efficient than comparable industries in other countries with more developed financial systems (the United States and Brazil). In sum, although Diaz used the rents created by the banking oligopoly to fund stability and greater economic progress than Mexico had achieved in the previous fifty-five years, this had long-term adverse implications on economic efficiency when compared to countries that did not commingle the role of politicians and bankers to the same degree.

The political-financial institutions established by Diaz were self-reinforcing and proved quite durable. After the horrendous violence and economic distress of the Mexican Revolution, President Calles reestablished order in the 1920s by reconstituting many of the same forces used under Diaz. The bankers were permitted to write a new banking law with extremely high barriers to entry. Furthermore, the government created the Comision Nacional Bancaria (CNB), which was charged with both regulating banks and reporting to congress. Unsurprisingly, the CNB was primarily composed of prominent bankers. This provided a convenient mechanism for bankers to coordinate their actions, lobby the government, and draft banking legislation. Finally, the government created Banixco in 1925, which had a monopoly on government lending and the issuance of paper money. Besides acting as the central bank, Banixco lent heavily to President Calles' companies, his relatives' companies, and companies owned by the Foreign Secretary, the Education Secretary, the Secretary of Industry Commerce and Labor, the Finance Secretary, and so on. Thus, the postrevolutionary structure was remarkably similar to that constructed under Diaz. To the detriment of economic efficiency, an autocratic political system allowed bankers to write the rules and the resulting rents from these rules were shared with politicians.

5.B.2. The United States

The history of banking in the early United States offers an illuminating contrast to that of Mexico. Under the 1789 Constitution, the states lost the right to tax international trade and to issue coin and paper money.[9] This hurt state revenues so state treasurers devised an alternative revenue source.

In return for providing financing, states granted banking licenses. Indeed, Bodenhorn (2003, p. 14) argues that although bankers frequently used bribery to elicit a charter, they were more likely to exploit chronic budgetary shortfalls in negotiating for a banking license. As discussed in Chapter 2, bank licensing became a significant form of revenue for a

---

[9] Hammond (1957, pp. 103–109; and 265) points out that there is nothing in the Constitution about banks and banking, and that the Constitution authorized the federal government to issue coin but was silent with respect to paper money. However, Supreme Court decisions "affirmed that Congress had power to incorporate and control a bank, and that the states had no power to interfere by taxation or otherwise." The Supreme Court also "removed whatever constitutional inhibition ever existed upon the power of Congress to authorize anything it wishes as money."

number of states, and the payments to the state took many forms, including direct cash payments, equity stakes in the bank, commitments to lend to the state at below market interest rates, and promises to fund state infrastructure projects (Sylla, Legler, and Wallis, 1987). Note that these cash payments, equity stakes, and loan agreements were between the state and the bank, not between individual politicians and the bank. The use of bank charters to raise revenues was sufficiently profitable that it expanded from the original thirteen states to Kentucky, Tennessee, Illinois, Arkansas, and Alabama as they entered the union. Thus, "[t]hroughout the country, banks were under specific requirements to lend to their state governments on special terms, and before 1820 the practice of exacting bonuses for the enactment or renewal of charters had become established..." Indeed, "[i]n February 1816, when some Massachusetts banks declined to lend to the state, an act was passed requiring them to do so, on penalty of two per cent a month of the sum the state wished to borrow" (Hammond, 1957, p. 188). Moreover, states did not want these rents competed away by the entry of non-chartered banks, so "... nearly all [states] passed laws that required private banks to obtain a corporate charter from the state government..." (Haber, 2004, p. 15).[10]

At first glance, the close ties between treasury revenues and banking monopolies reminds one of Mexico, but competition among political groups in the United States permitted competition among banks. Unsurprisingly given U.S. political history, Federalist-Republican tensions framed this competition. For example, Republican merchants in Philadelphia complained that the two existing "Federalist" banks funneled credit to Federalist-owned businesses. When Republicans gained a legislative majority in 1803, Republican bankers quickly petitioned for and gained a charter (Bodenhorn, 2003, p. 13).

A second example from New York illustrates that no single political-economic group had sufficient power to monopolize banking. Alexander Hamilton helped found the Bank of New York in 1791[11] and through his connections with the legislature fought off numerous attempts to start a "Republican" bank.[12] The Republican Aaron Burr (yes, that Aaron Burr), as a member of the state legislature, however, introduced a bill

---

[10] Also, see Hammond (1957, pp. 184–185). The Supreme Court affirmed the constitutionality of State bank charters in 1837 (Federal Reserve Staff, 1941, p. 8).

[11] The Bank of New York opened in 1784 but was not granted a corporate charter until 1791.

[12] "In New York City, from 1784 to 1791 there was no bank but the Bank of New York, and from 1791 to 1799 there was no other but the local office of the first Bank of United States. Both were Federalist" (Hammond, 1957, p. 149).

to charter a water company (the Manhattan Company) in 1799 with $2 million capital and slipped into the legislation a proviso that any capital not immediately necessary for the water project could be employed in moneyed transactions. That is, he successfully added a clause that established a bank (the Bank of the Manhattan Company). Although some have called this a great ruse, Bodenhorn (2003, pp. 133–135) suggests that the de facto granting of the banking license to Burr reflects two additional forces. There may have been blatant graft as politicians responded to the bribes of merchants seeking the new banking charter.[13] Also, the legislature may have been happy to look tricked because they recognized that New York's merchants needed greater access to credit but they did not want to vote for a new banking charter because the population was wary of banks. Bodenhorn (2003) offers these explanations because it was too easy for legislators to catch the clause that Burr added to the legislation (and some did) and the legislature kept making the same "mistake." Specifically, the legislature started many banks by granting charters to manufacturing firms, who then used the surplus capital to start and operate banks.[14] Whether through ruse or graft or some combination, the case of Bank of New York illustrates that no single group had sufficient political power in New York to stymie bank competition.

As a final example, the Browns of Providence, who were the Federalist owners of the only bank in town, Providence Bank, lost their monopoly when the Republicans came to power in 1800. "The surest procedure for any new group that wished to obtain a bank charter from a Jeffersonian state legislature was to cry out against monopoly in general and in particular against that of the Federalist bankers who would lend nothing, it was alleged, to good Republicans" (Hammond, 1957, p. 146). This type of argument was sufficiently persuasive to inject politics into banking

---

[13] According to Hammond (1957, p. 152), moreover, "[s]ince there were Federalists outside the legislature willing to put money in the project, it is not strange that there were Federalists inside willing to vote for it."

[14] There are two interesting twists to this story as recounted by Chernow (2004, pp. 585–589). New York suffered a terrible yellow-fever epidemic in 1798, primarily because New Yorkers relied on polluted wells. Thus, Burr gained Hamilton's support to create a water company that would pipe clean water from the Bronx River. Hamilton worked long hours in 1799 both in developing plans to obtain clean water and in lobbying the Federalist legislature to gain support for the plan. Thus, Burr had enlisted "his foe's mighty pen in a clandestine" plan to charter a Republican bank. Although successful in chartering a new bank, Burr's Manhattan (Water) Company did not fulfill its promise of clean water. It scraped its plan of piping in clean water and instead used contaminated water from old wells. Yellow fever returned to New York.

on the basis that "Jeffersonians, if they could not extirpate monopoly, could at least reduce its inequalities by seizing a share of its rewards" (Hammond, 1957, p. 146). Indeed, President Jefferson in 1803 wrote to his Treasury Secretary, ". . . as to the patronage of the republican bank in Providence, I am decidedly in favor of making all the banks republican by sharing [government] deposits amongst them in proportion to the dispositions they show" (quoted from Bodenhorn, 2003, p. 14). These examples simply indicate that one political party did not have sufficient control to thwart the emergence of new banks.

Political competition in conjunction with the fiscal needs of the state further undermined the ability of state governments to maintain monopoly banking in the United States. In Mexico with centralized political power, the granting of a banking monopoly meant in perpetuity, or at least a decade or more. In the United States, with more political competition, state legislatures developed much shorter time frames and quickly abrogated commitments to banking monopolies. Bodenhorn's (2003, p. 17) recounting of the Philadelphia Bank is illustrative. The Philadelphia Bank's chances of obtaining a charter in 1803 were slim because the state already held stock in the Pennsylvania Bank. To increase its chances, the Philadelphia Bank offered the state a very attractive financial package. The Pennsylvania Bank responded with an even more lucrative offer with the condition that the Philadelphia's petition be rejected. Back and forth went the bidding until the Philadelphia Bank won a charter in 1804, undercutting the Pennsylvania Bank's market position. Similarly, although the state of Virginia favored the Bank of Virginia in which it held a 20 percent ownership stake, it did charter new banks that paid a sufficiently sizable franchise tax to the state (Haber, 2004; Wallis, Sylla, and Legler, 1994). Louisiana followed this tradition, chartering new banks, as new infrastructure projects needed funding. The names of these banks illuminate the point: the Atchafalaya Railroad and Banking Company, New Orleans Gas Light and Banking Company, New Orleans Canal and Banking Company, and so on (Bodenhorn, 2003, pp. 231–232). More generally, ". . . banks were frequently chartered for the main purpose of financing some enterprise of a public nature, for example, a turnpike, a canal, a railway, or a toll bridge" (Federal Reserve Staff, 1941, p. 8). Furthermore, there was competition between the federal government and states. Indeed, antipathy by state banks toward the first Bank of the United States, and later toward the second Bank of the United States, helped defeat movements to renew their charters in 1812 and 1836, respectively (Haber, 2004, pp. 19–20, and Hammond, 1957, p. 355).

Competition for people also shaped banking policies in the United States (Haber, 2004, pp. 22–24). Each of the original thirteen states restricted the right to vote to those with sufficient resources to meet minimum property requirements or tax payments. As new states joined the union, however, all except for Louisiana had virtually no restrictions on the right to vote. To maintain their workforce, therefore, the original states were forced to reduce voting restrictions dramatically and many eliminated wealth-based qualifications. In essence, there was a bidding war for people, where the currency was political rights. The broadening of the right to vote undermined political coalitions that favored existing banking monopolies.

Thus, competition between states broadened political participation with material ramifications for banking sector policies. As voting rights spread from 1810 to 1840, the United States moved toward a free banking model.[15] Pennsylvania's Omnibus Banking Act of 1814 chartered forty-one new banks. By the 1820s, most New England states sold their shares in banks, regularly granted new banking charters to petitioners, and instead taxed bank capital and dividends to fill state coffers. Banking boomed. Between 1819 and 1830, the number of banks and bank capital more than doubled in New England (Haber, 2004, p. 24). Over time, most states of the United States had adopted de facto free banking, whereby bank charters no longer required a special legislative act. Based on the New York Free Banking Act of 1838, many states allowed anyone to obtain a charter and engage in the banking business by complying with certain general conditions.[16] Banks simply had to register with the state comptroller and deposit state or federal bonds with the comptroller if they wanted to issue notes. Whereas there were only 88 states banks in 1811, the number had increased to 901 in 1840, and still further to 1,562 in 1860 (Robertson, 1995, p. 16). Although some states implemented prudential regulations, including double liability for bank stockholders, competition in the United States clearly fostered a quite different banking system than in Mexico's oligarchic system.

---

[15] Bodenhorn (2004) stresses that the emergence of free banking in the United States is not fully explained by the rise of Jacksonian populism. Rather, he documents extensive corruption in the granting of banking charters and argues that this helped fuel a backlash against regulatory restrictions on entry that conformed to the "equality of treatment" political ideology of the 1830s.

[16] Eventually, even those state that prohibited banking (e.g., Florida and Texas) and those that maintained a system of branch banks comprising as a whole what was known as the "State Bank" (e.g., Indiana and Ohio) adopted free banking statutes (Federal Reserve Staff, p. 11).

Although the evidence clearly does not suggest that the United States in the middle of the nineteenth century had the ideal banking system, existing analyses do suggest that it was more competitive and efficient than the system in Mexico. A principal drawback was that the free banking era produced a huge number of small banks that were typically not permitted to branch. Indeed, in the late 1840s there were no branches of banks in any of the New England states, and only two for the State of New York (Robertson, 1995, p. 27). The inability of banks to branch reduced diversification, led to more than nine thousand different kinds of bank notes, and fostered close ties between local industries and the connected banks. At the same time, unlike in Mexico, no single group controlled the entry of new banks in the United States, so that elites had a more difficult time steering the flow of credit to narrow ends, which would have had detrimental effects on the overall economic efficiency. Thus, a more open, competitive political system reduced – although did not eliminate – the power of small elites.

This comparison of Mexico and the United States emphasizes the close links between political institutions and the operation and structure of the banking industry. Banks allocate society's savings to fund spending by consumers, business, and governments. Thus, people – and politicians – care about banks. To the extent that political institutions permit – or indeed foster – the formation of a small, uncontested coalition that creates and enforces banking policies, the history of Mexico suggests that this group will use its position to establish a banking system that acts in the interests of the ruling elite. To the extent that political institutions permit broader participation in policy making, the U.S. example suggests that it is more difficult for small groups to enact, enforce, and maintain policies that funnel bank credit to a few families. We now provide a broader conceptual basis for understanding the linkages between banking and political institutions, discuss alternative perspectives on the forces shaping banking policies, and present empirical evidence on the linkages between political institutions and bank supervision and regulation.

5.C. CONCEPTUAL FRAMEWORK

Two core questions emerged from our analyses in Chapter 4, which showed that bank supervision and regulation shape the level of banking development, the efficiency of bank operations, banking system stability, and the degree of corruption in bank lending.

(1) Why do some countries choose bank supervisory and regulatory policies that foster sound, efficient bank operations, while others choose policies that encourage inefficiencies, excessive risk-taking, and the allocation of credit based on political or corrupt connections?

(2) Will information, based on "best practice" judgments or research on what works best in bank supervision and regulation, influence policies, or do other factors dominate the choice of banking sector policies?

We apply Acemoglu, Johnson, and Robinson's (2005) analytical framework of the emergence of economic institutions in general to the emergence of bank supervisory and regulatory systems in particular. Consistent with the comparison of Mexico and the United States, we emphasize that the openness, competitiveness, and transparency of political systems shape bank supervision and regulation. We also describe several alternatives to this particular focus on political determinants of banking sector policies. To elaborate, some hold that policies reflect historical accidents. Others stress that policy makers make mistakes because they do not know what policies work best. Still others stress that given national tastes, countries choose optimal policies. And, some stress that public policies reflect the interests of small elites, which are able to achieve their objectives regardless of any specific political system. No doubt, each of these views has some validity. Nonetheless, we argue that both an appreciation of political forces is necessary for understanding cross-country differences in banking policies and current approaches by the international standard-setting community lack this crucial ingredient. In the next section, we take this framework to the data and assess whether cross-country differences in political institutions explain national choices of supervisory and regulatory policies.

5.C.1. Accidental or Limited Information Views of Bank Supervision and Regulation

We begin with the public interest view that governments choose banking policies to maximize social welfare, but have limited information on which policies actually do so. Under such circumstances, deviations of actual policies from optimal policies reflect imperfect information on what works best. From this perspective, credible, convincing research that identifies those bank supervisory and regulatory policies that improve banking system performance will induce countries to adopt better policies with positive benefits for welfare.

Similarly, banking sector policies may primarily reflect historical accidents, or the emulation of neighboring countries. Again, if historical accidents or emulation play prominent roles in causing actual policies to deviate from optimal ones, then a social welfare maximizing government will change policies once credible, convincing evidence accumulates on the benefits to be gained from alternative policies or once persuasive arguments for reform are made by international experts. Thus, in the presence of social welfare maximizing policy makers, convincing new findings on bank supervision and regulation will ignite policy reforms.

These presumptions – that policies reflect ignorance about which ones promote welfare or accidental choices – form the conceptual foundations for the work of international standard setting bodies, international financial institutions, and the bulk of policy-oriented research. For these organizations, the primary goals are to (1) collect information, (2) identify what works best in different countries and conditions, and (3) disseminate this information (along with some adjustment assistance) to policy makers around the world.[17] At times, they also may require countries to amend their regulatory framework as a condition of a loan. The presumption is that if each of these steps is successful, then countries will adopt better policies, poverty will fall, and welfare will improve. From this perspective, although cross-country differences in political institutions may influence the receptivity of countries to policy advice, these institutions are generally not a binding constraint on reform. Indeed, the 1944 Bretton Woods Agreement founding the International Monetary

---

[17] Each of these steps is very difficult. It is difficult to collect reliable information. We spent considerable time collecting information on bank supervision and regulations. And, as we discussed earlier, these data are fraught with problems and are only available in 1999 and 2003. It is very difficult to determine what works best with great confidence, especially when the implications of the same policy may differ under different circumstances. As discussed in Chapter 4, although we use different analytical methods and conduct an array of robustness checks, the presentation is filled with qualifications and notes on the limitations of the research to date. Finally, it is difficult to communicate what works best to policy makers and provide useful guidance on how to implement changes. Finding that information disclosure is an essential component for promoting efficient bank operations is useful, but making this happen in Haiti, or Indonesia, or Nigeria, or, as suggested by the Enron-World Com fiascos, in the United States, is not without its obstacles, even if policy makers want to reform.

Fund and the World Bank explicitly prohibits the use of political reform as a criterion for allocating assistance.

The presumption, however, that *"if we find what works best, countries will change"* seems demonstrably inadequate. Although it is essential to identify those policies that improve economic efficiency, this information alone will not necessarily promote reform. There are just too many counter examples to have much faith in the view that countries have socially suboptimal policies only because of accident or ignorance.

For example, consider Argentina. A British periodical (*British Observer*) remarked that,

"The Argentines alter their currency almost as frequently as they change presidents... No people in the world take a keener interest in currency experiments than the Argentines."

Given events at the turn of the twenty-first century, this quotation is by no means surprising. Argentina has suffered both macroeconomic and political instability since the collapse of the exchange rate against the dollar. What makes the quotation striking is that it was written in 1899! Clearly, Argentina has a deep-seated problem in establishing sound macroeconomic policies. It is possible that over one hundred years of macroeconomic instability reflects "ignorance." That is, Argentines may have consistently elected governments that produced this instability because the public has not deduced which policies produce socially inefficient levels of inflation. We are skeptical of this explanation, however. We doubt that more elaborate models and econometric evidence elucidating the adverse consequences of deficits, inflation, and misaligned exchange rates will solve Argentina's problems. It seems unlikely that Argentines know *less* about the causes and consequences of inflation than people in Japan, or France, or England. Rather, we believe that the evidence is much more consistent with the view that the structure and operation of the political system in Argentina has helped produce a century of macroeconomic instability.

As a second example, consider Burundi. Burundi's GDP per capita is somewhere around $200. This figure is so low that some may question its accuracy. Nevertheless, it seems safe to define Burundi as desperately poor. Moreover, this low level of income per capita is about 30 percent lower than it was over forty years ago when it gained independence. Burundi was poor and is getting poorer. For three-quarters of its independence, a Tutsi military dictatorship has systematically looted the economy by granting enormous state subsidies to enterprises controlled by ruling families and by providing extraordinarily lucrative civil service positions to members of these families. In such extreme conditions, pointing out that funneling credit to inefficient enterprises lowers economic efficiency, boosts poverty, and slows economic growth is unlikely to foster reforms. In such dire conditions, disseminating research results that excessively powerful bank supervisory officials may distort the flow of bank credit to politically connected constituents with adverse implications on overall economic efficiency is unlikely to have positive effects. Although accident and ignorance may partially explain cross-country differences in bank supervision and regulation, these are undoubtedly not the only explanations.

As a third example, consider Ghana. Ghana's major export crop is cocoa, which is produced in the Ashanti region. The Ashanti comprise only 13 percent of the population and enjoyed power for only two years from independence in 1957 to 2000.[18] Until the late 1980s, the various rulers have all agreed on taxing cocoa through ludicrously overvalued exchange rates and then rewarding their political supporters with the rights to import goods at the official exchange rate. Indeed, the black market premium reached 2,100 percent in 1982. By the 1980s, the Ashanti producers of cocoa were receiving only 6 percent of the world price of cocoa. Again, these policies were neither accidental nor a reflection of ignorance. They were quite deliberate. It seems unlikely that advice on social welfare improving policies will produce material change without changes in political forces and institutions in such a country.

Fourth, consider the discussion in Acemoglu, Johnson, and Robinson (2005) of North and South Korea. Before the separation, the two Koreas shared the same cultural and historical roots. At the time of the split, the two countries had about the same level of GDP per capita. If anything, the northern part of the country had better ports and had received the bulk of Japanese investment. By 2000, South Korea's income per capita was over $16,000, whereas North Korea's income per capita was only about $1,000. Ideology may have played a role in the original choices made by these countries. The divergence was so great by the 1980s, however, that differences of opinion about which policies will produce economic success simply cannot fully explain policy choices in North Korea. To extend this admittedly extreme example to banking, it seems safe to conclude (though we do not have data on North Korea) that the North Korean policy approach to financial intermediation is not based on private

---

[18] Since democratic elections in 2000, an Ashanti has held the presidency.

sector monitoring of banks. Nevertheless, our findings in Chapter 4 that a private monitoring approach to bank supervision improves the operation of banking systems is unlikely to resonate in North Korea even if (1) the information were disseminated widely and (2) there were no concerns about our data or methodologies. It seems clear that the North Korean leadership is not maximizing social welfare and the devastation that has transpired is neither an accident nor a mistake.

Fifth, in the 1980s and early 1990s, Rwanda offered preferential financing for coffee. Yet, from a risk management perspective, Rwanda's most significant financial risk was its exposure to coffee – then about 45 percent of GNP. From a risk-reduction perspective, therefore, social welfare considerations would have suggested directing subsidies toward activities with a negative correlation with coffee, not toward coffee. Although ignorance may have played some role, it is also plausible that the coffee growers used political influence to direct the flow of subsidies toward themselves, regardless of social considerations.

The purpose of these examples is not to argue that ignorance, chance, and differences of opinion about which policies will work best play no role in shaping banking policies. Rather, bank supervision and regulation almost certainly reflect both historical accidents and policy makers' best guesses about which policies are best for a country. Thus, we believe that collecting data on bank supervision and regulation, comparing what countries do, and assessing which banking sector policies enhance the performance of banks will improve the ability of policy makers to implement policies that benefit society at large. Nevertheless, these examples stress that political factors play a huge role in shaping banking sector policies. Thus, assembling data on bank supervision and regulation around the world and identifying which regulatory and supervisory strategies foster efficient bank operations are necessary steps but still only initial steps in producing socially efficient policy reforms.

5.C.2. A Coasian Theorem of Bank Supervision and Regulation

Another view is that countries construct bank supervisory and regulatory policies in an economically efficient manner, where economic efficiency is associated with output or wealth maximization, not Pareto Optimality (Acemoglu, Johnson, and Robinson, 2005). We use the phrase, "A Coasian Theorem of Bank Regulation," to characterize the view that politicians may contract for economically efficient policies. We apply this approach to the specific context of banking sector policies.

The title "A Coasian Theorem of Bank Regulation" is potentially misleading and we use it with care. Nobel Laureate Ronald Coase did not argue that writing and enforcing complex contracts were so inexpensive and certain that agents could contract for socially efficient outcomes. Rather, he showed that in many circumstances, one needed to make extraordinarily unrealistic assumptions about the contracting environment to conclude that private arrangements would produce socially efficient outcomes. Thus, Coase himself argued strenuously that to develop more realistic and useful models, we need to leave the frictionless world and embrace the importance of transactions costs. Hence, as nicely discussed by Glaeser, Johnson, and Shleifer (2001) in "Coase vs. the Coasians," there is a difference between Coasians, who focus on the benchmark case of zero transactions costs, and Coase, who emphasizes the gross limitations of this benchmark model and urged economists to develop theories based on nontrivial transactions costs. This distinction motivates us to use the phrase "A Coasian Theorem of Bank Regulation" to refer to a benchmark case and then to develop a social conflict theory of regulation that incorporates contracting costs and provides predictions about the relationship between political institutions and bank regulations.

The core logic underlying the Coasian Theorem of Bank Regulation is that when different groups in society can negotiate and contract at zero cost and when there is no cost or uncertainty associated with enforcing these contracts, externalities are internalized and societies construct efficient policies (Coase, 1960). Consider a situation in which new bank supervisory and regulatory policies will induce a reallocation of capital that produces more output with the same inputs. However, the extra output will accrue to group A whereas group B will receive less capital and produce less output under the new regulatory regime. Under a Coasian Theorem of Bank Regulation, group A can write a contract with group B: In exchange for group B supporting the bank supervisory and regulatory reform, group A will compensate group B for its loss. Thus, everyone is made better off by the policy reform.

Given a country's tastes, endowments, and economic structure, the Coasian Theorem of Bank Regulation implies that each nation chooses efficient bank supervisory and regulatory policies. End of story.

One key reason for questioning the usefulness of the Coasian Theorem of Bank Regulation is the absence of mechanisms for enforcing the types of contracts that are necessary for producing efficient policies. If the contracts cannot be enforced, they will not be negotiated. Countries will therefore be unable to construct efficient banking policies. In the example cited earlier, there may not exist mechanisms for enforcing group A's commitment to compensate group B once the regulatory reforms are enacted. Group B knows this ex ante and therefore never enters into the agreement. In sum, difficulties in enforcing agreements between different groups in society may prevent the implementation of socially efficient regulatory reforms.

This commitment problem further advertises the importance of politics. Perhaps a sufficiently well-developed political system could make the enforcement of intergroup agreements sufficiently credible that more efficient policies are feasible. Thus, there are linkages between the organization and operation of political systems and bank supervisory and regulatory policies.

The Coasian Theorem of bank regulation and supervision emphasizes a theme developed in Chapters 3 and 4 and that occupied much of our thinking during the initial stages of this research project: We expected to find that countries choose an optimal selection of policies depending on the sequencing of policy decisions and institutional capabilities. For example, if a country chooses generous deposit insurance, we expected that country to also choose stricter capital standards and more rigorous official supervisory practices. Similarly, we expected that countries with more generous deposit insurance would be more likely to restrict the ability of banks to engage in securities market activities, or the insurance business, or own nonfinancial firms to reduce the ability of the bank to exploit the deposit guarantee and assume greater risk. Or, if a country did not have the supervisory and regulatory capabilities to oversee banks and restrict risk-taking, we originally expected that this type of country would avoid granting generous deposit insurance. We expected to find many similar types of tradeoffs.

But, we did not find evidence consistent with policy makers choosing optimal combinations of policies, however. We did not find that countries with more generous deposit insurance, for example, were more likely to impose stricter capital standards, or have tougher official supervisory practices, or to enact more stringent information disclosure laws. Rather, we found that countries tended – albeit with great variance – to fall along a spectrum from those that incorporated a considerable degree of private monitoring and information disclosure as central components of bank supervision and regulation to those that focused almost exclusively on direct supervisory oversight of banks and government ownership of the bulk of the banking industry. These findings from Chapters 3 and 4 motivate an analysis of politics and political conflict in shaping bank supervision and regulation.

5.C.3. Politics: A Social Conflict View of
Bank Supervision and Regulation

5.C.3.i. Basics. Given the key role that banks play in allocating society's resources, and the impact of policies on the way they do business, it is not surprising that people frequently disagree sharply about banking sector policies. Existing banks tend to favor regulatory policies that restrict the entry of new banks. Those seeking to enter the market clearly have different views about entry regulations. Existing, well-connected firms may seek bank supervisory and regulatory policies that direct society's savings to them, not toward those enterprises with the highest risk-adjusted rates of return. Firms seeking to contest existing markets clearly have different views of bank policies. Particular ethnic, religious, or political groups may favor bank supervisory and regulatory policies that induce banks to support their clan, and stymie the aspirations of other groups. Given the critical role played by banks in determining who gets a chance at success and who does not, different political groups will almost surely form contentious views on national banking policies.

Although economic efficiency may influence the selection of bank supervisory and regulatory policies, political power ultimately arbitrates conflicts about policy. If one set of policies will produce more output with the same inputs than a different set of policies, this information will become an ingredient in choosing among bank supervisory and regulatory policies. Economic efficiency will not, however, be the only ingredient. Different groups in society care about the distribution of output, not just aggregate output (efficiency). Given conflicts about policies, resolution occurs in the political realm, based on distributional and political criteria, not simply based on economic efficiency criteria. The organization and operation of political systems, therefore, may play a prominent role in determining national banking policies.

Political power derives from two sources: political institutions and de facto political power. De facto political power stems from military power and the ability to bring pressure to bear on politicians (e.g., mass movements and protests, write-in campaigns, influence fundraising, etc). Political institutions (i.e., de jure political power) include the degree to which the political system (1) suppresses or encourages competitive political participation, (2) can grant a small group decisive sway over the selection of the chief executive or provides for democratic elections, (3) creates effective checks and balances on executive power or yields considerable discretionary power to the chief executive, and (4) holds political leaders accountable to the broad population. Both de facto power and political institutions influence the process for making policy choices and the choices themselves.

Political institutions are important because they shape, within bounds determined by de facto political power, the rules of the game for making decisions. For instance, democratic political institutions facilitate broader participation by the population than autocratic regimes. Checks and balances on executive discretion distribute power to other parts of the government and may limit the degree to which narrow special interests dominate public policy making. In contrast, a dictator makes decisions without necessarily incorporating the desires of many groups. The political institutions in Mexico permitted a very small portion of the population to establish a host of economic policies, including banking sector policies. Not surprisingly, governments (or countries) with political institutions that grant disproportionate power to a small group are more likely to choose policies that distribute economic resources to these ruling elites and place much less importance on promoting economic efficiency per se. As we discuss later, this has clear predictions regarding the choice of bank supervisory and regulatory policies.

Of course, both de facto political power and political institutions are endogenous. Indeed, economic policies influence the allocation of economic power, which in turn affect political power and the formation of political institutions. For our purposes, bank supervisory and regulatory policies influence the economic power of different groups, which in turn affects the distribution of political power, the shape of political institutions, and hence the process of making banking sector policies. Thus, there are dynamic interactions between political power and bank supervisory and regulatory policies. The Mexico example illustrates how bank supervisory policies reinforced the political power of ruling families. Similarly, the history of banking policies in the United States suggests that political competition permitted competition in banking, which distributed economic power broadly, with positive feedback on democratic political institutions. We discuss the endogenous formation of political institutions below. For now, we simply want to stress that a key (though many may argue obvious) component of a social conflict view of bank supervision and regulation is that conflicts over bank supervisory and regulatory policies are decided by politicians within the context of prevailing political institutions.

Thus, the basic arguments underlying this social conflict view of bank supervision and regulation are as follows. Bank supervision and regulation influence the allocation of capital and economic power, so that conflicts naturally arise over banking policies. Although overall economic efficiency influences the debate about policy, serious conflicts typically emerge over the distribution of resources. Since political institutions play a role in resolving conflicts over policy, the functioning of the political system will shape bank regulatory policies.

5.C.3.ii. Why Countries Choose Inefficient Policies. To gain a better understanding of this social conflict view of bank supervision and regulation, it is useful to address the question, why do political systems produce economically inefficient policies? Why are groups unable to agree to use economically efficient policies to produce the biggest economic pie possible, in which case conflict would be limited to distributing the output? Why are political institutions typically unable to separate efficiency from distribution?

To answer this question, the social conflict view stresses that the people who control the government are self-interested: They do not maximize social welfare; they maximize their own welfare and will therefore seek to satisfy powerful constituents. Thus, leaders care about distribution, not simply about efficiency. Bank supervisory and regulatory policies are not selected by the whole of society and they are not selected for the benefit of the whole of society. Instead, bank supervisory and regulatory policies are selected by those in power for the benefit of a narrow set of society, subject to the constraints of prevailing political institutions. From this perspective, informing policy makers that alternative bank supervisory and regulatory policies will produce more output with the same inputs will not necessarily spur policy reform because policy makers are not only guided by efficiency. Rather, new, credible information on those banking policies that work best to enhance social efficiency will only foster reform if policy makers believe this will improve their own welfare.

A theory of bank supervision and regulation that stresses the importance of political institutions and political power implies that those in power may choose and defend policies that adversely affect economic efficiency, with the overriding objective of maintaining their positions of power.[19] In the case of Mexico, the commingling of politicians and

---

[19] In an insightful discussion of how political interests change, Von Drehle (2003) describes how, in the wake of a terrible factory fire in New York City in 1911, a set of welfare enhancing reforms were pushed through notwithstanding the previous opposition of the political powers in Tammany Hall. The reforms happened precisely because a farsighted leader of the party political machine saw that immigration would be limiting his party's ability to survive if it persisted in putting narrow business interests first. Hence, his decision to bring in a new generation of political leaders and get in front of reforms was stimulated by political competition.

bankers and the granting of bank monopolies were designed to enrich and protect a small segment of society. The goal was not necessarily to design economically efficient policies that would expand the economic pie for everyone. The goal was to improve the welfare of the elite even if, short of a revolt, this led to less total output than could be produced with alternative policies. The key objective was the distribution of resources to the controlling group, not overall economic efficiency. The chosen banking sector policies were a calculated choice, not a mistake.

Some may suggest that there are ways to contract around inefficient banking policies. For example, the extra output produced by banking reforms that increase the size of the economic pie could be taxed and the proceeds used to compensate those hurt by the reform. This arrangement separates efficiency from distribution.

As discussed earlier, however, commitment problems make these types of arrangements impractical. First, the ruling group may be unable to make a credible commitment not to expropriate all of the gains from the reforming policies. Other groups know this, so the reforms may not induce them to borrow more from banks and undertake new activities. Monopoly political power, therefore, may preclude the realization of efficiency gains from reform. Thus, international differences in political institutions may help explain cross-country differences in bank supervisory and regulatory choices.

A second commitment problem that may bias those in power against undertaking reforms that increase the economic pie involves the potential loss of political power. If changes in existing bank supervisory and regulatory policies will enrich a group that is not in power, and if this newly enriched group were to win power in the future, it might then adopt policies focused on its own interests, not economic efficiency. This new group might even abrogate commitments to compensate the old rulers, and there would be no mechanism to enforce such contracts. Thus, this new group might simply replace the old group at the political helm with relatively little change otherwise.

Economic power influences military and political power. Thus, rulers might even violently oppose economically efficient reforms because they will enrich other groups and therefore jeopardize their own positions of power. Those in power take seriously distribution and hence are typically reluctant to undertake economically efficient reforms that may undermine their comparative economic, military, and political power.

History is replete with examples of political leaders opposing reforms that would increase economic efficiency because they fear losing political power (Acemoglu, Johnson, and Robinson, 2005). For instance, in both Russia and the Austro-Hungarian Empire, kings worried that industrialization would weaken their control and produce powerful competitors. Thus, the Russian monarchy consciously impeded the development of railway lines, except to ease court travel between Moscow and St. Petersburg. Indeed, it was only after the Crimean War that the monarchy permitted large-scale railway projects, the introduction of modern commercial laws that permitted industrialization, and freedom for the serfs. Similarly, the Hapsburg emperors (1) knew that the new technologies and production methods emerging in England would dramatically expand production and (2) blocked the adoption of these technologies because they knew it threatened the economic basis for their political power.[20] Rulers may therefore recognize that reform will boost output, but they also recognize that reform may undermine their economic and hence political power. Faced with this dilemma, the rulers may realize it is impossible to redistribute the gains of reform to themselves, so they oppose economically efficient reforms.[21]

In sum, countries may deliberately choose and maintain inefficient bank supervisory and regulatory policies that yield low output. People everywhere may recognize that the current policies produce socially inefficient outcomes and they may also recognize those reforms which would increase output with the same inputs. Nevertheless, these inefficient policies may protect the elites by limiting the economic and political power of other segments of society and thus persist.

5.C.3.iii. Predictions: Political Institutions and Bank Supervision and Regulation. This social conflict view provides predictions about the linkages between political regimes and banking sector policies. The broad predictions that we emphasize are consistent with a range of political economy models that stress the advantages of electoral competition (Besley and Coate, 1999; Dixit and Londregan, 1996, 1998; Grossman and Helpman, 1996), multiple veto players (North and Weingast, 2000), checks and balances (Persson, Roland, and Tabellini, 1997), the accountability and

---

[20] This is discussed in Acemoglu, Johnson, and Robinson (2005), who also provide historical references.

[21] These power arrangements are not immutable. After over a century of a financial system serving only the elites, Mexico liberalized restrictions on foreign bank ownership after the 1994–1995 crisis and the political system opened as the PRI lost its monopoly hold on the presidency. Although too early to judge, this may presage a period of welfare improving reforms.

credibility of candidates and politicians (Ferejohn, 1986), and a mixture of other factors that shape the degree to which narrow interests can effectively influence public policies (e.g., Dixit, 1996; Weingast and Marshall, 1988; Keefer, 2000). Thus, the social conflict approach to bank regulation is not the only framework for generating predictions about the relationship between political institutions and bank regulations. Although we evaluate broad empirical predictions that emerge from the social conflict framework, many of these other models will yield similar predictions about the basic linkages between political institutions and bank regulation and supervision.

At one extreme, some political systems focus on protecting and promoting the well-being of a small segment of society. These political systems suppress competitive political participation, grant the elite decisive sway over the selection of the chief executive, provide the chief executive considerable discretionary power, and limit the degree to which political leaders are directly accountable to the broad population. This type of political system will develop banking sector policies that facilitate the flow of society's savings toward the interests of the ruling elite.

Uncompetitive political systems that limit democratic input and grant extensive discretion to the chief executive, therefore, (1) will not tend to adopt bank supervisory and regulatory policies that promote private sector monitoring through information disclosure rules because transparency empowers the market in general, not only those in political control; and (2) will tend to erect barriers to bank entry in order to protect existing banks.[22]

Although the predictions regarding competition and information disclosure are straightforward, there are more ambiguous links between political institutions and other bank regulatory policies, such as official supervisory power, regulatory restrictions on bank activities, and government ownership of banks. Autocratic, uncompetitive, and closed political systems may construct powerful supervisory agencies that influence banks to lend to politically favored borrowers. From this same perspective, autocratic, uncompetitive, and closed political systems will

---

[22] Levine (2004) argues that restricting the entry of foreign banks is particularly important. The entry of new domestic banks may not generate less competition and contestability of the local market if large domestic banks can control the behavior of new domestic banks through a variety of local institutions. However, the entry of foreign banks may generate greater contestability of the local banking market than the emergence of new domestic banks if foreign banks are less prone to the influence of local institutions that are controlled by existing financial institutions.

favor regulatory restrictions on bank activities so that banks need to go to the government for special exemptions from those regulations. As a final example, this line of argument also suggests that political systems controlled by an elite group will develop government-owned banks that funnel society's savings toward the ruling group.

From an alternative perspective, if a powerful segment of society thoroughly controls the government, it may not need a powerful supervisory agency, regulatory restrictions, or government-owned banks to achieve its ends. Or, if the elite control the government and own the banks, the corresponding closed, autocratic political system may favor little formal government intervention in banking, except of course measures such as entry barriers to impede competition. More specifically, if the same societal group controls the banks and government, then this group will not need a powerful supervisory agency to induce banks to funnel credit to favored ends. It will simply need a compliant – and perhaps underfunded, understaffed, and unskilled – supervisory agency.[23] Similarly, if the political elites own the banks, they may not need government-owned banks to direct the flow of credit. Finally, if the political elites disproportionately control both the banks and political processes, regulatory restrictions on bank activities may be unnecessary or unattractive. Thus, theory provides conflicting predictions regarding the relationship between political structures and banking sector policies, including powerful official supervision, regulatory restrictions, and government ownership of banks.

Now consider a political system that facilitates political participation, provides for transparent, competitive, and democratic elections, has ample checks and balances on executive power, and makes political leaders accountable to the broad population. In such a political system, we would expect supervisory and regulatory systems that force banks to accurately disclose information to the public to facilitate private sector monitoring of banks. Stated differently, in an open, competitive, democratic political system, part of the policy response to market failures in banking will be to reduce those failures by lowering information and transactions costs. Furthermore, although there may be sound arguments for some limits on new bank entry, sufficiently open, competitive, and democratic political systems will not create regulatory barriers simply to protect existing bankers from competition.

---

[23] This may help explain why, in over a third of the countries in our database, bank supervisors still are not protected from civil lawsuits. The threat of lawsuits may be a convenient way for elites to keep bank supervisors on a short leash.

The social conflict theory also provides ambiguous predictions about the links between open, competitive, and democratic political institutions and official supervisory power, regulatory restrictions on bank activities, and government ownership of banks. On the one hand, open, competitive, and democratic political systems that fear the grabbing hand of government may be wary of (1) creating official supervisory agencies with sufficient power to induce banks to lend to politically favored ends, (2) enacting regulatory restrictions on bank activities that may encourage banks to bribe politicians to obtain exceptions to those regulations, or (3) establishing government-owned banks that favor connected parties. On the other hand, an open, competitive, democratic, and effective political system may function so well that there are few reasons to fear political failures (the grabbing hand) and greater reasons to believe that government agencies can directly ameliorate the market failures (see the discussion in Chapter 2 regarding Capie's [2004] description of U.K. financial regulation). Thus, if there are sufficiently sound institutions in place, (1) official supervisory agencies will reduce market failures, not divert the flow of capital to socially inefficient ends; (2) regulatory restrictions on bank activities will improve monitoring of banks, not create opportunities for predation; and (3) government-owned banks will overcome information and contract costs and produce socially desirable outcomes.

The discussion thus far inaccurately characterizes political systems as falling within a particular spectrum, from democracies to autocracies. Political systems may fall beyond these simple caricatures, however. As emphasized by Haber, Razo, and Maurer (2003), some political systems can be characterized by "roving banditry," in which there is virtually a complete breakdown in enforcing property rights and providing personal security. They emphasize that political systems characterized by political authoritarianism and rent-seeking coalitions that inefficiently allocate society's resources toward favored groups may be preferable to the chaos and violence associated with roving banditry. Using the case of Mexico from 1876 to 1929, these authors argue that Diaz (a stationary bandit) was an improvement over the instability associated with roving banditry before 1876. They stress that Mexico in 1876 could not have moved to an open, competitive, democratic political regime and that the Diaz government offered a dramatic improvement over the political system that had existed for fifty years. Acknowledging the diversity and complexity of political systems around the world does not invalidate the usefulness of examining whether international differences in political structure explain cross-country differences in banking sector policies. We therefore formulate and test some broad hypotheses about political structure and the adoption of bank regulations. However, this discussion emphasizes that we do not have a comprehensive, albeit exhaustive, taxonomy linking political system characteristics with regulatory outcomes. Indeed, our taxonomy is very limited and the results should be interpreted as suggestive of some broad patterns.

When turning to the data it is helpful to think of political systems as falling along a spectrum from those geared toward protecting and advancing the interests of small elites to those based on more open, competitive, democratic institutions. We test empirically whether movements along this political spectrum translate into predictable differences in approaches to bank supervision and regulation. As we move from countries with more closed, autocratic political systems to countries with more competitive, democratic institutions, do we find bank supervisory and regulatory regimes geared more toward private sector monitoring, information disclosure, and openness to new bank entry?

5.D. EMPIRICAL FRAMEWORK AND DATA

Turning from concepts and examples, we now use cross-country data to assess empirically the relationship between political systems and bank supervisory and regulatory systems. Operationally, there are three key data requirements. First, we need to select relevant bank supervisory and regulatory indicators. Second, we need to choose measures of cross-country differences in political systems. Finally, we must select instrumental variables for international differences in political systems because of potential endogeneity problems. In particular, if banking sector policies influence the distribution of income and this in turn shapes political institutions, then ordinary least squares regressions of banking sector policies on political institutions indicators will be biased. This subsection discusses the data and the econometric methodology. The next subsection presents the econometric results.

5.D.1. Indicators of Bank Regulation, Supervision, and Political Systems

We conduct the analyses with five bank supervisory and regulatory indicators. As in Chapter 4, we face the problem of selecting a manageable set of indicators from the large database of bank supervisory and indicators discussed in Chapter 3. We want policy variables that on a priori grounds are likely to reflect different approaches to the role of government in supervising and regulating banks. Although we defined these indicators in Chapters 3 and 4, we briefly describe each again and motivate its use in this investigation of the linkages between the organization and operation of the political system and banking sector policies.

First, we use five bank regulatory and supervisory variables defined and discussed in Chapter 4: **Private Monitoring Index**, **Entry Applications Denied**, **Official Supervisory Power**, **Activity Restrictions**, and **Government-Owned banks**. As stressed, the conceptual framework provides clear predictions about Private Monitoring Index and Entry Applications Denied. The concepts outlined above predict that political systems focused on protecting an entrenched group will not enact policies that force accurate information disclosure or that permit easy entry of new banks; rather they will seek to obscure bank activities and protect existing banks. Although it is feasible that an entrenched group's hold on power may be so secure that it is unconcerned about information disclosure and the entry of new banks, the political economy approach suggests that rulers will tend to be wary of anything that could jeopardize their position. The political economy framework provides more ambiguous predictions about Official Supervisory Power, Activity Restrictions, and Government-Owned banks. On the one hand, political systems that are focused on the elite may seek greater supervisory power, restrictions on bank activities, and government ownership of banks as mechanisms for defending and promoting the interest of the elite. On the other hand, these types of political regimes may not need these policies to funnel society's savings toward the powerful. Similarly, political systems geared more toward social welfare maximization may avoid these policies as they give government considerable power, which could be abused. Or governments with sufficient checks and balances will not abuse this power and will instead use supervisory power, regulatory restrictions, and government ownership to overcome market imperfections.

Second, we use four indicators of the political system to assess whether international differences in political structure influence the choice of bank supervisory and regulatory policies. These indicators provide information about where each country's political system falls along the spectrum from an open, competitive democracy that is accountable to the broad population to a closed, autocratic regime that is only responsive to a small group of leaders. We describe the indicators and the rationale for including them.

The first three indicators are from the Polity IV Project (Marshall and Jaggers, 2002), which provides a database on political regime characteristics from 1800–2002 for a broad cross-section of countries. We use political system data from 1998 so that they predate (or are roughly contemporaneous with) the bank supervision and regulation data.

The goal is to include information on:

1. The extent of formal constraints on the decision-making powers of chief executives,
2. The degree to which there are competitive elections of the executive relative to hereditary succession, and
3. Whether recruitment of the chief executive is open, in principle, to the public at large or whether there are institutionalized limits on political participation.

We chose these indicators because they align with the political economy theory of bank supervision and regulation that we outlined above. Political systems focused on protecting and promoting the well-being of elites will tend to avoid open, competitive elections and will seek to impose few constraints on an executive chosen by the elite, from the elite, to defend and advance the interests of the elite. The resultant political system will also choose bank supervisory and regulatory policies, along with other policies, to protect and promote the interests of the ruling elite.

Executive Constraints is an indicator of the degree to which there exist effective constraints on the chief executive's decision-making powers.[24] In some countries, the chief executive can ignore constitutional restrictions

---

[24] The variable is called XCONST in the Polity IV Project database. This variable measures the extent of institutionalized constraints on the decision-making powers of the chief executive in each country. The variable is coded on a 7-point scale, where higher values signify greater constraints. Specifically, one indicated that there are no regular limitations on the executive's actions. To the extent that a constitution provides some restrictions on executive actions, the legislature initiates some categories of legislation or blocks some executive acts, the ruling party initiates some legislation independently of the executive, or there is an independent judiciary, then XCONST is coded as a 3 (or a 2 if these constraints are very limited or a 3 if these constraints are more substantial). If there are substantial limitations on executive authority, such as the legislature modifies or defeats executive proposals, or the legislature sometimes refuses funds to the executive and makes important appointments to administrative posts, and so on, then XCONST is coded a 5 (or a 6 if these limitations are more extensive). Finally, XCONST is coded as 7 if accountable groups – legislature, ruling party, and so on – have effective authority equal to or greater than the executive in most key areas. This occurs when the legislature initiates most important legislation, or when the executive is chosen by the accountable group (as in parliamentary systems), and so on.

or revise the constitution when convenient. In some countries, there is no legislative assembly or the chief executive has the power to suspend it. At the other extreme, there are countries where the legislature initiates most important legislation and the chief executive relies on the continuous support of an elected group. The regressions here test whether cross-country variation in constraints on executive power shapes banking supervisory and regulatory policies as predicted by theory.

Executive Constraints varies from 1 to 7, where large values signify greater constraints on executive power. Based on 1998 values, many countries achieve values of 7. These countries range from Australia and Austria, to Latvia and Lesotho, to the United Kingdom and the United States. At the other extreme, Saudi Arabia, Qatar, and Nigeria have values of 1.

Executive Competition measures the degree of competition for the executive position in the last election.[25] Thus, chief executives may be selected through hereditary succession, or designated through rigged, unopposed elections. At the other extreme, competitive elections may produce the chief executive. Political systems designed to address the interests of a few will clearly develop undemocratic means for selecting the chief executive. We test whether the degree of competition in choosing the chief executive influences policies toward the banking industry in ways that are consistent with the conceptual framework outlined earlier.

Executive Competition varies from 0 to 3, where 3 implies greater competition. Again, many countries have values of 3, indicating open, competition elections. Many countries select executives based on hereditary rights, or through fixed elections. Countries with very low levels of Executive Competition in 1998 include Nigeria, Rwanda, Gambia, Burundi, Cambodia, and Ghana.

Executive Openness measures whether the position of chief executive is realistically open to the population at large.[26] In many countries, families

---

[25] The variable is called XRCOMP in the Polity IV Project database. This variable measures the extent that prevailing degree of competition for the position of chief executive. If changes in chief executive occur through forceful seizures of power, then XRCOMP is coded as 0. If chief executives are determined by hereditary succession, or through rigged, unopposed elections, then XRCOMP receives a value of 1. The variable is coded as 2 if there are dual chief executives, where one is chosen by hereditary succession and the other through competitive elections. Finally, XRCOMP is coded as 3 if the chief executives are typically chose in competitive elections with two or more major parties or candidates.

[26] The variable is called XROPEN in the Polity IV Project database. This measures the degree to which the position of chief executive is open to the population. XROPEN is

or small clans choose the chief executive as with kings, emirs, and so on. In other countries, open elections provide a mechanism for a broad segment of the population to participate in the political process.

Executive openness varies from 0 to 4, where 4 implies greater openness. Many countries achieve a value of 4, suggesting very open competition for the position of chief executive. In many other countries, institutional arrangements restrict the position of chief executive to only a small segment of society.

Finally, we use a political system indicator from a different data source.

Voice and Accountability measures the degree to which average citizens have a voice in the political process and the degree of accountability on the part of politicians (Kaufmann, Kraay, and Zoido-Lobaton, 1999). This index draws on data from six different data sources.[27] The index includes information on the degree of (1) free and fair elections and democratic accountability; (2) absence of the military from politics; (3) civil liberties, such as free speech, assembly, demonstration, and so on; (4) orderly changes of government; (5) political competition; and (6) independence of the media. Given our taxonomy of political systems, this is an appropriate indicator because it is designed to measure the degree to which the political system only represents and responds to the interest of a few. This indicator is substantively different from the others. The other indicators are measures of "institutions"; they directly measure rules regarding the operation of the political system. Voice and Accountability combines both measures of rules and measures people's subjective assessment of the degree of openness. Thus, Voice and Accountability both measures institutions that that may influence participation and people's beliefs about the degree of participation.

Voice and Accountability ranges from a low of -1.3 to a high of 1.7 in our sample. The means is 0.5 with a standard deviation of 0.87. Based on these data from 1997, some countries have political systems characterized as having very low levels of voice and accountability in the political

---

coded as 0 if the chief executive assumes power through forceful seizure and is coded as 1 if "selected" through hereditary succession. XROPEN is coded as 2 if there are dual executives with both a hereditary executive and an executive appointed through court selection. XROPEN is coded as 3 if there are dual executives, where one is selected through hereditary succession and the other through competitive elections. Finally, XROPEN is coded as 4 if chief executives are chosen in a competitive election.

[27] Kaufmann et al. (1999) provide details on the construction of the index, which uses information from the Economist Intelligence Unit, Freedom House, Political Risk Services, Political Economic Risk Consultancy, Institute for Management Development, and the World Bank Development Report.

process, such as Burundi, Nigeria, Rwanda, Indonesia, and Gambia. Many other countries have systems with open, free, competitive elections, with an independent media and ample freedoms of speech and political participation.

There is a high correlation across the different political system indicators. The correlations range from 0.52 to 0.81 and all are significant at the 1 percent level. Although high, these correlations suggest that the each of the four indicators provides some independent information. Thus, we conduct the analyses with each of these four different political system indicators to provide a more robust evaluation of the relationship between the political system and bank regulation.

In robustness tests, we examined additional political system indicators from a different database. For the period 1975–1995, Beck, Clarke, Groff, and Keefer (2001) construct measures of: (1) the competitiveness of legislative elections, (2) the competitiveness of executive elections, and (3) the number of veto players in the process of passing a new law.[28] When we use these indicators, we obtain the same results as those reported later.

5.D.2. Instrumental Variables: Extracting the Exogenous Part of Political System Indicators

To assess whether these political system indicators explain cross-country differences in bank supervision and regulation, we control for potential endogeneity. Bank supervisory and regulatory systems that enrich,

---

[28] The competitiveness of the legislative elections is scored as follows: If there is not legislature or the legislature is unelected, then the country receives a score of 1 or 2, respectively. If there were elections and there was one candidate or if there were multiple candidates but they were all from the same party, then the country receives a 3 or 4, respectively. If multiple parties are legal but only one party won seats, then the country receives a 5. If multiple parties won seats, but the largest part received more than 75 percent of the seats, then the country receives a 6. Finally, if multiple parties won seats but the largest party received less than 75 percent of the seats, then the country receives a 7.

The executive competitiveness indicator is scored in a similar way. For the number of veto players, the country receives a 1 if either the legislative or executive competitiveness is less than 5 and receives 2 if both are 5 or above. One is added if the executive competitiveness is 6 or 7. One is added if the opposition controls the legislature. In presidential systems, one is added for each chamber of the legislature unless the president's party has a majority in the lower house and a closed-list system is in effect (implying stronger presidential control of his/her party, and therefore of the legislature). In parliamentary systems, one is added for every party in the government coalition as long as the parties are needed to maintain a majority. In parliamentary systems, the prime minister's party is *not* counted as a veto player if there is a closed rule in place – the prime minister is presumed in this case to control the party fully.

empower, and protect a segment of society may facilitate the transformation of the political system in a way that reduces broad participation and accountability and instead intensifies the formation of political systems designed for the benefit of the few. Thus, there may be bi-directional causality between the operation of the political systems and banking sector policies. To control for this, we use instrumental variables to extract the exogenous component of the political system indicators. Note the use of instruments does not rule out that banking sector policies influence the political system. Rather, it allows us to address whether the political system influences bank supervision and regulation. Furthermore, as stressed in the comparison of the United States and Mexico, third factors – such as the lightly populated states to the west of the original colonies that competed for people – may influence both the political system and bank regulations. We use instrumental variables to draw as sharp a line as possible from exogenous variation in political system traits to national choices of bank regulatory policies.

Given the problems associated with identifying valid instrumental variables for differences in national political systems, we confirm the results using ordinary least squares (OLS) and assess the robustness of the results to employing different instruments. We obtain the same results when using OLS. Thus, if readers question the potential importance of reverse causality or if readers question our identification strategy, the simple OLS results alleviate some of this discomfort. The results also hold when using different instruments, as we discuss later.

In selecting instruments for the political variables, two characteristics are crucial. First, there needs to be a plausible explanation for how the instruments influence political institutions and hence banking sector policies. Based on theories of the historical development of political institutions, we use eight instrumental variables for the current political system. These choices are contentious because there is considerable debate about the sources of international differences in political institutions. We only provide a flavor of these debates below. Second, the instruments must be statistically valid. Specifically, the instruments must explain cross-country variation in the political indicators, but the instruments should not explain bank supervision and regulation beyond their ability to explain the political indicators. We test their statistical validity later.

Latitude equals the absolute value of the latitude of the country to proxy for geographical location of the country.[29] Small values imply that

---

[29] The latitude data are from La Porta et al. (1999).

the country is closer to the equator. Frequently, though with notable exceptions, small values of latitude indicate that the country may have a tropical environment. In contrast, countries with larger values of latitude tend to lie in temperate zones, and have correspondingly lower likelihood of having a tropical environment. Latitude is an appealing instrumental variable because it is an objective, exogenous, easily available, and unchanging variable; however, it is less appealing in this role because it is an imprecise measure of climate and the disease environment.

As discussed in Chapter 4, some theories suggest that natural resource endowments influence the construction of political institutions. For instance, Engerman and Sokoloff (1997) Acemoglu, Johnson, and Robinson (2001), and Easterly and Levine (2003) argue that the endowments encountered by European colonists influenced the political institutions they constructed. Because tropical climates were typically unattractive places for large numbers of Europeans to settle, the Europeans tended to establish institutions that facilitated the extraction and exploitation of natural resources using indigenous or slave labor overseen by a few Europeans. According to these theories, Europeans tended not to create open, competitive, democratic political institutions in the tropics. In contrast, more temperate climates were more likely to attract European settlers and therefore more likely to turn away from autocratic government and develop democratic political systems with limits on executive power. Furthermore, once in place, political institutions tend to endure even after countries gained their independence. Specifically, in autocratic, extractive regimes, local leaders frequently seized the reigns of power vacated by Europeans. So although subject to various critiques, we use Latitude as an instrumental variable for the political system.

Initial Executive Constraints/Competition/Openness equals the value of each of the three political system indicators from the Polity IV Database in 1800, or the first year of independence. We use these instruments to capture the initial political structure. Intuitively, historically determined political structures are likely to exert an enduring influence on current political structure. For instance, the political systems left by European colonists may continue to shape the operation of current political systems around the world. Statistically, it seems unlikely that the political system's structure in 1800 will influence current supervision and regulation beyond its influence through the current structure of the political system. Of course, some of our indicators of initial political structure are from the 1960s when countries gained their independence. To the extent that these initial conditions influence bank supervision and regulation beyond the current political system, then this would invalidate our instrumental variable results. Thus, we (1) confirm the results later when excluding the initial political system indicators as instruments and (2) test the statistical validity of the instruments.

Independence equals the percentage of years that the country has been independent since 1776. Although the initial political variable may shape the current political system, the link may be associated with how long the country has been free from colonial domination. Thus, countries that gained their independence in the eighteenth or early nineteenth centuries may have developed political systems that are substantively different from their colonial legacy and perhaps are more responsive to the broad population. In contrast, countries that gained their independence in the 1960s have had less time to develop distinct political institutions. We use information on independence from the CIA Factbook. Although some may question the usefulness and interpretability of using "Independence" in the analyses, the results hold when omitting Independence. Independence, however, helps explain the current political environment, such that higher levels of Independence are associated with more constraints on the executive, more competitive elections, and greater political participation. Moreover, we do not reject the validity of Independence as an instrument.

Religious Composition is four separate variables that capture, the percentage of the population that is Catholic, Muslim, Protestant, or belongs to another denomination. As in Chapter 4, the numbers are in percent and sum to 100, and Protestant is the omitted group. Thus, three variables for religious composition are included as instruments. According to some, Catholic and Muslim countries tend to create vertical bonds of authority that tend to centralize power in the hands of a strong executive (Landes, 1998; Putnam, 1993; Weber, 1958). Although undoubtedly subject to skepticism, we include this as an instrumental variable for the political system indicators. The religious composition variables significantly improve the fit of the first-stage regression. Furthermore, they are statistically valid. Moreover, we obtain the same results on the relationship between banking sector policies and the political environment regardless of the inclusion of the religious composition variables as instruments.

These instrumental variables do a good job of explaining cross-country variation in the political system indicators. The instruments explain Executive Constraints and Voice & Accountability particularly well. The F-test that the instruments do not explain Executive Constraints and Voice & Accountability is rejected at the 1 percent level. Moreover,

Latitude enters independently significantly at the 1 percent level and the religious dummy variables also enter jointly significantly. Furthermore, when we focus on the marginal explanatory power of the instruments in the first stage regressions that also include the exogenous explanatory variables in the second stage, we continue to find that the instruments significantly contribute to the explanatory power of the political system indicators. The instrumental variables also account for cross-country variability in Executive Competition. Again, the F-test that the instruments do not explain Executive Competition is rejected at the 1 percent level. The first stage results are less powerful for Executive Openness. Here, the F-test is rejected at the 8 percent level, so the results on Executive Openness should be treated with greater skepticism.

As a final note of caution and as a point of clarification, these instruments are useful, but we do not claim that they are the best or the only exogenous explanations of cross-country differences in political systems. We also have experimented with using the legal origin of each country as instruments and with using the ethnic diversity of a country as instruments. Including these does not change the results. Rather, using instrumental variables is a statistical method of addressing a legitimate concern that any relationship between political systems and banking sector policies simply reflects reverse causation. As we show later, the results are inconsistent with the view that any relationship found simply reflects reverse causation. Rather, the results confirm the conceptual arguments and examples given earlier. The degree to which countries have open, competitive, transparent political systems substantively shapes their selection of bank supervisory and regulatory policies in a theoretically predictable manner.

5.D.3. Methodology

To assess the impact of the political system on bank regulation, we use instrumental variables to extract the exogenous component of cross-country differences in political systems. Then, we test whether this exogenous part of political systems differences accounts for international differences in bank regulation. Specifically, we estimate the following system of equations using two-stage least squares and report heteroskedasticity-robust standard errors:

$$\text{Bank Regulation} = \alpha + \beta * \text{Political System} + \delta X + u \qquad (5.1)$$
$$\text{Political System} = \gamma Z + \varepsilon.$$

As noted earlier, we focus on five different measures of Bank Regulation: Private Monitoring Index, Entry Applications Denied, Official Supervisory Power, Activity Restrictions, or Government-Owned Banks. We examine these Bank Regulation indicators one at a time. Similarly, we focus on four measures of political system differences: Executive Constraints, Executive Competition, Executive Openness, and Voice and Accountability. Again, we examine these one at a time. As control variables in the second-stage regression, X, we include the three legal origin dummy variables for countries with a British common law, French Civil law, or German Civil law legal tradition, where the omitted category are countries with a Scandinavian legal heritage. We include the legal origin variables as La Porta et al. (1999) argue that cross-country differences in legal heritage shapes the degree of centralized government influence in the financial system. To the degree that British common law countries grant judges greater discretion and independence, this may influence the types of regulations that are enacted and the ways in which the courts interpret and enforce those regulations. We also included variables to capture the size of the country (e.g., the logarithm of population) and obtained similar results.[30] Finally, the instrumental variables, Z, are Latitude, Independence, Initial Executive Constraints/Competition/Openness, and Religious Composition. As noted, we obtain the same results using various combinations of these instrumental variables, or when adding ethnic diversity (or legal origin) as instrumental variables for political system characteristics as suggested by Easterly and Levine (1997).

To have confidence that we have extracted the exogenous component of political system differences across countries and not simply measuring the impact of bank regulations on the political system, the instrumental

---

[30] As one would expect, the results do not hold when controlling for income per capita. This finding, however, is not damning to the interpretation, and it is inappropriate to include income per capita in the regressions. It not damning to the interpretation because we find that historical forces shape current political institutions and these political institutions, as suggested in Chapter 2, shape bank supervisory and regulatory policies. Thus, we trace empirically a logical explanation running from exogenous factors, to current political institutions, and on to bank supervisory and regulatory policies. We do not claim, however, that the exogenous components of current political institutions are the only factors shaping bank supervision and regulation. It is inappropriate to include income per capita in the second stage regression because the level of economic development is clearly endogenous. Thus, one would need to use alternative instrumental variables to extract the exogenous component of income per capita. Nevertheless, we do recognize that there is an extraordinarily high degree of conceptual and statistical complexity associated with confidently identifying a logical chain running from exogenous factors to the political system and then to bank supervision and regulation.

variables must (1) explain political system differences and (2) not explain regulatory differences beyond their ability to explain political system differences. To assess the validity of the instrumental variables, we provide two pieces of information. First, we provide the p-value of the overidentifying restrictions (OIR-test). The null hypothesis is that the instruments are valid (i.e., the null hypothesis is that the instrumental variables are uncorrelated with the error term (u)). If the p-value is low, this signifies rejection of the null hypothesis that the instruments are valid. Second, we provide the p-value for the first-stage F-test where the null hypothesis is that the exogenous variables in the first-stage do not explain cross-country variation in the political system indicators. A low p-value signifies rejection of the null hypothesis that the instruments are weak. Thus, validity of the instruments requires rejection of the first-stage F-test and failure to reject the OIR-test. As shown below, the instrumental variables are appropriate.

5.D.4. Cross-Country Regression Results

We present the results on the relationship between political structure and bank supervision and regulation in a series of four tables and two figures. Tables 5.1–5.4 present the findings for each of the five bank policy indicators. The tables differ in that they each present the results using one of the four political system indicators. For each bank policy indicator, we present one regression that controls for legal origin and one that does not. In Figures 5.1 and 5.2, we illustrate the relationship between the Private Monitoring Index and the exogenous component of Executive Constraints and Voice & Accountability, respectively.

The results indicate that the exogenous component of current political structure – the component of the current political structure accounted for by the instrumental variables – helps explain bank supervisory and regulatory practices in ways that are consistent with the social conflict view discussed earlier.

First, consider the Private Monitoring Index regressions, where theory predicts a positive relationship between open, competitive, and democratic political systems and banking policies that foster private monitoring. Across Tables 5.1–5.4, each political structure indicator enters positively and significantly in the Private Monitoring Index regressions. Countries with more open, competitive, democratic political systems tend to adopt bank supervisory and regulatory practices that focus more on information disclosure.

Table 5.1. *Political System Determinants of Banking Policies: Executive Constraints*

	(1)	(2)	(3)	(4)	(5)	(6)	(7)	(8)	(9)	(10)
	Private Monitoring Index	Private Monitoring Index	Entry Applications Denied	Entry Applications Denied	Official Supervisory Power	Official Supervisory Power	Activity Restrictions	Activity Restrictions	Government-owned Banks	Government-owned Banks
Executive Constraints	0.380 (0.000)***	0.355 (0.001)***	−0.126 (0.004)***	−0.120 (0.008)***	−0.140 (0.209)	−0.116 (0.337)	−0.468 (0.000)***	−0.444 (0.000)***	−0.055 (0.036)**	−0.064 (0.031)**
Legal Origin–Common		−0.415 (0.273)		0.127 (0.143)		1.495 (0.000)***		0.103 (0.736)		0.054 (0.511)
Legal Origin–French		−0.146 (0.671)		−0.102 (0.136)		1.489 (0.000)***		0.189 (0.542)		0.012 (0.879)
Legal Origin–German		−0.058 (0.879)		−0.048 (0.112)		1.967 (0.000)***		0.041 (0.941)		0.141 (0.130)
Constant	−2.066 (0.001)***	−1.675 (0.031)**	0.934 (0.001)***	0.889 (0.005)***	0.718 (0.261)	−0.887 (0.296)	2.599 (0.000)***	2.333 (0.002)***	0.511 (0.003)***	0.518 (0.017)**
F-test (p-value)	0.00	0.00	0.00	0.00	0.00	0.00	0.00	0.00	0.00	0.00
O.I.R.	0.19	0.11	0.69	0.85	0.37	0.67	0.95	0.90	0.92	0.84
Observations	63	63	50	50	63	63	62	62	56	56

Notes: The dependent variable is listed at the top of each column.

The equations are estimated using Two Stage Least Squares.

Instruments used are (a) Latitude, (b) Independence, (c) Initial Executive Constraints, (d) Initial Executive Competition, (e) Initial Executive Openness, and (f) the fraction of the population that is Catholic, (g) the fraction of the population that is Muslim, and (h) the fraction of the population that is Non-Protestant. The omitted category is the fraction of the population that is Protestant.

P-values are in parentheses.

*, **, *** indicate significance at the 10, 5, and 1 percent, respectively.

O.I.R.: Test of over-identifying restrictions, that is, it assesses whether the instrumental variables are correlated with the dependent variable beyond their association with the endogenous variable in each equation. Thus, a low reported P-value rejects the validity of the instrumental variables.

F-test (p-value): Tests the null hypothesis that the instrumental variables do not explain cross-country variation in the endogenous regressor (the political system indicator). A low reported P-value rejects the hypothesis that the instruments are weak.

Table 5.2. Political System Determinants of Banking Policies: Executive Openness

	(1) Private Monitoring Index	(2) Private Monitoring Index	(3) Entry Applications Denied	(4) Entry Applications Denied	(5) Official Supervisory Power	(6) Official Supervisory Power	(7) Activity Restrictions	(8) Activity Restrictions	(9) Government-owned Banks	(10) Government-owned Banks
Executive Openness	0.780 (0.001)***	0.706 (0.002)***	-0.230 (0.027)**	-0.196 (0.042)**	-0.156 (0.487)	-0.155 (0.484)	-0.980 (0.003)***	-0.839 (0.003)***	-0.108 (0.059)*	-0.109 (0.045)**
Legal Origin – Common		-0.582 (0.113)		0.174 (0.056)*		1.584 (0.000)***		0.332 (0.267)		0.076 (0.389)
Legal Origin – French		-0.353 (0.298)		-0.009 (0.896)		1.592 (0.000)***		0.443 (0.133)		0.059 (0.430)
Legal Origin – German		0.235 (0.691)		-0.025 (0.371)		1.909 (0.000)***		-0.305 (0.651)		0.097 (0.355)
Constant	-2.658 (0.003)***	-2.012 (0.035)**	1.028 (0.014)**	0.836 (0.031)**	0.469 (0.550)	-1.077 (0.228)	3.378 (0.006)***	2.580 (0.022)**	0.571 (0.010)***	0.510 (0.026)**
F-test (p-value)	0.04	0.08	0.04	0.14	0.04	0.08	0.05	0.09	0.06	0.11
O.I.R.	0.33	0.33	0.82	0.79	0.24	0.58	0.97	0.95	0.95	0.91
Observations	63	63	50	50	63	63	62	62	56	56

Notes: The dependent variable is listed at the top of each column.

The equations are estimated using Two Stage Least Squares.

Instruments used are (a) Latitude, (b) Independence, (c) Initial Executive Constraints, (d) Initial Executive Competition, (e) Initial Executive Openness, and (f) the fraction of the population that is Catholic, (g) the fraction of the population that is Muslim, and (h) the fraction of the population that is Non-Protestant. The omitted category is the fraction of the population that is Protestant.

P-values are in parentheses.

*, **, *** indicate significance at the 10, 5, and 1 percent, respectively.

O.I.R.: Test of over-identifying restrictions, that is, it assesses whether the instrumental variables are correlated with the dependent variable beyond their association with the endogenous variable in each equation. Thus, a low reported P-value rejects the validity of the instrumental variables.

F-test (p-value): Tests the null hypothesis that the instrumental variables do not explain cross-country variation in the endogenous regressor (the political system indicator). A low reported P-value rejects the hypothesis that the instruments are weak.

Table 5.3. *Political System Determinants of Banking Policies: Executive Competition*

	(1)	(2)	(3)	(4)	(5)	(6)	(7)	(8)	(9)	(10)
	Private Monitoring Index	Private Monitoring Index	Entry Applications Denied	Entry Applications Denied	Official Supervisory Power	Official Supervisory Power	Activity Restrictions	Activity Restrictions	Government-owned Banks	Government-owned Banks
Executive Competition	0.840	0.744	-0.264	-0.217	-0.189	-0.145	-1.057	-0.962	-0.123	-0.134
	(0.001)***	(0.002)***	(0.009)***	(0.024)**	(0.436)	(0.565)	(0.000)***	(0.000)***	(0.041)**	(0.025)**
Legal Origin – Common		-0.459		0.142		1.568		0.138		0.049
		(0.221)		(0.122)		(0.000)***		(0.649)		(0.553)
Legal Origin – French		-0.221		-0.041		1.574		0.230		0.025
		(0.512)		(0.472)		(0.000)***		(0.429)		(0.741)
Legal Origin – German		0.130		-0.025		1.938		-0.206		0.107
		(0.803)		(0.371)		(0.000)***		(0.743)		(0.289)
Constant	-1.938	-1.419	0.861	0.703	0.376	-1.262	2.476	2.111	0.490	0.474
	(0.003)***	(0.059)*	(0.003)***	(0.016)**	(0.524)	(0.100)	(0.000)***	(0.006)***	(0.003)***	(0.013)**
F-test (p-value)	0.00	0.01	0.00	0.02	0.00	0.01	0.00	0.01	0.01	0.03
O.I.R.	0.32	0.17	0.92	0.74	0.26	0.57	0.99	0.99	0.97	0.94
Observations	63	63	50	50	63	63	62	62	56	56

Notes: The dependent variable is listed at the top of each column.

The equations are estimated using Two Stage Least Squares.

Instruments used are (a) Latitude, (b) Independence, (c) Initial Executive Constraints, (d) Initial Executive Competition, (e) Initial Executive Openness, and (f) the fraction of the population that is Catholic, (g) the fraction of the population that is Muslim, and (h) the fraction of the population that is Non-Protestant. The omitted category is the fraction of the population that is Protestant.

P-values are in parentheses.

*, **, *** indicate significance at the 10, 5, and 1 percent, respectively.

O.I.R.: Test of over-identifying restrictions, that is, it assesses whether the instrumental variables are correlated with the dependent variable beyond their association with the endogenous variable in each equation. Thus, a low reported P-value rejects the validity of the instrumental variables.

F-test (p-value): Tests the null hypothesis that the instrumental variables do not explain cross-country variation in the endogenous regressor (the political system indicator). A low reported P-value rejects the hypothesis that the instruments are weak.

Table 5.4. *Political System Determinants of Banking Policies: Voice & Accountability*

	(1)	(2)	(3)	(4)	(5)	(6)	(7)	(8)	(9)	(10)
	Private Monitoring Index	Private Monitoring Index	Entry Applications Denied	Entry Applications Denied	Official Supervisory Power	Official Supervisory Power	Activity Restrictions	Activity Restrictions	Government-owned Banks	Government-owned Banks
Voice & Accountability	0.661	0.709	-0.206	-0.222	-0.358	-0.296	-0.827	-0.864	-0.093	-0.128
	(0.000)***	(0.000)***	(0.000)***	(0.000)**	(0.057)*	(0.176)	(0.000)***	(0.000)***	(0.011)**	(0.005)***
Legal Origin – Common		-0.093		0.032		1.315		-0.274		-0.003
		(0.800)		(0.666)		(0.001)***		(0.394)		(0.968)
Legal Origin – French		0.352		-0.202		1.307		-0.268		-0.068
		(0.339)		(0.009)***		(0.000)***		(0.409)		(0.440)
Legal Origin – German		0.145		-0.096		1.877		-0.205		0.105
		(0.726)		(0.027)**		(0.000)***		(0.679)		(0.261)
Constant	-0.188	-0.337	0.322	0.411	0.115	-1.218	0.354	0.625	0.241	0.280
	(0.175)	(0.385)	(0.000)***	(0.000)***	(0.416)	(0.001)***	(0.003)***	(0.050)**	(0.000)***	(0.004)**
F-test (p-value)	0.00	0.00	0.00	0.00	0.00	0.00	0.00	0.00	0.00	0.00
O.I.R.	0.34	0.12	0.33	0.59	0.50	0.82	0.77	0.73	0.70	0.68
Observations	65	65	52	52	65	65	64	64	58	58

Notes: The dependent variable is listed at the top of each column.

The equations are estimated using Two Stage Least Squares.

Instruments used are (a) Latitude, (b) Independence, (c) Initial Executive Constraints, (d) Initial Executive Competition, (e) Initial Executive Openness, and (f) the fraction of the population that is Catholic, (g) the fraction of the population that is Muslim, and (h) the fraction of the population that is Non-Protestant. The omitted category is the fraction of the population that is Protestant.

P-values are in parentheses.

*, **, *** indicate significance at the 10, 5, and 1 percent, respectively.

O.I.R.: Test of over-identifying restrictions, that is, it assesses whether the instrumental variables are correlated with the dependent variable beyond their association with the endogenous variable in each equation. Thus, a low reported P-value rejects the validity of the instrumental variables.

F-test (p-value): Tests the null hypothesis that the instrumental variables do not explain cross-country variation in the endogenous regressor (the political system indicator). A low reported P-value rejects the hypothesis that the instruments are weak.

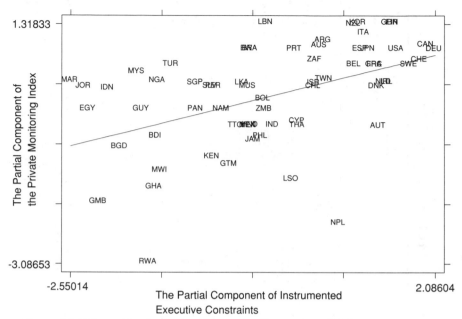

Figure 5.1. Private Monitoring and Executive Constraints. This is the partial scatter plot of regression 1 in Table 5.1, which is a two-stage least squares regression of Private Monitoring against Executive Constraints. In this simple regression, there are no included exogenous variables in the second stage. The excluded instrumental variables are Latitude, Independence, Initial Executive Constraints, Initial Executive Competition, and Initial Executive Openness. To construct this figure, first compute the predicted value of Executive Constraints from the first stage regression. Second, regress Private Monitoring on a constant and collect the residuals. This is called the partial component of Private Monitoring. Third, regress the predicted values of Executive Constraints from the first stage regression on a constant and collect the residuals. This is called the partial component of the instrumented Executive Constraints. Finally, plot the partial component of Private Monitoring against the partial component of Instrumented Executive Constraints. This represents the two-dimensional representation of the regression plane in Private Monitoring–Executive Constraints space while controlling for the endogeneity of Executive Constraints.

Figures 5.1 and 5.2 further illustrate the close relationship between Private Monitoring and both Executive Constraints and Voice & Accountability. Given the similarity of results across the Private Monitoring regressions, we simply present partial scatter plots for the Executive Constraints and Voice & Accountability regressions. Figure 5.1 presents the partial scatter plot of regression 1 in Table 5.1, which is a two-stage least squares regression of the Private Monitoring Index in

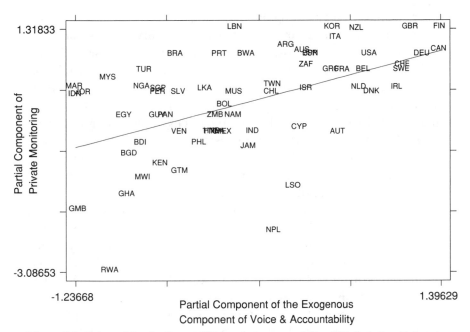

Figure 5.2. Private Monitoring and Voice & Accountability. This is the partial scatter plot of regression 1 in Table 5.4, which is a two-stage least squares regression of Private Monitoring against Voice and Accountability. In this simple regression, there are no included exogenous variables in the second stage. The excluded instrumental variables are Latitude, Independence, Initial Executive Constraints, Initial Executive Competition, and Initial Executive Openness. To construct this figure, first compute the predicted value of Voice and Accountability from the first stage regression. Second, regress Private Monitoring on a constant and collect the residuals. This is called the partial component of Private Monitoring. Third, regress the predicted values of Voice and Accountability from the first stage regression on a constant and collect the residuals. This is called the partial component of the instrumented Voice and Accountability. Finally, plot the partial component of Private Monitoring against the partial component of Instrumented Voice and Accountability. This represents the two-dimensional representation of the regression plane in Private Monitoring–Voice and Accountability space while controlling for the endogeneity of Voice and Accountability.

1999 against Executive Constraints. To construct Figure 5.1, first compute the predicted value of Executive Constraints from the first stage regression. Second, after removing the sample means, plot Private Monitoring against the predicted values of Executive Constraints. This represents the two-dimensional representation of the regression plane in Private Monitoring – Executive Constraints space while controlling for the endogeneity of Executive Constraints. Although there are some outliers, the

figure demonstrates a strong positive relationship between greater constraints on the chief executive and bank supervisory policies that foster
accurate information disclosure to the public. Figure 5.2 presents the partial scatter plot of regression 1 in Table 5.4, which considers the relationship between the Private Monitoring Index and Voice & Accountability.
Again, we observe a strong positive relationship. In both cases, removing
influential observations – outliers – strengthens the positive relationship.
The data clearly indicate that more constraints on the executive and political systems where the public has greater voice and politicians face direct
accountability are more likely to enact banking sector policies that foster
private monitoring through information disclosure.

The regression results also indicate that the impact of political systems
on banking system policies is very large. For example, Egypt is a country that imposes few constraints on its executive. Executive Constraints
equals 3 in Egypt. Egypt also has a very low value of the Private Monitoring Index of -0.13. In contrast, Greece, Turkey, and Portugal all have
extensive constraints on the chief executive, so that Executive Constraints
equals the maximum of 7. All of these countries are in the top quarter of
the sample in terms of the Private Monitoring Index. Indeed, all but three
of the top twenty countries based on the Private Monitoring Index have
values of 7 for Executive Constraints. The regression results suggest that
if Egypt had the same level of Executive Constraints as Greece, Turkey,
and Portugal, it would have even higher levels of Private Monitoring than
these countries.[31]

Similarly, each political structure indicator enters negatively and significantly in the Entry Applications Denied regressions. Countries with
open, competitive and democratic political systems are less likely to deny
a high percentage of entry applications than countries with more autocratic political systems that are unresponsive to the population at large.
Thus, consistent with intuition, political systems that are geared toward
advancing the interests of a small, powerful elite are less likely to favor
transparent information disclosure about banks and more likely to protect
existing banks by denying a high fraction of new bank entry applications.

Furthermore, the results shed empirical light on areas of bank
supervision and regulation in which political economy theory provides

---

[31] These examples suggest that the relationship between political institutions and bank
supervision and regulation is economically meaningful. These examples, however, are not
exploitable elasticities. They do not explain how to change constraints on the executive.
They are simply illustrative examples of the size of the linkages.

ambiguous predictions. In terms of Official Supervisory Power, we find that the political system indicators never enter significantly. As suggested by theory, democratic political systems may be either (1) wary of the potential corrupting influence of bank supervisory power or (2) keen to overcome market failures with strong official supervision. As Madison might have argued, democratic political systems might have a public interest desire to ameliorate market failures, but worry that establishing a powerful supervisory agency will facilitate private interest activities. Similarly, comparatively autocratic political regimes may either (1) eagerly construct powerful supervisory agencies to funnel the flow of bank credit toward favored ends or (2) not see the need for powerful supervision as the elite already control both the banks and government. Thus, theory provides ambiguous predictions and the empirical evidence in Tables 5.1–5.4 confirms that there is not a reliable relationship between the political system indicators and bank supervisory power.

Some simple observations confirm these formal statistical results. Although countries with comparatively competitive, democratic political systems – such as Canada, Denmark, Finland, and Sweden – have low levels of Official Supervisory Power, other countries with democratic political systems – such as the United States and Portugal – have very high levels of Official Supervisory Power. Similarly, while relatively autocratic regimes – such as Burundi and Jordan – have low Official Supervisory Power, Gambia, Rwanda, and Nigeria have high Official Supervisory Power. Thus, countries may choose to have powerful or weak supervisory agencies for very different reasons.

In terms of regulatory restrictions on bank activities and government ownership of banks, the empirical work in Tables 5.1–5.4 distinguishes between competing predictions. Open, competitive, democratic political systems that are responsive to the population at large are less likely to impose regulatory restrictions on bank activities and less likely to have large state-owned banks. Rather, autocratic regimes are much more likely to have large government-owned banks and limit bank activities. These results are consistent with the view that autocratic political regimes establist government-owned banks to funnel credit toward the interest of the ruling elite. Similarly, the results are consistent with the view that closed political systems that are unaccountable to the public at large will tend to create regulatory restrictions so that bankers need to lobby politicians for special exemptions. In turn, the results are inconsistent with the view that autocratic political regimes do not need government banks and regulatory restrictions.

5.E. SUMMARY REMARKS

The core finding is that the organization and operation of political systems shape bank supervisory and regulatory practices. At a more detailed level, the regressions indicate that more open, competitive, democratic political systems tend to choose bank supervisory and regulatory strategies that rely more on private monitoring, accept a higher fraction of new bank entry applications, impose fewer regulatory restrictions on what banks can do, and have less of a role for government-owned banks. We did not find a reliable link between the political system indicators and official supervisory power.

These results emphasize that, in many countries, improving bank supervision and regulation requires more than identifying those bank supervisory and regulatory policies that improve the operation of banks and enhance social welfare. Clearly, a crucial component of implementing policies that maximize social welfare is to discover which policies will do just that. But, if policy makers are not maximizing social welfare, it is just as clear that discovering the "best" policies will not necessarily convince policy makers to adopt those policies unless it is in the interests of policy makers, too. To put it bluntly, socially efficient regulatory reform will tend to subvert the interests of powerful segments in society, which makes effective reform extraordinarily challenging. Thus, the finding that political systems substantively shape bank regulation implies that successfully implementing banking sector reform requires country-level customization that appreciates the political economy differences of each country.

SIX

Rethinking Bank Regulation

"I cannot expect to have escaped statistical errors and oversights, although I hope that none of them is serious enough to affect descriptions or conclusions substantially. All I can do is to take comfort in the proverb, 'Nothing ventured, nothing gained,' and to put my faith in those who will plow the field over again and may produce a richer harvest, in particular obtaining a higher yield per hour for their labor."

Goldsmith (1969, p. x)

6.A. APPROACH AND CONTEXT

Joseph Schumpeter (1912, p. 74) argued that the banker authorizes the entrepreneur, in the name of society, to innovate. He meant that banks mobilize society's savings and decide who gets to use them. If banks make good decisions, this will maximize the chances that the economy will innovate and thrive. Thus, bank regulation and supervision matter. As illustrated by the differences between the United States and Mexico during the nineteenth century, banking policies can either underwrite growth that benefits society at large, or they can fortify a political fortress that simultaneously enriches the elite while thwarting the aspirations of the many.

To contribute to the understanding of bank regulation and its impact on societies, we construct a new database on banking policies around the world. Within international policy circles, official regulators and supervisors have relied on their experience to formulate best practice recommendations. Clearly, practical experience is essential for designing sound policies. Just as clearly, however, providing cross-country evidence on the efficacy of bank regulatory and supervisory practices will contribute to the development of socially beneficial policies. Similarly, the experts that set best practices are typically from a few high-income countries and rely on practices from their home countries when establishing international norms. But what works well in one country may not succeed in other countries with different political and legal systems.[1] By assembling data on a wide range of countries, we expand the analytical horizons for assessing banking policies. That is, we make it possible to test the conditions under which particular regulations and supervisory procedures work best and under which conditions the same policies will produce undesirable outcomes. Finally, many economists study bank regulation and supervision with theoretical models, or with data from a few countries, especially the United States.[2] Our data allow researchers to test the predictions from these models and to confirm, reject, or modify past findings by using experiences from a fuller set of countries at all levels of income and in all parts of the world.

We take a comparatively expansive approach by assessing regulation and supervision within a political economy context and by looking beyond banking system stability. For instance, many treatments of regulation, especially since the Mexican and East Asian crises, have taken for granted that stability is the prime goal of regulation. Although this is an understandable reaction to crises, we investigate the impact of bank regulation and supervision on a broader set of variables. Besides stability, we examine the impact on financial sector development, the efficiency of intermediation, the integrity of the lending process, and bank governance. This is critical for societies. Banks should not simply be safe places to put savings. Well-functioning banks play a pivotal role in mobilizing society's savings and deciding who gets to use those resources. Thus, policy makers

---

[1] In an insightful critique of the so-called Washington Consensus, Rodrik (2004) argues that the Augmented Consensus (do more, and do it better) essentially requires developing countries to follow in the footsteps of what rich countries look like today, which is very different from what they looked like when they were developing. He also worries that the new consensus is inherently unfalsifiable – the checklist of recommendations is so long that it is always possible to claim that implementation fell short of 100 percent, and the response is to add more things to the checklist. As a result, international experts can feel more satisfied that their approach is comprehensive, while developing country officials still have little idea of what to do first.

[2] Although some of this literature is cited in Chapter 2, we emphasize here that our unique contribution is the data, not our conclusions. Many others have cautioned against relying on official supervision and urged policy makers to focus on strengthening private monitoring (e.g., see Calomiris (1992, 1997), Calomiris and Powell (2000), Herring (2003), Kane (1997), Demirgüç-Kunt and Kane (2002), Kaufman (1991), Kaufman and Kroszner (1997), and various Shadow Financial Regulatory Committee publications).

should not assess banking policies only along the metric of stability. They also should examine which policies encourage banks to operate efficiently and to make sound capital-allocation decisions.

Similarly, many – although by no means all – treatments of bank regulation and supervision focus on deriving uniform standards for banks everywhere and do not assess banking policies within a broader political economy context. We instead follow an influential strand of the literature that stresses the connections between banking and politics. In particular, we stress that the public has a difficult time inducing politicians to behave in the best interests of the population, and politicians sometimes cannot control bank regulators. Bank regulators in turn frequently lack the resources, expertise, and will to supervise and discipline powerful banks. These relationships are made more complex by potential corruption, as the economically and politically powerful seek to tip the "financial" game in their favor. Throughout the book, therefore, we stress that a comprehensive understanding of bank regulation and supervision must consider the political, legal, and cultural context in which all of these forces operate to influence bank behavior.

6.B. LESSONS AND IMPLICATIONS

Before reviewing the findings, we emphasize that this book represents a first, tentative step toward examining a crucial set of policies with a new global database. As a caveat, we cannot improve on the quotation by Raymond Goldsmith that introduces this chapter. Although we have done our best, we cannot expect to have avoided all mistakes or satisfactorily addressed all methodological pitfalls. In the end, we hope that our efforts both lower the marginal costs and increase the marginal benefits of future research on bank regulation and supervision, and thereby assist policy makers in deciding how best to regulate the operations of banks.

So what have we learned? First, we use our new database to provide a picture of the diversity of regulatory systems around the world and demonstrate one way to aggregate some of the raw data into broader indices that characterize national regulatory systems. We document an important, although perhaps obvious, point: countries do not pick and choose individual rules and procedures in isolation. Rather, bank regulations and supervisory practices appear to reflect national approaches to the role of government in the economy. Thus, countries that choose to have the government own a large percentage of the banking industry also heavily regulate bank activities and the entry of new banks. In contrast, countries that avoid imposing official restrictions on banks also tend to promote and facilitate private sector monitoring of banks.

Second, an approach to bank supervision and regulation that stresses private monitoring tends to boost the operation of banks more effectively than an approach based on direct, official oversight of and restrictions on banks. Bank supervisory practices and regulations that: (1) require reliable information disclosure, (2) do not discourage private monitoring through generous deposit insurance, and (3) empower private equity and debt holders tend to: (a) boost bank development, (b) increase bank efficiency, (c) improve the corporate governance of banks, and (d) reduce corruption in bank lending. There also is evidence that information disclosure is more effective at improving bank operations in countries with well-functioning legal systems. Or, put differently, to be effective, market discipline requires both information and the means of using that information to influence bank behavior. Similarly, policies – such as generous deposit insurance – that reduce the incentives of the private sector to assess and discipline banks tend to increase the probability that the country will suffer a systemic financial crisis. Although there are methodological shortcomings with each of this book's investigations, the different econometric techniques and analyses speak with a single voice: empowering private monitoring of banks improves their operation.

Within the context of this central finding, the results raise a cautionary flag regarding reliance on direct official oversight of banks, government ownership of banks, generous government deposit insurance, and regulations that restrict bank activities and impede the entry of new domestic and foreign banks. Indeed, countries that emphasize the role of official supervisors by giving them greater discretion (to force a bank to change its internal organizational structure, suspend dividends, stop bonuses, halt management fees, force banks to provision against actual or potential loses as determined by the supervisory agency, supersede the legal rights of shareholders, remove and replace managers and directors, obtain information from external auditors, and take legal action against auditors for negligence) tend to have (a) lower levels of bank development and (b) greater corruption in bank lending. Similarly, governments that heavily regulate bank activities, restrict entry into banking, and own large proportions of the banking industry tend to hurt bank performance. Furthermore, these policies do not enhance stability. On the contrary, we find that restricting banks from diversifying into nonlending activities, prohibiting banks from lending abroad, and providing generous government deposit insurance tend to increase banking system fragility.

We do find that some regulations have positive outcomes. For instance, minimum diversification guidelines encourage banks to diversify their lending portfolios, with positive ramifications on bank stability, and regulations that mandate reliable information disclosure foster better capital allocation. But even in these cases, the results support an approach to bank regulation and supervision focused on encouraging and facilitating private sector governance of banks, not an approach based on direct official oversight.

Third, this book has important messages about the relative importance that countries should place on the three pillars of Basel II, whose first and most developed pillar emphasizes capital regulation. Of course, we do not directly test Pillar I, because this is only a proposal that has not been implemented. Nevertheless, across a wide assortment of analyses, we find little impact of the stringency of capital regulations on bank development, bank efficiency, bank stability, the governance of banks, or corruption. Although there were some variants in which capital regulation was linked with more stable banking systems, this link was not statistically robust. It may be that the uniformity of countries' approaches to capital regulation makes it difficult to detect an empirically meaningful relationship. Or, some might say that the lack of clear evidence on the beneficial effects of capital regulation advertises the inadequacy of the Basel I Capital Accord and the need for the advances of Basel II. Others may instead claim that banks evade official capital regulations whenever they are sufficiently inconvenient. Our results simply demonstrate the absence of a robust statistical relationship between the stringency of capital regulations and the performance of national banking systems.

The second major pillar of Basel II is official supervision, but, as already noted, our findings contradict this standard "best practice" recommendation. For most countries, the data indicate that following Basel II's recommendations regarding the strengthening of official supervisory powers will make things worse, not better. Unless the country is a "top ten" country in terms of the development of its political institutions, the evidence suggests that strengthening official supervisory powers will tend to hurt bank development, impede the flow of credit to worthy firms, and lead to greater corruption in bank lending without robust evidence of any compensating positive effects. Some may view these results as simply emphasizing that countries need to develop well-functioning institutions – with ample checks and balances on government officials and an active, independent media scrutinizing politicians – to enjoy the benefits, and avoid the costs, of strong official supervision. We agree, but hasten to add that (1) it may take a long time to create a well-functioning democracy and (2) our findings indicate that recommending that official supervisory agencies be granted greater powers *before* the country has already developed well-functioning political institutions lacks any empirical support and, if implemented, is likely to produce bad outcomes.

Instead, our results advertise the efficacy of Basel II's sometimes forgotten third pillar: market discipline.[3] As stressed earlier, we find that regulations that require informational transparency and that strengthen the ability and incentives of the private sector to monitor banks tend to promote sound banking. This does not support a laissez faire attitude toward banking. Our findings do not suggest that there is no constructive role for official supervisors. Rather, our findings indicate that supervision works best when it facilitates market monitoring. Perhaps the most important supportive role is to have supervisors require the dissemination of high-quality information about banks and to ensure that private investors have available to them the legal tools to exert effective corporate governance over banks. Some may go further and recommend that supervisors be publicly accountable for verifying the data released by banks. Others would undoubtedly counter that this would supplant the market and reduce incentives for private investors to assess banks independently. Still others might respond that, given the extent of information asymmetries in banking, it is useful to have both public and private entities verifying the information disclosed by banks.[4] Our analyses do not distinguish among these more subtle strategies for improving market monitoring but, rather, simply stress the positive impact of improved market monitoring on the functioning of banking systems.

We recognize that many will reject the policy implications that emerge from our findings on Basel II as impractical. Do we really recommend reliance on market monitoring in a country with a dictator and single government-owned bank? Our response is that creating more elaborate capital regulations and giving official supervisors more power are also unlikely to improve the operation of the banking system in such

---

[3] As mentioned in Chapter 2, perhaps this inattention is sensible if the focus were just on the G-10 countries, where market monitoring is relatively well developed.

[4] As mentioned in Chapter 2, a mandatory subordinated debt requirement, by motivating this class of creditors to monitor banks closely, could make a key contribution in improving the oversight of banks. See the World Bank (2001), various publications by the Shadow Financial Regulatory Committee, Calomiris (1997), and Horvitz (1984).

an environment! Moreover, strengthening supervisory power may simply enhance the tools available to the government for directing society's resources toward politically advantageous ends. Others will argue that the expert advice embodied in Basel II's first two pillars will improve banking if applied sensibly and maintain that this more extensive checklist of best practice recommendations is a practical step toward ensuring that countries sensibly implement sound bank regulations. Although at one level this argument is tautological depending on how one interprets "sensibly," the reality is that best practice recommendations are ultimately implemented by national governments after international experts have departed. For example, in Basel I, the credit risk weight on government debt was set at zero and this scheme was followed by developing countries, even by those whose debt was trading at much less than par in international markets. This misguided application of Basel weakened banking systems, as in the case of Argentina, and provided a false sense of comfort to investors purchasing bank securities. Clearly, an international expert would say – especially ex post – that if countries applied their guidance sensibly, with a higher risk weight where warranted, all would be well. Unfortunately, even assuming that the "best practice" is a good one, this recommendation overlooks the power of politicians, who have a clear preference that banks purchase government securities at artificially high prices, which they can enjoy by applying the popular interpretation of Basel I (a low risk weight for government paper). As we stress later, the ability of politicians to circumvent the best intentions of international experts seems to far outstrip the ability of these experts to develop capital regulations and official supervisory practices that induce countries to implement best practices sensibly. For our purposes, the bottom line is tied relentlessly to empirical evidence: We find little support for the first two pillars of Basel II and noteworthy evidence supporting the efficacy of Pillar III.

Fourth, although this book is about bank supervision and regulation, it is also a case study in the debate about the role of government in society. If one views the government as benevolent, then this leads to a public interest view of government: the government will fix problems in the economy and produce a socially optimal outcome. As Madison might have put it today, if angels were to govern men, or if checks and balances were to work so perfectly that government officials behaved like angels, then there would be good reasons to believe that powerful official bank supervisors would always work to improve the functioning of banks and hence boost human welfare. The countervailing view of government, however, holds that government officials act to maximize their own welfare, not necessarily to promote national prosperity. At a more sophisticated level, this private interest view holds that political institutions in most countries do not induce politicians to behave like angels. From this perspective, regulatory restrictions on bank activities, impediments to the entry of new banks, limits on banks investing abroad, government ownership of banks, and strengthening the discretionary power of official supervisors will produce more cronyism, greater corruption, intensified collusion, and hence less efficient banking. As Madison put it, the great difficulty lies in obliging the government to control itself. In the context of bank supervision and regulation, this view holds that strengthening private monitoring of banks is the most efficacious way of improving the operation of banks to the benefit of society while controlling the grabbing-hand of government.

The data provide ample support for the private interest view of government and surprisingly little support for the public interest view. Thus, from the laboratory of bank supervision and regulation, angels do not govern! Across the world there are insufficient checks and balances on government officials to induce them to behave in a way that boosts the functioning of banks. As stressed, we find that the bulk of "hands-on" policies by the government tends to hinder bank development, reduce bank efficiency, intensify banking system fragility, and increase corruption in lending. These results are inconsistent with the public interest view. As noted, we do find that regulatory policies that actively promote information disclosure and private sector governance lead to better functioning banks, but the effectiveness of these public policies actually validates the predictions of the private interest view, not those of the public interest view. In sum, the evidence is consistent with the view that politicians and government officials frequently act to promote their own private interests even if this hurts society in general.

Finally, we provide suggestive evidence that the approach toward bank supervision and regulation directly reflects political institutions. Specifically, the data indicate that countries with more open, competitive, democratic political institutions that have effective constraints on executive power tend to adopt an approach to bank supervision and regulation that relies more on private monitoring, imposes fewer regulatory restrictions on bank activities and bank entry, and has less of a role for government-owned banks. In contrast, countries with more closed, uncompetitive, autocratic political institutions that impose ineffective constraints on the executive tend to rely less on private monitoring, impose more restrictions on bank actions and new bank entry, and create a bigger role for government banks.

These results on (1) the private-public interest debate and (2) political system determinants of bank regulation have important policy implications. One way to see this is through the eyes of a well-intentioned supervisor, who must operate within the political, legal, and cultural context of her country. Do politicians support the supervisor with good salaries and provide her with the tools and incentives to promote social welfare? Or do politicians pressure the supervisor to achieve political or personal goals? Does the legal system protect the supervisor from civil lawsuits for doing her job and decide cases expeditiously and fairly? Or can elites threaten an individual supervisor with expensive lawsuits, bribe judges, and tie up cases indefinitely? Do independent media investigate political corruption and inspect supervisory behavior? Or do the same people that own the banks also own the media? The answers to these broad questions about national institutions shape the individual supervisor's behavior. At the country level, our findings emphasize that policy recommendations no matter how well intentioned will not produce socially beneficial change unless they incorporate an appreciation of the country's political and legal institutions. At the extreme, no matter how impressive the international team of experts or the econometric results on which they base their recommendations, we doubt that Porfirio Diaz would have eased his stranglehold on the Mexican financial system (discussed in Chapter 5). For socially beneficial reforms to be implemented successfully, political leaders must see the reforms as being in their own interests. This can either result from successful democratic institutions that align the interests of politicians with those of the public, or from designing reforms that both promote the public interest and appeal to those in power. We doubt that international organizations can effectively achieve beneficial banking reforms in a country against the wishes of those in power. As suggested by Madison, the great difficulty lies in creating political and legal institutions that control government officials and inducing them to act in the best interests of society. From our perspective, these lessons suggest that although international agencies, banking experts, and evidence from cross-country regressions can provide useful information on which broad approaches to banking policies tend to work best, both the impetus for reform and the detailed design of bank regulations and supervisory practices depend on the political and legal institutions operating in each individual country.

In sum, we find that political systems shape bank regulatory and supervisory policies, and these policies in turn influence the level of development of the banking sector, the efficiency with which banks intermediate savings, the fragility of the national banking system, bank governance and the extent to which corruption impedes the allocation of society's savings. Given our findings regarding the connections between the operation of the political system and both the selection and influence of banking policies, our work sheds a skeptical light on attempts by international agencies to develop uniform best practice checklists for countries. Moreover, our findings suggest that the all too common recommendation by official supervisors to rely on official supervision is misguided, at least "Till Angels Govern." Rather, our findings suggest that countries with political, legal, and regulatory systems that focus on improving and empowering the private market's ability to monitor and discipline banks are rewarded with well-functioning banking systems.

APPENDICES

Guide to the 2003 World Bank Survey

This guide summarizes the questions from the World Bank Survey. It provides a shortened and condensed version of the original survey questions. An asterisk indicates that the question is new to this survey.

1. Entry into Banking

1.1. What body/agency grants commercial banking licenses?

    1.1.1. Is there more than one body/agency that grants licenses to banks?*

    1.1.2. Is more than one license required (e.g., one for each banking activity, such as commercial banking, securities operations, insurance, etc.)?*

1.2. How many commercial banks were there at year-end 2001?

    1.2.1. What are the total assets of all commercial banks at year-end 2001?*

    1.2.2. What are the total deposits of all commercial banks at year-end 2001?*

1.3. What are the minimum capital entry requirements (in U.S. $ and/or domestic currency)?

    1.3.1. Is this minimum capital entry requirement the same for a foreign branch and subsidiary?*

1.4. Is it legally required that applicants submit information on the source of funds to be used as capital?

1.5. Are the sources of funds to be used as capital verified by the regulatory/supervisory authorities?

1.6. Can the initial disbursement or subsequent injections of capital be done with assets other than cash or government securities?

1.7. Can initial disbursement of capital be done with borrowed funds?

1.8. Which of the following are legally required to be submitted before issuance of the banking license?

    1.8.1. Draft by-laws?

    1.8.2. Intended organization chart?

    1.8.3. Financial projections for first three years?

    1.8.4. Financial information on main potential shareholders?

    1.8.5. Background/experience of future directors?

    1.8.6. Background/experience of future managers?

    1.8.7. Sources of funds to be disbursed in the capitalization of new bank?

    1.8.8. Market differentiation intended for the new bank?

1.9. In the past five years, how many applications for commercial banking licenses have been received from domestic entities?

    1.9.1. How many of those applications have been denied?

1.10. In the past five years, how many applications for commercial banking licenses have been received from foreign entities? And how many have been denied?*

    1.10.1. Number of applications from foreign entities to enter through the acquisition of domestic bank?*

    1.10.2. Number of applications from foreign entities to enter through new, capitalized subsidiary?*

    1.10.3. Number of applications from foreign entities to enter through opening a branch?*

    1.10.4. Number of applications from foreign entities to enter through some other means?*

1.11. What were the primary reasons for denial of the applications in 1.9 and 1.10?

    1.11.1. Capital amount or quality?

    1.11.2. Banking skills?

    1.11.3. Reputation?

    1.11.4. Incomplete application?

    1.11.5. Other reasons(s). Please list.

1.12. Are foreign entities prohibited from entering through:*

    1.12.1. Acquisition?*

    1.12.2. Subsidiary?*

    1.12.3. Branch?*

2. Ownership

2.1. Is there a maximum percentage of bank capital that can be owned by a single owner?

    2.1.1. If yes, what is the percentage?

2.2. Can related parties own capital in a bank?

    2.2.1. If yes, what are the maximum percentages associated with the total ownership by a related party group (e.g., family, business associates, etc.)?

    2.2.2. Are there penalties for violating this rule?

2.3. What is the level of regulatory restrictiveness for nonfinancial firms ownership of banks:

    Unrestricted – A nonfinancial firm may own 100 percent of the equity in a bank?

    Permitted – Unrestricted with prior authorization or approval?

    Restricted – Limits are placed on ownership, such as a maximum percentage of a bank's capital or shares?

    Prohibited – No equity investment in a bank?

2.4. What fraction of capital in the largest ten banks is owned by commercial/industrial and/or financial conglomerates? If there are fewer than ten banks, use that number in your answer.*

2.5. What is the level of regulatory restrictiveness for nonbank financial firms (e.g., insurance companies, finance companies, etc.) ownership of banks:

    Unrestricted – A non-bank financial firm may own 100 percent of the equity in a bank?

    Permitted – Unrestricted with prior authorization or approval?

    Restricted – Limits are placed on ownership, such as a maximum percentage of a bank's capital or shares?

    Prohibited – No equity investment in a bank?

2.6. Of commercial banks in your country, what fraction of:

    2.6.1. deposits is held by the five (5) largest banks at year-end 2001?

    2.6.2. assets is held by the five (5) largest banks at year-end 2001?*

2.7. Of all deposit-taking institutions in your country, what fraction of their assets is held by just commercial banks?*

3. Capital

3.1. What is the minimum capital-asset ratio requirement?

    3.1.1. Is this ratio risk weighted in line with the Basel guidelines?

3.2. Does the minimum ratio vary as a function of an individual bank's credit risk?

3.3. Does the minimum ratio vary as a function of market risk?

3.4. What is the actual risk-adjusted capital ratio in banks as of year-end 2001, using the 1988 Basel Accord definitions?*

    3.4.1. What is the actual equity capital ratio (i.e., not risk-adjusted) of banks as of year-end 2001?*

3.5. Is subordinated debt allowable as part of capital?

3.6. Is subordinated debt required as part of capital?

3.7. What fraction of revaluation gains is allowed as part of capital?

3.8. What fraction of the banking system's assets is in banks that are:

    3.8.1. 50 percent or more government owned as of year-end 2001?

    3.8.2. 50 percent or more foreign owned as of year-end 2001?

3.9. Before minimum capital adequacy is determined, which of the following are deducted from the book value of capital:

    3.9.1. Market value of loan losses not realized on accounting books?

    3.9.2. Unrealized losses in securities portfolios?

    3.9.3. Unrealized foreign exchange losses?

3.10. Are accounting practices for banks in accordance with International Accounting Standards (IAS)?*

3.11. Are accounting practices for banks in accordance with U.S. Generally Accepted Accounting Standards (GAAS)?*

4. Activities

4.1. What is the level of regulatory restrictiveness for bank participation in securities activities (the ability of banks to engage in the business of securities underwriting, brokering, dealing, and all aspects of the mutual fund industry):

    Unrestricted – A full range of activities in the given category can be conducted directly in the bank?

    Permitted – A full range of activities can be conducted, but all or some must be conducted in subsidiaries?

    Restricted – Less than a full range of activities can be conducted in the bank or subsidiaries?

    Prohibited – The activity cannot be conducted in either the bank or subsidiaries?

4.2. What is the level of regulatory restrictiveness for bank participation in insurance activities (the ability of banks to engage in insurance underwriting and selling):

    Unrestricted – A full range of activities in the given category can be conducted directly in the bank?

Permitted – A full range of activities can be conducted, but all or some must be conducted in subsidiaries?

Restricted – Less than a full range of activities can be conducted in the bank or subsidiaries?

Prohibited – The activity cannot be conducted in either the bank or subsidiaries?

4.3. What is the level of regulatory restrictiveness for bank participation in real estate activities (the ability of banks to engage in real estate investment, development, and management):

Unrestricted – A full range of activities in the given category can be conducted directly in the bank?

Permitted – A full range of activities can be conducted, but all or some must be conducted in subsidiaries?

Restricted – Less than a full range of activities can be conducted in the bank or subsidiaries?

Prohibited – The activity cannot be conducted in either the bank or subsidiaries?

4.4. What is the level of regulatory restrictiveness for bank ownership of nonfinancial firms:

Unrestricted – A bank may own 100 percent of the equity in any nonfinancial firm?

Permitted – A bank may own 100 percent of the equity in a nonfinancial firm, but ownership is limited based on a bank's equity capital?

Restricted – A bank can only acquire less than 100 percent of the equity in a nonfinancial firm?

Prohibited – A bank may not acquire any equity investment in a nonfinancial firm?

5. External Auditing Requirements

5.1. Is an external audit a compulsory obligation for banks?

5.2. Are specific requirements for the extent or nature of the audit spelled out?

5.3. Are auditors licensed or certified?

5.4. Do supervisors get a copy of the auditor's report?

5.5. Does the supervisory agency have the right to meet with external auditors to discuss their report without the approval of the bank?

5.6. Are auditors required by law to communicate directly to the supervisory agency any presumed involvement of bank directors or senior managers in illicit activities, fraud, or insider abuse?

5.7. Can supervisors take legal action against external auditors for negligence?

5.8. Has action been taken against an auditor in the last five years?

6. Internal Management/Organizational Requirements

6.1. Can the supervisory authority force a bank to change its internal organizational structure?

6.2. Has this power been utilized in the last five years?

7. Liquidity & Diversification Requirements

7.1. Are there explicit, verifiable, and quantifiable guidelines regarding asset diversification (for example, are banks required to have some minimum diversification of loans among sectors, or are there sectoral concentration limits)?*

7.2. Are banks prohibited from making loans abroad?

7.3. Are banks required to hold either liquidity reserves or any deposits at the Central Bank?

   7.3.1. If so, what are these requirements?

7.4. Do these reserves earn any interest?

   7.4.1. What interest is paid on these reserves?

7.5. Are banks allowed to hold reserves in foreign denominated currencies or other foreign denominated instruments? If yes, please state the ratio.*

7.6. Are banks required to hold reserves in foreign denominated currencies or other foreign denominated instruments? If yes, please state the ratio.*

7.7. What percent of the commercial banking system's assets is foreign-currency denominated?*

7.8. What percent of the commercial banking system's liabilities is foreign-currency denominated?*

7.9. What percent of the commercial banking system's assets is in central government bonds?*

7.10. What percent of the commercial banking system's assets is funded with deposits?*

   7.10.1. What percent of the commercial banking system's assets is funded with insured deposits?*

8. Depositor (Savings) Protection Schemes

8.1. Is there an explicit deposit insurance protection system?
   If no, you may skip to question 8.2. If yes:

   8.1.1. Is it funded by (check one): the government, the banks, or both?

8.1.2. Are premia collected regularly (ex ante)
only when there is a need (ex post)
or both?*

8.1.3. Do deposit insurance fees charged to banks vary based on some assessment of risk?*

8.1.4. If pre-funded, what is the ratio of accumulated funds to total bank assets?

8.1.5. What is the deposit insurance limit per account (in US$ and local currency)?

8.1.5.1. US$:

8.1.5.2. Domestic currency:

8.1.6. Is there a limit per person?

8.1.6.1. If yes, what is that limit (in domestic currency)?

8.1.7. Is there formal coinsurance, that is, are depositors only insured for some percentage of their deposits, either absolutely or above some floor and/or up to some limit?*

8.1.8. Does the deposit insurance scheme also cover foreign currency deposits?*

8.1.9. Are interbank deposits covered?*

8.1.10. Does the deposit insurance authority make the decision to intervene a bank?*

8.1.10.1. If no, who does?

8.1.11. Does the deposit insurance authority have the legal power to cancel or revoke deposit insurance for any participating bank?*

8.2. As a share of total assets, what is the value of large denominated debt liabilities of banks – subordinated debt, bonds, and so on – that are definitely not covered by any explicit or implicit savings protection scheme?

8.3. As part of failure resolution, how many banks closed or merged in the last five years?

8.4. Were depositors wholly compensated (to the extent of legal protection) the last time a bank failed?

8.4.1. On average, how long does it take to pay depositors in full?

8.4.2. What was the longest that depositors had to wait in the last five years?

8.5. Were any deposits not explicitly covered by deposit insurance at the time of the failure compensated when the bank failed (excluding funds later paid out in liquidation procedures)?

8.6. Can the deposit insurance agency/fund take legal action against bank directors or other bank officials?

8.7. Has the deposit insurance agency/fund ever taken legal action against bank directors or other bank officials?

8.8. Are non-residents treated differently than residents with respect to deposit insurance scheme coverage?*

8.9. Who manages the insurance fund? Is it managed:*
   a. solely by the private sector?
   b. jointly by private-public officials?
   c. solely by public sector?

8.10. Is participation in the deposit insurance system compulsory for all banks?*

9. Provisioning Requirements

9.1. Is there a formal definition of a "nonperforming loan"?
   9.1.1. The primary system for loan classification is based on (PLEASE PICK ONE):
      (a) the number of days a loan is in arrears
      (b) a forward looking estimate of the probability of default
      (c) other

9.2. How many days is a loan in arrears classified as:
   9.2.1. Substandard?
   9.2.2. Doubtful?
   9.2.3. Loss?

9.3. What is the minimum provisioning required as loans become:
   9.3.1. Substandard?
   9.3.2. Doubtful?
   9.3.3. Loss?

9.4. What is the ratio of nonperforming loans to total assets as of year-end 2001?

9.5. If a customer has multiple loans and one loan is classified as non-performing, are the other loans automatically classified as non-performing?

9.6. What is the aggregate net interest margin-to-asset ratio as of year-end 2001?*

9.7. What is the aggregate overhead costs-to-asset ratio as of year-end 2001?*

9.8. What is the tax deductibility of provisions:*
   9.8.1. Specific provisions can be deducted?*
   9.8.2. General provisions can be deducted?*
   9.8.3. Provisions cannot be deducted?*

10. Accounting/Information Disclosure Requirements

10.1. Does accrued, though unpaid, interest/principal enter the income statement while the loan is still performing?

    10.1.1. Does accrued, although unpaid, interest/principal enter the income statement while the loan is nonperforming?

10.2. After how many days in arrears must interest income accrual cease?

10.3. Are financial institutions required to produce consolidated accounts covering all bank and any nonbank financial subsidiaries?

10.4. Are off-balance sheet items disclosed to supervisors?

    10.4.1. Are off-balance sheet items disclosed to the public?

10.5. Must banks disclose their risk management procedures to the public?

10.6. Are bank directors legally liable if information disclosed is erroneous or misleading?

    10.6.1. What are the penalties, if applicable?

    10.6.2. Have penalties been enforced?

10.7. Do regulations require credit ratings for commercial banks?

    10.7.1. What percentage of the top ten banks are rated by international credit rating agencies (e.g., Moody's, Standard and Poor)?

    10.7.2. How many of the top ten banks are rated by domestic credit rating agencies?

    10.7.3. Which bank activities are rated?

        10.7.3.1. Bonds?

        10.7.3.2. Commercial paper?

        10.7.3.3. Other activity (e.g., issuance of bank certificates of deposit, pension and mutual funds, insurance companies, financial guarantees, etc.)?

11. Discipline/Problem Institutions/Exit

11.1. Are there any mechanisms of cease and desist-type orders, whose infraction leads to the automatic imposition of civil and penal sanctions on the banks directors and managers?

    11.1.1. Are bank regulators/supervisors required to make public formal enforcement actions, which include cease-and-desist orders and written agreements between a bank regulatory/supervisory body and a banking organization?*

11.2. Can the supervisory agency order the bank's directors or management to constitute provisions to cover actual or potential losses?

11.3. Can the supervisory agency suspend the directors' decision to distribute:

11.3.1. Dividends?

11.3.2. Bonuses?

11.3.3. Management fees?

11.4. Have any such actions been taken in the last five years?

11.5. Which laws address bank insolvency?

11.6. Can the supervisory agency legally declare – such that this declaration supersedes the rights of bank shareholders – that a bank is insolvent?

11.7. Does the Banking Law give authority to the supervisory agency to intervene – that is, suspend some or all ownership rights – a problem bank?

11.8. Does the Law establish predetermined levels of solvency deterioration that forces automatic actions (such as intervention)?

11.9. Regarding bank restructuring and reorganization, can the supervisory agency or any other government agency do the following:

11.9.1. Supersede shareholder rights?

11.9.2. Remove and replace management?

11.9.3. Remove and replace directors?

11.9.4. Forbear certain prudential regulations?

11.9.5. Insure liabilities beyond any explicit deposit insurance scheme?

11.10.

11.10.1. During the last five years, how many banks have been resolved in the following way, and what was the percentage of assets of the banking system accounted for by each:

a. Closure and liquidation?*

b. Intervention and open bank assistance?*

c. Transfer of assets and liabilities (incl. purchase and assumption) or merger and acquisition?

d. Other (please specify)?*

11.10.2. What percentage of total bank assets did each of these solution methods account for?*

11.10.3. How many months did each of these resolution techniques take on average, from the moment of intervention by the responsible authority to the moment of resolution?*

11.11. Who is responsible for appointing and supervising a bank liquidator/receiver?*

11.12. Is court approval required for supervisory actions, such as superseding shareholder rights, removing and replacing management, removing and replacing directors, or license revocation?*

11.13. Is court order required to appoint a receiver/liquidator in the event of liquidation?*

11.14. Can the bank shareholders appeal to the court against a decision of the bank supervisor?*

12. Supervision

12.1. What body/agency supervises banks?

12.1.1. Is there more than one supervisory body?*

12.1.2. Is there a single financial supervisory agency for the financial sector?*

12.2. To whom are the supervisory bodies responsible or accountable?

12.2.1. How is the head of the supervisory agency (and other directors) appointed?

12.2.2. Does the head of the supervisory agency (and other directors) have a fixed term? If yes, how long is the term?*

12.2.3. The head of the supervisory agency can be removed by:

a: the decision of the head of government (e.g., president, prime minister)?*

b: the decision of the finance minister or other cabinet level authority?*

c: a simple majority of a legislative body (Parliament or Congress)?*

d: a supermajority (e.g., 60 percent, 75 percent) of a legislative body?*

e: other?*

12.3. Are there important differences between what the supervisory agency is expected to do and what is mandated by law?

12.4. How many professional bank supervisors are there in total?

12.5. How many on-site examinations per bank were performed in the last five years?

12.6. What is the total budget for supervision in local currency or dollars (please specify) in 2002?

12.7. How frequently are OSE inspections conducted in large and medium size banks (annually, every two years, less frequently)?

12.8. How many of the total bank supervisors have more than ten years of experience in bank supervision?

   12.8.1. What is the average tenure of current supervisors (i.e., what is the average number of years current supervisors have been supervisors)?

12.9. If an infraction of any prudential regulation is found by a supervisor, must it be reported?

   12.9.1. Are there mandatory actions in these cases?

   12.9.2. Who authorizes exceptions to such actions?

   12.9.3. How many exceptions were granted last year?

12.10. Are supervisors legally liable for their actions (e.g., if a supervisor takes actions against a bank can he/she be sued)?

Quantification of Different Dimensions of Bank Regulation and Supervision

Variable	Definition	Source and Quantification	World Bank Guide Questions
1. Bank Activity Regulatory Variables			
(a) Securities Activities	The extent to which banks may engage in underwriting, brokering and dealing in securities, and all aspects of the mutual fund industry.	WBG 4.1 (higher values, more restrictive) Unrestricted = 1 = full range of activities can be conducted directly in the bank; Permitted = 2 = full range of activities can be conducted, but some or all must be conducted in subsidiaries; Restricted = 3 = less than full range of activities can be conducted in the bank or subsidiaries; and Prohibited = 4 = the activity cannot be conducted in either the bank or subsidiaries.	4.1 What is the level of regulatory restrictiveness for bank participation in securities activities (the ability of banks to engage in the business of securities underwriting, brokering, dealing, and all aspects of the mutual fund industry)?
(b) Insurance Activities	The extent to which banks may engage in insurance underwriting and selling.	WBG 4.2 (higher values, more restrictive) Unrestricted = 1 = full range of activities can be conducted directly in the bank;	4.2 What is the level of regulatory restrictiveness for bank participation in insurance activities (the ability of banks to engage in

(continued)

Appendix 2 (*continued*)

Variable	Definition	Source and Quantification	World Bank Guide Questions
		Permitted = 2 = full range of activities can be conducted, but some or all must be conducted in subsidiaries; Restricted = 3 = less than full range of activities can be conducted in the bank or subsidiaries; and Prohibited = 4 = the activity cannot be conducted in either the bank or subsidiaries.	insurance underwriting and selling)?
(c) Real Estate Activities	The extent to which banks may engage in real estate investment, development, and management.	WBG 4.3 (higher values, more restrictive) Unrestricted = 1 = full range of activities can be conducted directly in the bank; Permitted = 2 = full range of activities can be conducted, but some or all must be conducted in subsidiaries; Restricted = 3 = less than full range of activities can be conducted in the bank or subsidiaries; and Prohibited = 4 = the activity cannot be conducted in either the bank or subsidiaries.	4.3 What is the level of regulatory restrictiveness for bank participation in real estate activities (the ability of banks to engage in real estate investment, development, and management)?

(d) Overall Activities Restrictiveness

Sum of (a) + (b) + (c) Higher values indicate greater restrictiveness.

2. Financial Conglomerate Variables

(a) Banks Owning Nonfinancial Firms

The extent to which banks may own and control nonfinancial firms.

WBG 4.4 (higher values, more restrictive)

Unrestricted = 1 = a bank may own 100 percent of the equity in any nonfinancial firm;
Permitted = 2 = a bank may own 100 percent of the equity of a nonfinancial firm, but ownership is limited based on a bank's equity capital;
Restricted = 3 = a bank can only acquire less than 100 percent of the equity in a nonfinancial firm; and
Prohibited = 4 = a bank may not acquire any equity investment in a nonfinancial firm whatsoever.

4.4 What is the level of regulatory restrictiveness for bank ownership of nonfinancial firms?

(b) Nonfinancial Firms Owning Banks

The extent to which nonfinancial firms may own and control banks.

WBG 2.3 (higher values, more restrictive)

Unrestricted = 1 = a nonfinancial firm may own 100 percent of the equity

2.3 What is the level of regulatory restrictiveness of ownership by nonfinancial firms of banks?

(continued)

333

Appendix 2 (continued)

Variable	Definition	Source and Quantification	World Bank Guide Questions
		in a bank; Permitted = 2 = unrestricted with prior authorization or approval; Restricted = 3 = limits are placed on ownership, such as a maximum percentage of a bank's capital or shares; and Prohibited = 4 = no equity investment in a bank.	
(c) Nonbank Financial Firms Owning Banks	The extent to which nonbank financial firms may own and control banks.	WBG 2.5 (higher values, more restrictive) Unrestricted = 1 = a nonfinancial firm may own 100 percent of the equity in a bank; Permitted = 2 = unrestricted with prior authorization or approval; Restricted = 3 = limits are placed on ownership, such as a maximum percentage of a bank's capital or shares; and Prohibited = 4 = no equity investment in a bank.	2.5 What is the level of regulatory restrictiveness of ownership by nonfinancial firms of banks?
(d) Overall Financial Conglomerates Restrictiveness		Sum of (a) + (b) + (c) Higher values indicate greater restrictiveness.	

3. Competition Regulatory Variables

Variable	Description	Definition
(a) Limitations on Foreign Bank Entry/Ownership	Whether foreign banks may own domestic banks and whether foreign banks may enter a country's banking industry.	WBG 1.12.1–1.12.3 Yes = 0; No = 1 Lower values indicate greater stringency.
	1.12 Are foreign entities prohibited from entering through	
	1.12.1 Acquisitions (Yes, prohibited; No, not prohibited)	
	1.12.2 Subsidiary (Yes, prohibited; No, not prohibited)	
	1.12.3 Branch (Yes, prohibited; No, not prohibited)	
(b) Entry into Banking Requirements	Whether various types of legal submissions are required to obtain a banking license.	WBG 1.8.1–1.8.8 Yes = 1; No = 0 Higher values indicate greater stringency.
	1.8 Which of the following are legally required to be submitted before issuance of the banking license?	
	1.8.1 Draft by-laws? Yes/No	
	1.8.2 Intended organization chart? Yes/No	
	1.8.3 Financial projections for first three years? Yes/No	
	1.8.4 Financial information on main potential shareholders? Yes/No	
	1.8.5 Background/experience of future directors? Yes/No	
	1.8.6 Background/experience of future managers? Yes/No	

(continued)

335

Appendix 2 (continued)

Variable	Definition	Source and Quantification	World Bank Guide Questions
			1.8.7 Sources of funds to be disbursed in the capitalization of new banks? Yes/No
			1.8.8 Market differentiation intended for the new bank? Yes/No
(c) Fraction of Entry Applications Denied	The degree to which applications to enter banking are denied.	WBG (1.9.1 + 1.10 (denied))/(1.9 + 1.10 (received)) (percent)	1.9 In the past five years, how many applications for commercial banking licenses have been received from domestic entities?
			1.9.1 How many of those applications have been denied?
			1.10 In the past five years, how many applications for commercial banking licenses have been received from foreign entities? And how many have been denied?
(1) Domestic Denials	The degree to which domestic applications to enter banking are denied.	WBG 1.9.1/1.9 (percent)	1.9 In the past five years, how many applications for banking licenses have been received from domestic entities?
			1.9.1 How many of those applications have been denied?

(2) Foreign Denials	The degree to which foreign applications to enter banking are denied.	WBG 1.10 (denied/received) (percent)	1.10 In the past five years, how many applications for banking licenses have been received from foreign entities? And how many have been denied?
4. Capital Regulatory Variables			
(a) Overall Capital Stringency	Whether the capital requirement reflects certain risk elements and deducts certain market value losses from capital before minimum capital adequacy is determined.	WBG 3.1.1 + 3.2 + 3.3 + 3.9.1 + 3.9.2 + 3.9.3 + (1 if 3.7 < 0.75) Yes = 1; No = 0 Higher values indicating greater stringency.	3.1.1 Is the minimum capital-asset ratio requirement risk weighted in line with the Basel I guidelines? Yes/No 3.2 Does the minimum ratio vary as a function of an individual bank's credit risk? Yes/No 3.3 Does the minimum ratio vary as a function of market risk? Yes/No 3.9 Before minimum capital adequacy is determined, which of the following are deducted from the book value of capital?

(continued)

337

Appendix 2 (continued)

Variable	Definition	Source and Quantification	World Bank Guide Questions
			3.9.1 Market value of loan losses not realized in accounting books? Yes/No 3.9.2 Unrealized losses in securities portfolios? Yes/No 3.9.3 Unrealized foreign exchange losses? Yes/No 3.7 What fraction of revaluation gains is allowed as part of capital?
(b) Initial Capital Stringency	Whether certain funds may be used to initially capitalize a bank and whether they are officially verified.	WBG 1.5: Yes = 1, No = 0: WBG 1.6&1.7: Yes = 0, No = 1. Higher values indicating greater stringency.	1.5 Are the sources of funds to be used as capital verified by the regulatory/supervisory authorities? Yes/No 1.6 Can the initial disbursement or subsequent injections of capital be done with assets other than cash or government securities? Yes/No 1.7 Can initial disbursement of capital be done with borrowed funds? Yes/No
(c) Capital Regulatory Index	The sum of (a) and (b).	(a) + (b) Higher values indicate greater stringency.	

5. *Official Supervisory Action Variables*

(a) Official Supervisory Power

Whether the supervisory authorities have the authority to take specific actions to prevent and correct problems.

WBG $5.5 + 5.6 + 5.7 + 6.1 + 10.4 + 11.2 + 11.3.1 + 11.3.2 + 11.3.3 + 11.6 + 11.7 + 11.9.1 + 11.9.2 + 11.9.3$

For questions 5.5, 5.6, 5.7, 6.1, 10.4, 11.2, 11.3.1, 11.3.2 and 11.3.3:

$Yes = 1; No = 0$

For questions 11.6, 11.7 and 11.9:

Bank supervisor $= 1$; Deposit insurance agency $= 0.5$; Bank restructuring or Asset Management Agency $= 0.5$; 0 otherwise.

Sum of these assigned values, with higher values indicating greater power.

5.5 Does the supervisory agency have the right to meet with external auditors to discuss their report without the approval of the bank? Yes/No

5.6 Are auditors required by law to communicate directly to the supervisory agency any presumed involvement of bank directors or senior managers in elicit activities, fraud, or insider abuse? Yes/No

5.7 Can supervisors take legal action against external auditors for negligence? Yes/No

6.1 Can the supervisory authority force a bank to change its internal organizational structure? Yes/No

10.4 Are off-balance sheet items disclosed to supervisors? Yes/No

(continued)

Appendix 2 *(continued)*

Variable	Definition	Source and Quantification	World Bank Guide Questions
			11.2 Can the supervisory agency order the bank's directors or management to constitute provisions to cover actual or potential losses? Yes/No
			11.3 Can the supervisory agency suspend the directors' decision to distribute:
			11.3.1 Dividends? Yes/No
			11.3.2 Bonuses? Yes/No
			11.3.3 Management fees? Yes/No
			11.6 Who can legally declare – such that this declaration supercedes the some of the rights of shareholders – that a bank is insolvent:
			11.6.1 Bank supervisor – Yes/No
			11.6.2 Court – Yes/No
			11.6.3 Deposit insurance agency – Yes/No
			11.6.4 Bank restructuring or Asset Management Agency – Yes/No
			11.6.5 Other – Yes/No

11.7 According to the Banking Law, who has authority to intervene – that is, suspend some or all ownership rights – a problem bank?

11.7.1 Bank supervisor – Yes/No

11.7.2 Court – Yes/No

11.7.3 Deposit insurance agency – Yes/No

11.7.4 Bank restructuring or Asset Management Agency – Yes/No

11.7.5 Other – Yes/No

11.9 Regarding bank restructuring and reorganization, can the supervisory agency or any other government agency do the following:

11.9.1 Supersede shareholder rights?

11.9.1.1 Bank supervisor – Yes/No

11.9.1.2 Court – Yes/No

11.9.1.3 Deposit insurance agency – Yes/No

11.9.1.4 Bank restructuring or Asset Management Agency – Yes/No

(continued)

Variable	Definition	Source and Quantification	World Bank Guide Questions
			11.9.1.5 Other – Yes/No
			11.9.2 Remove and replace management?
			11.9.2.1 Bank supervisor – Yes/No
			11.9.2.2 Court – Yes/No
			11.9.2.3 Deposit insurance agency – Yes/No
			11.9.2.4 Bank restructuring or Asset Management Agency – Yes/No
			11.9.2.5 Other – Yes/No
			11.9.3 Remove and replace directors?
			11.9.3.1 Bank supervisor – Yes/No
			11.9.3.2 Court – Yes/No
			11.9.3.3 Deposit insurance agency – Yes/No
			11.9.3.4 Bank restructuring or Asset Management Agency – Yes/No
			11.9.3.5 Other – Yes/No
(1) Prompt Corrective Power	Whether the law establishes predetermined levels of bank solvency deterioration that force automatic actions, such as intervention.	WBG 11.8 * (11.1 + 11.2 + 11.3.1 + 11.3.2 + 11.3.3 + 6.1) Yes = 1; No = 0 Sum of the assigned values for the items in parenthesis	11.8 Does the Law establish predetermined levels of solvency deterioration which forces automatic actions (like intervention)? Yes/No

	multiplied by 1 if there is a legally predetermined level of solvency deterioration forcing automatic actions and by 0 if not.		11.1 Are there any mechanisms of cease and desist-type orders, whose infraction leads to the automatic imposition of civil and penal sanctions on the bank's directors and managers? Yes/No 11.2 Can the supervisory agency order the bank's directors or management to constitute provisions to cover actual or potential losses? Yes/No 11.3 Can the supervisory agency suspend the directors' decision to distribute: 11.3.1 Dividends? Yes/No 11.3.2 Bonuses? Yes/No 11.3.3 Management fees? Yes/No 6.1 Can the supervisory authority force a bank to change its internal organizational structure? Yes/No
(2) Restructuring Power	Whether the supervisory authorities have the power to restructure and reorganize a troubled bank.	WBG 11.9.1 + 11.9.2 + 11.9.3 Bank supervisor = 1; Deposit insurance agency = 0.5;	11.9 Regarding bank restructuring and reorganization, can the

(continued)

343

Appendix 2 (continued)

Variable	Definition	Source and Quantification	World Bank Guide Questions
		Bank restructuring or Asset Management Agency = 0.5; 0 otherwise. Higher values indicate greater restructuring power.	supervisory agency or any other government agency do the following: 11.9.1 Supersede shareholder rights? 11.9.1.1 Bank supervisor – Yes/No 11.9.1.2 Court – Yes/No 11.9.1.3 Deposit insurance agency – Yes/No 11.9.1.4 Bank restructuring or Asset Management Agency – Yes/No 11.9.1.5 Other – Yes/No 11.9.2 Remove and replace management? 11.9.2.1 Bank supervisor – Yes/No 11.9.2.2 Court – Yes/No 11.9.2.3 Deposit insurance agency – Yes/No 11.9.2.4 Bank restructuring or Asset Management Agency – Yes/No 11.9.2.5 Other – Yes/No

11.9.3 Remove and replace directors?

11.9.3.1 Bank supervisor – Yes/No

11.9.3.2 Court – Yes/No

11.9.3.3 Deposit insurance agency – Yes/No

11.9.3.4 Bank restructuring or Asset Management Agency – Yes/No

11.9.3.5 Other – Yes/No

11.6 Who can legally declare – such that this declaration supercedes the some of the rights of shareholders – that a bank is insolvent:

11.6.1 Bank supervisor – Yes/No

11.6.2 Court – Yes/No

11.6.3 Deposit insurance agency – Yes/No

11.6.4 Bank restructuring or Asset Management Agency – Yes/No

11.6.5 Other – Yes/No

11.7 According to the Banking Law, who has authority to intervene – that is, suspend some or all ownership rights–a problem bank?

(continued)

| (3) Declaring Insolvency Power | Whether the supervisory authorities have the power to declare a deeply troubled bank insolvent. | WBG 11.6 + 11.7 Bank supervisor = 1; Deposit insurance agency = 0.5; Bank restructuring or Asset Management Agency = 0.5; 0 otherwise. Higher values indicate greater power. |

Appendix 2 *(continued)*

Variable	Definition	Source and Quantification	World Bank Guide Questions
			11.7.1 Bank supervisor – Yes/No 11.7.2 Court – Yes/No 11.7.3 Deposit insurance agency – Yes/No 11.7.4 Bank restructuring or Asset Management Agency – Yes/No 11.7.5 Other – Yes/No
(b) Supervisory Forbearance Discretion	Whether the supervisory authorities may engage in forbearance when confronted with violations of laws and regulations or other imprudent behavior.	WBG 11.9.4 + (11.8 – 1) * (−1) + (12.9 – 1) * (−1) + (12.9.1 – 1) * (−1) Bank supervisor = 1; Deposit insurance agency = 0.5; Bank restructuring or Asset Management Agency = 0.5; 0 otherwise. Sum of these assigned values such that higher values indicate greater discretion.	11.9.4 Regarding bank restructuring and reorganization, can the supervisory agency or any other government agency forbear certain prudential regulations? Yes/No 11.9.4.1 Bank supervisor – Yes/No 11.9.4.2 Court – Yes/No 11.9.4.3 Deposit insurance agency – Yes/No 11.9.4.4 Bank restructuring or Asset Management Agency – Yes/No

| (c) Court Involvement | The degree to which the court dominates the supervisory authority. | 11.9.4.5 Other – Yes/No
11.8 Does the Law establish predetermined levels of solvency deterioration which forces automatic actions (like intervention)? Yes/No
12.9 If an infraction of any prudential regulation is found by a supervisor, must it be reported? Yes/No
12.9.1 Are there mandatory actions in these cases? Yes/No

11.12 Is court approval required for supervisory actions, such as superceding shareholder rights, removing and replacing management, removing and replacing directors, or license revocation?
11.13 Is court order required to appoint a receiver/liquidator in the event of liquidation?
11.14 Can the bank shareholders appeal to the court against a decision of the bank supervisor? | WBG 11.12–11.14
Yes = 1; No = 0
Sum of these assigned values such that higher values mean less supervisory discretion. |

(continued)

Appendix 2 (*continued*)

Variable	Definition	Source and Quantification	World Bank Guide Questions
(d) Loan Classification Stringency	The classification of loans in arrears as substandard, doubtful, and loss.	WBG 9.2.1–9.2.3 (days) If there is a loan classification system, the actual minimum number of days beyond which a loan in arrears must be classified as substandard, then doubtful, and finally loss are summed. Higher values indicate less stringency.	9.2 Classification of loans in arrears based on their quality: after how many days is a loan in arrears classified as: 9.2.1 Substandard? 9.2.2 Doubtful? 9.2.3 Loss?
(e) Provisioning Stringency	The minimum required provisions as loans become substandard, doubtful, and loss.	WBG 9.3.1–9.3.3 (percent) The sum of the minimum required provisioning percentages when a loan is successively classified as substandard, doubtful, and loss. If a range is provided, the minimum percentage is used. Higher values indicate greater stringency.	9.3 What are the minimum required provisions as loans become: 9.3.1 Substandard? 9.3.2 Doubtful? 9.3.3 Loss?
(f) Diversification Index	Whether there are explicit, verifiable, quantifiable guidelines for asset diversification, and banks are allowed to make loans abroad.	WBG 7.1 + (7.2 –1) * (–1) Yes = 1; No = 0 Sum of these assigned values, with higher values indicating more diversification.	7.1 Are there explicit, verifiable, and quantifiable guidelines regarding asset diversification? Yes/No 7.2 Are banks prohibited from making loans abroad? Yes/No

6. Official Supervisory Structural Variables

(a) Supervisor Tenure	The average tenure of a professional bank supervisor.	WBG 12.8.1 (years)	12.8.1 What is the average tenure of current supervisors (i.e., what is the average number of years current supervisors have been supervisors)?
(b) Independence of Supervisory Authority-Political	The degree to which the supervisory authority is independent within the government from political influence.	WBG 12.2 12.2(c) = 1; other = 0 Higher values signify greater independence.	12.2 To whom are the supervisory bodies responsible or accountable? (a) the Prime Minister – Yes/No (b) the Finance Minister or other cabinet level official – Yes/No (c) a legislative body, such as Parliament or Congress – Yes/No (d) other – Yes/No
(c) Independence of Supervisory Authority – Banks	The degree to which the supervisory authority is protected by the legal system from the banking industry.	WBG 12.10 Yes = 0; No = 1	12.10 Are supervisors legally liable for their actions (e.g., if a supervisor takes actions against a bank can he/she be sued)?
(d) Independence of Supervisory Authority – Fixed Term	The degree to which the supervisory authority is able to make decisions independently of political considerations.	WBG 12.2.2 Less than 4 years or no fixed term = 0; a fixed term of 4 years or greater = 1.	12.2.2 Does the head of the supervisory agency (and other directors) have a fixed term? Yes/No If yes, how long is the term?

(continued)

Appendix 2 (*continued*)

Variable	Definition	Source and Quantification	World Bank Guide Questions
(e) Independence of Supervisory Authority – Overall	The degree to which the supervisory authority is independent from the government and legally protected from the banking industry.	WBG (b) + (c) + (d) Higher values signify greater independence.	
(f) Multiple Supervisors	This variable indicates whether there is a single official regulator of banks, or whether multiple supervisors share responsibility for supervising the nation's banks.	This variable is assigned a value of 1 if there is more than one supervisor and 0 otherwise.	12.1 What body/agency supervises banks? 12.1.1 Is there more than one supervisory body?
(g) Single vs. Multiple Financial Supervisory Authority	This variable indicates whether or not there is a single financial supervisory authority.	WBG 12.1.2 Yes = 1; No = 0	12.1.2 Is there a single financial supervisory agency for financial sector?
7. Private Monitoring Variables			
(a) Certified Audit Required	Whether there is a compulsory external audit by a licensed or certified auditor.	WBG 5.1 * 5.3 (Yes = 1; No = 0)	5.1 Is an external audit a compulsory obligation for banks? Yes/No 5.3 Are auditors licensed or certified? Yes/No
(b) Percentage of Ten Biggest Banks Rated by International Credit Rating Agencies	The percentage of the top ten banks that are rated by international credit rating agencies.	WBG 10.7.1 (percent)	10.7.1 What percentage of the top ten banks are rated by international credit rating agencies (e.g., Moody's, Standard and Poor)?
(c) Percentage of Ten Biggest Banks Rated by Domestic Credit Rating Agencies	The percentage of the top ten banks that are rated by domestic credit rating agencies.	WBG 10.7.2 (percent)	10.7.2 How many of the top ten banks are rated by domestic credit rating agencies?

| (d) No Explicit Deposit Insurance Scheme | Whether there is an explicit deposit insurance scheme and, if not, whether depositors were fully compensated the last time a bank failed. | 8.1 Is there an explicit insurance protection system? Yes/No
8.4 Were depositors wholly compensated (to the extent of legal protection) the last time a bank failed? Yes/No | WBG 1 if 8.1 = 0 and/or 8.4 = 0; 0 otherwise
Yes = 1; No = 0
Higher values indicate more private supervision. |
| (e) Bank Accounting | Whether the income statement includes accrued or unpaid interest or principal on performing and nonperforming loans and whether banks are required to produce consolidated financial statements. | 10.1 Does accrued, though unpaid interest/principal enter the income statement while the loan is still performing?
10.1.1 Does accrued, though unpaid interest/principal enter the income statement while the loan is still nonperforming?
10.3 Are financial institutions required to produce consolidated accounts covering all bank and any nonbank financial subsidiaries?
10.6 Are bank directors legally liable if information disclosed is erroneous or misleading? | WBG $10.1 + (10.1.1 - 1) \ast (-1) + 10.3 + 10.6$
Yes = 1; No = 0
Sum of assigned values, with higher values indicating more informative bank accounts. |

(continued)

351

Appendix 2 (continued)

Variable	Definition	Source and Quantification	World Bank Guide Questions
(f) Private Monitoring Index	Whether (a) occurs, (b) equals 100%, (c) equals 100%, (d) occurs, (e) occurs, subordinated debt is allowable as a part of regulatory capital, subordinated debt is required as a part of regulatory capital, off-balance sheet items are disclosed to supervisors, off-balance sheet items are disclosed to the public, and banks must disclose risk management procedures to the public.	WBG: (a) + [1 if (b) equals 100%; 0 otherwise] + [1 if (c) equals 100%; 0 otherwise] + (d) + (e) + (1 if 3.5 or 3.6 equals "yes") + 10.4.1 + 10.5 + 11.1.1 Yes = 1; No = 0 Higher values indicating more private monitoring.	3.5 Is subordinated debt allowable as part of capital? Yes/No 3.6 Is subordinated debt required as part of capital? Yes/No 10.4.1 Are off-balance sheet items disclosed to the public? Yes/No 10.5 Must banks disclose their risk management procedures to the public? Yes/No 11.1.1 Are bank regulators/supervisors required to make public formal enforcement actions, which include cease-and-desist orders and written agreements between a bank regulatory/supervisory body and a banking organization?

8. Deposit Insurance Scheme Variables

(a) Deposit Insurer Power	Whether the deposit insurance authority has the authority to make the decision to intervene in a bank, take legal action against bank directors or officials, and has ever taken any legal action against bank directors or officers.	WBG 8.1.10 + 8.1.11 + 8.6 + 8.7 Yes = 1; No = 0 Sum of assigned values, with higher values indicating more power.	8.1.10 Does the deposit insurance authority make the decision to intervene a bank? Yes/No 8.1.11 Does the deposit insurance authority have the legal power to cancel or revoke deposit insurance for any participating bank? Yes/No 8.6 Can the deposit insurance agency/fund take legal action against bank directors or other bank officials? Yes/No 8.7 Has the deposit insurance agency/fund ever taken legal action against bank directors or other bank officials? Yes/No
(b) Deposit Insurance Funds-to-Total Bank Assets	The size of the deposit insurance fund relative to total bank assets.	WBG 8.1.4 (percent)	8.1.4 If pre-funded, what is the ratio of accumulated funds to total bank assets?
(c) Funding with Insured Deposits (percent)	The degree to which moral hazard exists.	WBG 7.10.1 Higher values indicate more moral hazard.	7.10.1 What percent of the commercial banking system's assets is funded with insured deposits?

(continued)

353

Appendix 2 (continued)

Variable	Definition	Source and Quantification	World Bank Guide Questions
(d) Various Factors Mitigating Moral Hazard	Degree to which actions taken to mitigate moral hazard.	WBG 8.1.1 + 8.1.3 + 8.17 Yes = 1; No = 0 and 1 if funded by banks, 0 otherwise Higher values indicate greater mitigation of moral hazard.	8.1.1 Is it funded by (check one) the government, the banks, or both? 8.1.3 Do deposit insurance fees charged to banks vary based on some assessment of risk? Yes/ No 8.1.7 Is there formal co-insurance, that is, are depositors only insured for some percentage of their deposits, either absolutely or above some floor and/or up to some limit? Yes/ No

9. External Governance Variables

Variable	Definition	Source and Quantification	World Bank Guide Questions
(a) Strength of External Audit	The effectiveness of external audits of banks.	WBG 5.1 + 5.2 + 5.3 + 5.4 + 5.5 + 5.6 + 5.7 Yes = 1; No = 0 Higher values indicate better strength of external audit.	5.1 Is an external audit a compulsory obligation for banks? Yes/No 5.2 Are specific requirements for the extent or nature of the audit spelled out? Yes/No 5.3 Are auditors licensed or certified? Yes/No 5.4 Do supervisors get a copy of the auditor's report? Yes/No

5.5 Does the supervisory agency have the right to meet with external auditors to discuss their report without the approval of the bank? Yes/No

5.6 Are auditors required by law to communicate directly to the supervisory agency any presumed involvement of bank directors or senior managers in illicit activities, fraud, or insider abuse? Yes/No

5.7 Can supervisors take legal action against external auditors for negligence? Yes/No

10.1 Does accrued, though unpaid interest/principal enter the income statement while the loan is still performing?

10.3 Are financial institutions required to produce consolidated accounts covering all bank and any nonbank financial subsidiaries?

(b) Financial Statement Transparency | The transparency of bank financial statements practices. | WBG 10.1 + 10.3 + 10.4.1 + 10.5 + 10.6 + (10.1.1 − 1) * (−1)
Yes = 1; No = 0
Higher values indicate better transparency.

355

(continued)

Appendix 2 (continued)

Variable	Definition	Source and Quantification	World Bank Guide Questions
			10.4.1 Are off-balance sheet items disclosed to the public? Yes/No
			10.5 Must banks disclose their risk management procedures to the public? Yes/No
			10.6 Are bank directors legally liable if information disclosed is erroneous or misleading?
			10.1.1 Does accrued, though unpaid, interest/principal enter the income statement while the loan is still nonperforming? Yes/No
(c) Accounting Practices	The type of accounting practices used.	WBG 3.10 or 3.11 Yes = 1; No = 0 Higher values indicate better practices.	3.10 Are accounting practices for banks in accordance with International Accounting Standards (IAS)?
			3.11 Are accounting practices for banks in accordance with U.S. Generally Accepted Accounting Standards (GAAS)?

Component	Description	Questions / Scoring
(d) External Ratings and Creditor Monitoring	The evaluations by external rating agencies and incentives for creditors of the bank to monitor bank performance.	WBG $3.5 + 3.6 + 10.7 + (1$ if $10.7.1$ equals 100%; 0 otherwise$) + (1$ if $10.7.2$ equals 100%; 0 otherwise$)$ Yes $= 1$; No $= 0$ Higher values indicate better credit monitoring.	3.5 Is subordinated debt allowable as part of capital? Yes/No 3.6 Is subordinated debt required as part of capital? Yes/No 10.7 Do regulations require credit ratings for commercial banks? 10.7.1 What percent of the top ten banks are rated by international credit rating agencies (e.g., Moody's, Standard and Poor)? 10.7.2 How many of the top ten banks are rated by domestic credit rating agencies?
(e) External Governance Index	The degree of stringent corporate governance measures.	Sum of (a) + (b) + (c) + (d) Higher values indicating better corporate governance.	

357

Key International Standards for Sound Financial Systems

Area	Key Standard	International Issuing Body
Financial Regulation and Supervision		
Banking Supervision	Core Principles for Effective Banking Supervision	Basel Committee on Banking Supervision
Securities Regulation	Objectives and Principles of Securities Regulation	International Organization of Securities Commissions
Insurance Supervision	Insurance Core Principles	International Association of Insurance Supervisors
Institutional and Market Infrastructure		
Insolvency	Principles and Guidelines on Effective Insolvency and Creditor Rights Systems	World Bank
Corporate Governance	Principles of Corporate Governance	Organization for Economic Cooperation and Development
Accounting	International Accounting Standards (IAS)	International Accounting Standards Board
Auditing	International Standards on Auditing (ISA)	International Federation of Accountants
Payment and Settlement	Core Principles for Systemically Important Payment Systems	Committee on Payment and Settlement Systems
Market Integrity (Money Laundering)	The Forty Recommendations of the Financial Action Task Force on Money Laundering	Financial Action Task Force
Macroeconomic Policy and Data Transparency		
Monetary and Financial Policy Transparency	Code of Good Practices on Transparency in Monetary and Financial Policies	International Monetary Fund
Fiscal Policy Transparency	Code of Good Practices on Fiscal Transparency	International Monetary Fund
Data Dissemination	Special Data Dissemination Standard, General Data Dissemination System	International Monetary Fund

Source: Financial Stability Forum (2001).

Core Principles for Effective Banking Supervision

The Basel Core Principles comprise twenty-five basic principles that need to be in place for a supervisory system to be effective. The Principles relate to:

Objectives, autonomy, powers and resources

CP 1 is divided into six parts:

CP 1.1 deals with the definition of responsibilities and objectives for the supervisory agency.

CP 1.2 deals with, skills, resources and independence of the supervisory agency.

CP 1.3 deals with the legal framework.

CP 1.4 deals with enforcement powers.

CP 1.5 requires adequate legal protection for supervisors.

CP 1.6 deals with information sharing.

Licensing and structure

CP 2 deals with permissible activities of banks.

CP 3 deals with licensing criteria and the licensing process.

CP 4 requires supervisors to review, and have the power to reject, all significant transfers of ownership in banks.

CP 5 requires supervisors to review major acquisitions and investments by banks.

Prudential regulations and requirements

CP 6 deals with minimum capital adequacy requirements. For internationally active banks, these must not be less stringent than those in the Basel Capital Accord.

CP 7 deals with the granting and managing of loans and the making of investments.

CP 8 sets out requirements for evaluating asset quality, and the adequacy of loan loss provisions and reserves.

CP 9 sets forth rules for identifying and limiting concentrations of exposures to single borrowers, or to groups of related borrowers.

CP 10 sets out rules for lending to connected or related parties.

CP 11 requires banks to have policies for identifying and managing country and transfer risks.

CP 12 requires banks to have systems to measure, monitor and control market risks.

CP 13 requires banks to have systems to measure, monitor and control all other material risks.

CP 14 calls for banks to have adequate internal control systems.

CP 15 sets out rules for the prevention of fraud and money laundering.

Methods of ongoing supervision

CP 16 defines the overall framework for on-site and off-site supervision.

CP 17 requires supervisors to have regular contacts with bank management and staff, and to fully understand banks' operations.

CP 18 sets out the requirements for off-site supervision.

CP 19 requires supervisors to conduct on-site examinations, or to use external auditors for validation of supervisory information.

CP 20 requires the conduct of consolidated supervision.

Information requirements

CP 21 requires banks to maintain adequate records reflecting the true condition of the bank, and to publish audited financial statements.

Remedial measures and exit

CP 22 requires the supervisor to have, and promptly apply, adequate remedial measures for banks when they do not meet prudential requirements, or are otherwise threatened.

Cross-border banking

CP 23 requires supervisors to apply global consolidated supervision over internationally active banks.

CP 24 requires supervisors to establish contact and information exchange with other supervisors involved in international operations, such as host country authorities.

Source: Cesare Calari and Stefan Ingves, "Implementation of the Basel Core Principles for Effective Banking Supervision, Experiences, Influences, and Perspectives," *International Monetary Fund and World Bank* (September 2002), p. 13.

APPENDIX 5

Information on Different Dimensions of Bank Regulation and Supervision: Averages by Income Level and Development Status

	High Income (45 Countries)	Upper Middle Income (32 Countries)	Lower Middle Income (41 Countries)	Low Income (35 Countries)	Advanced Economies (29 Countries)	Developing Countries (124 Countries)
1. Banking Activity Regulatory Variables						
(a) Securities	1.5	1.6	2.1	2.0	1.4	1.9
(b) Insurance	2.5	2.7	2.7	3.3	2.5	2.8
(c) Real Estate	2.5	2.8	2.9	2.5	2.3	2.7
(d) Overall Activities Restrictiveness	6.5	7.2	7.6	7.8	6.3	7.4
2. Financial Conglomerate Variables						
(a) Banks Owning Nonfinancial Firms	2.3	2.4	2.7	2.8	2.2	2.6
(b) Nonfinancial Firms Owning Banks	2.2	2.0	2.2	2.2	2.1	2.1
(c) Nonbank Financial Firms Owning Banks	2.1	2.0	2.3	2.2	2.0	2.2
(d) Overall Financial Conglomerate Restrictiveness	6.6	6.5	7.1	7.1	6.3	7.0
3. Competition Regulatory Variables						
(a) Limitations on Foreign Bank Entry/Ownership	3.0	2.8	2.7	2.9	3.0	2.8
(b) Entry into Banking Requirements	7.2	7.5	7.6	7.8	7.1	7.6

(continued)

Appendix 5 (*continued*)

	High Income (45 Countries)	Upper Middle Income (32 Countries)	Lower Middle Income (41 Countries)	Low Income (35 Countries)	Advanced Economies (29 Countries)	Developing Countries (124 Countries)
(c) Fraction of Entry Applications Denied (percent)	5.2	13.4	38.2	44.0	7.1	28.2
(1) Domestic Denials (percent)	9.9	32.4	26.4	42.3	11.9	30.9
(2) Foreign Denials (percent)	8.3	17.4	38.3	42.3	10.4	28.2
4. Capital Regulatory Variables						
(a) Overall Capital Stringency	4.5	3.4	3.7	4.3	4.4	3.9
(b) Initial Capital Stringency	2.0	2.3	2.4	2.1	1.7	2.3
(c) Capital Regulatory Index	6.5	5.7	6.1	6.4	6.1	6.2
5. Official Supervisory Variables						
(a) Official Supervisory Power	10.5	9.9	10.4	11.1	10.0	10.6
(1) Prompt Corrective Power	1.6	2.4	2.9	2.7	1.3	2.6
(2) Restructuring Power	2.3	2.5	2.6	2.7	2.2	2.6
(3) Declaring Insolvency Power	1.2	1.3	1.5	1.3	1.1	1.4
(b) Supervisory Forbearance Discretion	1.8	1.7	1.1	1.6	1.9	1.5
(c) Court Involvement	1.6	1.8	1.6	1.3	1.5	1.6
(d) Loan Classification Stringency (Days)	499.3	526.0	538.6	570.4	428.8	541.0
(e) Provisioning Stringency (Percent)	190.0	164.3	165.5	164.2	205.0	166.3
(f) Diversification Index	1.5	1.4	1.1	1.3	1.4	1.3

6. Official Supervisory Structural Variables

(a) Supervisor Tenure (Years)	7.7	7.2	7.5	6.0	8.5	6.9
(b) Independence of Supervisory Authority – Political	0.4	0.2	0.4	0.2	0.4	0.3
(c) Independence of Supervisory Authority – Banks	0.7	0.6	0.6	0.7	0.6	0.6
(d) Independence of Supervisory Authority – Fixed Term	0.6	0.8	0.7	0.5	0.6	0.6
(e) Independence of Supervisory Authority – Overall	1.7	1.6	1.6	1.4	1.7	1.6
(f) Multiple Supervisors	0.2	0.3	0.2	0.0	0.2	0.2
(g) Single vs. Multiple Financial Supervisor Authority	0.4	0.2	0.3	0.3	0.4	0.3

7. Private Monitoring Variables

(a) Certified Audit Required	0.9	1.0	1.0	1.0	1.0	1.0
(b) Percentage of Ten Biggest Banks Rated by International Credit Rating Agencies	72.8	55.8	42.5	10.0	81.4	37.9
(c) Percentage of Ten Biggest Banks Rated by Domestic Credit Rating Agencies	22.6	21.7	20.7	6.3	34.0	14.4
(d) No Explicit Deposit Insurance Scheme	0.3	0.5	0.5	0.4	0.2	0.5
(e) Bank Accounting	3.8	3.8	3.6	3.6	3.7	3.7
(f) Private Monitoring Index	8.3	8.1	7.3	7.0	8.4	7.5

(continued)

Appendix 5 *(continued)*

	High Income (45 Countries)	Upper Middle Income (32 Countries)	Lower Middle Income (41 Countries)	Low Income (35 Countries)	Advanced Economies (29 Countries)	Developing Countries (124 Countries)
8. *Deposit Insurance Variables*						
(a) Deposit Insurer Power	1.3	1.1	1.0	1.8	1.2	1.2
(b) Deposit Insurance Funds-to-Total Bank Assets (percent)	0.3	2.3	1.2	0.6	0.3	1.5
(c) Funding with Insured Deposits (percent)	43.3	37.6	37.9	46.3	36.8	41.6
(d) Various Factors Mitigating Moral Hazard	1.9	1.5	1.2	1.5	1.8	1.4
9. *External Governance Variables*						
(a) Strength of External Audit	6.0	5.6	5.6	6.2	6.2	5.8
(b) Financial Statement Transparency	5.2	4.7	4.5	4.5	5.3	4.6
(c) Accounting Practices	0.6	0.9	0.8	0.9	0.5	0.9
(d) External Ratings and Credit Monitoring	1.9	1.8	1.6	1.2	2.0	1.5
(e) External Governance Index	14.0	13.8	12.4	13.2	14.1	13.2

Information on Different Dimensions of Bank Regulation and Supervision: Averages by Region

	Americas (35 Countries)	East Asia and Pacific (18 Countries)	Europe and Central Asia (50 Countries)	Middle East and North Africa (14 Countries)	South Asia (4 Countries)	Sub-Saharan Africa (31 Countries)
1. Banking Activity Regulatory Variables						
(a) Securities	2.0	1.7	1.7	1.6	2.0	1.9
(b) Insurance	2.6	2.7	2.7	2.7	3.3	3.0
(c) Real Estate	2.9	3.2	2.4	2.9	3.8	2.3
(d) Overall Activities Restrictiveness	7.5	7.5	6.8	7.3	9.0	7.2
2. Financial Conglomerate Variables						
(a) Banks Owning Nonfinancial Firms	2.6	2.6	2.2	2.8	3.0	2.8
(b) Nonfinancial Firms Owning Banks	2.2	2.2	2.1	2.1	2.8	2.0
(c) Nonbank Financial Firms Owning Banks	2.2	2.3	2.1	2.1	2.8	2.0
(d) Overall Financial Conglomerate Restrictiveness	7.1	7.0	6.4	7.0	8.5	6.8

(continued)

365

Appendix 6 (continued)

	Americas (35 Countries)	East Asia and Pacific (18 Countries)	Europe and Central Asia (50 Countries)	Middle East and North Africa (14 Countries)	South Asia (4 Countries)	Sub-Saharan Africa (31 Countries)
3. Competition Regulatory Variables						
(a) Limitations on Foreign Bank Entry/Ownership	2.8	2.8	2.9	2.9	3.0	2.9
(b) Entry into Banking Requirements	7.5	7.5	7.4	7.1	7.3	7.7
(c) Fraction of Entry Applications Denied (percent)	20.5	37.4	11.1	18.6	52.0	48.3
(1) Domestic Denials (percent)	27.5	33.3	15.8	14.3	57.2	43.6
(2) Foreign Denials (percent)	20.6	32.9	13.6	25.8	12.5	57.6
4. Capital Regulatory Variables						
(a) Overall Capital Stringency	3.5	4.0	4.2	4.2	5.3	3.9
(b) Initial Capital Stringency	2.4	1.8	2.2	2.5	2.0	2.2
(c) Capital Regulatory Index	5.9	5.8	6.3	6.7	7.3	6.1

5. Official Supervisory Variables

(a) Official Supervisory Power	9.2	11.3	10.3	12.5	10.3	11.0
(1) Prompt Corrective Power	2.1	2.1	2.4	4.1	2.5	2.1
(2) Restructuring Power	2.4	2.4	2.4	2.5	2.5	2.7
(3) Declaring Insolvency Power	1.2	1.4	1.3	1.5	1.5	1.3
(b) Supervisory Forbearance Discretion	1.6	1.6	1.4	1.1	1.8	1.9
(c) Court Involvement	1.7	1.6	1.6	1.5	2.0	1.3
(d) Loan Classification Stringency (Days)	513.6	531.5	395.3	622.8	967.3	640.4
(e) Provisioning Stringency (Percent)	160.6	170.0	181.7	160.0	180.0	165.4
(f) Diversification Index	1.2	1.3	1.4	1.5	1.5	1.3
6. Official Supervisory Structural Variables						
(a) Supervisor Tenure (Years)	7.5	6.4	6.9	8.9	7.8	6.6
(b) Independence of Supervisory Authority – Political	0.2	0.3	0.6	0.4	0.3	0.1
(c) Independence of Supervisory Authority – Banks	0.5	0.7	0.6	0.5	0.8	0.9

(continued)

Appendix 6 (continued)

	Americas (35 Countries)	East Asia and Pacific (18 Countries)	Europe and Central Asia (50 Countries)	Middle East and North Africa (14 Countries)	South Asia (4 Countries)	Sub-Saharan Africa (31 Countries)
(d) Independence of Supervisory Authority – Fixed Term	0.7	0.5	0.7	0.8	0.0	0.6
(e) Independence of Supervisory Authority – Overall	1.4	1.5	1.8	1.7	1.0	1.5
(f) Multiple Supervisors	0.3	0.3	0.2	0.1	0.0	0.0
(g) Single vs. Multiple Financial Supervisory Agency	0.3	0.6	0.3	0.2	0.3	0.2
7. Private Monitoring Variables						
(a) Certified Audit Required	1.0	0.9	1.0	0.9	1.0	1.0
(b) Percentage of Ten Biggest Banks Rated by International Credit Rating Agencies	57.8	70.0	53.0	71.7	36.7	7.2
(c) Percentage of Ten Biggest Banks Rated by Domestic Credit Rating Agencies	44.3	43.3	5.4	14.5	20.0	5.8

(d) No Explicit Deposit Insurance Scheme	0.6	0.4	0.2	0.6	0.3	0.5
(e) Bank Accounting	3.8	3.6	3.6	3.8	3.8	3.6
(f) Private Monitoring Index	7.6	8.7	7.4	8.9	7.3	7.3
8. Deposit Insurance Variables						
(a) Deposit Insurer Power	1.3	1.2	1.1	1.0	1.0	3.0
(b) Deposit Insurance Funds-to-Total Bank Assets (percent)	1.3	0.3	1.4	0.7	0.3	0.9
(c) Funding with Insured Deposits (percent)	31.1	87.0	40.5	38.7	43.7	56.0
(d) Various Factors Mitigating Moral Hazard	1.5	0.5	1.7	2.0	0.5	1.5
9. External Governance Variables						
(a) Strength of External Audit	5.2	5.8	6.0	6.4	6.0	6.2
(b) Financial Statement Transparency	4.4	5.1	4.8	5.5	5.0	4.6
(c) Accounting Practices	0.8	0.9	0.6	0.9	0.8	0.9
(d) External Ratings and Credit Monitoring	2.2	2.1	1.5	1.9	1.3	1.1
(e) External Governance Index	12.9	14.1	13.1	14.8	13.0	13.3

APPENDIX 7

Information on Different Dimensions of Bank Regulation and Supervision: Averages by Economic and Currency Unions Status

	Old EU (15 Countries)	Non-Old EU* (137 Countries)	Old & New EU (25 Countries)	Non-Old & New EU (127 Countries)	EMU (12 Countries)	Non-EMU (140 Countries)
1. Banking Activity Regulatory Variables						
(a) Securities	1.3	1.8	1.4	1.9	1.2	1.8
(b) Insurance	2.5	2.8	2.5	2.8	2.7	2.8
(c) Real Estate	1.9	2.7	2.3	2.7	1.8	2.7
(d) Overall Activities Restrictiveness	5.7	7.4	6.2	7.4	5.7	7.3
2. Financial Conglomerate Variables						
(a) Banks Owning Nonfinancial Firms	1.9	2.6	2.2	2.6	2.0	2.6
(b) Nonfinancial Firms Owning Banks	1.9	2.2	1.9	2.2	1.9	2.2
(c) Nonbank Financial Firms Owning Banks	1.9	2.2	1.9	2.2	1.9	2.2
(d) Overall Activities Restrictiveness	5.7	6.9	6.0	7.0	5.8	6.9
3. Competition Regulatory Variables						
(a) Limitations on Foreign Bank Entry/Ownership	3.0	2.9	3.0	2.8	3.0	2.9

(b) Entry into Banking Requirements	7.0	7.5	7.2	7.5	6.8	7.5
(c) Fraction of Entry Applications Denied (percent)	7.1	25.6	8.3	27.6	7.5	25.4
(1) Domestic Denials (percent)	6.4	29.6	16.3	28.8	5.5	29.1
(2) Foreign Denials (percent)	18.3	24.9	12.3	27.4	20.1	24.6
4. Capital Regulatory Variables						
(a) Overall Capital Stringency	4.5	3.9	4.2	3.9	4.5	3.9
(b) Initial Capital Stringency	1.8	2.3	2.0	2.3	2.0	2.2
(c) Capital Regulatory Index	6.3	6.2	6.2	6.2	6.5	6.1
5. Official Supervisory Variables						
(a) Official Supervisory Power	9.6	10.6	10.4	10.5	9.7	10.6
(1) Prompt Corrective Power	0.7	2.6	2.2	2.4	0.8	2.5
(2) Restructuring Power	2.1	2.5	2.4	2.5	2.0	2.5
(3) Declaring Insolvency Power	1.1	1.3	1.3	1.3	1.0	1.3
(b) Supervisory Forbearance Discretion	2.1	1.5	1.6	1.6	1.9	1.5
(c) Court Involvement	1.5	1.6	1.6	1.5	1.6	1.5
(d) Loan Classification Stringency (Days)	630.0	534.9	424.9	545.5	630.0	534.9
(e) Provisioning Stringency (Percent)	248.8	166.1	196.6	166.0	248.8	166.1
(f) Diversification Index	1.4	1.3	1.6	1.3	1.5	1.3

(continued)

371

Appendix 7 (continued)

	Old EU (15 Countries)	Non-Old EU (137 Countries)	Old & New EU (25 Countries)	Non-Old & New EU (127 Countries)	EMU (12 Countries)	Non-EMU (140 Countries)
6. Official Supervisory Structural Variables						
(a) Supervisor Tenure (Years)	8.7	7.1	7.9	7.1	9.1	7.1
(b) Independence of Supervisory Authority – Political	0.4	0.3	0.6	0.3	0.5	0.3
(c) Independence of Supervisory Authority – Banks	0.5	0.6	0.7	0.6	0.5	0.6
(d) Independence of Supervisory Authority – Fixed Term	0.7	0.6	0.7	0.6	0.8	0.6
(e) Independence of Supervisory Authority – Overall	1.6	1.6	1.9	1.5	1.8	1.6
(f) Multiple Supervisors	0.1	0.2	0.2	0.2	0.1	0.2
(g) Single vs. Multiple Financial Supervisory Agency	0.3	0.3	0.3	0.3	0.3	0.3
7. Private Monitoring Variables						
(a) Certified Audit Required	0.9	1.0	1.0	1.0	0.9	1.0
(b) Percentage of Ten Biggest Banks Rated by International Credit Rating Agencies	79.3	43.8	71.7	42.0	81.8	44.5
(c) Percentage of Ten Biggest Banks Rated by Domestic Credit Rating Agencies	9.1	18.9	10.5	19.5	0.0	19.5

(d) No Explicit Deposit Insurance Scheme	0.5	0.0	0.5	0.2	0.1
(e) Bank Accounting	3.7	3.6	3.7	3.7	3.6
(f) Private Monitoring Index	7.7	7.6	7.6	7.9	7.6
8. Deposit Insurance Variables					
(a) Deposit Insurer Power	1.2	1.4	1.2	1.3	1.3
(b) Deposit Insurance Funds-to-Total Bank Assets (percent)	1.2	0.3	0.9	1.6	0.4
(c) Funding with Insured Deposits (percent)	40.4	39.7	37.3	46.7	39.7
(d) Various Factors Mitigating Moral Hazard	1.4	2.2	1.3	2.0	2.0
9. External Governance Variables					
(a) Strength of External Audit	5.8	6.4	5.8	6.3	6.3
(b) Financial Statement Transparency	4.8	4.9	4.7	5.2	5.0
(c) Accounting Practices	0.8	0.2	0.9	0.4	0.2
(d) External Ratings and Credit Monitoring	1.6	1.6	1.6	1.6	1.6
(e) External Governance Index	13.3	13.4	13.3	13.7	13.5

*Refer to all the countries in our database except the 15 "old" EU members.

Information on Different Dimensions of Bank Regulation and Supervision: Averages by OECD, WTO, and Offshore Status

	OECD (30 Countries)	Non-OECD (122 Countries)	WTO (123 Countries)	Non-WTO (29 Countries)	Offshore Centers (27 Countries)	Non-Offshore Centers (125 Countries)
1. Banking Activity Regulatory Variables						
(a) Securities	1.5	1.9	1.8	1.9	1.5	1.8
(b) Insurance	2.5	2.8	2.8	2.7	2.6	2.8
(c) Real Estate	2.3	2.8	2.6	2.9	3.0	2.6
(d) Overall Activities Restrictiveness	6.3	7.4	7.1	7.5	7.1	7.2
2. Financial Conglomerate Variables						
(a) Banks Owning Nonfinancial Firms	2.1	2.6	2.6	2.3	2.2	2.6
(b) Nonfinancial Firms Owning Banks	2.0	2.2	2.1	2.2	2.3	2.1
(c) Nonbank Financial Firms Owning Banks	1.9	2.2	2.1	2.4	2.3	2.1
(d) Overall Financial Conglomerate Activities	6.0	7.0	6.8	7.0	7.0	6.8
3. Competition Regulatory Variables						
(a) Limitations on Foreign Bank Entry/Ownership	3.0	2.8	2.9	2.8	3.0	2.8
(b) Entry into Banking Requirements	7.3	7.5	7.5	7.5	7.7	7.4

(c) Fraction of Entry Applications Denied (percent)	8.2	28.1	24.2	21.4	10.6	25.9
(1) Domestic Denials (percent)	14.7	30.2	28.0	17.0	33.3	25.3
(2) Foreign Denials (percent)	11.0	28.2	22.9	28.7	13.8	26.1
4. Capital Regulatory Variables						
(a) Overall Capital Stringency	4.1	3.9	4.0	4.0	3.9	4.0
(b) Initial Capital Stringency	1.9	2.3	2.2	2.3	2.5	2.2
(c) Capital Regulatory Index	6.0	6.2	6.2	6.3	6.5	6.1
5. Official Supervisory Variables						
(a) Official Supervisory Power	10.2	10.6	10.5	10.4	9.1	10.8
(1) Prompt Corrective Power	2.0	2.5	2.4	2.2	1.1	2.7
(2) Restructuring Power	2.3	2.5	2.5	2.5	2.4	2.5
(3) Declaring Insolvency Power	1.2	1.3	1.3	1.3	1.0	1.4
(b) Supervisory Forbearance Discretion	1.7	1.5	1.6	1.6	2.2	1.4
(c) Court Involvement	1.4	1.6	1.5	1.9	2.0	1.5
(d) Loan Classification Stringency (Days)	498.7	539.2	566.2	433.2	597.3	521.3
(e) Provisioning Stringency (Percent)	191.5	166.4	170.5	165.1	179.2	167.2
(f) Diversification Index	1.5	1.3	1.4	1.3	1.3	1.3

(continued)

Appendix 8 (*continued*)

	OECD (30 Countries)	Non-OECD (122 Countries)	WTO (123 Countries)	Non-WTO (29 Countries)	Offshore Centers (27 Countries)	Non-Offshore Centers (125 Countries)
6. *Official Supervisory Structural Variables*						
(a) Supervisor Tenure (Years)	7.9	7.0	7.5	6.0	6.1	7.5
(b) Independence of Supervisory Authority – Political	0.4	0.3	0.3	0.4	0.3	0.3
(c) Independence of Supervisory Authority – Banks	0.6	0.6	0.7	0.5	0.7	0.6
(d) Independence of Supervisory Authority – Fixed Term	0.7	0.6	0.6	0.7	0.7	0.6
(e) Independence of Supervisory Authority – Overall	1.7	1.6	1.6	1.5	1.7	1.6
(f) Multiple Supervisors	0.2	0.2	0.2	0.2	0.4	0.1
(g) Single vs. Multiple Financial Supervisory Agency	0.4	0.3	0.3	0.4	0.4	0.3
7. *Private Monitoring Variables*						
(a) Certified Audit Required	1.0	1.0	1.0	1.0	0.9	1.0
(b) Percentage of Ten Biggest Banks Rated by International Credit Rating Agencies	85.2	36.3	51.0	30.5	38.0	49.2
(c) Percentage of Ten Biggest Banks Rated by Domestic Credit Rating Agencies	27.3	15.6	21.3	1.6	1.5	20.1

(d) No Explicit Deposit Insurance Scheme	0.2	0.5	0.4	0.6	0.7	0.4
(e) Bank Accounting	3.7	3.7	3.7	3.5	3.8	3.6
(f) Private Monitoring Index	8.3	7.5	7.9	6.8	7.4	7.7
8. Deposit Insurance Variables						
(a) Deposit Insurer Power	1.3	1.1	1.2	1.4	1.6	1.1
(b) Deposit Insurance Funds-to-Total Bank Assets (percent)	0.4	1.5	1.2	0.5	0.3	1.2
(c) Funding with Insured Deposits (percent)	38.9	41.0	41.8	31.6	53.6	38.7
(d) Various Factors Mitigating Moral Hazard	1.9	1.4	1.5	1.7	2.2	1.5
9. External Governance Variables						
(a) Strength of External Audit	6.2	5.8	5.9	5.6	4.9	6.1
(b) Financial Statement Transparency	5.2	4.7	4.9	4.3	4.5	4.8
(c) Accounting Practices	0.5	0.9	0.8	0.9	1.0	0.7
(d) External Ratings and Credit Monitoring	2.0	1.5	1.7	1.3	1.5	1.6
(e) External Governance Index	14.1	13.2	13.6	12.1	12.9	13.4

APPENDIX 9

Country Names and Country Codes

Code	Country Names	Code	Country Names	Code	Country Names
ARG	Argentina	IRL	Ireland	OMN	Oman
AUS	Australia	ISR	Israel	PAN	Panama
AUT	Austria	ITA	Italy	PER	Peru
BGD	Bangladesh	JAM	Jamaica	PHL	Philippines
BEL	Belgium	JPN	Japan	POL	Poland
BOL	Bolivia	JOR	Jordan	PRT	Portugal
BWA	Botswana	KEN	Kenya	ROM	Romania
BRA	Brazil	KOR	Korea	RWA	Rwanda
BDI	Burundi	KWT	Kuwait	SLV	Salvador, El
CAN	Canada	LVA	Latvia	SAU	Saudi Arabia
CHL	Chile	LSO	Lesotho	SGP	Singapore
CHN	China	LTU	Lithuania	SVN	Slovenia
CYP	Cyprus	LUX	Luxembourg	ZAF	South Africa
CZE	Czech Republic	MWI	Malawi	ESP	Spain
DNK	Denmark	MYS	Malaysia	LKA	Sri Lanka
EGY	Egypt	MDV	Maldives	SWE	Sweden
EST	Estonia	MLT	Malta	CHE	Switzerland
FIN	Finland	MUS	Mauritius	THA	Thailand
FRA	France	MEX	Mexico	TTO	Trinidad & Tobago
DEU	Germany	MDA	Moldova	TUR	Turkey
GRC	Greece	MAR	Morocco	GBR	United Kingdom
GTM	Guatemala	NAM	Namibia	USA	United States
HND	Honduras	NPL	Nepal	VEN	Venezuela
HUN	Hungary	NLD	Netherlands	VNM	Vietnam
IND	India	NZL	New Zealand		
IDN	Indonesia	NGA	Nigeria		

References

Abrams, Burton A., and Russell F. Settle. 1993. "Pressure-group influence and Institutional Change: Branch Banking Legislation during the Great Depression," *Public Choice*, 77, 687–705.

Acemoglu, Daron, Simon Johnson, and James A. Robinson. 2001. "The Colonial Origins of Comparative Development: An Empirical Investigation," *American Economic Review*, 91(5), 1369–1401.

Adams, Renée, and Hamid Mehran. 2003. "Is Corporate Governance Different for Bank Holding Companies?," *Economic Policy Review*, 9 (Special Issue, April), Federal Reserve Bank of New York, 123–142.

Adams, Renée, and Joao Santos. 2004. "Identifying the Effect of Managerial Control on Firm Performance," mimeo, Federal Reserve Bank of New York.

Akerlof, George. 1970. "The Market for Lemons: Quality Uncertainty and the Market Mechanism," *Quarterly Journal of Economics*, 89, 488–500.

Alexander, G. J., and A. M. Baptista. 2001. "A VaR-Constrained Mean-Variance Model: Implications for Portfolio Selection and the Basle Capital Accord," mimeo, University of Minnesota.

Alexander, Kern. 2002. "The World Trade Organization and Financial Stability: The Need to Resolve the Tension between Liberalization and Prudential Regulation," Working Paper No. 5, ESRC Centre for Business Research, Cambridge University.

Allen, Franklin, and Douglas Gale. 2003. "Capital Adequacy Regulation: In Search of a Rationale," in R. Arnott, B. Greenwald, R. Kanbur, and B. Nalebuff, eds., *Economics for an Imperfect World: Essays in Honor of Joseph Stiglitz* (Cambridge, MA: MIT Press).

Alston, Philip. 1997. "The Myopia of the Handmaidens: International Lawyers and Globalization," *European Journal of International Law*, 8(2), 435–441.

Ang, J. S., and T. Richardson. 1994. "The Underpricing Experience of Commercial Bank Affiliates Prior to the Glass-Steagall Act: A Re-examination of Evidence for Passage of the Act," *Journal of Banking and Finance*, 18, 351–395.

379

Armstrong, Lawrin. 2003. "Usury," in Joel Mokyr, ed., *The Oxford Encyclopedia of Economic History* (New York: Oxford University Press).

Arner, Douglas, Zhongfei Zhou, Mattheo Bushehri, Berry F. C. Hsu, Jianbo Lou, and Wei Wang. 2004. "Financial Regulation and the WTO: Liberalization and Restructuring in China Two Years Post-Accession," EAIEL Policy Paper no. 1. East Asian International Economic Law & Policy Programme, University of Hong Kong.

Atkinson, Andrew B., and Joseph E. Stiglitz. 1980. *Lectures on Public Economics* (London: McGraw-Hill).

Austin-Smith, David, and John Wright. 1992. "Competitive Lobbying for a Legislator's Vote," *Social Choice and Welfare*, 9, 229–257.

Austin-Smith, David, and John Wright. 1994. "Counteractive Lobbying," *American Journal of Political Science*, 38, 25–44.

Banerjee, Abhijit V., Shawn Cole, and Esther Duflo. 2004. "Banking Reform in India," mimeo, Massachusetts Institute of Technology, http://econ-www.mit.edu/faculty/index.htm?prof_id=banerjee&type=paper.

Baron, David. 1991. "Majoritarian Incentives, Pork Barrel Programs and Procedural Control," *American Journal of Political Science*, 35, 57–90.

Baron, David. 1994. "Electoral Competition with Informed and Uniformed Voters," *American Political Science Review*, 8, 33–47.

Baron, David, and John Ferejohn. 1989. "Bargaining in Legislatures," *American Political Science Review*, 83, 1181–1206.

Barron, John M., and Michael Staten. 2003. "The Value of Comprehensive Credit Reports: Lessons from the U.S. Experience," in Margaret J. Miller, ed., *Credit Reporting Systems and the International Economy* (273–310) (Cambridge, MA: MIT Press).

Barth, James R., Joseph J. Cordes, and Anthony M. J. Yezer. 1983. "An Analysis of Informational Restrictions on the Lending Decisions of Financial Institutions," *Economic Inquiry*, 21(3), 349–360.

Barth, James R., Padma Gotur, Neela Manage, and Anthony M. J. Yezer. 1983. "The Effect of Government Regulations on Personal Loan Markets: A Tobit Estimation of a Microeconomic Model," *The Journal of Finance*, 38(4), 1233–1251.

Barth, James R., R. Dan Brumbaugh, Jr., Daniel Sauerhaft, and George H. K. Wang. 1985. "Thrift-Institution Failures: Causes and Policy Issues," Working Paper for presentation at the conference on Bank Structure and Competition, Federal Reserve Bank of Chicago, May 1–3.

Barth, James R., R. Dan Brumbaugh, Jr., Daniel Sauerhaft, and George H. K. Wang. 1989. "Thrift-Institution Failures: Estimating the Regulator's Closure Rule," in George G. Kaufman, ed., *Research in Financial Services*, Vol. 1, 1–23 (London: JAI Press Inc.).

Barth, James R. 1990. "Deposit Insurance Reform," in Deposit Insurance Reform and Financial Modernization, Hearings before the Committee on Banking, Housing, and Urban Affairs, United States Senate, Vol. II of III, 58–67 (Washington, D.C.: U.S. Government Printing Office).

Barth, James R., Philip F. Bartholomew, and Michael G. Bradley. 1990. "Determinants of Thrift Institution Resolution Costs," *The Journal of Finance*, 45(3), 731–754.

Barth, James R. 1991. *The Great Savings and Loan Debacle* (Washington, DC: The AEI Press).

Barth, James R., and R. Dan Brumbaugh, Jr. 1994a. "Moral-Hazard and Agency Problems: Understanding Depository Institution Failure Costs," in George G. Kaufman, ed., *Research In Financial Services: Public and Private Policy*, Vol. 6, 61–102 (London: JAI Press Ltd.).

Barth, James R., and R. Dan Brumbaugh, Jr. 1994b. "Risk Based Capital: Informational and Political Issues," in Charles A. Stone and Anne Zissu, eds., *Global Risk Based Capital Regulations, Volume I: Capital Adequacy*, 363–399 (New York: Irwin Professional Publishing).

Barth, James R., and R. Dan Brumbaugh, Jr. 1996. "The Condition and Regulation of Madison Guaranty Savings and Loan Association in the 1980s: A Case Study of Regulatory Failure," in George G. Kaufman, ed., *Research In Financial Services: Public and Private Policy*, Vol. 8, 73–96 (London: JAI Press Ltd.).

Barth, James R., Ray Chou, and John S. Jahera, Jr. 1999. "The U.S. Banking Industry in Transition," in Jerry Haar and Krishnan Dandapani, eds., *Banking in North America: NAFTA and Beyond*, 53–80 (Amsterdam and New York: Pergamon).

Barth, James R., R. Dan Brumbaugh, and James A. Wilcox. 2000. "The Repeal of Glass-Steagall and the Advent of Broad Banking," *Journal of Economic Perspectives*, 14(2), 191–204.

Barth, James R., Daniel E. Nolle, and Tara N. Rice. 2000. "Commercial Banking Structure, Regulation and Performance: An International Comparison," in Dimitri B. Papadimitriou, ed., *Modernizing Financial Systems*, 119–251 (New York: St. Martin's Press).

Barth, James R., Gerard Caprio, and Ross Levine. 2001a. "Banking Systems Around the Globe: Do Regulations and Ownership Affect Performance and Stability?," in Frederic S. Mishkin, ed., *Prudential Supervision: What Works and What Doesn't*, 31–96 (Chicago: University of Chicago Press).

Barth, James R., Gerard Caprio, and Ross Levine. 2001b. "The Regulation and Supervision of Bank Around the World: A New Database," in Robert E. Litan and Richard Herring, eds., *Integrating Emerging Market Countries into the Global Financial System*, Brookings-Wharton Papers on Financial Services, 183–240 (Washington, D.C.: Brookings Institution Press).

Barth, James R., L. G. Dopico, Daniel E. Nolle, and J. A. Wilcox. 2002. "An International Comparison and Assessment of the Structure of Bank Supervision" in J. Lin and D. Arner, eds., *Financial Regulation: A Guide to Structural Reform*, 57–92 (Hong Kong: Sweet & Maxwell).

Barth, James R., Daniel E. Nolle, Triphon Phumiwasana, and Glenn Yago. 2003. "A Cross-Country Analysis of the Bank Supervisory Framework and Bank Performance," *Financial Markets, Institutions & Instruments*, New York University Solomon Center 12(2), 67–120.

Barth, James R., Gerard Caprio, and Ross Levine. 2004. "Bank Regulation and Supervision: What Works Best?," *Journal of Financial Intermediation*, 13(2), 205–248.

Barth, James R., Rob Koepp, and Zhongfei Zhou. 2004. "Institute View: Disciplining China's Banks," *Milken Institute Review: Journal of Economic Policy*, 2nd Quarter, 83–92.

Barth, James R., Lawrence Goldberg, Daniel E. Nolle, and Glenn Yago. 2004. "Financial Supervision and Crisis Management: U.S. Experience and Lessons for Emerging Market Economies," prepared for the 2004 EWC/KDI Conference, Honolulu, July 29–30.

Basel Committee on Bank Supervision. 2004. "International Convergence of Capital Measurement and Capital Standards: A Revised Framework," mimeo, Bank for International Settlements, http://www.bis.org/bcbs/index.htm.

Baumann, Ursel, and Erlend Nier. 2003. "Market Discipline and Financial Stability: Some Empirical Evidence," *Financial Stability Review*, 14: 134–141.

Beatty, Anne L., and Anne Gron. 2001. "Capital, Portfolio, and Growth: Bank Behavior under Risk-based Capital Guidelines," *Journal of Financial Services Research*, 20(1), 5–31.

Beck, Thorsten. 2002. "Deposit Insurance as a Private Club: The Case of Germany," *Quarterly Review of Economics and Finance*, 42(4), 701–719.

Beck, Thorsten, Asli Demirgüç-Kunt, Luc Laeven, and Ross Levine. 2004. "Finance, Firm Size, and Growth". National Bureau of Economic Research Working Paper, No. 10983, Cambridge, MA.

Beck, Thorsten, Asli Demirgüç-Kunt, and Ross Levine. 2000. "A New Database on the Structure and Development of the Financial Sector," *The World Bank Economic Review*, 14, 597–605.

Beck, Thorsten, Asli Demirgüç-Kunt, and Ross Levine. 2001. "Legal Theories of Financial Development," *Oxford Review of Economic Policy*, 17, 483–501.

Beck, Thorsten, Asli Demirgüç-Kunt, and Ross Levine. 2003a. "Law, Endowments, and Finance," *Journal of Financial Economics*, 70, 137–181.

Beck, Thorsten, Asli Demirgüç-Kunt, and Ross Levine. 2003b. "Bank Supervision and Corporate Finance," National Bureau of Economic Research Working Paper No. 9620, Cambridge, MA.

Beck, Thorsten, Asli Demirgüç-Kunt, and Ross Levine. 2004a. "Law and Finance: Why Does Legal Origin Matter?," *Journal of Comparative Economics*, 31, 653–675.

Beck, Thorsten, Asli Demirgüç-Kunt, and Ross Levine. 2004b. "Finance, Inequality, and Poverty: Cross-Country Evidence," National Bureau of Economic Research Working Paper, No. 10979, Cambridge, MA.

Beck, Thorsten, Asli Demirgüç-Kunt, and Ross Levine. 2005a. "Law and Firms' Access to Finance," *American Law and Economics Review*, 7, 211–252.

Beck, Thorsten, Asli Demirgüç-Kunt, and Ross Levine. 2005b. "Bank Supervision and Corruption in Lending," National Bureau of Economic Research Working Paper, No. 11498, Cambridge, MA.

Beck, Thorsten, Asli Demirgüç-Kunt, and Ross Levine. 2006a. "Bank Concentration, Competition, and Crises: First Results," *Journal of Banking and Finance*, forthcoming.

Beck, Thorsten, Asli Demirgüç-Kunt, and Ross Levine. 2006b. "Bank Concentration and Fragility: Impact and Mechanics," in Mark Carey and Rene Stulz, ed., *Risks of Financial Institutions*, Cambridge, MA: National Bureau of Economic Research, forthcoming.

Beck, Thorsten, and Ross Levine. 2004. "Stock Markets, Banks, and Growth: Correlation and Causality," *Journal of Banking and Finance*, 28, 423–442.

Beck, Thorsten, and Ross Levine. 2005. "Legal Institutions and Financial Development," in Claude Menard and Mary Shirley, eds., *Handbook of New Institutional Economics* 251–278 (The Netherlands: Springer).

Beck, Thorsten, Ross Levine, and Norman Loayza. 2000. "Finance and the Sources of Growth," *Journal of Financial Economics*, 58, 261–300.

Becker, Gary S. 1983. "A Theory of Competition among Pressure Groups for Political Influence," *Quarterly Journal of Economics*, 98, 371–400.

Bennedsen, Morten, and Daniel Wolfenzon. 2000. "The Balance of Power in Closely Held Corporations," *Journal of Financial Economics*, 58(1–2), 113–139.

Benston, George J., and George G. Kaufman. 1988. "Risk and Solvency Regulation of Depository Institutions: Past Policies and Current Options," in *Monograph Series in Finance and Economics*, No. 1988-1, Salomon Brothers Center for the Study of Financial Institutions (New York: New York University).

Benston, George, Michael Bromwich, Robert Litan, and Alfred Wagenhofer. 2003. *Following the Money: the Enron Failure and the State of Corporate Disclosure* (Washington, DC: AEI-Brookings Joint Center for Regulatory Studies).

Berger, Allen, and Gregory Udell. 1996. "Universal Banking and the Future of Small Business Lending," in I. Walter and A. Saunders, eds., *Universal Banking: Financial System Design Reconsidered* (559–627) (Chicago: Irwin).

Berger, Allen, and Gregory Udell. 2002. "Small Business Credit Availability and Relationship Lending: The Importance of Bank Organisational Structure," *Economic Journal*, 112(477), 32–53.

Berger, Allen, Sally Davies, and Mark Flannery. 2000. "Comparing Market and Supervisory Assessments of Bank Performance: Who Knows What When?," *Journal of Money, Credit, and Banking* (August), Part 2: 641–667.

Berger, Allen, Asli Demirgüç-Kunt, Joel G. Haubrich, and Ross Levine. 2004. "Bank Concentration and Competition," *Journal of Money, Credit, and Banking*, 36(3), 433–452.

Berger, Allen, Richard J. Herring, and Giorgio P. Szegö. 1995. "The Role of Capital in Financial Institutions," *Journal of Banking and Finance*, 19, 257–276.

Bernanke, Ben. 2004. "The Implementation of Basel II: Some Issues for Cross-Border Banking," remarks from the *Institute of International Bankers' Annual Breakfast Dialogue*, Washington, DC, October 4.

Besanko, D., and G. Kanatas. 1996. "The Regulation of Bank Capital: Do Capital Standards Promote Bank Safety?," *The Journal of Finance Intermediation*, 5(4), 160–183.

Besley, Timothy, and Stephen Coate. 1996. "Lobbying and Welfare in a Representative Democracy," mimeo, London School of Economics.

Besley, Timothy, and Stephen Coate. 1997. "An Economic Model of Representative Democracy," *Quarterly Journal of Economics*, 112, 85–114.

Besley, Timothy, and Stephen Coate. 1998. "Sources of Inefficiency in a Representative Democracy: A Dynamic Analysis," *American Economic Review*, 88, 139–156.

Bhattacharya, Sudipo, Arnoud W. A. Boot, and Anjan V. Thakor. 1998. "The Economics of Bank Regulation," *Journal of Money Credit and Banking*, 30(4), 745–770.

Bishop, Matthew. 2002. "The Regulator Who Isn't There," *Economist*, May 16, 12–16.

Blanchard, Olivier, and Mark Watson. 1982. "Bubbles, Rational Expectations, and Financial Markets," in Paul Wachtel, ed., *Crises in the Economic and Financial Structure* (Lexington, MA: Lexington Books).

Bliss, Robert R. 2003. "Market Discipline: Players, Processes, and Purposes," paper presented at "Market Discipline: The Evidence across Countries and Industries," Sixth Annual Global Conference, Cosponsored by the Bank for International Settlements and the Federal Reserve Bank of Chicago, Chicago, IL, October 30–November 1, 2003.

Blum, Jurg. 1999. "Do Bank Capital Adequacy Requirements Reduce Risks," *Journal of Banking and Finance*, 23, 755–771.

Bodenhorn, Howard. 2003. State *Banking in Early America: A New Economic History* (Oxford: Oxford University Press).

Boot, Arnoud. 2003. "Regulatory and Supervisory Arrangements in the EMU: Some Issues," mimeo, University of Amsterdam and CEPR.

Boot, Arnoud, and Anjan Thakor. 1997. "Financial System Architecture," *Review of Financial Studies*, 10(3), 693–733.

Boot, Arnoud, and Anjan Thakor. 2000. "Can Relationship Banking Survive Competition?," *Journal of Finance*, 55(2), 679–713.

Borio, Claudio, William Hunter, George Kaufman, and Kostas Tsatsaronis. 2004. *Market Discipline across Countries and Industries* (Cambridge, MA: MIT Press).

Boyd, John H., Chun Chang, and Bruce D. Smith. 1998. "Moral Hazard under Commercial and Universal Banking," *Journal of Money, Credit, and Banking* 30(2), 426–468.

Boyd, John H., and Gianni De Nicolo. 2005. "The Theory of Bank Risk-Taking and Competition Revisited," *Journal of Finance*, 60(3), 1329–1343.

Boyd, John H., Ross Levine, and Bruce D. Smith. 2001. "The Impact of Inflation on Financial Sector Performance," *Journal of Monetary Economics*, 47, 221–248.

Boyd, John H., and Edward C. Prescott. 1986. "Financial Intermediary-Coalitions," *Journal of Economic Theory*, 38, 211–232.

Briault, Clive. 1999. "The Rationale for a Single National Financial Services Regulator," Financial Services Authority Occasional Paper, Series 2.

Brumbaugh, R. Dan Jr. 1988. *Thrifts Under Siege: Restoring Order to American Banking* (Cambridge, MA: Ballinger Publishing).

Buch, Claudia, and Ralph Heinrich. 2002. "Financial Integration in Europe and Banking Sector Performance," mimeo, Kiel Institute for World Economics, January.

Buchanan, James J., and Gordon Tullock. 1962. *The Calculus of Consent: Logical Foundation of Constitutional Democracy* (Ann Arbor: University of Michigan Press).

Burkart, Mike, Denis Gromb, and Fausto Panunzi. 1997. "Large Shareholders, Monitoring, and Fiduciary Duty," *Quarterly Journal of Economics*, 112, 693–728.

Burkart, Mike, Denis Gromb, and Fausto Panunzi. 1998. "Why Higher Takeover Premia Protect Minority Shareholders," *Journal of Political Economy*, 106, 172–204.

Bushman, Robert M., and Abbie J. Smith. 2003. "Transparency, Financial Accounting Information, and Corporate Governance," *Economic Policy Review*, 9(1), 65–90.

Calomiris, Charles W. 1992. "Getting the Incentives Right in the Current Deposit Insurance System: Successes from the Pre-FDIC Era," in James R. Barth and R. Dan Brumbaugh, eds., *The Reform of Federal Deposit Insurance: Disciplining the Government and Protecting Taxpayers*, 13–35 (New York: Harper Business).

Calomiris, Charles. 1997a. "Universal Banking and the Financing of Industrial Development," in Gerard Caprio, Jr. and Dimitri Vittas, eds., *Reforming Financial Systems: Historical Implications for Policy* (Cambridge and New York: Cambridge University Press).

Calomiris, Charles. 1997b. *The Postmodern Bank Safety Net: Lessons from Developed and Developing Countries* (Washington, DC: The AEI Press).

Calomiris, Charles. 1997c. "Contagion and Bank Failures during the Great Depression: The June 1932 Chicago Banking Panic," *American Economic Review*, 87, 863–883.

Calomiris, Charles. 2003. "Modern Banking," in Joel Mokyr, ed., *The Oxford Encyclopedia of Economic History* (New York: Oxford University Press).

Calomiris, Charles W., and Charles Kahn. 1991. "The Role of Demandable Debt in Structuring Optimal Banking Arrangements," *American Economic Review*, 81(3), 497–513.

Calomiris, Charles, and Joseph Mason. 2003. "Fundamentals, Panics, and Bank Distress during the Depression," *American Economic Review*, 93(5), 1615–1647.

Calomiris, Charles W., and Andrew Powell. 2000. "Can Emerging Market Bank Regulators Establish Credible Discipline? The Case of Argentina," mimeo, Washington, DC, The World Bank. http://www.worldbank.org/research/interest/intrstweb.htm.

Calomiris, Charles, and Carlos Ramirez. 2002. "The Political Economy of Bank Entry Restrictions: Theory and Evidence from the US in the 1920s," mimeo, Columbia Business School.

Calomiris, Charles, and Eugene N. White. 1994. "The Origins of Federal Deposit Insurance," in Claudia Goldin and Gary Libecap, eds., *The Regulated Economy: A Historical Approach to Political Economy* (145–188) (Chicago: University of Chicago Press).

Camdessus, M. 1997. "The Challenges of a Sound Banking System," in C. Enoch and J. H. Green, eds., *Banking Soundness and Monetary Policy* (535–539) (Washington, DC: International Monetary Fund).

Capie, Forrest. 1997. "The Evolution of Central Banking," in G. Caprio and D. Vittas, eds., *Reforming Financial Systems: Historical Implications for Policy* (Cambridge: Cambridge University Press).

Capie, Forrest. 2004. *The Political Economy of Financial Regulation over the Long Run,* mimeo, Cass Business School, London, January.

Caprio, Gerard, James A. Hanson, and Patrick Honohan. 2001. "Introduction and Overview: the Case for Liberalization and Some Drawbacks," in Gerard Caprio, Patrick Honahan, and Joseph E. Stiglitz, eds., *Financial Liberalization: How Far, How Fast?* (3–30) (New York: Cambridge University Press).

Caprio, Gerard, and Patrick Honohan. 2004. "Can the Unsophisticated Market Provide Discipline?," in Claudio Borio, William Hunter, George Kaufman, and Kostas Tsatsaronis, eds., *Market Discipline Across Countries and Industries* (349–362) (Cambridge, MA: The MIT Press).

Caprio, Gerard, Jr., and Daniela Klingebiel. 1997. "Bank Insolvency: Bad Luck, Bad Policy, or Bad Banking?," in Michael Bruno and Boris Pleskovic, eds., *Annual Bank Conference on Development Economics 1996* (29–62), The World Bank.

Caprio, Gerard, Jr., and Daniela Klingebiel. 1999. "Episodes of Systematic and Borderline Financial Distress," mimeo, The World Bank.

Caprio, Gerard, Daniela Klingebiel, Luc Laeven, and Guillermo Noguera. 2003. "An Update of the Caprio-Klingebiel Database," mimeo, the World Bank, http://www.worldbank.org/finance/html/database_sfd.html.

Caprio, Gerard, Luc Laeven, and Ross Levine. 2003. "Governance and Bank Valuation," National Bureau of Economic Research, Working Paper No. 10158.

Caprio, Gerard Jr., and Ross Levine. 2002. "Corporate Governance in Finance: Concepts and International Observations," in Robert E. Litan, Michael Pomerleano, and V. Sundararajan, eds., *Financial Sector Governance: The Roles of the Public and Private Sectors* (17–50) (Washington, DC: Brookings Institution Press).

Caprio, Gerard Jr., and Lawrence Summers. 1996. "Financial Reform: Beyond Laissez Faire," in Dimitri Papadimitriou, ed., *Stability of the Financial System,* (400–422) (New York: Macmillan Press).

Carkovic, Maria, and Ross Levine. 2002. "Finance and Growth: New Evidence and Policy Analyses for Chile," in Norman Loayza and Raimundo Soto, eds., *Economic Growth: Sources, Trends, and Cycles* (343–376) (Santiago, Chile: Central Bank of Chile).

Center for Medieval and Renaissance Studies, University of California, Los Angeles. 1979. *The Dawn of Modern Banking* (New Haven, CT: Yale University Press).

Centre for the Study of Financial Innovation. 2005. *Banana Skins 2005: CSFI's Annual Survey of the Risks Facing Banks* (London: Centre for the Study of Financial Innovation and PriceWaterhouseCoopers).

Cetorelli, Nicola, and M. Gambera. 2001. "Banking Market Structure, Financial Dependence and Growth: International Evidence from Industry Data," *Journal of Finance*, 56(2), 617–648.

Cetorelli, Nicola, and Philip Strahan, 2005. "Finance as a Barrier to Entry: Bank Competition and Industry Structure in Local U.S. Markets," forthcoming, *Journal of Finance.*

Chen, A. H., and S. C. Mazumdar. 1994. "Impact of Regulatory Interactions on Bank Capital Structure," *Journal of Financial Services Research*, 8, 283–300.

Claessens, Stijn, Simeon Djankov, and Larry Lang. 2000. "The Separation of Ownership and Control in East Asian Corporations," *Journal of Financial Economics*, 58 (1–2), 81–112.

Claessens, Stijn, Asli Demirgüç-Kunt, and Harry Huizinga. 2001. "How Does Foreign Entry Affect Domestic Banking Markets?," *Journal of Banking and Finance*, 25(5), 891–911.

Claessens, Stijn, Simeon Djankov, Joseph Fan, and Larry Lang. 2002. "Disentangling the Incentive and Entrenchment Effects of Large Shareholdings," *Journal of Finance*, 57(6), 2741–2771.

Claessens, Stijn, and Daniela Klingebiel, 1999. "Alternative Frameworks for Providing Financial Services, World Bank Policy Research Working Paper 2189, November.

Claessens, Stijn, and Luc Laeven. 2003. "Financial Development, Property Rights, and Growth," *Journal of Finance*, 58, 2401–2436.

Coase, Ronald H. 1960. "The Problem of Social Cost," *The Journal of Law and Economics*, 3, 1–44.

Collier, Berna. 2004. "Australia's Regulatory Response to Financial Consolidation in the Context of Globalization," prepared for the 2004 EWC/KDI Conference, Honolulu, July 29–30.

Cornwall, Rupert. 1983. *God's Banker: An Account of the Life and Death of Roberto Calvi* (London: V. Gollancz).

Courtis, Neil, ed. 2002. *How Countries Supervise Their Banks, Insurers, and Securities Markets 2003* (London: Central Banking Publishing Ltd).

Crockett, Andrew. 2001. "Banking Supervision and Regulation: International Trends," paper presented at the 64th Banking Convention of the Mexican Bankers' Association, Acapulco, March 30, http://www.bis.org/speeches/sp010330.htm.

Crockett, Andrew, Trevor Harris, Frederic Mishkin, and Eugene White. 2004. *Conflicts of Interest in the Financial Services Industry: What Should We Do about Them?* (Geneva: International Centre for Monetary and Banking Studies, London: Centre for Economic Policy Research).

Cull, Robert, Lemma Senbet, and Marco Sorge. 2005. "Deposit Insurance and Financial Development," *Journal of Money, Credit, and Banking*, 37(1), February, 43–82.

Cull, Robert, Lance Davis, Naomi Lamoreaux, and Jean-Laurent Rosenthal. 2004. "Historical Financing of SMEs," mimeo, The World Bank.

Dale, Richard. 1994. "Issues in International Banking Regulation: Global Policies for Global Markets," *Financial Review*, 32, 118–150.

Darlap, Patrick, and Grünbichler Andreas. 2004. "Regulation and Supervision of Financial Markets and Institutions: A European Perspective," paper presented at the 2004 European Financial Management Association, Basel, Switzerland, June 30–July 3.

Das, Udaibir, Marc Quintyn, and Kina Chenard. 2004. "Does Regulatory Governance Matter for Financial System Stability? An Empirical Analysis," IMF Working Paper, May.

DeLong, Bradford. 1991. "Did J. P. Morgan's Men Add Value? An Economist's Perspective on Financial Capitalism," in P. Temin, ed., *Inside the Business Enterprise: Historical Perspectives on the Use of Information* (205–250) (Chicago: University of Chicago Press).

Demirgüç-Kunt, Asli, and Enria Detragiache. 1998. "The Determinants of Banking Crises in Developing and Developed Countries," *The International Monetary Fund Staff Papers*, 45(1), 81–109.

Demirgüç-Kunt, Asli, and Enrica Detragiache. 2002. "Does Deposit Insurance Increase Banking System Stability? An Empirical Investigation," *Journal of Monetary Economics*, 49(7), 1373–1406.

Demirgüç-Kunt, Asli, and Harry Huizinga. 2004. "Market Discipline and Deposit Insurance," *Journal of Monetary Economics*, 51(2) 375–399.

Demirgüç-Kunt, Asli, and Edward Kane. 2002. "Deposit Insurance Around the Globe: Where Does it Work?," *Journal of Economic Perspectives*, 16(2), 175–195.

Demirgüç-Kunt, Asli, Edward J. Kane, and Luc Laeven. 2005. "Determinants of Deposit Insurance: Adoption and Design," mimeo, The World Bank.

Demirgüç-Kunt, Asli, Luc Laeven, and Ross Levine. 2004. "Regulations, Market Structure, Institutions, and the Cost of Financial Intermediation," *Journal of Money, Credit and Banking*, 36(3, Pt.2), 593–622.

Demirgüç-Kunt, Asli, Ross Levine, and Hong-Ghi Min. 1998. "Opening to Foreign Banks: Issues of Stability, Efficiency and Growth," in Seongtae Lee, ed., *The Implications of Globalization of World Financial Markets* (83–105) (Seoul: Bank of Korea).

Dermine, Jean. 2002. "European Banking: Past, Present and Future," paper presented at the Second ECB Central Banking Conference, Frankfurt, Germany, October 24–25.

Dewatripont, Mathias, and Jean Tirole. 1993. *The Prudential Regulation of Banks* (Cambridge: Cambridge University Press).

Díaz-Alejandro, Carlos F. 1985. "Goodbye Financial Repression, Hello Financial Crash," *Journal of Development Economics*, 19(September/October), 1–24.

Diamond, Douglas. 1984. "Financial Intermediation and Delegated Monitoring," *Review of Economic Studies*, 51(3), 393–414.

Diamond, Douglas, and Philip Dybvig. 1983. "Bank Runs, Deposit Insurance, and Liquidity," *Journal of Political Economy*, 91, 401–419.

Diamond, Jared. 1997. *Guns, Germs, and Steel: The Fates of Human Societies* (New York: W.W. Norton).

Dinc, Serdar, and Criag O'Neil Brown. 2004. "The Politics of Bank Failures: Evidence from Emerging Markets," mimeo, University of Michigan Business School.

Dixit, Avinash, Gene Grossman, and Elhanan Helpman. 1997. "Common Agency and Coordination: General Theory and Application to Government Policy Making," *Journal of Political Economy*, 105, 752–769.

Dixit, Avinash, and John Londregan. 1996. "The Determinants of Success of Special Interests in Redistributive Politics," *Journal of Politics*, 58, 1132–1155.

Dixit, Avinash, and John Londregan. 1998. "Ideology, Tactics, and Efficiency in Redistributive Politics," *Quarterly Journal of Economics*, 113, 497–529.

Djankov, S., R. La Porta, F. Lopez-de-Silanes, and A. Shleifer. 2002. "The Regulation of Entry," *Quarterly Journal of Economics*, 117(1), 1–37.

Djankov, Simeon, Caralee McLiesh, Tatiana Nenova, and Andrei Shleifer. 2003. "Who Owns the Media," *Journal of Law and Economics*, 46, 341–383.

Easterly, William. 2006. "The White Man's Burden: The Wacky Ambition of the West to Transform the Rest," New York: Penguin, forthcoming.

Easterly, William, and Ross Levine. 1997. "Africa's Growth Tragedy: Policies and Ethnic Divisions," *Quarterly Journal of Economics*, 112, 1203–1250.

Easterly, William, and Ross Levine. 2003. "Tropics, Germs, and Crops," *Journal of Monetary Economics*, 50, 3–39.

Economides, Nicolas, R. Glenn Hubbard, and Darius Palia. 1996. "The Political Economy of Branching Restrictions and Deposit Insurance," *Journal of Law and Economics*, 29, 667–704.

Edwards, Franklin R. 1979. "Banks and Securities Activities: Legal and Economic Perspective on the Glass-Steagall Act," in L. Goldberg and L. J. White, eds., *The Deregulation of Banking Securities Activities* (273–294) (Lexington, MA: Lexington Books).

Edwards, Franklin R. 1987. "Can Regulatory Reform Prevent the Impending Disaster in Financial Markets?," in *Restructuring the Financial System* (1–17) (Kansas City: Federal Reserve Bank of Kansas City).

Ehrenberg, Richard. 1928. *Capital and Finance in the Age of the Renaissance: A Study of the Fuggers and Their Connections* (New York: Harcourt, Brace, and Co.).

Eisenbeis, R., and L. D. Wall. 1984. "Risk Considerations in Deregulating Bank Activities," *Federal Reserve Bank of Atlanta Economic Review*, 69, 6–19.

Engerman, Stanley L., and Kenneth L. Sokoloff. 1997. "Factor Endowments, Institutions, and Differential Paths of Growth among New World Economies," in Stephen Haber, ed., *How Latin America Fell Behind* (260–304) (Stanford, CA: Stanford University Press).

Engerman, Stanley L., and Kenneth L. Sokoloff. 2002. "Factor Endowments, Inequality, and Paths of Development among New World Economies," *Economia* 3 (Fall): 41–102.

Engerman, Stanley L., and Kenneth L. Sokoloff. 2005. "The Evolution of Suffrage Institutions in the New World," *Journal of Economic History*, forthcoming.

Eppendorfer, Carsten, Rainer Beckmann, and Markus Neimke. 2002. Background paper to the study "The Benefits of a Working European Retail Market for Financial Services," European Financial Services Round Table.

Eppendorfer, Carsten, Rainer Beckmann, and Markus Neimke. 2005. "Banking: McCreevy Asks Italy to Confirm Equal Treatment for Foreign Banks," *European Report*, February 9.

Federal Reserve Deposit Insurance Corporation. 1984. *The First Fifty Years* (Washington, DC: Federal Deposit Insurance Corporation).

Federal Reserve Staff. 1941. *Banking Studies*, Members of the Staff Board of Governors of the Federal Reserve System (Baltimore: Waverly Press).

Ferejohn, John. 1986. "Incumbent Performance and Electoral Control," *Public Choice*, 50, 5–26.

Ferguson, Niall. 2001. *The Cash Nexus: Money and Power in the Modern World, 1700–2000* (New York: Basic Books).

Financial Stability Institute. 2004. "Implementation of the New Capital Adequacy Framework in Non-Basel Committee Member Countries," Occasional Paper Number 4, Basel: Bank for International Settlements.

Flandreau, Marc. 2003. *The Money Doctors: The Experience of International Financial Advising 1850–2000* (London and New York: Routledge).

Flannery, Mark. 1984. "The Social Costs of Unit Banking Restrictions," *Journal of Monetary Economics*, 13, 239–242.

Flannery, Mark. 1989. "Capital Regulation and Insured Banks' Choices of Individual Loan Default Rates," *Journal of Monetary Economics*, 24, 235–258.

Flannery, Mark, Simon H. Kwan, and M. Nimalendran. 2004. "Market Evidence on the Opaqueness of Banking Firms' Assets," *Journal of Financial Economics*, 71(3), 419–614.

Flannery, Mark, Robert De Young, William Lang, and Sorin Sorescu. 2001. "The Informational Content of Bank Exam Ratings and Subordinated Debt Prices," *Journal of Money, Credit, and Banking*, November, 900–925.

Foot, Michael. 2004. "Paper 1: Legal Reforms of Financial Regulations: Case of the United Kingdom," prepared for the 2004 EWC/KDI Conference, Honolulu, July 29–30.

Freixas, Xavier. 2002. "An Overall Perspective on Banking Regulation," Federal Reserve Bank of Philadelphia Working Paper No. 02-1.

Furfine, Craig. 2001. "Bank Portfolio Allocation: The Impact of Capital Requirements, Regulatory Monitoring, and Economic Conditions," *Journal of Financial Services Research*, 20(1), 33–56.

Furlong, F. T., and M. C. Keeley. 1989. "Capital Regulation and Bank Risk-Taking: A Note," *Journal of Banking and Finance*, 13, 883–891.

Garber, Peter. 2000. *Famous First Bubbles: The Fundamentals of Early Manias* (Cambridge, MA: MIT Press).

Genotte, G., and D. Pyle. 1991. "Capital Controls and Bank Risk," *Journal of Banking and Finance*, 15(5), 805–924.

Gerschenkron, A. 1962. *Economic Backwardness in Historical Perspective: A Book of Essays* (Cambridge, MA: Belknap Press of Harvard University Press).

Glaeser, Edward L., and Andrei Shleifer. 2003. "The Rise of the Regulatory State," *Journal of Economic Literature*, 41(2), 401–425.

Glaessner, Thomas, Thomas Kellermann, and Valerie McNevin. 2004. "Electronic Safety and Soundness: Securing Finance in a New Age," Working Paper No. 26, The World Bank.

Goldsmith, Raymond. 1969. *Financial Structure and Development* (New Haven, CT: Yale University Press).

Goodhart, Charles. 2002. "Financial Integration and Prudential Control Segmentation: What Kind of Coordination Does Prudential Policy Need in the Integrated European Financial Market?," Unpublished paper, Financial Markets Group, London School of Economics.

Goodhart, Charles, and Dirk Schoenmaker. 1995. "Should the Functions of Monetary Policy and Banking Supervision be Separated?," *Oxford Economic Papers* 47: 539–560.

Goodhart, Charles, Dirk Schoenmaker, and Paolo Dasgupta. 2001. "The Skill Profile of Central Bankers and Supervisors," *FMG Discussion Papers* (London: United Kingdom).

Gorton, Gary. 1984. "Private Clearinghouses and the Origins of Central Banking," *Federal Reserve Bank of Philadelphia Business Review* (January-February), 3–12.

Gorton, Gary. 1985. "Clearinghouses and the Origins of Central Banking in the United States," *Journal of Economic History*, 45, 277–283.

Gorton, Gary, and Lixin Huang. 2001. "Banking Panics and the Origin of Central Banking," Working Paper, Wharton Financial Institutions Center.

Gorton, Gary, and Andrew Winton. 1999. "Liquidity Provision, and Cost of Bank Capital, and the Macroeconomy," International Monetary Fund Seminar Series Paper, No. 2000-22:1–43.

Greenspan, Alan. 1998. "The Role of Capital in Optimal Banking Supervision and Regulation," in "Financial Services at the Crossroads: Capital Regulation in the Twenty-First Century, Proceedings of a Conference," *FRBNY Economic Policy Review*, 4(3), 163–168.

Grossman, Gene M., and Elhanan Helpman. 1994. "Protection for Sale," *Amercian Economics Review*, 84, 833–850.

Grossman, Gene M., and Elhanan Helpman. 1995. "The Politics of Free-Trade Agreements," *American Economic Review*, 85, 667–690.

Grossman, Gene M., and Elhanan Helpman. 1996. "Electoral Competition and Special Interest Politics," *Review of Economic Studies*, 63, 265–286.

Grossman, Gene M., and Elhanan Helpman. 2001. *Special Interest Politics* (Cambridge, MA: MIT Press).

Grossman, Sanford, and Oliver Hart. 1988. "One Share One Vote and the Market for Corporate Control," *Journal of Financial Economics*, 20, 175–202.

Grossman, Sanford, and Joseph Stiglitz. 1980. "On the Impossibility of Informationally Efficient Markets," *American Economic Review*, 70, 393–408.

Guiso, Luigi, Paola Sapienza, and Luigi Zingales. 2004. "Does Local Financial Development Matter?," *Quarterly Journal of Economics*, 119, 929–969.

Haber, Stephen. 2004. "Political Institutions and Economic Development: Evidence from the Banking Systems of the United States and Mexico," mimeo, Stanford University.

Haber, Stephen, Armando Razo, and Noel Maurer. 2003. *The Politics of Property Rights: Political Instability, Credible Commitments, and Economic Growth in Mexico* (Cambridge: Cambridge University Press).

Hahm, Joon-Ho, and Joon-Kyung Kim. 2004. "Risks and Supervisory Challenges of Financial Conglomerates in Korea," prepared for the EWC/KDI Conference, Honolulu, Hawaii, July 29–30.

Hamilton, Alexander, John Jay, and James Madison. 1788. *The Federalist Papers* (Reprinted in C. Rossiter, ed., *The Federalist Papers*, New York: New American Library, 1961).

Hammond, Bray. 1957. *Banks and Politics in America: From the Revolution to the Civil War* (Princeton: Princeton University Press).

Hanson, James. 2003. "Banking in Developing Countries in the 1990s," World Bank Policy Research Working Paper 3168, The World Bank.

Hanson, James, Patrick Honohan, and Giovanni Majnoni, eds. 2003. *Globalization and National Financial Systems* (Washington, DC: The World Bank).

Hanson, James. 2001. "Indonesia and India: Contrasting Approaches to Repression and Liberalization," in Gerard Caprio, Patrick Honahan, and Joseph E. Stiglitz, eds., *Financial Liberalization: How Far, How Fast?* (233–264) (New York: Cambridge University Press).

Haubrich, Joseph G., and João A. Santos. 2003. "Alternative Forms of Mixing Banking with Commerce: Evidence from American History," *Financial Markets, Institutions & Instruments*, 12(2), 121–164.

Haubrich, Santos, and Joseph Haubrich. 2005. "Banking and Commerce: A Liquidity Approach," *Journal of Banking and Finance*, 29(2), 271–294.

Hawke, John. 2003. "Basel II: a Brave New World for Financial Institutions?," mimeo, Office of the Comptroller of the Currency, http://www.occ.gov/ftp/release/2003–99a.pdf.

Hayek, Friedrich A. 1960. *The Constitution of Liberty* (Chicago: University of Chicago Press).

Heinemann, Friedrich, and Mathias Jopp. 2002. "The Benefits of a Working European Retail Market for Financial Services," Report to European Financial Services Round Table, February.

Hellman, J., G. Jones, Daniel Kaufmann, and M. Schankerman. 2000. "Measuring Governance and State Capture: The Role of Bureaucrats and Firms in Shaping the Business Environment," European Bank for Reconstruction and Development, WP 51.

Hellmann, Thomas, Kevin Murdoch, and Joseph Stiglitz. 2000. "Liberalization, Moral Hazard in Banking and Prudential Regulation: Are Capital Requirements Enough?," *American Economic Review*, 90(1), 147–165.

Hellmann, Thomas, Kevin Murdoch, and Joseph Stiglitz. 2002. "Franchise Value and the Dynamics of Financial Liberalization: The Use of Capital Requirements and Deposit Rate Controls for Prudential Regulation," in Anna Meyendorff and Anjan Thakor, eds., *Financial Systems in Transition: The Design of Financial Systems in Central Europe* (111–127) (Cambridge, MA: MIT Press).

Herring, Richard. 2004. "How Can the Invisible Hand Prudential Supervision? and How Can Prudential Supervision Strengthen the Invisible Hand?," in Claudio Borio, William Hunter, George Kaufman, and Kostas Tsatsaronis, eds., *Market Discipline Across Countries and Industries* 363–380 (Cambridge, MA: MIT Press).

Hibbert, Christopher. 2003. *The House of Medici: Its Rise and Fall* (New York: Perennial).

HM Treasury. 2004. "After the EU Financial Services Plan: A New Strategic Approach," HM Treasury, England, May.

HM Treasury. 2004. "After the EU Financial Services Plan: UK Response to the Reports of the Four Independent Expert Groups," HM Treasury, England, September.

Homer, Sidney, and Richard Sylla. 1996. *A History of Interest Rates* (New Brunswick, NJ: Rutgers University Press).

Honohan, Patrick. 2004. "Financial Sector Policy and the Poor: Selected Findings and Issues," World Bank Working Paper No. 43, The World Bank.

Honohan, Patrick, and Daniela Klingebiel. 2000. "Controlling the Fiscal Costs of Banking Crisis," Policy Research Working Paper 2441, The World Bank.

Honohan, Patrick, and Luc Laeven. 2005. *Systemic Financial Crises: Containment and Resolution* (Cambridge: Cambridge University Press).

Horvitz, Paul. 1984. "Subordinated Debt Is Key to New Bank Capital Requirements," in *American Banker*, page 5, December 31.

Hunter, William C., George G. Kaufman, and Michael Pomerleano. 2003. *Asset Price Bubbles: The Implications for Monetary, Regulatory, and International Policies* (Cambridge, MA: MIT Press).

Ingves, Stefan, and Carol S. Carson. 2003. "Offshore Financial Center Program: A Progress Report." Prepared by the Monetary and Exchange Affairs and Statistics Departments, International Monetary Fund, March.

Institute of International Bankers. 2003. *Global Survey of Regulatory and Market Developments in Banking, Securities and Insurance* (New York: Institute of International Bankers).

International Monetary Fund. 2000. "Offshore Financial Centers," IMF Background Paper, International Monetary Fund, June 23.

International Monetary Fund. 2000. "Offshore Financial Centers," mimeo, International Monetary Fund.

International Monetary Fund. 2001. *International Capital Markets* (Washington, DC: International Monetary Fund).

International Monetary Fund. 2002. "Offshore Financial Center Program," A Progress Report, International Monetary Fund, March 28.

International Monetary Fund. 2004. *International Financial Statistics* (Washington, DC: International Monetary Fund).

Jackson, Howell. 2004. "An American Perspective on the U.K. Financial Services Authority: Politics, Goals & Regulatory Intensity," prepared for the 2004 EWC/KDI Conference, Honolulu, July 29–30.

James, John A. 1978. *Money and Capital Markets in Postbellum America* (Princeton, NJ: Princeton University Press).

Jameson, Rob. 2001. "Between Raroc and a Hard Place," *Erisk*, February, 1–5.

Jayaratne, Jith, and Philip E. Strahan. 1996. "The Finance Growth Nexus: Evidence from Bank Branch Deregulation," *Quarterly Journal of Economics*, 101, 639–670.

Jayaratne, Jith, and Philip E. Strahan. 1998. "Entry Restrictions, Industry Evolution and Dynamic Efficiency: Evidence from Commercial Banking," *Journal of Law and Economics*, 49, 239–274.

Jensen, Michael, and William Meckling. 1976. "Theory of the Firm, Managerial Behavior, Agency Costs and Ownership Structure," *Journal of Financial Economics*, 3, 305–360.

John, Kose, Teresa A. John, and Anthony Saunders. 1994. "Universal Banking and Firm Risk Taking," *Journal of Banking and Finance*," 18(2), January, 307–323.

Johnson, Simon, John McMillan, and Christopher Woodruff. 2002b. "Property Rights and Finance, *American Economic Review*, 92, 1335–1356.

Kahane, Y. 1977. "Capital Adequacy and the Regulation of Financial Intermediaries," *Journal of Banking and Finance*, 1, 207–218.

Kahn, C. M., and João A. C. Santos. 2004. "Allocating the Lender of Last Resort and Supervision in the Euro Area," in V. Alexander, J. Melitz, and G. M. von Furstenberg, eds., *Monetary Unions and Hard Pegs – Effects on Trade, Financial Development, and Stability* (347–360) (Oxford and New York: Oxford University Press).

Kahn, Charles M., and João A. C. Santos. 2005. "Allocating Bank Regulatory Powers: Lender of Last Resort, Deposit Insurance and Supervision," *European Economic Review*, forthcoming.

Kahneman, D., and Andrei Tversky. 1979. "Prospect Theory: An Analysis of Decision under Risk," *Econometrica*, 47, 263–291.

Kane, Edward J. 1977. "Good Intentions and Unintended Evil," *Journal of Money Credit in Banking* (February), 55–69.

Kane, Edward J. 1981. "Accelerating Inflation, Technological Innovation, and the Decreasing Effectiveness of Banking Regulation," *Journal of Finance*, 36(2), 355–367.

Kane, Edward J. 1984. "Technological and Regulatory Forces in the Developing Fusion of Financial Services Competition," Columbus: Ohio State University, WPS 84–4.

Kane, Edward J. 1989. *The S&L Insurance Mess: How Did It Happen?* (Washington, DC: Urban Institute Press).

Kane, Edward J. 1996. "De Jure Interstate Banking: Why Only Now?," *Journal of Money, Credit and Banking*, 28, 141–161.

Kane, Edward J. 1997. "Ethical Foundations of Financial Regulation," National Bureau of Economic Research Working Paper 6020.

Kane, Edward J., and Berry Wilson. 1998. "A Contracting-Theory Interpretation of the Origins of Federal Deposit Insurance," National Bureau of Economic Research Working Paper W6451.

Kane, Edward J. 2000. "The Dialectical Role of Information and Disinformation in Regulation and Used Banking Crises," *Pacific Basin Finance Journal*, 8, 285–308.

Kane, Edward J. 2002. "Using Deferred Compensation to Strengthen the Ethics of Financial Regulation," *Journal of Banking and Finance*, 26 (September), 1919–1933.

Kane, Edward J. 2004. "Financial Regulation and Bank Safety Nets: An International Comparison," mimeo, Boston College.

Kashyup, Anil, and Jerome Stein. 2004. "Cyclical Implications of the Basel-II Capital Standards," Federal Reserve Bank of Chicago, *Economic Perspectives*, First Quarter, 18–31.

Kaufmann, D., A. Kraay, and P. Zoido-Lobaton. 1999. "Governance Matters," Policy Research Working Paper 2196, The World Bank.

Kaufman, George. 1994. "Bank Contagion: A Review of the Theory and Evidence," *Journal of Financial Services Research*, 8(2), 123–150.

Kaufman, George, and Randall Kroszner. 1997. "How Should Financial Institutions and Markets Be Structured?," in Liliana Rojas-Suarez, ed., *Safe and Sound Financial Systems: What Works for Latin America?* (97–122) (Washington, DC: Inter-American Development Bank).

Kaufman, George G. 1999. "Helping to Prevent Banking Crises: Taking the 'State' out of State Banks," *Review of Pacific Basin Financial Markets and Policies*, 2, 83–98.

Kaufman, George G. 1991. "Capital in Banking: Past, Present and Future," *Journal of Financial Services Research*, 5, 385–402.

Keefer, Philip. 2000. "When do Special Interest Run Rampant? Disentangling the Role of Elections, Incomplete Information, and Checks and Balances in Banking Crises," mimeo, The World Bank.

Keeley, M. C. 1990. "Deposit Insurance, Risk, and Market Power in Banking," *American Economic Review*, 80(5), 1183–1200.

Keeley, M. C., and F. T. Furlong. 1990. "A Reexamination of Mean-Variance Analysis of Bank Capital Regulations," *Journal of Banking and Finance*, 14, 69–84.

Key, Sydney. 2003. *The Doha Round and Financial Services Negotiations* (Washington, DC: AEI Press).

Khan, B. Zorina, and Kenneth L. Sokoloff. 2004. The Innovation of Patent Systems in the Nineteenth Century: A Comparative Perspective, National Bureau of Economic Research, Working Paper.

Khwaja, Asim Ijaz, and Atif Mian. 2004. "Do Lenders Favor Politically Connected Firms? Rent Provision in an Emerging Financial Market," mimeo, University of Chicago.

Kim, D., and A. M. Santomero. 1988. "Risk in Banking and Capital Regulation," *The Journal of Finance*, 35, 1219–1233.

Kindleberger, Charles P. 1978, 1996. *Manias, Panics, and Crashes: A History of Financial Crises* (New York: John Wiley and Sons).

Kindleberger, Charles P. 1986. *The World in the Depression, 1929–1939* (Berkeley: University of California Press).

Kindleberger, Charles P. 1984. *A Financial History of Western Europe* (London: Allen & Unwin).

King, Robert G., and Ross Levine. 1993a. "Finance and Growth: Schumpeter Might Be Right," *Quarterly Journal of Economics*, 108, 717–738.

King, Robert G., and Ross Levine. 1993b. "Finance, Entrepreneurship, and Growth: Theory and Evidence," *Journal of Monetary Economics*, 32, 513–542.

Koehn, M., and A. M. Santomero. 1980. "Regulation of Bank Capital and Portfolio Risk," *Journal of Finance*, 35, 1235–1250.

Kohn, Meir. 1999. "Early Deposit Banking," draft chapter of Finance, Business, and Government before the Industrial Revolution, Dartmouth College, http://www.dartmouth.edu/~mkohn/.

Kohn, Meir. 2004. *Financial Institutions and Markets* (New York and Oxford: Oxford University Press).

Kornai, Janos. 1979. "Resource-Constrained vs. Demand-Constrained Systems," *Econometrica*, 49, 801–819.

Kroszner, Randall S. 1997. "Free Banking: The Scottish Experience as a Model for Emerging Economies," in Gerard Caprio and Dimitri Vittas, eds., *Reforming Financial Systems: Historical Implications for Policy* (41–64) (New York: Cambridge University Press).

Kroszner, Randall S. 1998. "On the Political Economy of Banking in Financial Regulatory Reform in Emerging Markets," mimeo, University of Chicago.

Kroszner, Randall S. 2001. "The Motivations behind Banking Reform," *Regulation*, 24(2), 36–41.

Kroszner, Randall S., and Douglas Irwin. 1999. "Interest, Institutions, and Ideology in Securing Policy Change: The Republican Conversion to Trade Liberalization after Smoot-Hawley," *Journal of Law and Economics*, 643–673.

Kroszner, Randall S., and Raghuram G. Rajan. 1994. "Is the Glass-Steagall Act Justified? A Study of the US Experience with Universal Banking before 1933," *American Economic Review*, 84, 810–832.

Kroszner, Randall S., and Raghuram G. Rajan. 1997. "Organization Structure and Credibility: Evidence from Commercial Bank Securities Activities before the Glass-Steagall Act," *Journal of Monetary Economics*, 29, 475–516.

Kroszner, Randall S., and Philip Strahan. 1999. "What Drives Deregulation? Economics and Politics of the Relaxation of Bank Branching Restrictions," *Quarterly Journal of Economics*, 1437–1467.

Kroszner, Randall, and Philip Strahan. 2001. "Obstacles to Optimal Policy: The Interplay of Politics and Economics in Shaping Bank Supervision and Regulation Reforms," in Frederic Mishkin, ed., *Prudential Supervision: What Works and What Doesn't* (233–266) (Chicago: University of Chicago Press).

Kroszner, Randall S., and Thomas Stratmann. 1998. "Interest Group Competition and the Organization of Congress: Theory and Evidence from Financial Services Political Action Committees," *American Economic Review*, 1163–1187.

Kupiec, Paul, and James O'Brien. 1995. "A Pre-Commitment Approach to Capital Requirements for Market Risk," *Finance and Economics Discussion Paper Series, No. 1997-14* (Washington, DC: Board of Governors of the Federal Reserve).

Kupiec, Paul, and James O'Brien. 1997. "The Pre-Commitment Approach: Using Incentives to Set Market Risk Capital Requirements," Board of Governors of the Federal Reserve System, Finance and Economics Discussion Paper Series, 1997/14, March.

Kuran, Timur. 2004. "Islam and Mammon," *Milken Institute Review*, Third Quarter, 61–81.

Kwan, S. H., and E. S. Laderman. 1999. "On the Portfolio Effects of Financial Convergence – A Review of the Literature," *Federal Reserve Bank of San Francisco*, 2, 18–31.

Laeven, Luc. 2002. "Bank Risk and Deposit Insurance," *World Bank Economic Review*, 16, 109–137.

Laeven, Luc. 2002a. "The Pricing of Deposit Insurance," World Bank Policy Research Working Paper 2871.

Laeven, Luc. 2002b. "Insider Lending and Bank Ownership: The Case of Russia," *Journal of Comparative Economics*, 29(2), 207–229.

Laeven, Luc. 2004. "The Political Economy of Deposit Insurance," *Journal of Financial Services Research*, 26, 201–224.

Laeven, Luc, and Ross Levine. 2005. "Is There a Diversification Discount in Financial Conglomerates?," Journal of Financial Economics forthcoming.

Lam, C. H., and A. H. Chen. 1985. "Joint Effects of Interest Rate Deregulation and Capital Requirements on Optimal Bank Portfolio Adjustments," *Journal of Finance*, 45(2), 563–575.

Lamoreaux, N. 1994. *Insider Lending: Banks, Personal Connections, and Economic Development in Industrial New England* (Cambridge and New York: Cambridge University Press).

Landes, David. 1998. *The Wealth and Poverty of Nations* (New York: W.W. Norton).

Lannoo, Karel. 2000. "Challenges to the Structure of Financial Supervision in the EU," CEPS Working Party Report, Centre for European Policy Studies (Chairman: David Green).

La Porta, Rafael, Florencio Lopez-de-Silanes, and Andrei Shleifer. 2002. "Government Ownership of Commercial Banks," *The Journal of Finance*, 57(1), 265–301.

La Porta, Rafael, Florencio Lopez-de-Silanes, and Andrei Shleifer. 2005. "What Works in Securities Laws?," *Journal of Finance*, forthcoming.

La Porta, Rafael, Florencio Lopez-de-Silanes, Andrei Shleifer, and Robert W. Vishny. 1997. "Legal Determinants of External Finance," *Journal of Finance*, 52, 1131–1150.

La Porta, Rafael, Florencio Lopez-de-Silanes, Andrei Shleifer, and Robert W. Vishny. 1998. "Law and Finance," *Journal of Political Economy*, 106, 1113–1155.

La Porta, Rafael, Florencio Lopez-de-Silanes, Andrei Shleifer, and Robert W. Vishny. 1999. "The Quality of Government," *Journal of Law, Economics and Organization*, 15, 222–279.

La Porta, Rafael, Florencio Lopez-de-Silanes, Andrei Shleifer, and Robert W. Vishny. 2002. "Investor Protection and Corporate Valuation," *Journal of Finance*, 57, 1147–1170.

La Porta, Rafael, Florencio Lopez-de-Silanes, and Guillermo Zamarripa. 2003. "Related Lending," *The Quarterly Journal of Economics*, 118(1), 231–268.

Lastra, Rosa. 2003. "The Governance Structure for Financial Regulation and Supervision in Europe," Financial Market Group Special Paper 149, May.

Le Goff, Jacques. 1990. *Your Money or Your Life: Economy and Religion in the Middle Ages*, trans. Patricia Ranum (Cambridge, MA: MIT Press).

Levine, Ross. 1997. "Financial Development and Economic Growth: Views and Agenda," *Journal of Economic Literature*, 35, 688–726.

Levine, Ross. 1998. "The Legal Environment, Banks, and Long-run Economic Growth," *Journal of Money, Credit, and Banking*, 30, 596–620.

Levine, Ross. 1999. "Law, Finance, and Economic Growth," *Journal of Financial Intermediation*, 8, 36–67.

Levine, Ross. 2002. "Bank-Based or Market-Based Financial Systems: Which Is Better?," *Journal of Financial Intermediation*, 11, 398–428.

Levine, Ross. 2004. "Denying Foreign Bank Entry: Implications for Bank Interest Margins," in Luis Antonio Ahumada and J. Rodrigo Fuentes, eds., *Bank Market Structure and Monetary Policy* (271–292) (Santiago: Banco Central de Chile).

Levine, Ross. 2005a. "Finance and Growth: Theory and Evidence," in *Handbook of Economic Growth*. Eds. Philippe Aghion and Steven Durlauf, Amsterdam: North-Holland Elsevier Publishers, forthcoming.

Levine, Ross. 2005b. "Law, Endowments, and Property Rights," *Journal of Economic Perspectives*, forthcoming.

Levine, Ross, Norman Loayza, and Thorsten Beck. 2000. "Financial Intermediation and Growth: Causality and Causes," *Journal of Monetary Economics*, 46, 31–77.

Levine, R., and Sara Zervos. 1993. "What Have We Learned about Policy and Growth from Cross-country Regressions?," *The American Economic Review*, 83(2), 426–430.

Levine, Ross, and Sara Zervos. 1998. "Stock Markets, Banks, and Economic Growth," *American Economic Review*, 88, 537–558.

Lewis, Arthur. 1950. *The Principles of Economic Planning* (London: G. Allen & Unwin).

Lindgren, Carl-Johan, Gillian Garcia, and Matthew I. Saal. 1996. *Bank Soundness and Macroeconomic Policy* (Washington, DC: International Monetary Fund).

Lown, Cara, Donald P. Morgan, and Sonali Rohatgi. 2000. "Listening to Loan Officers: The Impact of Commercial Credit Standards on Lending and Output," *Economic Policy Review, Federal Reserve Bank of New York*, 6(2), 1–16.

Macey, Jonathan R. 2003. Regulatory Globalization as a Response to Regulatory Competition, *Emory Law Journal*, 52(3), 1353–1379.

Macey, Jonathan R., and Maureen O'Hara. 2003. "The Corporate Governance of Banks," *Economic Policy Review, Federal Reserve Bank of New York* 9 (Special Issue), 91–108.

Marchetti, Juan A. 2003. "What Should Financial Regulators Know About the GATS?," mimeo, paper presented at the Central Banking seminar, Cambridge University, England, 7–11.

Marshall, Monty, and Keith Jaggers. 2002. "Data Users' Manual," *Polity IV Project*, Center for International Development and Conflict Management, University of Maryland. http://www.cidcm.umd.edu/inscr/polity/index.htm

Martínez, José de Luna, and Thomas A. Rose. 2003. "International Survey of Integrated Supervision," in Douglas Arner and Jan-Juy Lin, eds., *Financial Regulation: A Guide to Structural Reform* (3–39) (Hong Kong: Sweet & Maxwell Asia).

Martinez-Peria, Maria Soledad, and Sergio Schmukler. 2001. "Do Depositors Punish Banks for 'Bad' Behavior? Market Discipline, Deposit Insurance and Banking Crises," *The Journal of Finance*, 56(3), 1029–1051.

Mathieson, Donald, and Jorge Roldos. 2001. "The Role of Foreign Banks in Emerging Markets," presented at the 3rd Annual Financial Markets and Development Conference, New York, New York, April 19–21.

Mauro, Paolo. 1995. "Corruption and Growth," *Quarterly Journal of Economics*, 110, 681–712.

McCraw, Thomas K. 1984. *The Prophets of Regulation* (Cambridge, MA: Harvard University Press).

Mian, Atif. 2003. "Foreign, Domestic Private, and Government Banks: New Evidence from Emerging Markets," mimeo, Graduate School of Business, University of Chicago.

Milne, Alistair. 2004. "The Inventory Perspective on Bank Capital," mimeo, City University, London.

Mishan, E. J. 1969. *Welfare Economics: An Assessment* (Amsterdam and London: North Holland Publishing Company).

Morgan, Donald. 2002. "Rating Banks: Risk and Uncertainty in an Opaque Industry," *American Economic Review*, 92, 874–888.

Morner, Anna. 1997. "Banking Law Reform in Central and Eastern Europe – The Influence of European Union Banking Legislation," Essays in International Financial & Economic Law, No.11, London Institute of International Banking, Finance, & Development Law, England.

Myrdal, Gunnar. 1968. *Asian Drama* (New York: Pantheon).

Nenovsky, Nikolay, and Kalina Dimirova. 2003. "Deposit Insurance During EU Accession," William Davidson Institute Working Paper Number 617, October.

North, Douglass C., and Barry R. Weingast. 1989. "Constitutions and Commitment: The Evolution of Institutions Governing Public Choice in Seventeenth-Century England," *Journal of Economic History*, 49(4), 803–832.

North, Douglass C., William Summerhill, and Barry Weingast. 2000. "Order, Disorder, and Economic Change: Latin America Versus North America," in Bruce Bueno de Mesquita and Hilton L. Root, eds., *Governing for Prosperity*, 17–58 (New Haven, CT: Yale University Press).

Office of the Comptroller of the Currency. 2003. *Detecting Red Flags in Board Reports: A Guide for Directors* (Washington, DC: Office of the Comptroller of the Currency).

Olson, Mancur. 1965. *The Logic of Collective Action* (Cambridge, MA: Harvard University Press).

Pages, H., and J. A. C. Santos. 2001. "Optimal Supervisory Policies and Depositor-Preference Laws," mimeo, Federal Reserve Bank of New York.

Palia, Darius, and Robert Porter. 2003. "Contemporary Issues in Regulatory Risk Management of Commercial Banks," *Financial Markets, Institutions & Instruments*, 12(4), 223–289.

Peek, Joseph, and Eric Rosengren. 2000. "Collateral Damage: Effects of the Japanese Bank Crisis on Real Activity in the United States," *American Economic Review*, 90(1), 30–45.

Peltzman, Sam. 1976. "Toward a More General Theory of Regulation," *Journal of Law and Economics*, 10, 109–148.

Peltzman, Sam. 1989. "The Economic Theory of Regulation after a Decade of Deregulation," *Brookings Papers: Microeconomics*, 1–41.

Persson, Torsten, Gerard Roland, and Guido Tabellini. 1997. "Separation of Powers and Political Accountability," *Quarterly Journal of Economics*, 112, 1163–1202.

Persson, Torsten, and Guido Tabellini. 2000. *Political Economics: Explaining Economic Policy* (Cambridge, MA: MIT Press).

Persson, Torsten, and Guido Tabellini. 2002. "Political Economics and Public Finance," in A. Auerbach and M. Feldstein, eds., *Handbook of Public Economics, Volume 3* (1549–1650) (Amsterdam: North-Holland).

Peterson, Mitchell, and Raghuram Rajan. 1994. "The Benefits of Lending Relationships: Evidence from Small Business Data," *The Journal of Finance*, 49, 3–37.

Philipps, Ronnie J. 1995. *The Chicago Plan and New Deal Banking Reform* (Armonk, NY: M. E. Sharpe).

Pigou, Arthur C. 1938. *The Economics of Welfare, 4th edition* (London: Macmillan).

Poole, Keith, and Howard Rosenthal. 1997. *Congress: A Political-Economic History of Roll Call Voting* (Oxford: Oxford University Press).

Posner, Richard A. 1974. "Theories of Economic Regulation," *The Bell Journal of Economics and Management Science*, 5(2), 3–21.

Powell, Andrew. 2004. "Basel II and Developing Countries: Sailing through the Sea of Standards," mimeo, Universidad Torcuato di Tella and The World Bank.

Puri, M. 1996. "Commercial Banks in Investment Banking: Conflict of Interest or Certification Role?," *Journal of Financial Economics*, 40, 373–401.

Putnam, Robert. 1993. *Making Democracy Work: Civic Traditions in Modern Italy* (Princeton, NJ: Princeton University Press).

Quintyn, Marc, and Taylor, Michael W. 2004. "Should Financial Sector Regulators Be Independent?," *Economic Issues*, 32, International Monetary Fund.

Rajan, Raghuram, and Luigi Zingales. 2003. *Saving Capitalism from the Capitalists: Unleashing the Power of Financial Markets to Create Wealth and Spread Opportunity* (New York: Crown).

Ramirez, C. 1995. "Did J. P. Morgan's Men Add Liquidity? Corporate Investment, Cash-Flow, and Financial Structure at the Turn of the Century," *Journal of Finance*, 50, 661–678.

Ramirez, Carlos. 1999. "Did Bank Security Affiliates Add Value? Evidence from the Commercial Banking Industry During the 1920s," mimeo, George Mason University.

Robertson, Ross M. 1995. *The Comptroller and Bank Supervision: A Historical Appraisal* (Washington, D.C.: The Office of the Comptroller of the Currency, Administrator of National Banks).

Rochet, Jean-Charles. 2003. "Rebalancing the 3 Pillars of Basel 2," mimeo, paper prepared for Columbia University – N.Y. Federal Reserve Bank Conference, Beyond Pillar Three in International Bank Regulation.

Rochet, Jean-Charles. 1992. "Capital Requirements and the Behavior of Commercial Banks," *European Economic Review*, 36(5), 1137–1170.

Rodrik, Dani. 2004. "Rethinking Growth Policies in the Developing World," mimeo, Harvard University.

Rodrik, Dani, Arvind Subramanium, and Francesco Trebbi. 2002. "Institutions Rule: The Privacy of Institutions over Geography and Integration in Economic Development," mimeo, Harvard University.

Roe, Mark J. 1994. *Strong Managers Weak Owners: The Political Roots of American Corporate Finance* (Princeton, NJ: Princeton University Press).

Roosevelt, Franklin D. 1933. "Franklin D. Roosevelt's First Fireside Chat," The Fireside Chats of Franklin Delano Roosevelt, March 12. http://www. blackmask.com/ books93c/fdrfc.htm.

Rosen, Richard J. 2003. "Is Three a Crowd? Competition among Regulators in Banking," *Journal of Money, Credit & Banking*, 35(6), 967–998.

De Roover, Raymond. 1966. *The Rise and Fall of the Medici Bank, 1397–1494* (New York: W.W. Norton).

Rousseau, Peter L., and Richard Sylla. 2003. "Financial Systems, Economic Growth, and Globalization," in Michael D. Bordo, Alan M. Taylor and Jeffrey G. Williamson, eds., *Globalization in Historical Perspective* (373–413) (Chicago: University of Chicago Press).

Santos, João A. C. 1998a. "Banking and Commerce: How Does the United States Compare to Other Countries?," *Federal Reserve Bank of Cleveland Economic Review*, 34(4), 14–26.

Santos, João A. C. 1998b. "Commercial Banks in the Securities Business: A Review," *Journal of Financial Services Research*, 14(1), 35–59.

Santos, João A. C. 1999. "Bank Capital and Equity Investment Regulations," *Journal of Banking and Finance*, 23(7), 1095–1120.

Santos, João A. C. 2001. "Bank Capital Regulation in Contemporary Banking Theory: A Review of the Literature," *Financial Markets, Institutions and Instruments*, 10(2), 41–84.

Santos, João A. C. 2004. "Do Markets Discipline All Banks Equally," mimeo, Federal Reserve Bank of New York.

Saunders, Anthony, and Berry Wilson. 1999. "The Impact of Consolidation and Safety-net Support on Canadian, U.S., and U.K. Banks: 1893–1992," *Journal of Banking and Finance*, 23, 537–571.

Saunders, Anthony. 1994. "Banking and Commerce: An Overview of the Public Policy Issues," *Journal of Banking and Finance*, 18(2), 231–254.

Schüler, Martin. 2003a. "How Do Banking Supervisors Deal with Europe-wide Systemic Risk," Discussion Paper No. 03-03, Centre for European Economic Research.

Schüler, Martin. 2003b. "Incentive Problems in Banking Supervision – The European Case," Discussion Paper No. 03-62, Center for European Economic Research, Mannheim, Germany, October.

Schumpeter, Joseph A. 1912. "Theorie der Wirtschaftlichen Entwicklung. Leipzig: Dunker & Humblot," *The Theory of Economic Development*, translated by R. Opie. Cambridge, MA: Harvard University Press, 1934.

Shadow Financial Regulatory Committee. 1999. The Basel Committee's New Capital Adequacy Framework, Statement Number 156, September 27, http://www.aei.org/research/shadow/publications/pageID.241,projectID.15/default.asp.

Shaffer. Sherrill. 1993. "Market Conduct and Excess Capacity in Banking: A Cross-country Comparison," Federal Reserve Bank of Philadephia, Working Papers No. 93-28:1–41.

Shiller, Robert. 2003. *The New Financial Order* (Princeton, NJ: Princeton University Press).

Shin, Hyun Song, Felix Muennich, Charles Goodhart, Paul Embrechts, Jon Danielsson, and Con Keating. 2001. "An Academic Response to Basel II," FMG Special Papers SP130, Financial Markets Group, London School of Economics.

Shleifer, Andrei. 2000. *Inefficient Markets: An Introduction to Behavioral Finance* (New York: Oxford University Press).

Shleifer, Andrei. 2005. "Understanding Regulation," mimeo, Harvard University, and *European Financial Management*, forthcoming.

Shleifer, Andrei, and Lawrence Summers. 1990. "The Noise Trader Approach to Finance," *Journal of Economic Perspectives*, 4(2), 19–33.

Shleifer, Andrei, and R. Vishny. 1993. "Corruption," *Quarterly Journal of Economics*, 108, 599–617.

Shleifer, Andrei, and R. Vishny. 1994. "Politicians and Firms," *Quarterly Journal of Economics*, 109, 995–1025.

Shleifer, Andrei, and Robert W. Vishny. 1997. "A Survey of Corporate Governance," *The Journal of Finance*, 52(2), 737–783.

Shleifer, Andrei, and Robert W. Vishny. 1998. *The Grabbing Hand: Government Pathologies and Their Cures* (Cambridge, MA: Harvard University Press).

Shleifer, Andrei, and Daniel Wolfenzon. 2002. "Investor Protection and Equity Markets," *Journal of Financial Economics*, 66(1), 3–27.

Singer, David, A. 2003. "Capital Rules: The Domestic Politics of International Regulatory Harmonization," mimeo, August 15.

Sokoloff, Kenneth L., and Stanley L. Engerman. 2000. "History Lessons: Institutions, Factor Endowments, and Paths of Development in the New World," *Journal of Economic Perspectives*, 14(3), 217–232.

Song, Inwon. 2004. "Foreign Banking Supervision and Challenges to Emerging Market Supervisors," IMF Working Paper, May.

Staff report. 2002. "Legal Framework Must for Governing Islamic Financial Institutions," *Daily Times Pakistan*, November 11, 2002,

Steil, Benn. 1994. "Introduction: Effective Public Policy in a World of Footloose Finance," in Benn Steil, ed., *International Financial Market Regulation* (1–14) Wiley Publishers.

Stevens, E. 2000. "Evolution in Banking Supervision," *Economic Commentary*, Federal Reserve Bank of Cleveland, http://www.clevelandfed.org/research/com2000/0301.htm.

Stigler, George J. 1971. "The Theory of Economic Regulation" *The Bell Journal of Economics and Management Science*, 2(1), 3–21.

Stigler, George. 1975. *The Citizen and the State: Essays on Regulation* (Chicago: University of Chicago Press).

Stiglitz, Joseph. 1994. *Whither Socialism* (Cambridge, MA: MIT Press).

Stiglitz, Joseph E., and Andrew Weiss. 1981. "Credit Rationing in Markets with Imperfect Information," *American Economic Review*, 71, 393–410.

Stulz, Rene. 1988. "Managerial Control of Voting Rights: Financial Policies and the Market for Corporate Control," *Journal of Financial Economics*, 20, 25–54.

Stulz, Rene, and Rohan Williamson. 2003. "Culture, Openness, and Finance," *Journal of Financial Economics*, 313–349, December.

Sundararajan, V., and Luca Errico. 2002. "Islamic Financial Institutions and Products in the Global Financial System: Key Issues in Risk Management and Challenges Ahead," IMF Working Paper No. 02/192.

Sundararajan, V., David Marston, and Ritu Basu. 2001. "Financial System Standards and Financial Stability – The Case of Basel Core Principles," IMF Working Paper No. 01/62.

Swamy, P. A. V. B., James R. Barth, Ray Y. Chou, and John S. Jahera, Jr. 1996. "Determinants of U.S. Commercial Bank Performance: Regulatory and Econometric Issues," in Andrew H. Chen, ed., *Research in Finance, Volume 14*, 117–156 (London: JAI Press Inc.).

Sylla, Richard E. 1975. *The American Capital Market, 1846–1914: A Study of the Effects of Public Policy on Economic Development* (New York: Arno Press).

Sylla, Richard, John Legler, and John Wallis. 1987. "Banks and State Public Finance in the New Republic: The United States, 1790–1860," *Journal of Economic History*, 47, 391–403.

Tabellini, Guido. 2004. "Culture and Institutions: Economic Development in the Regions of Europe," mimeo, IGIER, Bocconi University.

Tadesse, Soloman. 2004. "Banking Fragility and Disclosure: International Evidence," mimeo, University of South Carolina (Moore School of Business).

Tarullo, Daniel. "Banking on Basel: the Future of International Financial Regulation," Washington, DC: Institute for International Economics, forthcoming.

Taylor, Edward. 2005. "Europe's Banks Find Bold Moves Lead to Outcry; Drive to Match U.S. Rivals Stokes Fears of Losing Jobs as well as National Pride," *Wall Street Journal* (Eastern Edition), page A9, February 11.

Temin, Peter, and Hans Joachim Voth. 2004. "Riding the South Sea Bubble," *American Economic Review*, 94(5), 1654–1668.

Thakor, Anjan. 1996. "The Design of Financial Systems: An Overview," *Journal of Banking and Finance*, 20, 917–948.

Thakor, Anjan, and Patricia Wilson, 1995. "Capital Requirements, Loan Renegotiation and the Borrower's Choice of Financing Source," *Journal of Banking and Finance*, 19, 693–711.

T. Hart, Marjolein, Joost Jonker, and Jan Luiten Van Zanden. 1997. *A Financial History of the Netherlands* (Cambridge: Cambridge University Press).

Townsend, Robert M. 1979. "Optimal Contracts and Competitive Markets with Costly State Verification," *Journal of Economic Theory*, 21(2), 265–293.

Tsebelis, George. 1999. "Veto Players and Law Production in Parliamentary Democracies: An Empirical Analysis," *American Political Science Review*, 93(3), 591–608.

Tullock, Gordon. 1959. "Some Problems of Majority Voting," *Journal of Political Economy*, 67, 571–579.

Vennet, R. V. 1999. "Costs and Profit Dynamics in Financial Conglomerates and Universal Banks in Europe," mimeo, University of Gent.

Udell, Gregory F. 1989. "Loan Quality, Commercial Loan Review and Loan Officer Contracting," *Journal of Banking and Finance*, 13, 367–382.

U.S. Department of State. 2004. "Offshore Financial Centers," International Narcotic Control Strategy Report-2003, released by the Bureau for International Narcotics and Law Enforcement Affairs, March.

Von Thadden, Eric L. 2004. "Introduction to Bank Capital Adequacy Regulation Under the New Basel Accord," *Journal of Financial Intermediation*, 13, 90–95.

Wallis, John. 2004. "The Concept of Systematic Corruption in American History," in Edward L. Glaeser and Claudia Goldin, eds., *Corruption and Reform: Lessons from America's History*, forthcoming, University of Chicago Press.

Weber, Max. 1958. *The Protestant Ethic and the Spirit of Capitalism* (New York: Charles Scribner's Sons).

Weingast, Barry R., and William Marshall. 1988. "The Industrial Organization of Congress," *Journal of Political Economy*, 96, 132–163.

Weingast, Barry R., Kenneth Shepsle, and Christopher Johnsen. 1981. "The Political Economy of Benefits and Costs: A Neoclassical Approach to Distributive Politics," *Journal of Political Economy*, 89, 642–664.

White, Eugene. 1982. "The Political Economy of Banking Regulation, 1864–1933," *The Journal of Economic History*, 42(1), 33–40.

White, Eugene. 1983. *The Regulation and Reform of the American Banking System, 1900–1929* (Princeton, NJ: Princeton University Press).

White, Eugene. 1986. "Before the Glass-Steagall Act: An Analysis of the Investment Banking Activities of Commercial Banks," *Explorations in Economic History*, 23, 33–55.

White, Eugene. 1997. "Deposit Insurance," in Gerard Caprio and Dimitri Vittas, eds., *Reforming Financial Systems: Historical Implications for Policy* (85–100) (New York: Cambridge University Press).

White, Eugene. 2005. "The Evolution of Banking Regulation in Twentieth Century Colombia," mimeo, Rutgers University, http://econweb.rutgers.edu/white/.

White, Lawrence J. 1991. *The S&L Debacle: Public Policy Lessons for Bank and Thrift Regulation* (Oxford: Oxford University Press).

White, Lawrence H. 1995. *Free Banking in Britain: Theory, Experience, and Debate, 1800–1845, 2nd edition* (London: Institute of Economic Affairs).

Wittman, Donald N. 1995. *The Myth of Democratic Failure* (Chicago: University of Chicago Press).

World Bank. 1995. *Bureaucrats in Business*, A World Bank Policy Research Report (Oxford: Oxford University Press).

World Bank. 2001. *Finance for Growth: Policy Choices in a Volatile World*, A World Bank Policy Research Report (Oxford: Oxford University Press).

Wurgler, Jeffrey. 2000. "Financial Markets and the Allocation of Capital," *Journal of Financial Economics*, 58, 187–214.

Wyplosz, Charles. 2001. "Financial Restraints and Liberalization in Postwar Europe," in Gerard Caprio, Patrick Honohan, and Joseph E. Stiglitz, eds., *Financial Liberalization: How Far, How Fast?* (125–158) (New York and Cambridge: Cambridge University Press).

Zimmerman, Gary. 1996. "Integrating Banking Markets in the EC," *FRBSF Economic Letter*, April, www.sf.frb.org/econrsrch/wklylty/el9612.html.

Zingales, Luigi. 2004. "The Costs and Benefits of Financial Market Regulation," European Corporate Governance Institute, Working Paper No. 21/2004.

Index